ANNE RICE
SERVANT OF THE BONES

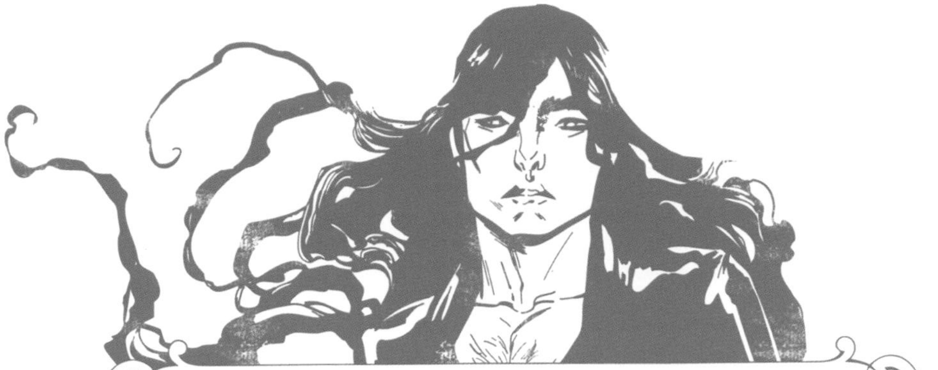

Written by Anne Rice
Adapted by Mariah McCourt
Art by Renae De Liz and Ray Dillon

Lettering by Shawn Lee
Original Series Edited by
Chris Ryall and Mariah Huehner

Collection Cover by Renae De Liz and Ray Dillon
Collection Edits by Justin Eisinger and Alonzo Simon
Collection Design by Shawn Lee

Special thanks to Becket Ghioto for his invaluable assistance

IDW founded by Ted Adams, Alex Garner, Kris Oprisko, and Robbie Robbins | International Rights Representative, Christine Meyer: christine@gfloystudio.com

ISBN: 978-1-61377-173-0 ISBN: 978-1-61377-185-3 (Signed Edition) 15 14 13 12 1 2 3 4

IDW

Ted Adams, CEO & Publisher
Greg Goldstein, President & COO
Robbie Robbins, EVP/Sr. Graphic Artist
Chris Ryall, Chief Creative Officer/Editor-in-Chief
Matthew Ruzicka, CPA, Chief Financial Officer
Alan Payne, VP of Sales

Become our fan on Facebook **facebook.com/idwpublishing**
Follow us on Twitter **@idwpublishing**
Check us out on YouTube **youtube.com/idwpublishing**
www.IDWPUBLISHING.com

Originally published as SERVANT OF THE BONES Issues #1–6.

uys, dolls, transsexuals, extraterrestrials, and all of the readers: Well, here it is! SERVANT OF THE BONES brought to you in this gorgeous graphic novel.

You know, I was really thrilled with SERVANT. This story was tremendously exciting for me to write because, as you may or may not be aware, it was my first novel involving a ghost. It was a book I wrote that had no involvement with either vampires or witches. Those supernatural heroes I have loved with great devotion, but writing about ghosts and hauntings without my beloved Lestat or Lasher or the Mayfair clan was a breath of fresh air! Coming from New Orleans, I grew up hearing good old fashion ghost stories. And a ghost story this is!

Of course, I never write a story unless it comes to me like a swarm of bees surrounding my head. The preparation was unlike any other. For years I have had a passion for archaeology. I go to great lengths to be as historically accurate as possible. The research I conducted for SERVANT OF THE BONES was extensive. I studied the Hebrew exile in Babylon; I studied ancient Sumer and the Temple of Marduk; I also visited Jerusalem and encountered many Jewish readers who provided good and honest answers to my endless questions. I yearned then as I still do today to make all aspects of my writing as real as possible.

To bring history into focus, during the time I wrote SERVANT, there was much global turmoil. The subtext of the story speaks about the differences and similarities between East and West. In a sense I was saying that, although we can be politically, economically, spiritually divided, we have a kind of oneness in a shared sense of Gothic lore. I was saying that both cultures are truly united in loving the beauty of form and movement, loving goose bumps on the back of your neck, loving a good ghost story!

The characters were an obsession for me. Esther was not the inspiration for the story, but she was the catalyst for the narrative. I liked her character a great deal. For a time I actually walked in Esther's shoes. I visited the diamond district in New York City. I spoke with several merchants; I listened to how they talked to me; I observed how they interacted with other haggling clientele. I found a lovely necklace that Esther would have liked, though nowhere near as expensive as one she would have purchased. But I had to have such rituals. I had to have something that she would have had. It helped me know her better.

Gregory Belkin, the villain, had what we called in my family "black Irish" blood, a reference to the Elizabethan period when the Spanish Armada crash landed on the Irish coast and intermarried with the locals, thoroughly mixing the gene pool. That was the idea behind Gregory Belkin, with his pure black eyes. His black Irish blood didn't make him sinister; it made his villainous features more attractive and believable.

But Azriel was my dark hero in this story, and his character began with his name. I love to investigate the root and meaning of names. No good name in any of my stories is an accident, and Azriel certainly fell into that category. I chose his name because it was very common for BC Hebrews, and also because it seemed very uncommon for the modern English-speaker; the name was beautiful and mysterious; and for me at least, it described my dark new hero character perfectly. I found myself haunted by the idea that Azriel has all of Lestat's courage, but is liberated from the curse of the vampires. Azriel is locked out of heaven, an outcast among us in search of his own soul. He is a true ghost and there are things that Azriel can do that Lestat can't do and I have the eerie feeling that I fell in love with Azriel the way I was in love with Lestat.

If this sounds like a sales pitch, what can I do but burst into tears! I'd love you to read about my heroes–I want you to love my ghost in this absolutely amazing graphic novel retelling.

Love to all,

Anne Rice

Chapter One

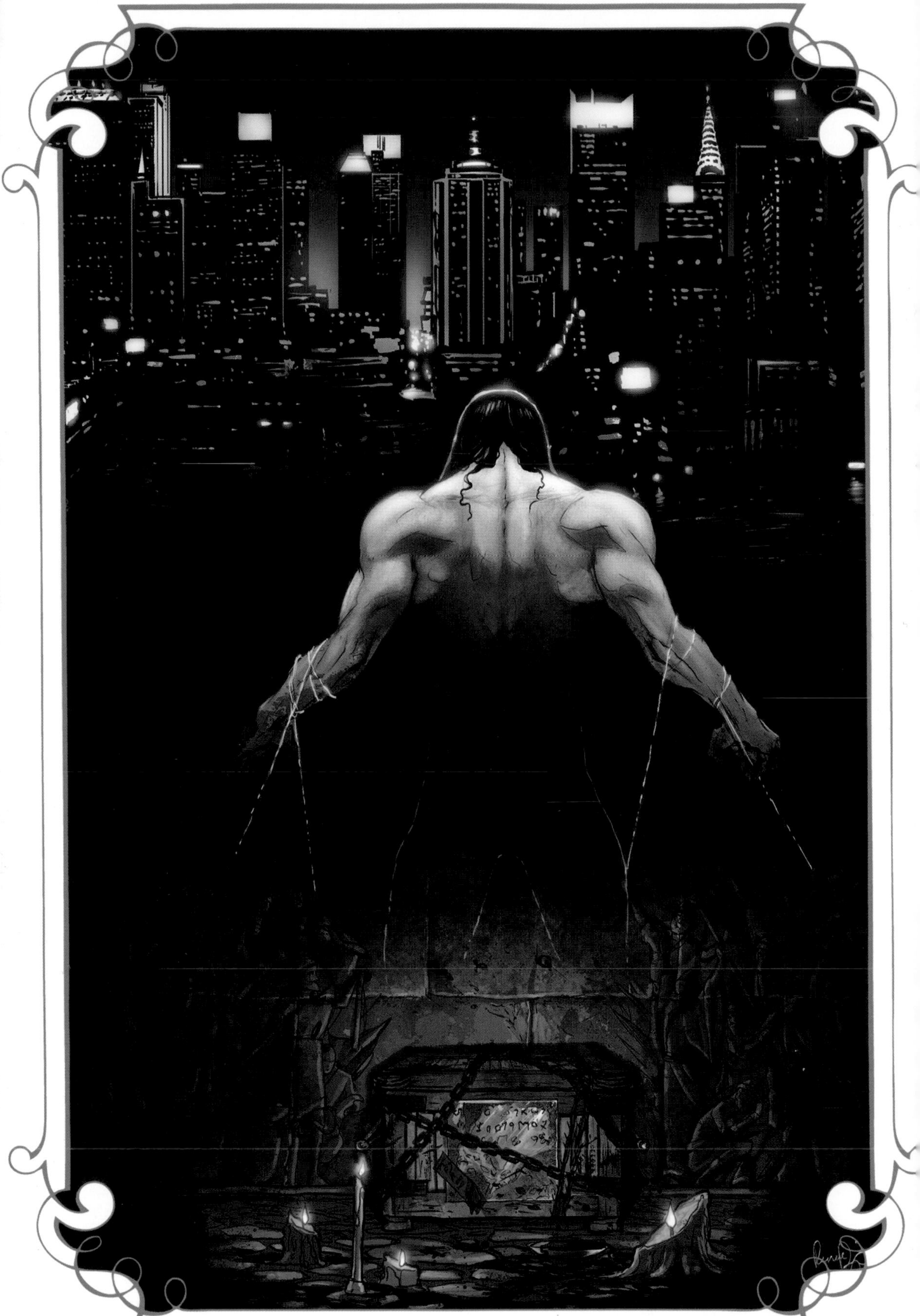

Art by Renae De Liz • Colors by Ray Dillon

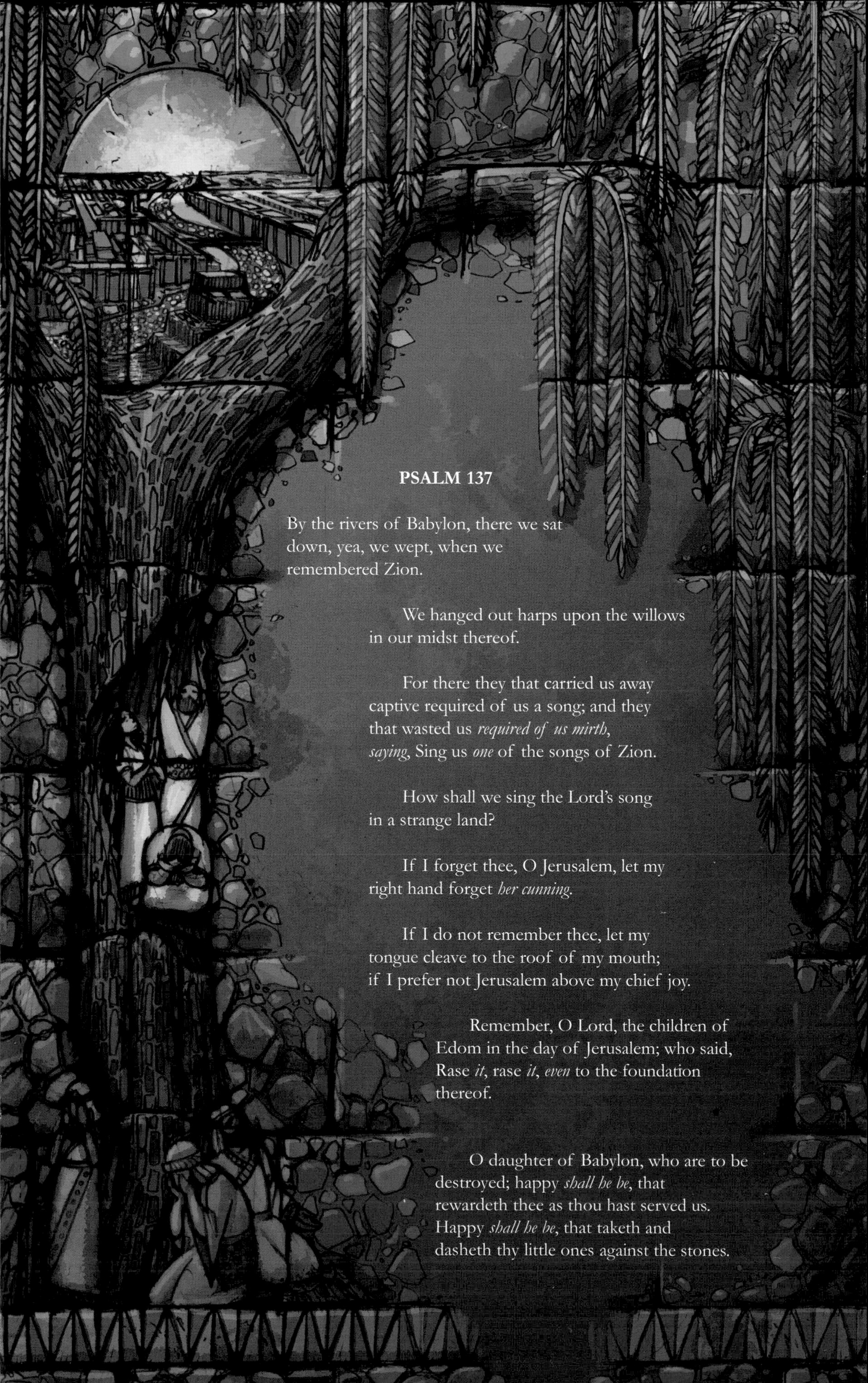

PSALM 137

By the rivers of Babylon, there we sat down, yea, we wept, when we remembered Zion.

We hanged out harps upon the willows in our midst thereof.

For there they that carried us away captive required of us a song; and they that wasted us *required of us mirth*, *saying*, Sing us *one* of the songs of Zion.

How shall we sing the Lord's song in a strange land?

If I forget thee, O Jerusalem, let my right hand forget *her cunning*.

If I do not remember thee, let my tongue cleave to the roof of my mouth; if I prefer not Jerusalem above my chief joy.

Remember, O Lord, the children of Edom in the day of Jerusalem; who said, Rase *it*, rase *it*, *even* to the foundation thereof.

O daughter of Babylon, who are to be destroyed; happy *shall he be*, that rewardeth thee as thou hast served us. Happy *shall he be*, that taketh and dasheth thy little ones against the stones.

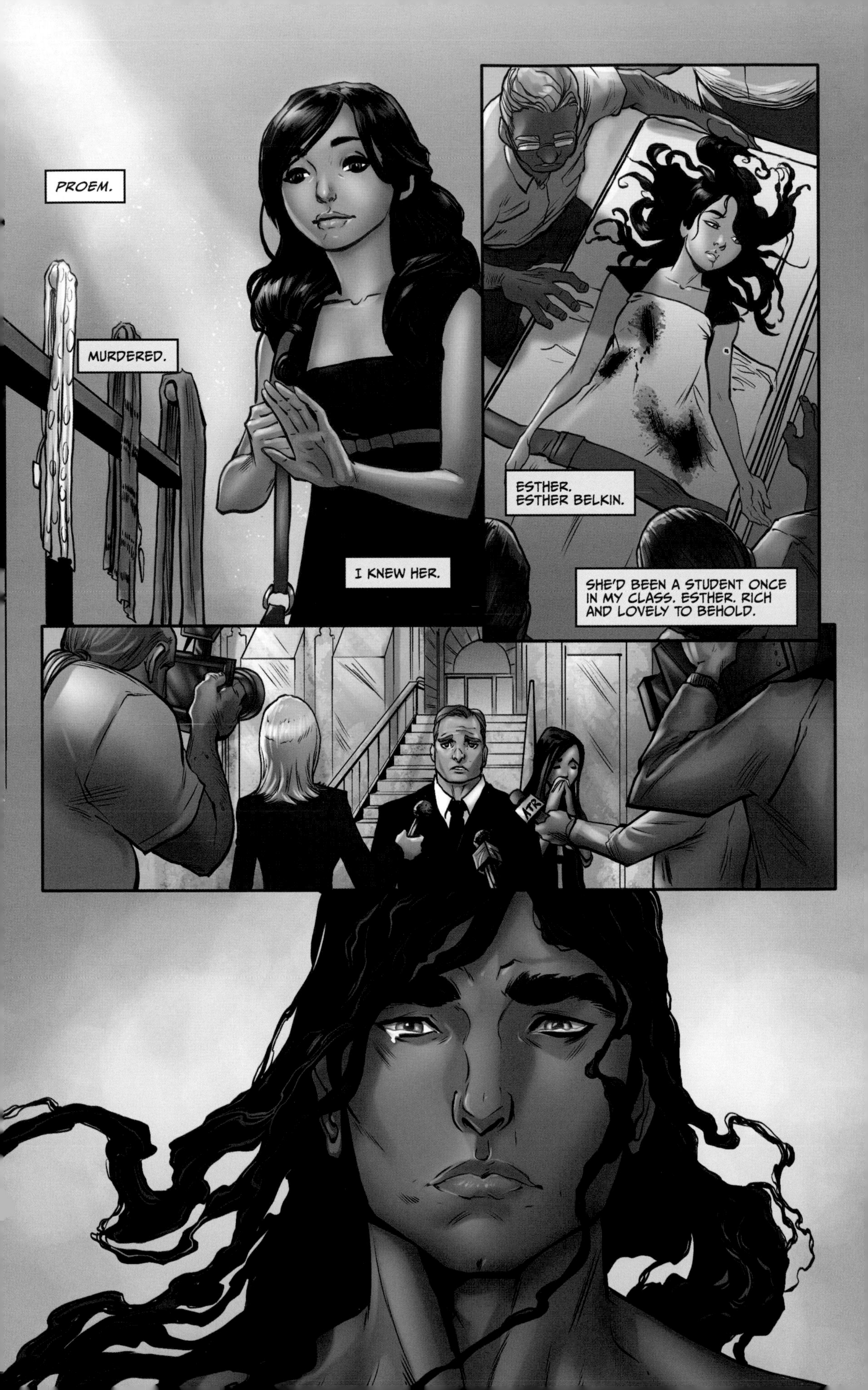
PROEM.
MURDERED.
I KNEW HER.
ESTHER.
ESTHER BELKIN.
SHE'D BEEN A STUDENT ONCE IN MY CLASS. ESTHER. RICH AND LOVELY TO BEHOLD.
ATR

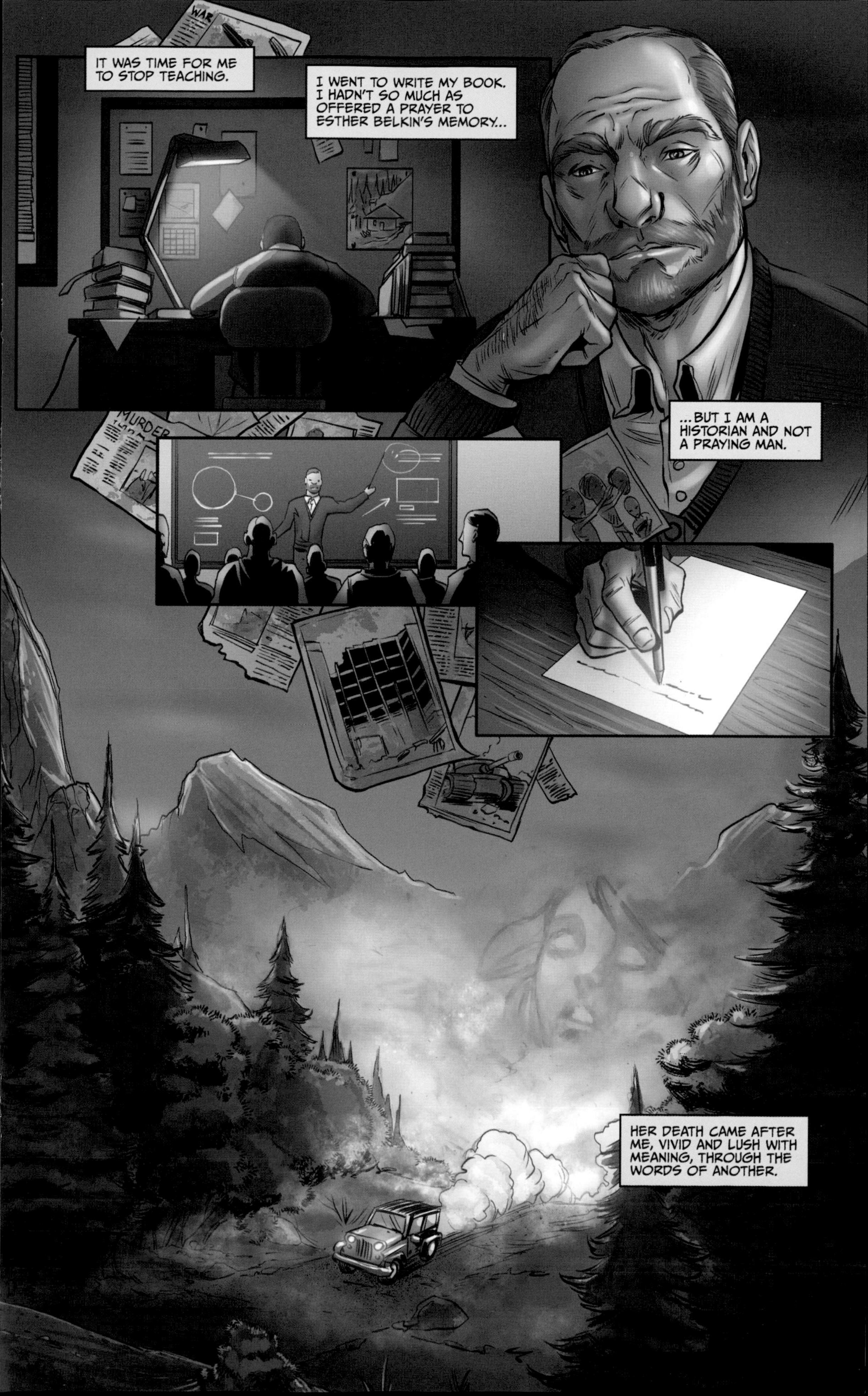
IT WAS TIME FOR ME TO STOP TEACHING.
I WENT TO WRITE MY BOOK. I HADN'T SO MUCH AS OFFERED A PRAYER TO ESTHER BELKIN'S MEMORY...
...BUT I AM A HISTORIAN AND NOT A PRAYING MAN.
HER DEATH CAME AFTER ME, VIVID AND LUSH WITH MEANING, THROUGH THE WORDS OF ANOTHER.

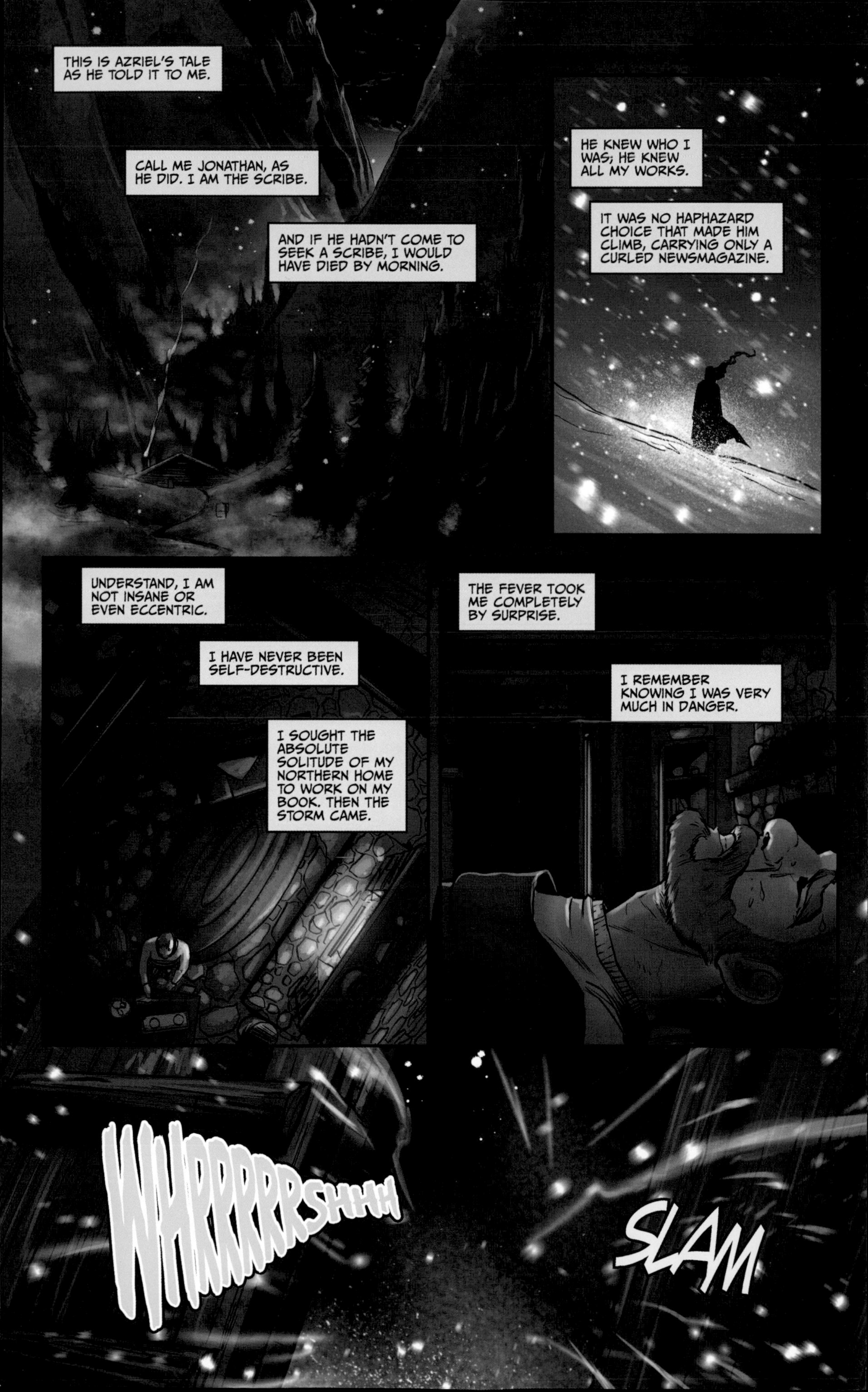
THIS IS AZRIEL'S TALE AS HE TOLD IT TO ME.
CALL ME JONATHAN, AS HE DID. I AM THE SCRIBE.
AND IF HE HADN'T COME TO SEEK A SCRIBE, I WOULD HAVE DIED BY MORNING.
HE KNEW WHO I WAS; HE KNEW ALL MY WORKS.
IT WAS NO HAPHAZARD CHOICE THAT MADE HIM CLIMB, CARRYING ONLY A CURLED NEWSMAGAZINE.
UNDERSTAND, I AM NOT INSANE OR EVEN ECCENTRIC.
I HAVE NEVER BEEN SELF-DESTRUCTIVE.
I SOUGHT THE ABSOLUTE SOLITUDE OF MY NORTHERN HOME TO WORK ON MY BOOK. THEN THE STORM CAME.
THE FEVER TOOK ME COMPLETELY BY SURPRISE.
I REMEMBER KNOWING I WAS VERY MUCH IN DANGER.
WHRRRRRRSHHHH
SLAM

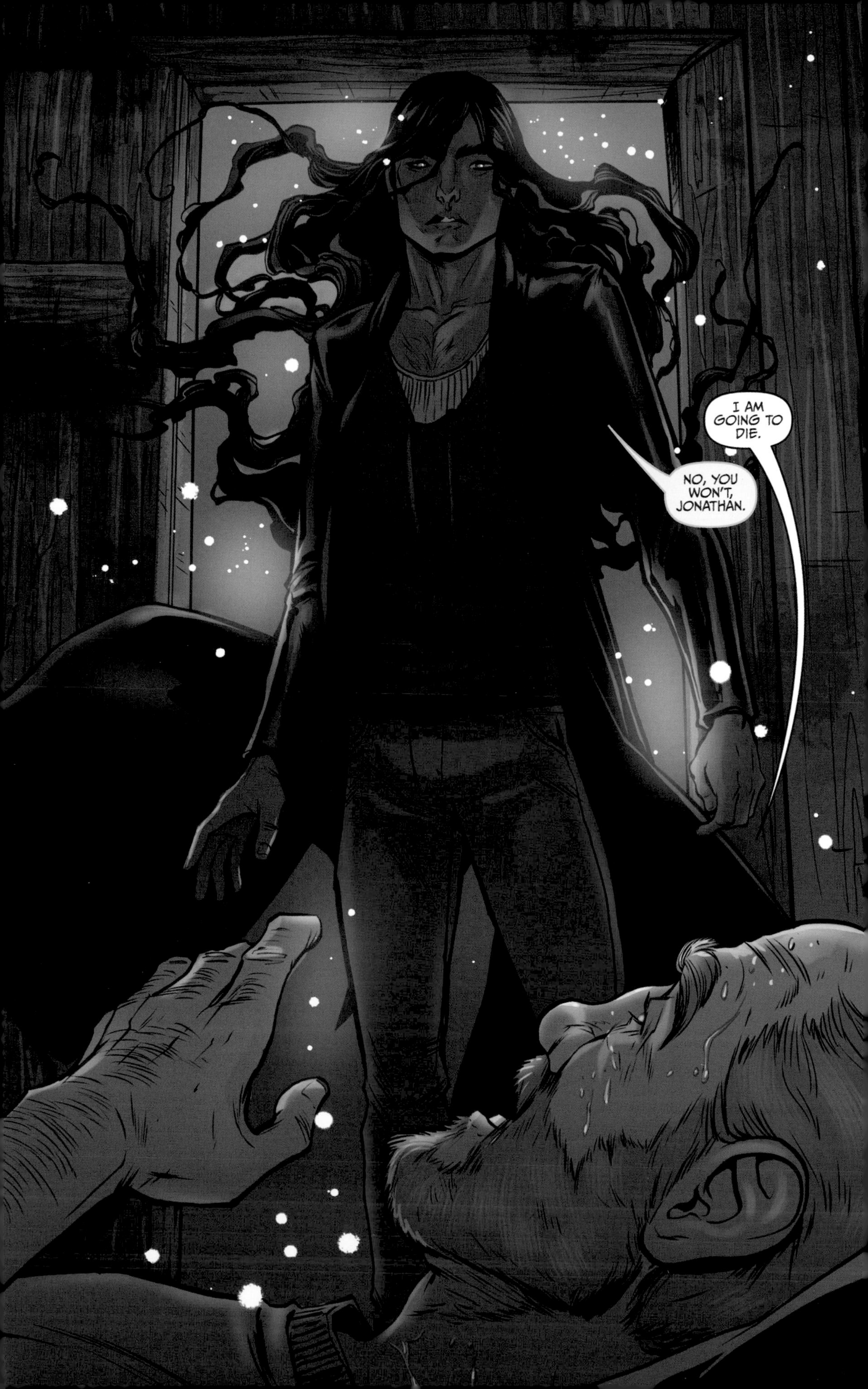
I AM GOING TO DIE.
NO, YOU WON'T, JONATHAN.

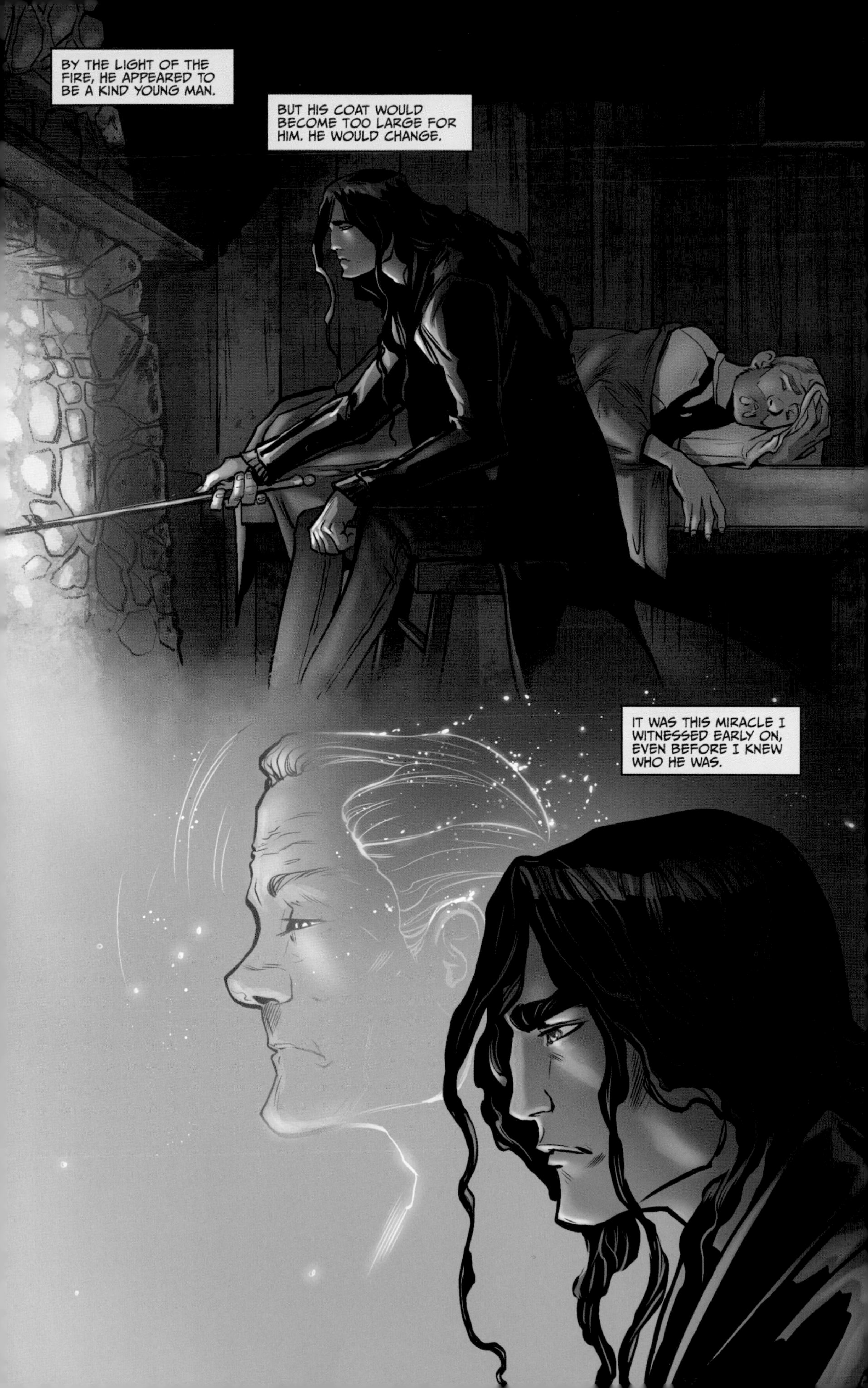
BY THE LIGHT OF THE FIRE, HE APPEARED TO BE A KIND YOUNG MAN.
BUT HIS COAT WOULD BECOME TOO LARGE FOR HIM. HE WOULD CHANGE.
IT WAS THIS MIRACLE I WITNESSED EARLY ON, EVEN BEFORE I KNEW WHO HE WAS.

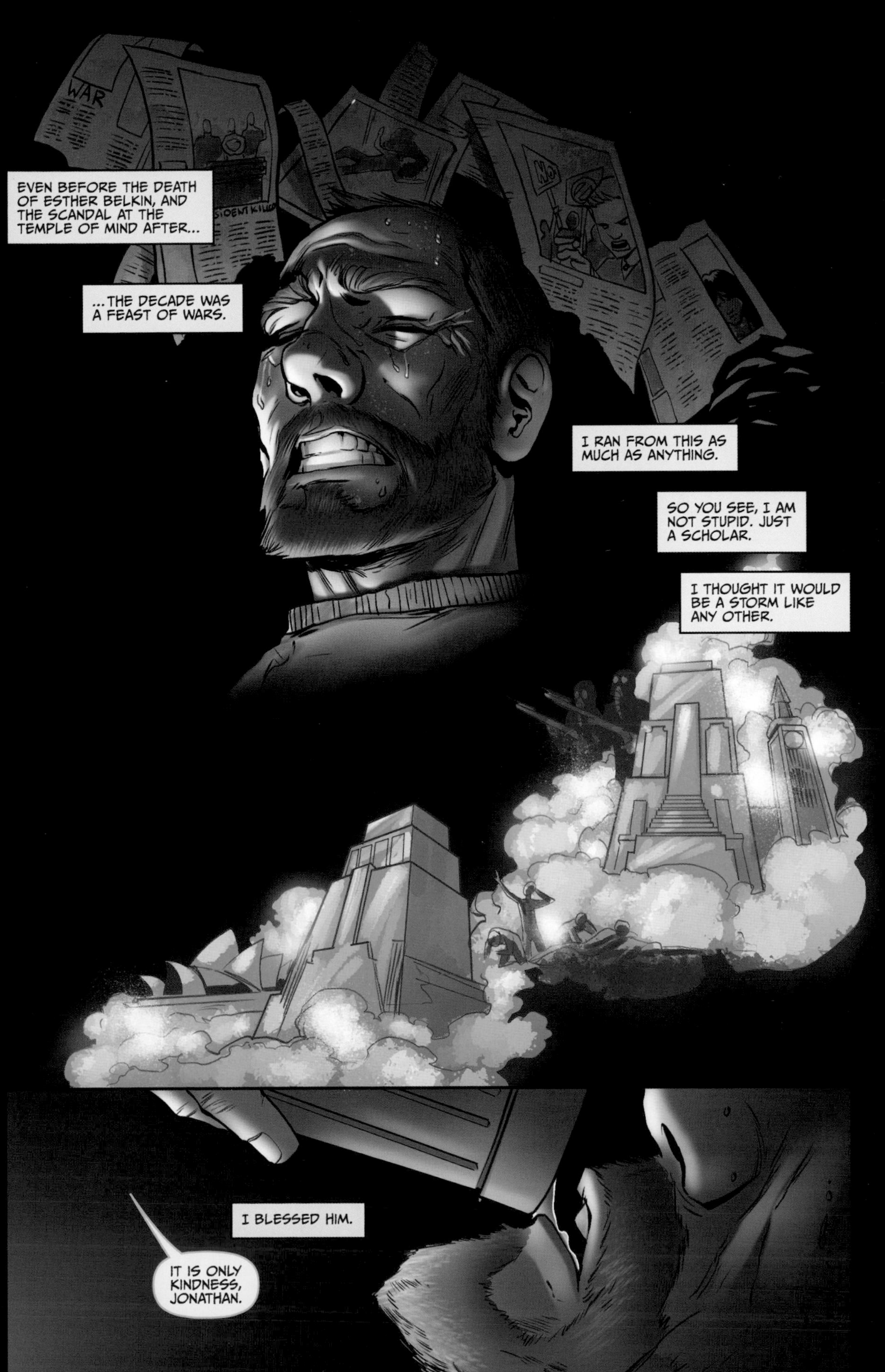
WAR
EVEN BEFORE THE DEATH OF ESTHER BELKIN, AND THE SCANDAL AT THE TEMPLE OF MIND AFTER...
...THE DECADE WAS A FEAST OF WARS.
I RAN FROM THIS AS MUCH AS ANYTHING.
SO YOU SEE, I AM NOT STUPID. JUST A SCHOLAR.
I THOUGHT IT WOULD BE A STORM LIKE ANY OTHER.
I BLESSED HIM.
IT IS ONLY KINDNESS, JONATHAN.

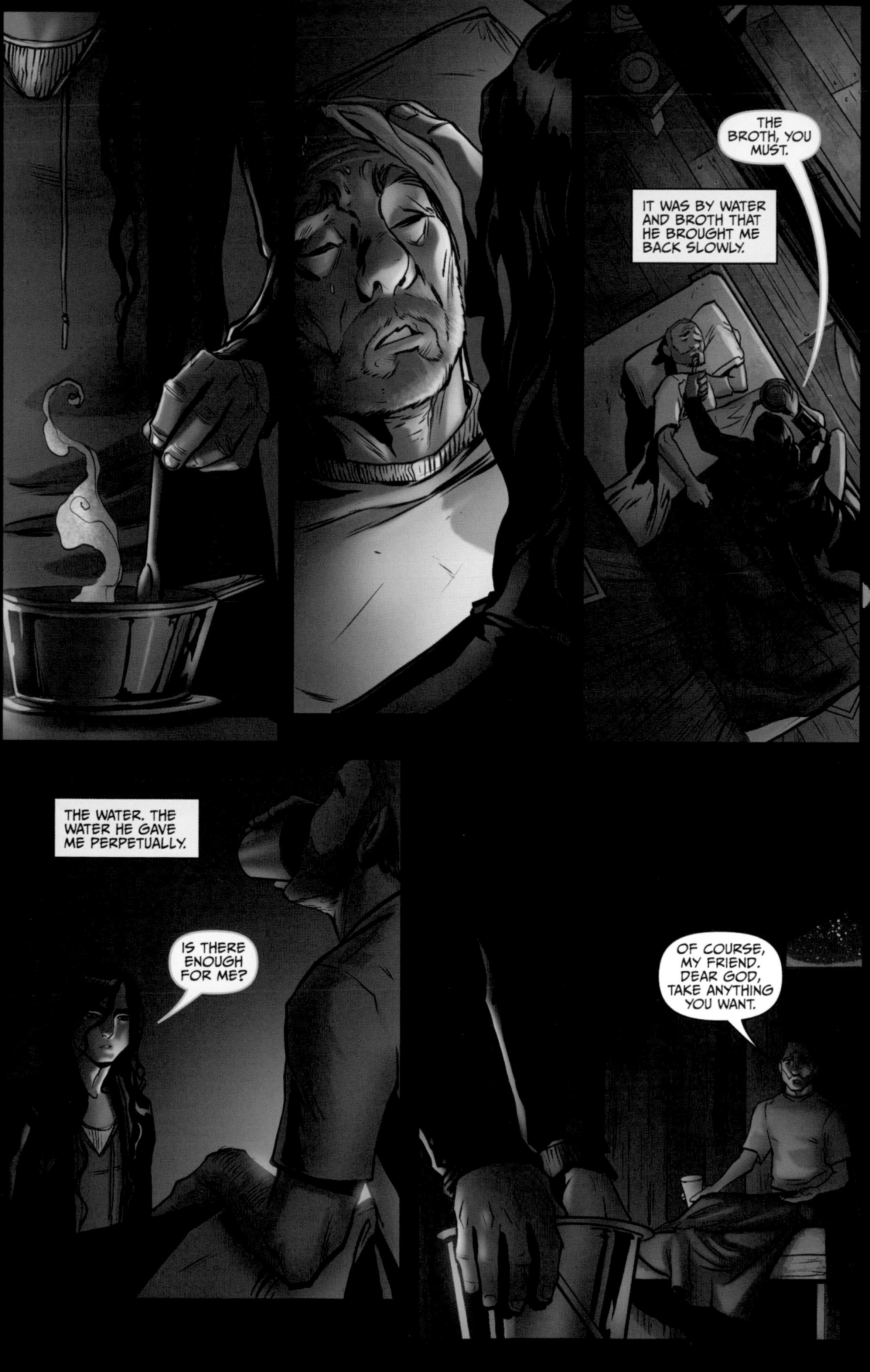
THE BROTH, YOU MUST.
IT WAS BY WATER AND BROTH THAT HE BROUGHT ME BACK SLOWLY.
THE WATER. THE WATER HE GAVE ME PERPETUALLY.
IS THERE ENOUGH FOR ME?
OF COURSE, MY FRIEND. DEAR GOD, TAKE ANYTHING YOU WANT.

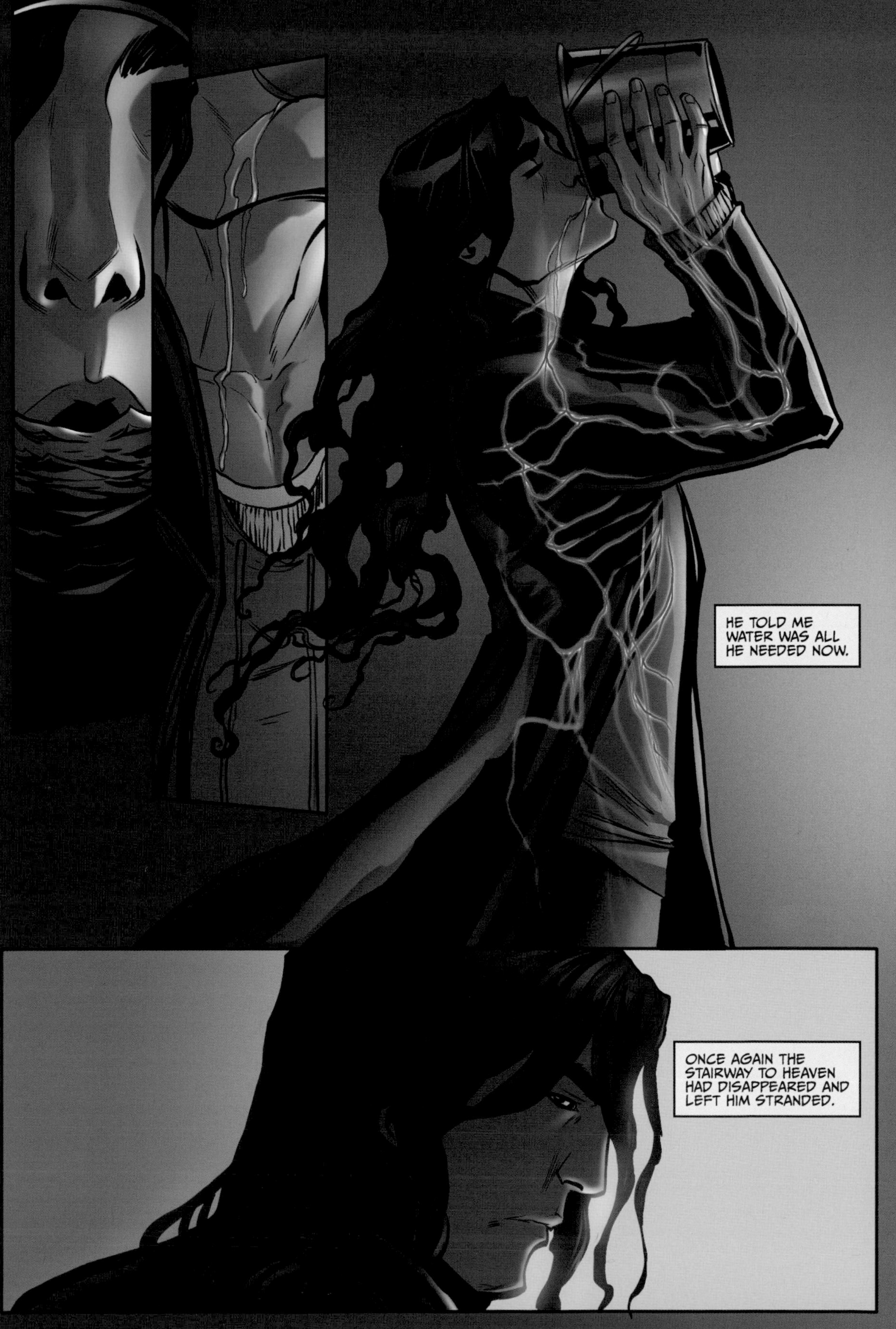
HE TOLD ME WATER WAS ALL HE NEEDED NOW.
ONCE AGAIN THE STAIRWAY TO HEAVEN HAD DISAPPEARED AND LEFT HIM STRANDED.

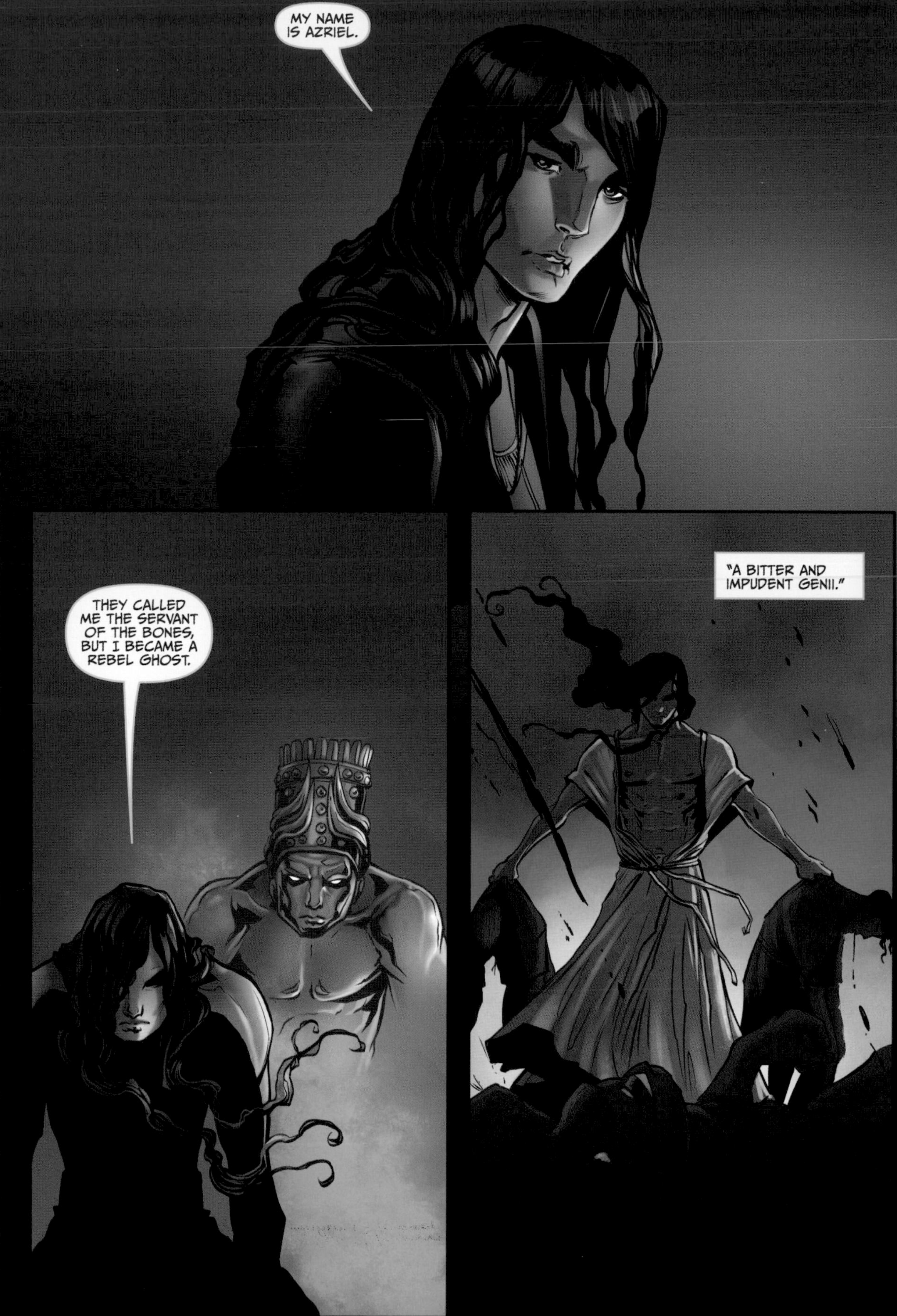
MY NAME IS AZRIEL.
THEY CALLED ME THE SERVANT OF THE BONES, BUT I BECAME A REBEL GHOST.
"A BITTER AND IMPUDENT GENII."

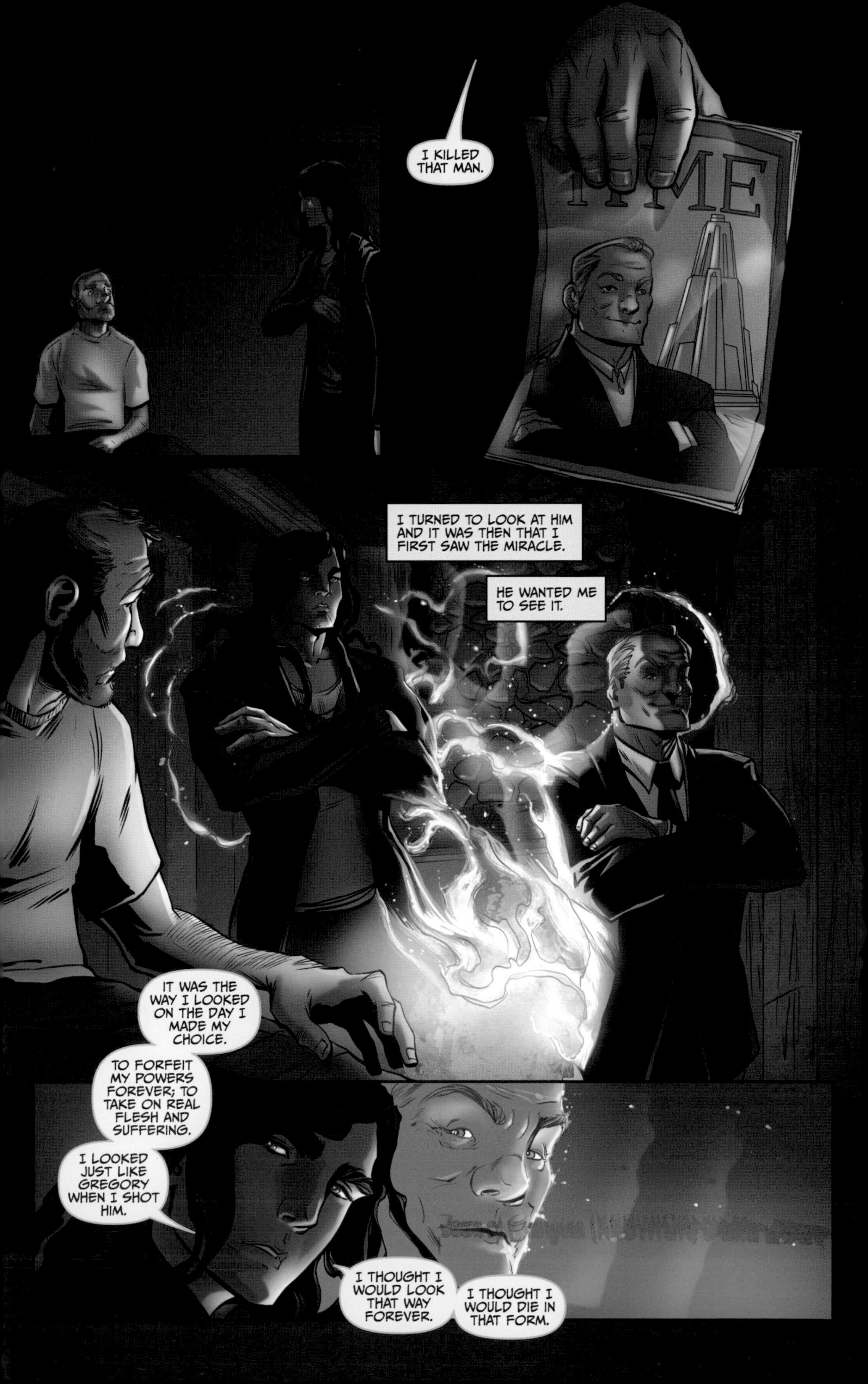
I KILLED THAT MAN.
I TURNED TO LOOK AT HIM AND IT WAS THEN THAT I FIRST SAW THE MIRACLE.
HE WANTED ME TO SEE IT.
IT WAS THE WAY I LOOKED ON THE DAY I MADE MY CHOICE.
TO FORFEIT MY POWERS FOREVER; TO TAKE ON REAL FLESH AND SUFFERING.
I LOOKED JUST LIKE GREGORY WHEN I SHOT HIM.
I THOUGHT I WOULD LOOK THAT WAY FOREVER.
I THOUGHT I WOULD DIE IN THAT FORM.

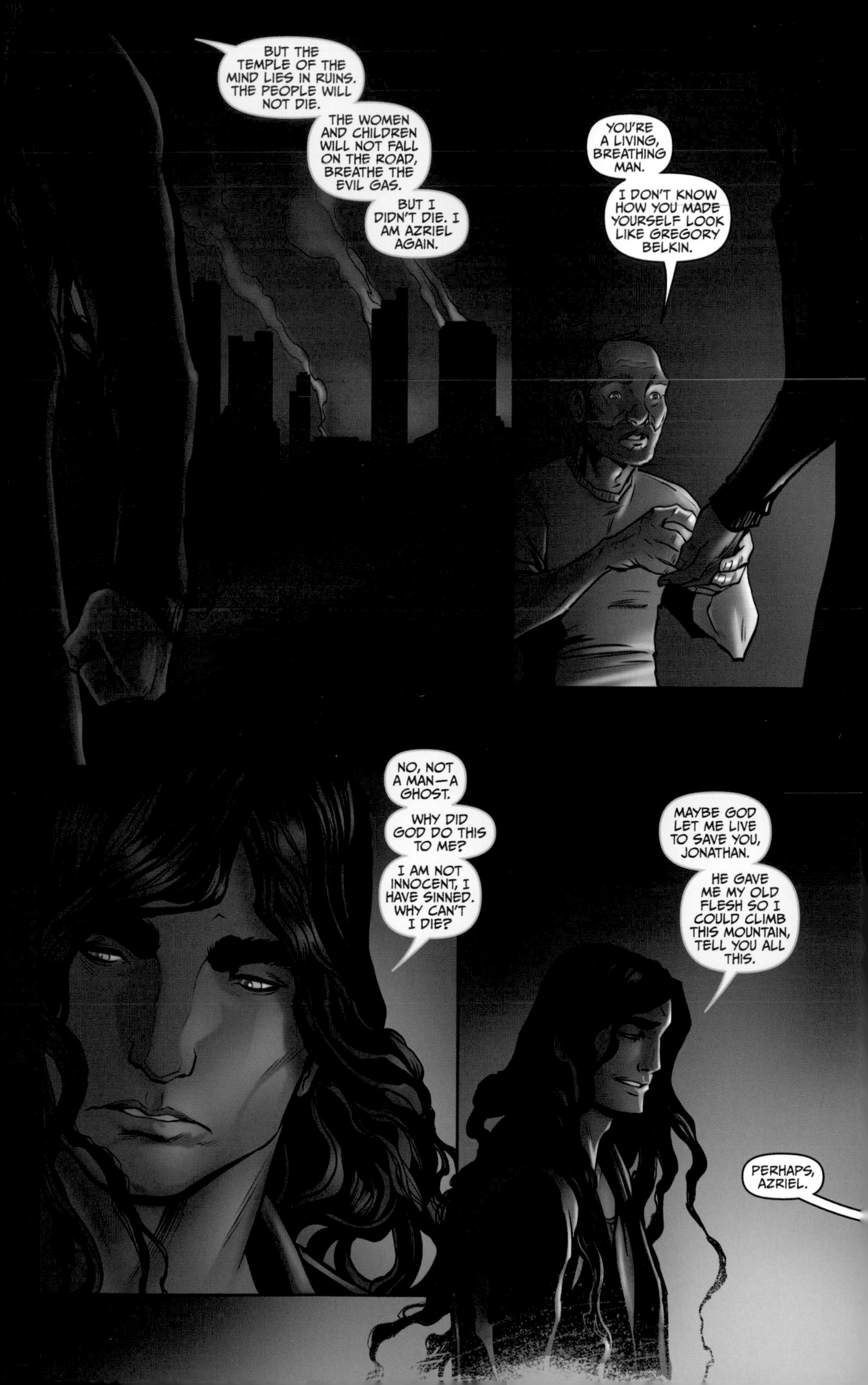
BUT THE TEMPLE OF THE MIND LIES IN RUINS. THE PEOPLE WILL NOT DIE.
THE WOMEN AND CHILDREN WILL NOT FALL ON THE ROAD, BREATHE THE EVIL GAS.
BUT I DIDN'T DIE. I AM AZRIEL AGAIN.
YOU'RE A LIVING, BREATHING MAN.
I DON'T KNOW HOW YOU MADE YOURSELF LOOK LIKE GREGORY BELKIN.
NO, NOT A MAN—A GHOST.
WHY DID GOD DO THIS TO ME?
I AM NOT INNOCENT, I HAVE SINNED. WHY CAN'T I DIE?
MAYBE GOD LET ME LIVE TO SAVE YOU, JONATHAN.
HE GAVE ME MY OLD FLESH SO I COULD CLIMB THIS MOUNTAIN, TELL YOU ALL THIS.
PERHAPS, AZRIEL.

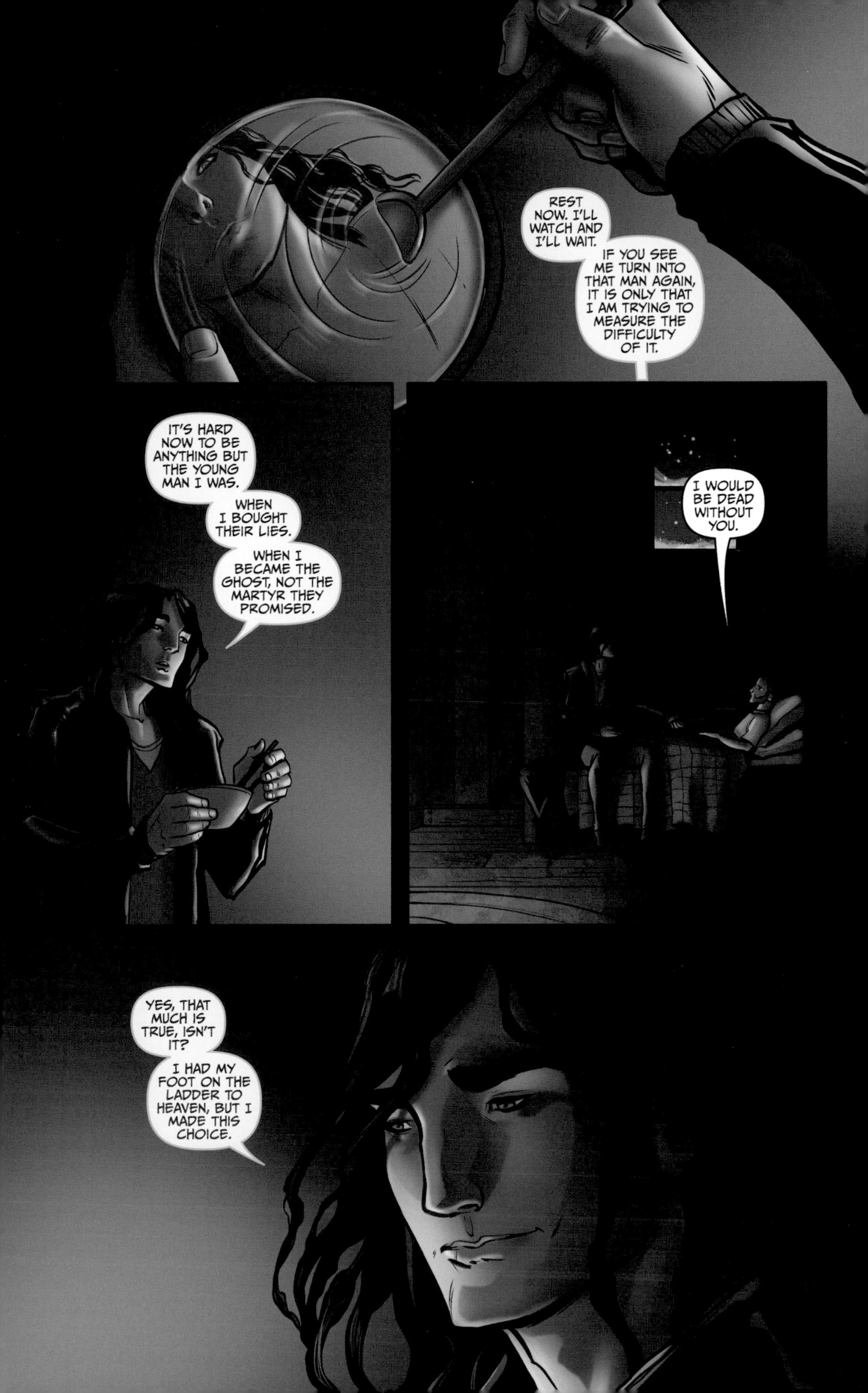
REST NOW. I'LL WATCH AND I'LL WAIT.
IF YOU SEE ME TURN INTO THAT MAN AGAIN, IT IS ONLY THAT I AM TRYING TO MEASURE THE DIFFICULTY OF IT.
IT'S HARD NOW TO BE ANYTHING BUT THE YOUNG MAN I WAS.
WHEN I BOUGHT THEIR LIES.
WHEN I BECAME THE GHOST, NOT THE MARTYR THEY PROMISED.
I WOULD BE DEAD WITHOUT YOU.
YES, THAT MUCH IS TRUE, ISN'T IT?
I HAD MY FOOT ON THE LADDER TO HEAVEN, BUT I MADE THIS CHOICE.

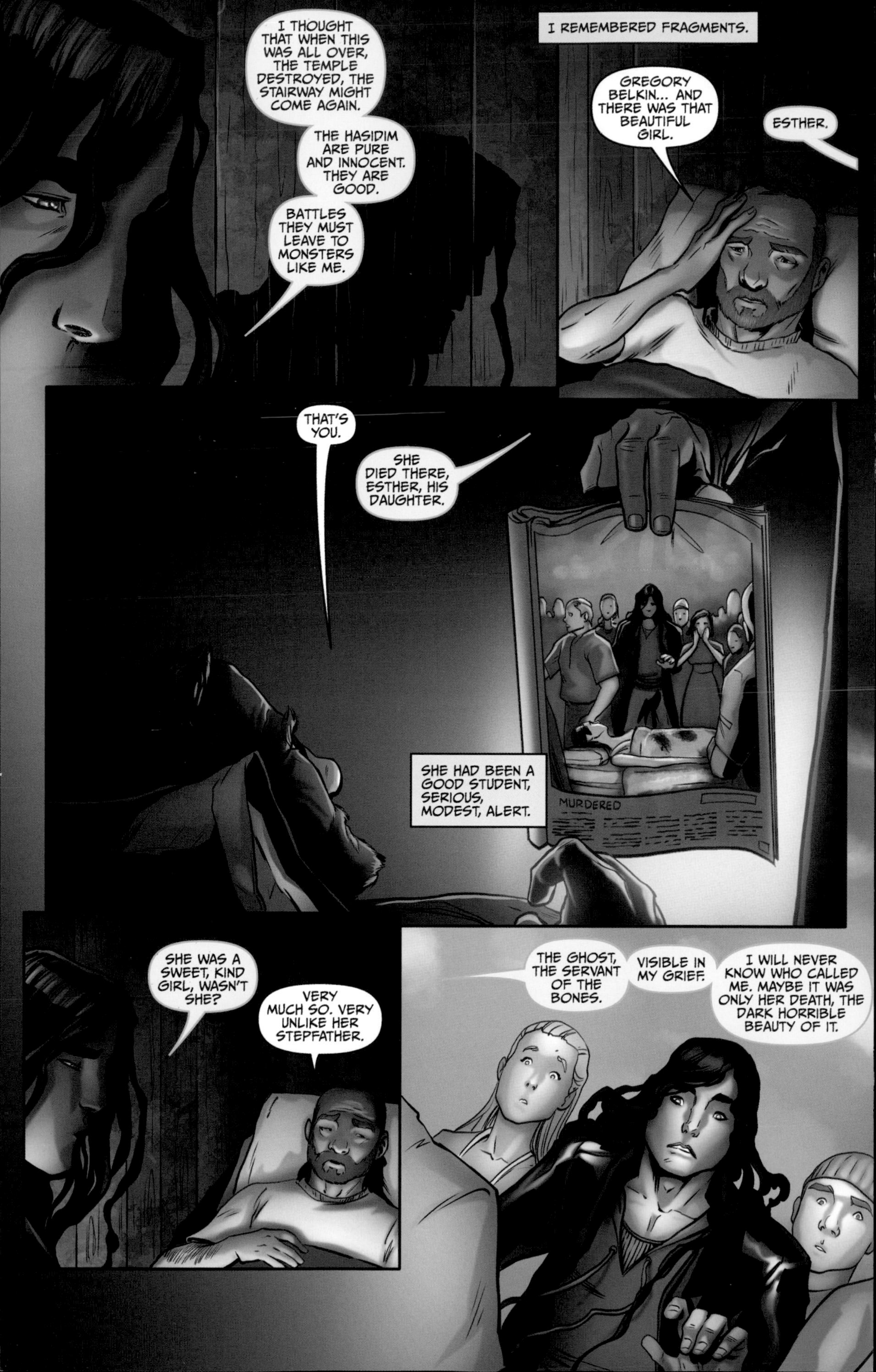
I THOUGHT THAT WHEN THIS WAS ALL OVER, THE TEMPLE DESTROYED, THE STAIRWAY MIGHT COME AGAIN.
THE HASIDIM ARE PURE AND INNOCENT. THEY ARE GOOD.
BATTLES THEY MUST LEAVE TO MONSTERS LIKE ME.
I REMEMBERED FRAGMENTS.
GREGORY BELKIN... AND THERE WAS THAT BEAUTIFUL GIRL.
ESTHER.
THAT'S YOU.
SHE DIED THERE, ESTHER, HIS DAUGHTER.
MURDERED
SHE HAD BEEN A GOOD STUDENT, SERIOUS, MODEST, ALERT.
SHE WAS A SWEET, KIND GIRL, WASN'T SHE?
VERY MUCH SO. VERY UNLIKE HER STEPFATHER.
THE GHOST, THE SERVANT OF THE BONES.
VISIBLE IN MY GRIEF.
I WILL NEVER KNOW WHO CALLED ME. MAYBE IT WAS ONLY HER DEATH, THE DARK HORRIBLE BEAUTY OF IT.

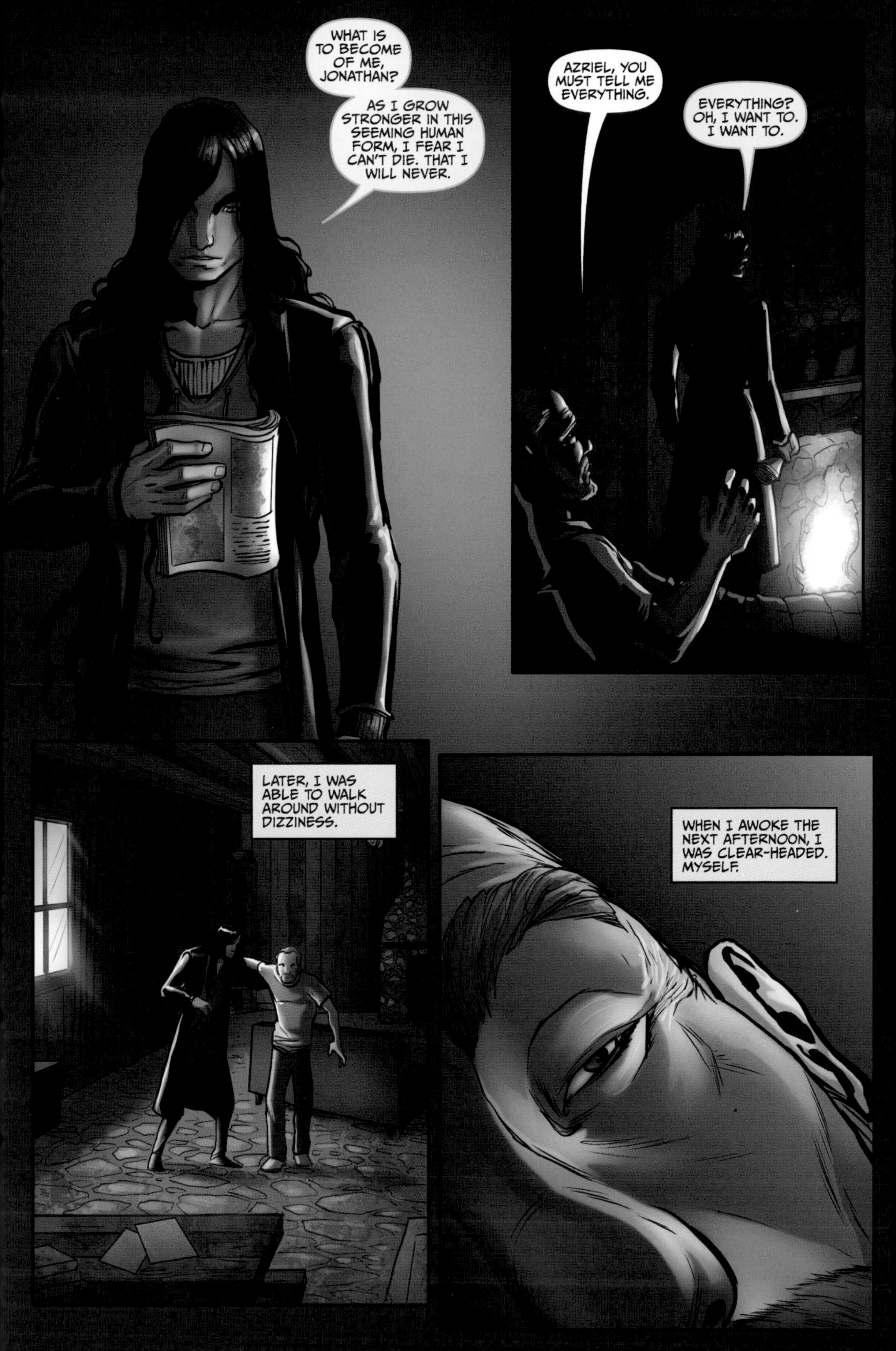
WHAT IS TO BECOME OF ME, JONATHAN?
AS I GROW STRONGER IN THIS SEEMING HUMAN FORM, I FEAR I CAN'T DIE. THAT I WILL NEVER.
AZRIEL, YOU MUST TELL ME EVERYTHING.
EVERYTHING? OH, I WANT TO. I WANT TO.
LATER, I WAS ABLE TO WALK AROUND WITHOUT DIZZINESS.
WHEN I AWOKE THE NEXT AFTERNOON, I WAS CLEAR-HEADED. MYSELF.

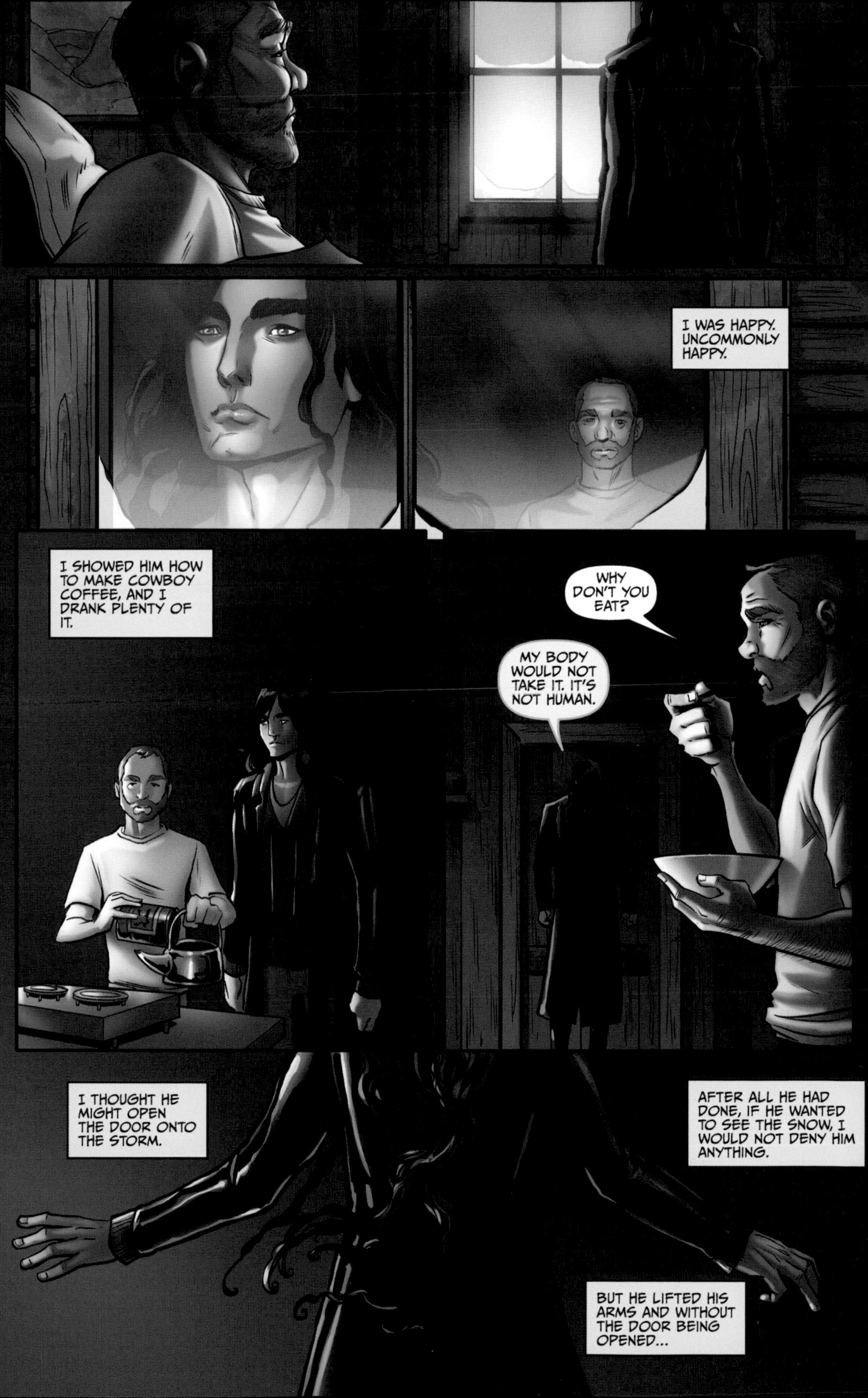
I WAS HAPPY. UNCOMMONLY HAPPY.
I SHOWED HIM HOW TO MAKE COWBOY COFFEE, AND I DRANK PLENTY OF IT.
WHY DON'T YOU EAT?
MY BODY WOULD NOT TAKE IT. IT'S NOT HUMAN.
I THOUGHT HE MIGHT OPEN THE DOOR ONTO THE STORM.
AFTER ALL HE HAD DONE, IF HE WANTED TO SEE THE SNOW, I WOULD NOT DENY HIM ANYTHING.
BUT HE LIFTED HIS ARMS AND WITHOUT THE DOOR BEING OPENED...

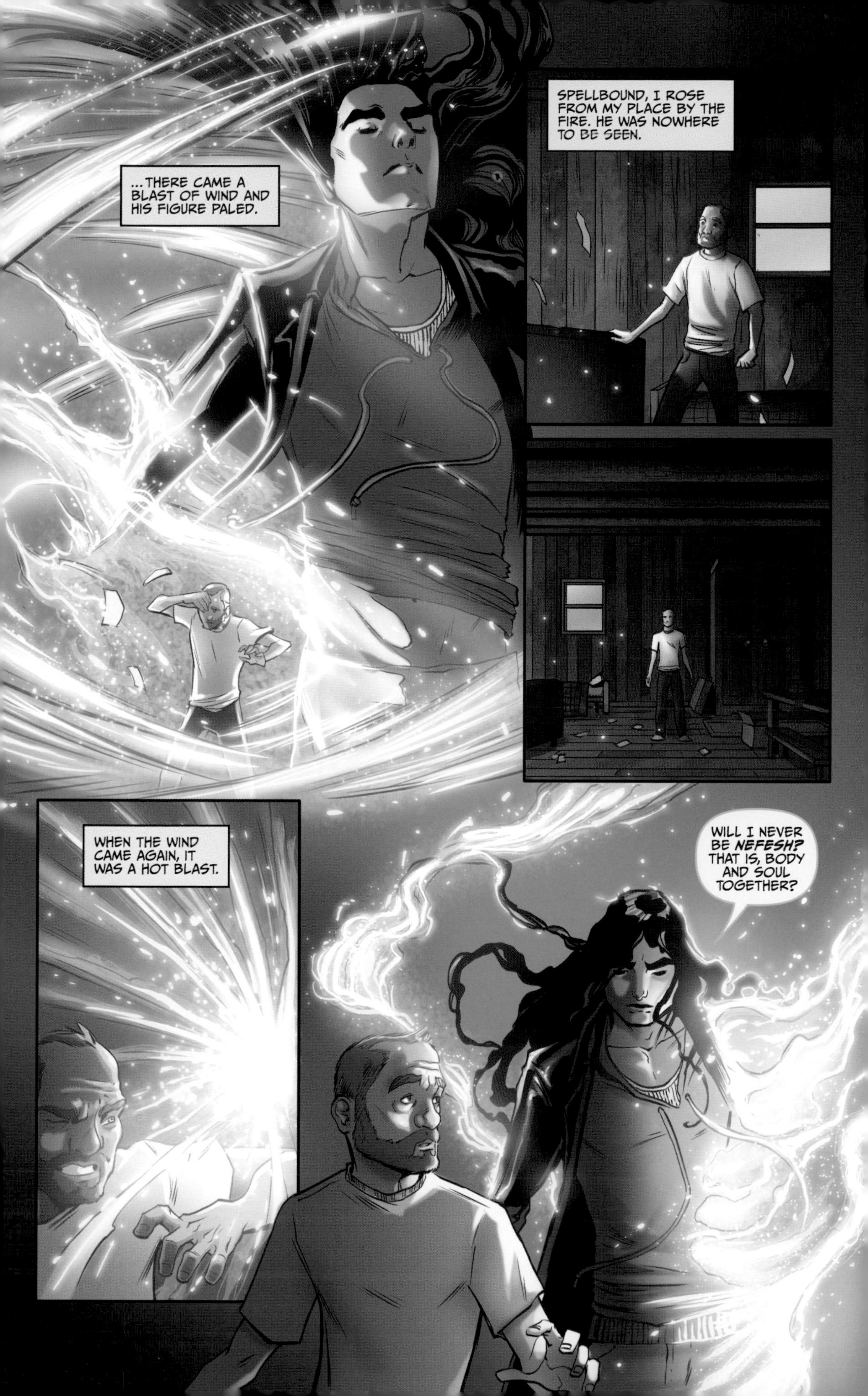
...THERE CAME A BLAST OF WIND AND HIS FIGURE PALED.
SPELLBOUND, I ROSE FROM MY PLACE BY THE FIRE. HE WAS NOWHERE TO BE SEEN.
WHEN THE WIND CAME AGAIN, IT WAS A HOT BLAST.
WILL I NEVER BE NEFESH? THAT IS, BODY AND SOUL TOGETHER?

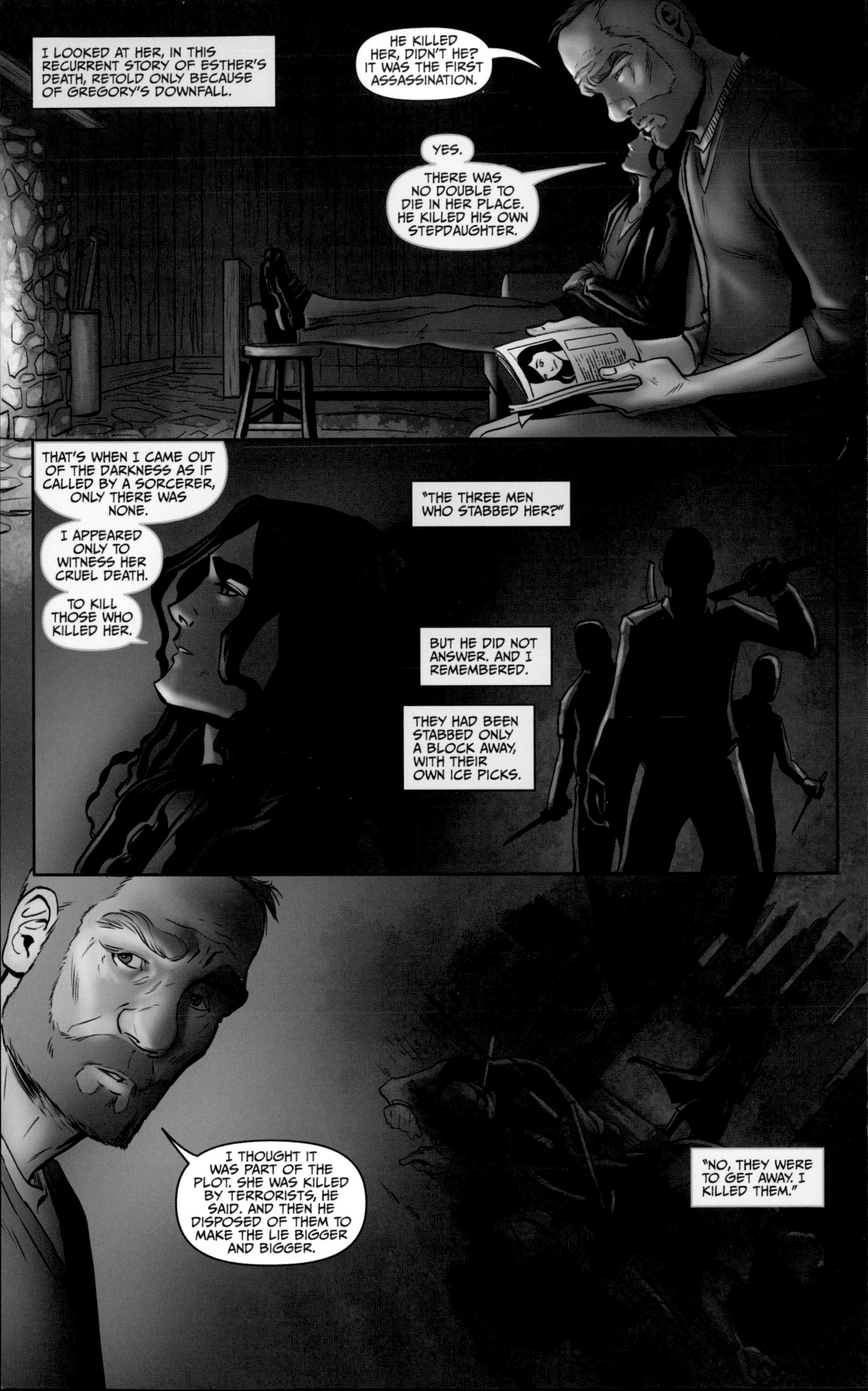
I LOOKED AT HER, IN THIS RECURRENT STORY OF ESTHER'S DEATH, RETOLD ONLY BECAUSE OF GREGORY'S DOWNFALL.
HE KILLED HER, DIDN'T HE? IT WAS THE FIRST ASSASSINATION.
YES.
THERE WAS NO DOUBLE TO DIE IN HER PLACE. HE KILLED HIS OWN STEPDAUGHTER.
THAT'S WHEN I CAME OUT OF THE DARKNESS AS IF CALLED BY A SORCERER, ONLY THERE WAS NONE.
I APPEARED ONLY TO WITNESS HER CRUEL DEATH.
TO KILL THOSE WHO KILLED HER.
"THE THREE MEN WHO STABBED HER?"
BUT HE DID NOT ANSWER. AND I REMEMBERED.
THEY HAD BEEN STABBED ONLY A BLOCK AWAY, WITH THEIR OWN ICE PICKS.
I THOUGHT IT WAS PART OF THE PLOT. SHE WAS KILLED BY TERRORISTS, HE SAID. AND THEN HE DISPOSED OF THEM TO MAKE THE LIE BIGGER AND BIGGER.
"NO, THEY WERE TO GET AWAY. I KILLED THEM."

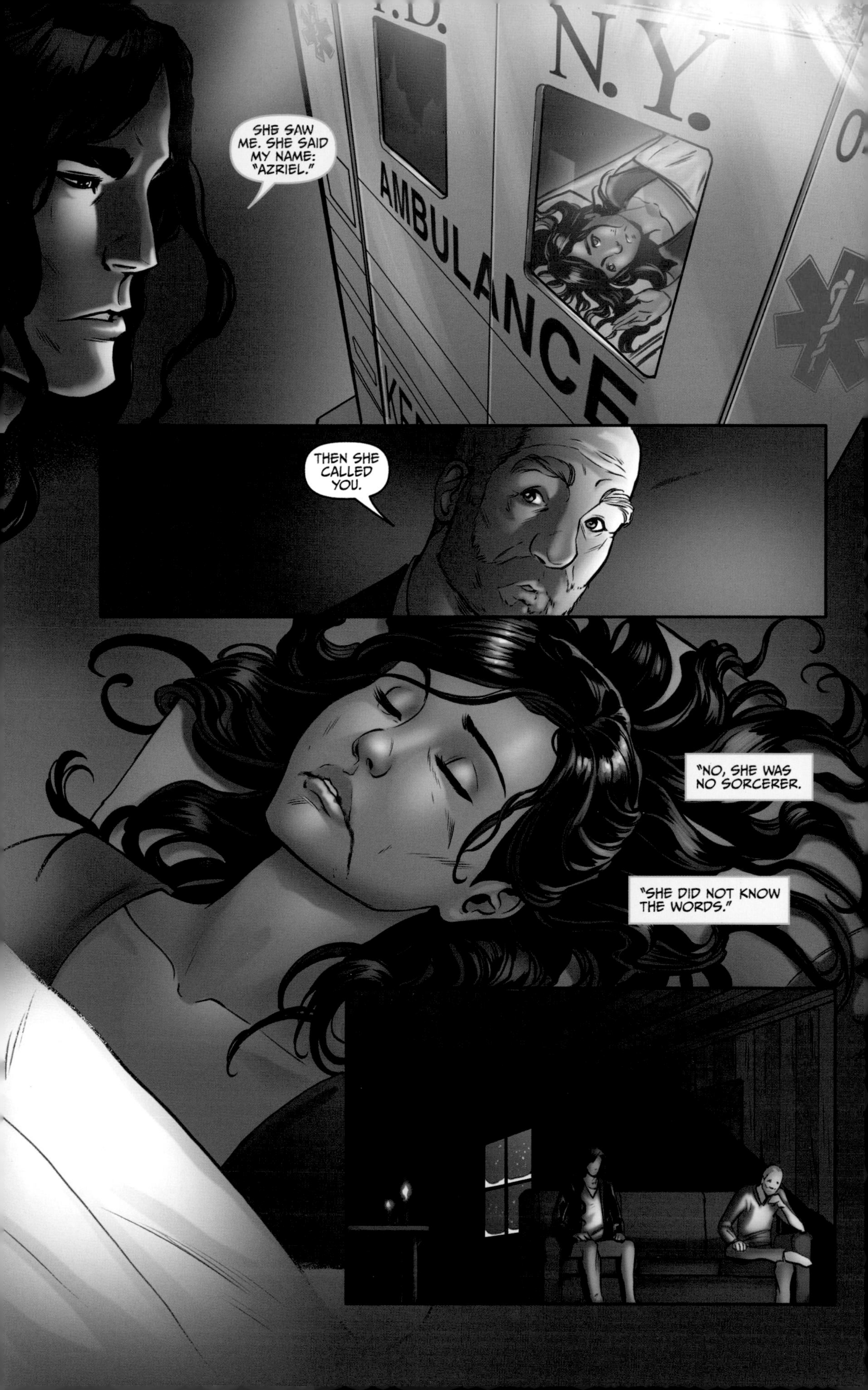
SHE SAW ME. SHE SAID MY NAME: "AZRIEL."
N.Y.
AMBULANCE
THEN SHE CALLED YOU.
"NO, SHE WAS NO SORCERER.
"SHE DID NOT KNOW THE WORDS."

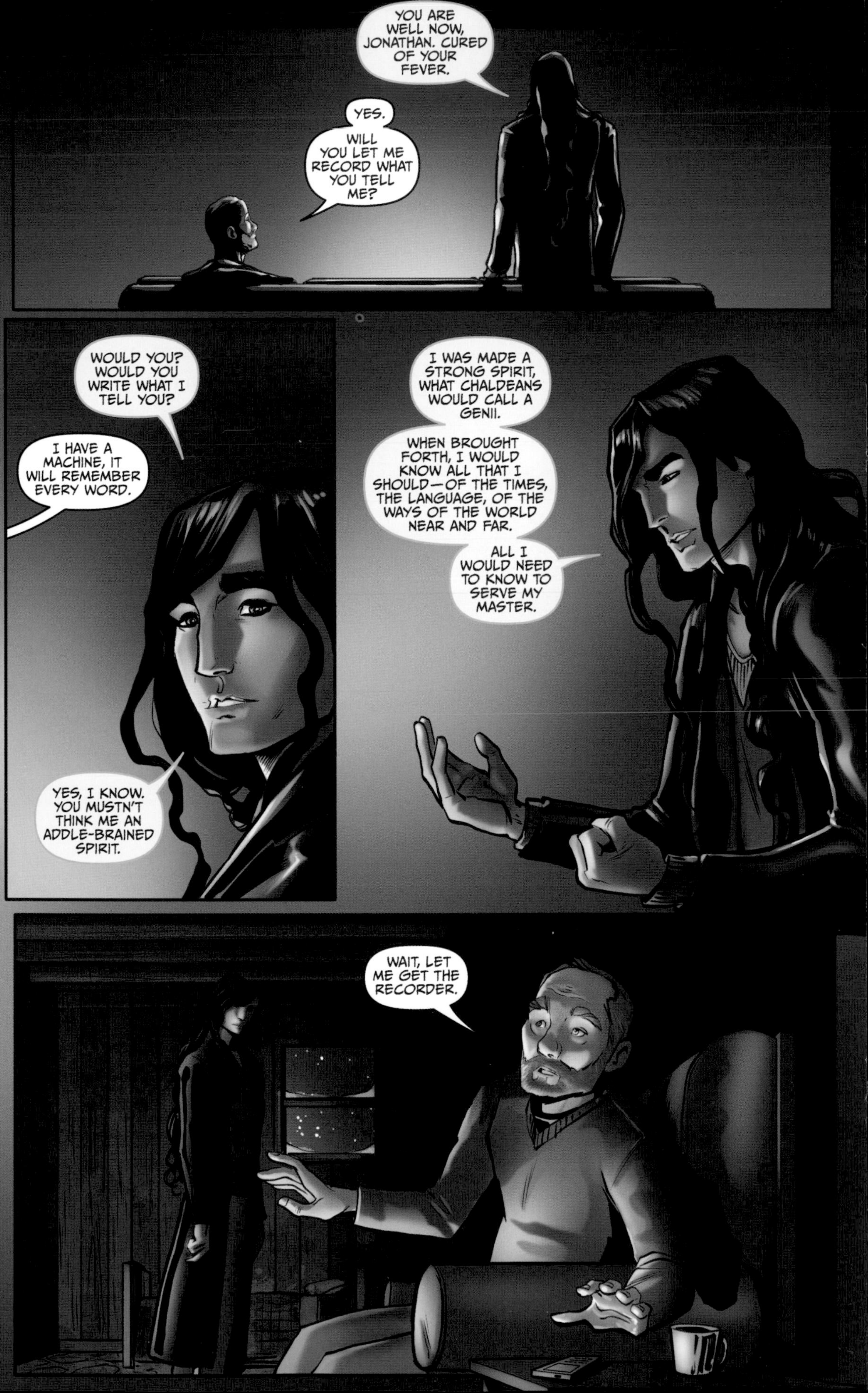
YOU ARE WELL NOW, JONATHAN. CURED OF YOUR FEVER.
YES.
WILL YOU LET ME RECORD WHAT YOU TELL ME?
WOULD YOU? WOULD YOU WRITE WHAT I TELL YOU?
I HAVE A MACHINE, IT WILL REMEMBER EVERY WORD.
YES, I KNOW. YOU MUSTN'T THINK ME AN ADDLE-BRAINED SPIRIT.
I WAS MADE A STRONG SPIRIT, WHAT CHALDEANS WOULD CALL A GENII.
WHEN BROUGHT FORTH, I WOULD KNOW ALL THAT I SHOULD—OF THE TIMES, THE LANGUAGE, OF THE WAYS OF THE WORLD NEAR AND FAR.
ALL I WOULD NEED TO KNOW TO SERVE MY MASTER.
WAIT, LET ME GET THE RECORDER.

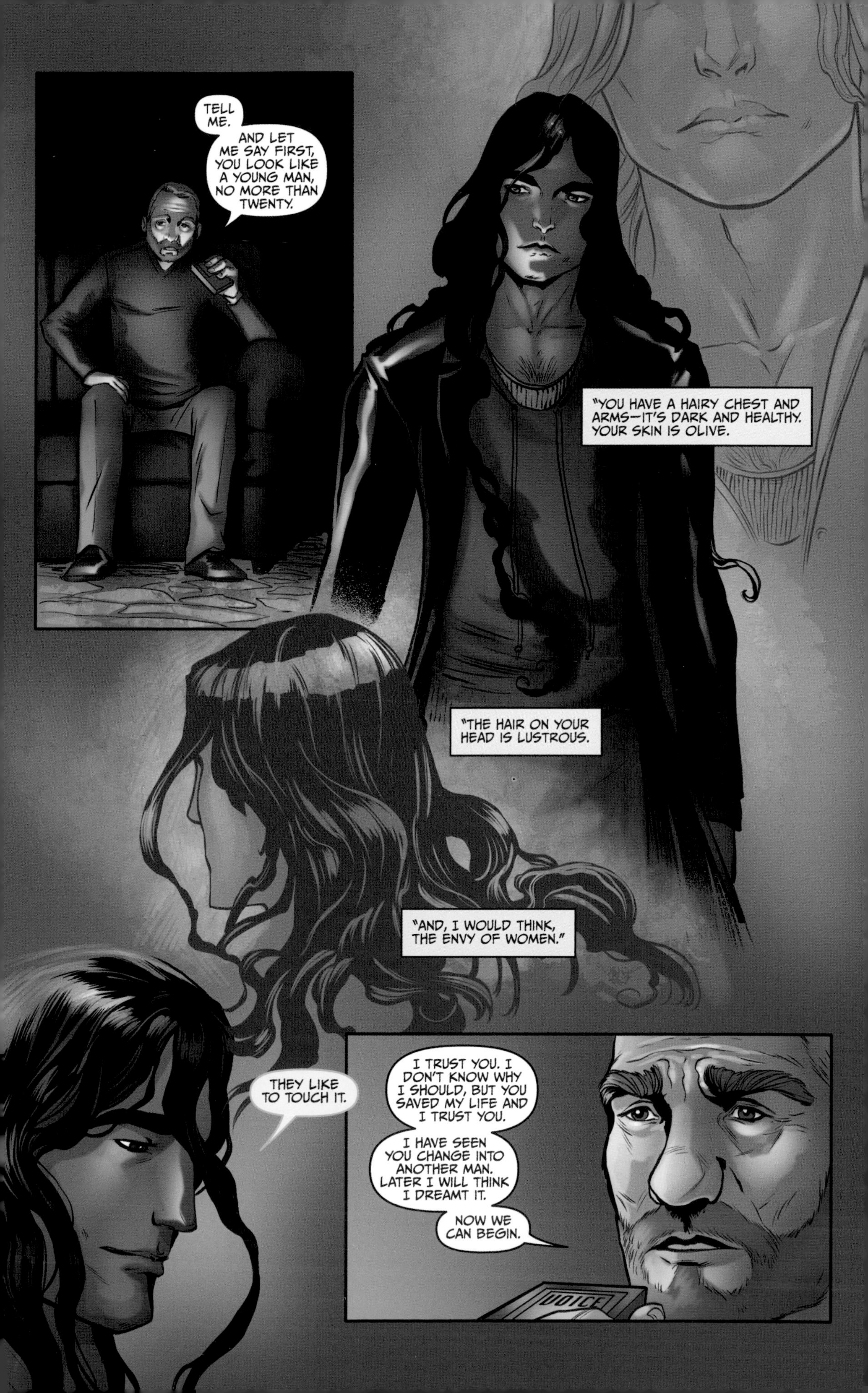
TELL ME.
AND LET ME SAY FIRST, YOU LOOK LIKE A YOUNG MAN, NO MORE THAN TWENTY.
"YOU HAVE A HAIRY CHEST AND ARMS—IT'S DARK AND HEALTHY. YOUR SKIN IS OLIVE.
"THE HAIR ON YOUR HEAD IS LUSTROUS.
"AND, I WOULD THINK, THE ENVY OF WOMEN."
THEY LIKE TO TOUCH IT.
I TRUST YOU. I DON'T KNOW WHY I SHOULD, BUT YOU SAVED MY LIFE AND I TRUST YOU.
I HAVE SEEN YOU CHANGE INTO ANOTHER MAN. LATER I WILL THINK I DREAMT IT.
NOW WE CAN BEGIN.
VOICE

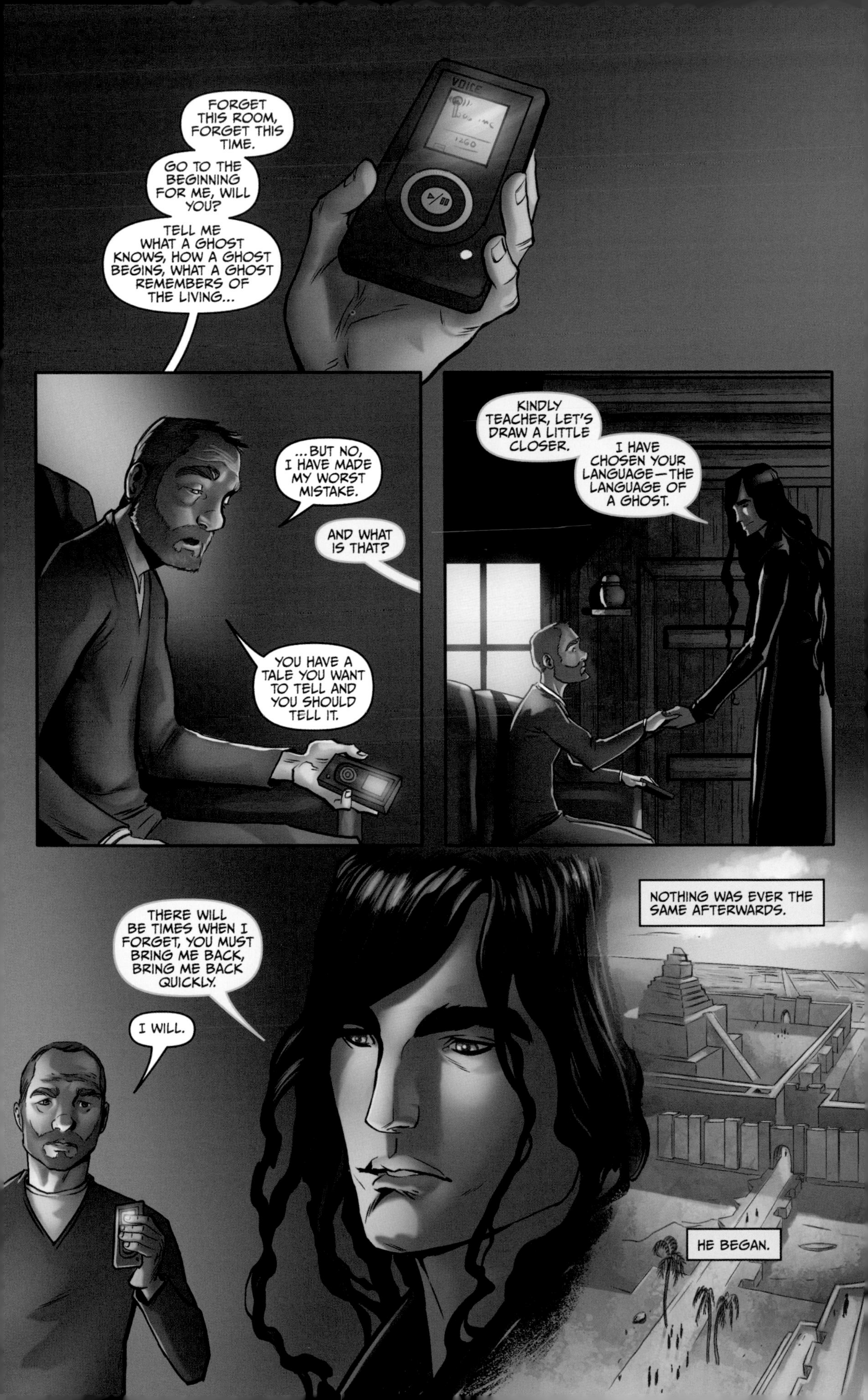
FORGET THIS ROOM, FORGET THIS TIME.
GO TO THE BEGINNING FOR ME, WILL YOU?
TELL ME WHAT A GHOST KNOWS, HOW A GHOST BEGINS, WHAT A GHOST REMEMBERS OF THE LIVING...
...BUT NO, I HAVE MADE MY WORST MISTAKE.
AND WHAT IS THAT?
YOU HAVE A TALE YOU WANT TO TELL AND YOU SHOULD TELL IT.
KINDLY TEACHER, LET'S DRAW A LITTLE CLOSER.
I HAVE CHOSEN YOUR LANGUAGE—THE LANGUAGE OF A GHOST.
THERE WILL BE TIMES WHEN I FORGET, YOU MUST BRING ME BACK, BRING ME BACK QUICKLY.
I WILL.
NOTHING WAS EVER THE SAME AFTERWARDS.
HE BEGAN.

THE BONES OF WOE

Golden are the bones of woe.
Their brilliance has no place to go.
It plunges inward,
Spikes through snow.

Of weeping fathers whom we drink
And mother's milk and final stink
We can dream but cannot think.
Golden bones encrust the brink.

Golden silver copper silk.
Woe is water shocked by milk.
Heart attack, assassin, cancer.
Who would think these bones such dancers.

Golden are the bones of woe.
Skeleton holds skeleton.
Words of ghosts are not to know.
Ignorance is what we learn.

Stan Rice, *Some Lamb* **1975**

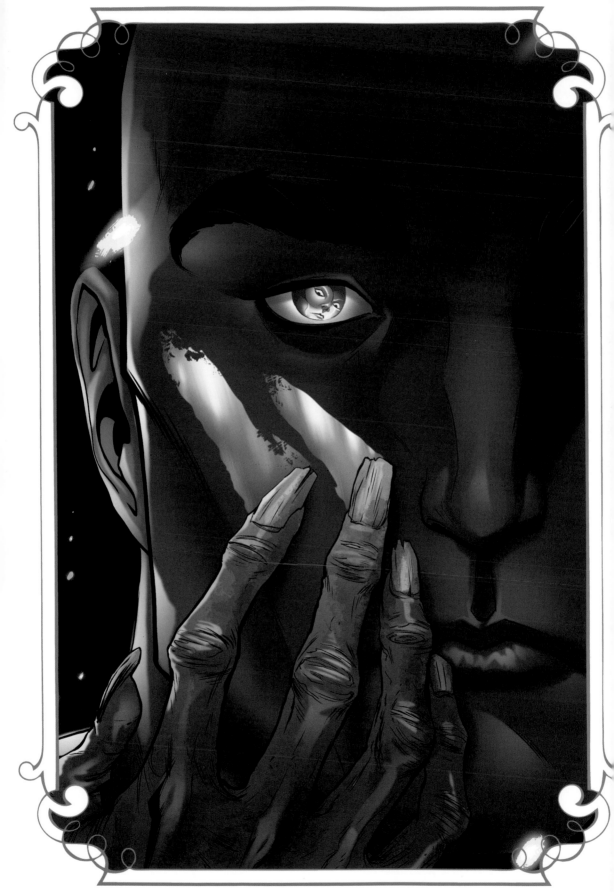

Art by Renae De Liz • Colors by Ray Dillon

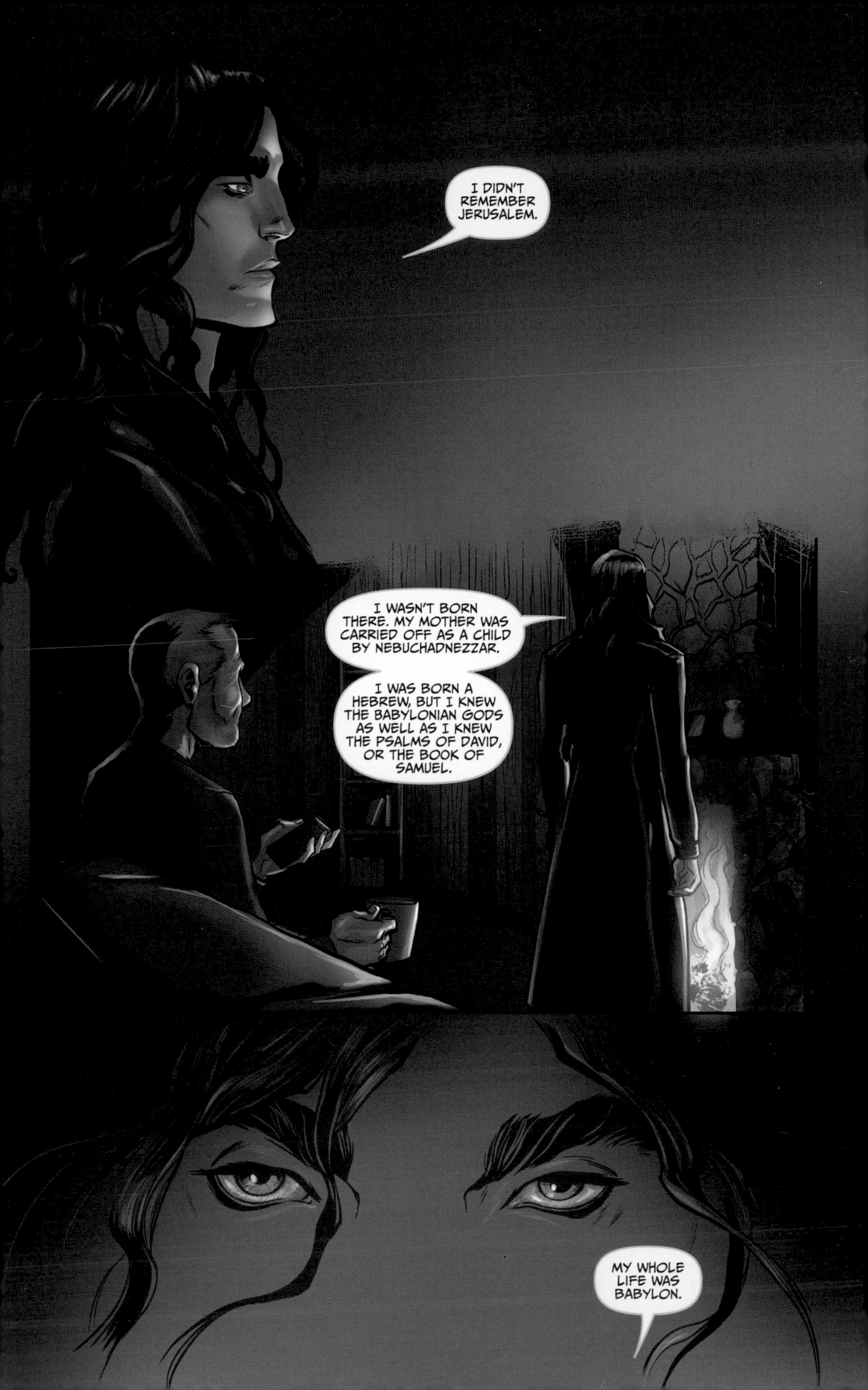
I DIDN'T REMEMBER JERUSALEM.
I WASN'T BORN THERE. MY MOTHER WAS CARRIED OFF AS A CHILD BY NEBUCHADNEZZAR.
I WAS BORN A HEBREW, BUT I KNEW THE BABYLONIAN GODS AS WELL AS I KNEW THE PSALMS OF DAVID, OR THE BOOK OF SAMUEL.
MY WHOLE LIFE WAS BABYLON.

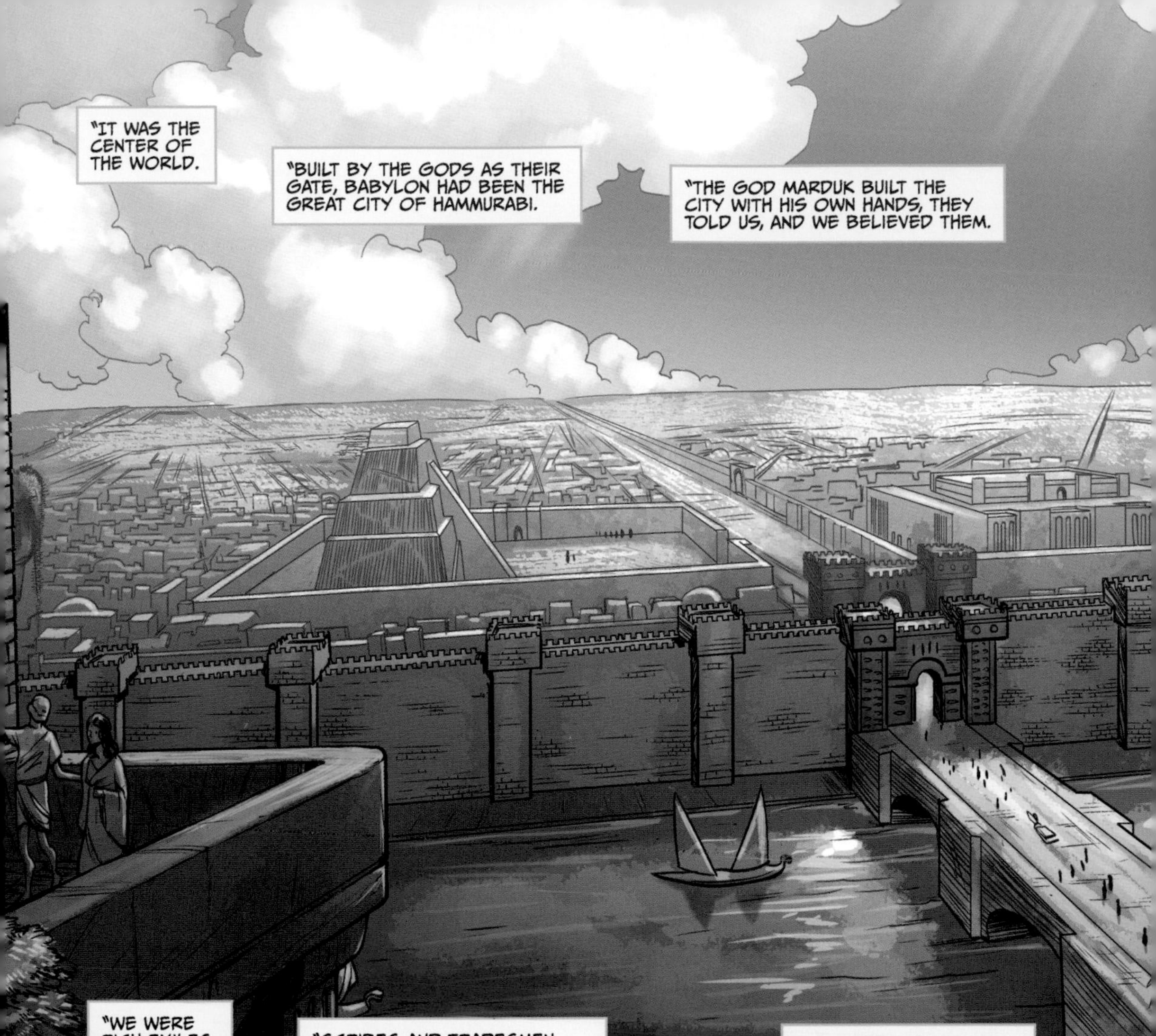
"IT WAS THE CENTER OF THE WORLD.
"BUILT BY THE GODS AS THEIR GATE, BABYLON HAD BEEN THE GREAT CITY OF HAMMURABI.
"THE GOD MARDUK BUILT THE CITY WITH HIS OWN HANDS, THEY TOLD US, AND WE BELIEVED THEM.

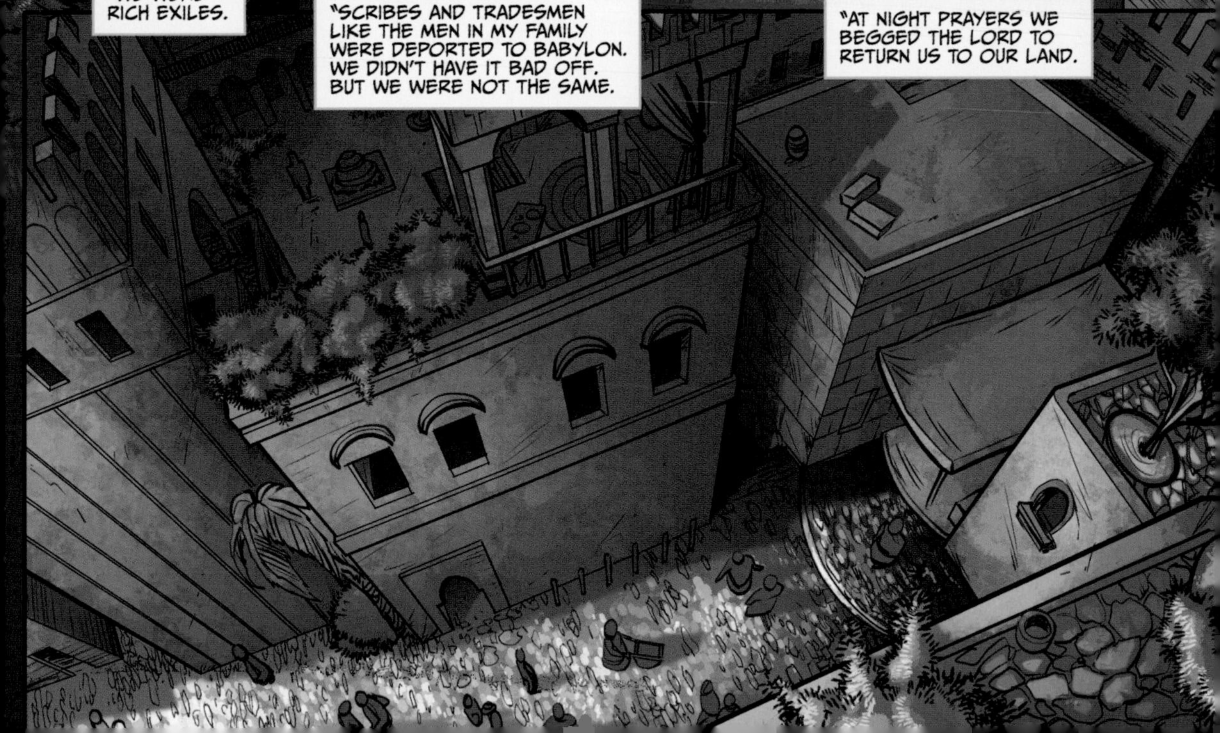
"WE WERE RICH EXILES.
"SCRIBES AND TRADESMEN LIKE THE MEN IN MY FAMILY WERE DEPORTED TO BABYLON. WE DIDN'T HAVE IT BAD OFF. BUT WE WERE NOT THE SAME.
"AT NIGHT PRAYERS WE BEGGED THE LORD TO RETURN US TO OUR LAND.

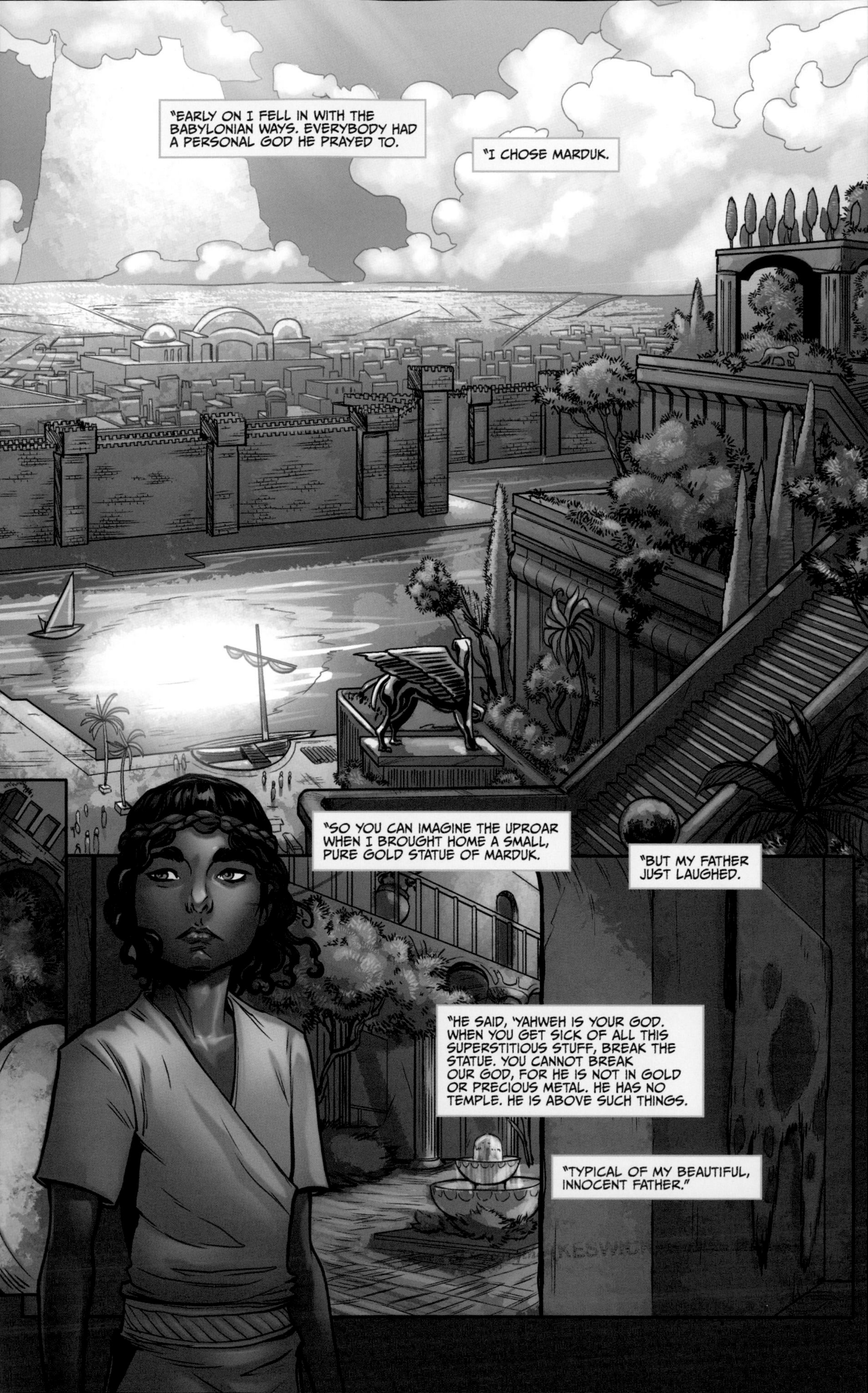
"EARLY ON I FELL IN WITH THE BABYLONIAN WAYS. EVERYBODY HAD A PERSONAL GOD HE PRAYED TO.
"I CHOSE MARDUK.
"SO YOU CAN IMAGINE THE UPROAR WHEN I BROUGHT HOME A SMALL, PURE GOLD STATUE OF MARDUK.
"BUT MY FATHER JUST LAUGHED.
"HE SAID, 'YAHWEH IS YOUR GOD. WHEN YOU GET SICK OF ALL THIS SUPERSTITIOUS STUFF, BREAK THE STATUE. YOU CANNOT BREAK OUR GOD, FOR HE IS NOT IN GOLD OR PRECIOUS METAL. HE HAS NO TEMPLE. HE IS ABOVE SUCH THINGS.
"TYPICAL OF MY BEAUTIFUL, INNOCENT FATHER."

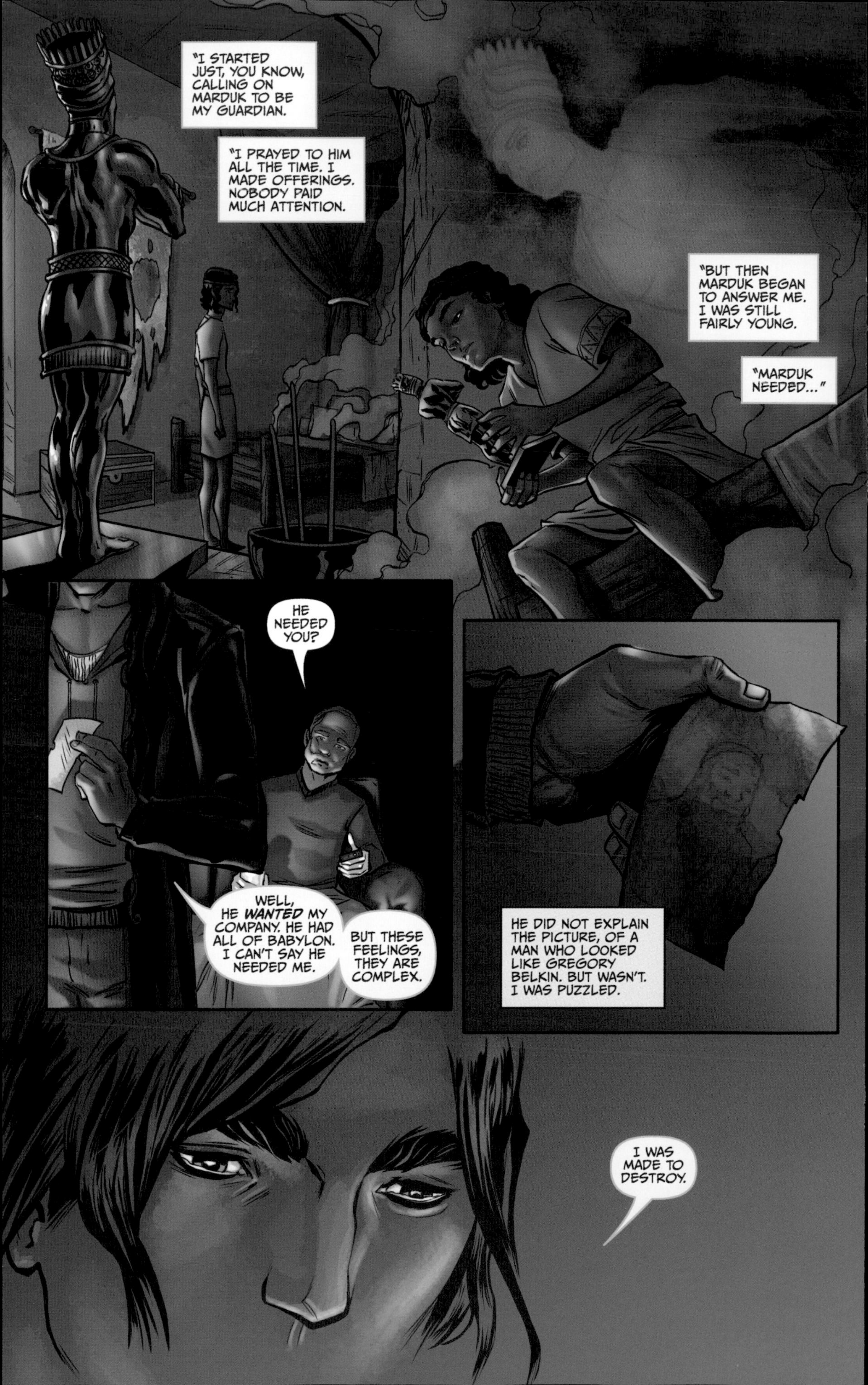
"I STARTED JUST, YOU KNOW, CALLING ON MARDUK TO BE MY GUARDIAN.
"I PRAYED TO HIM ALL THE TIME. I MADE OFFERINGS. NOBODY PAID MUCH ATTENTION.
"BUT THEN MARDUK BEGAN TO ANSWER ME. I WAS STILL FAIRLY YOUNG.
"MARDUK NEEDED..."
HE NEEDED YOU?
WELL, HE ***WANTED*** MY COMPANY. HE HAD ALL OF BABYLON. I CAN'T SAY HE NEEDED ME.
BUT THESE FEELINGS, THEY ARE COMPLEX.
HE DID NOT EXPLAIN THE PICTURE, OF A MAN WHO LOOKED LIKE GREGORY BELKIN. BUT WASN'T. I WAS PUZZLED.
I WAS MADE TO DESTROY.

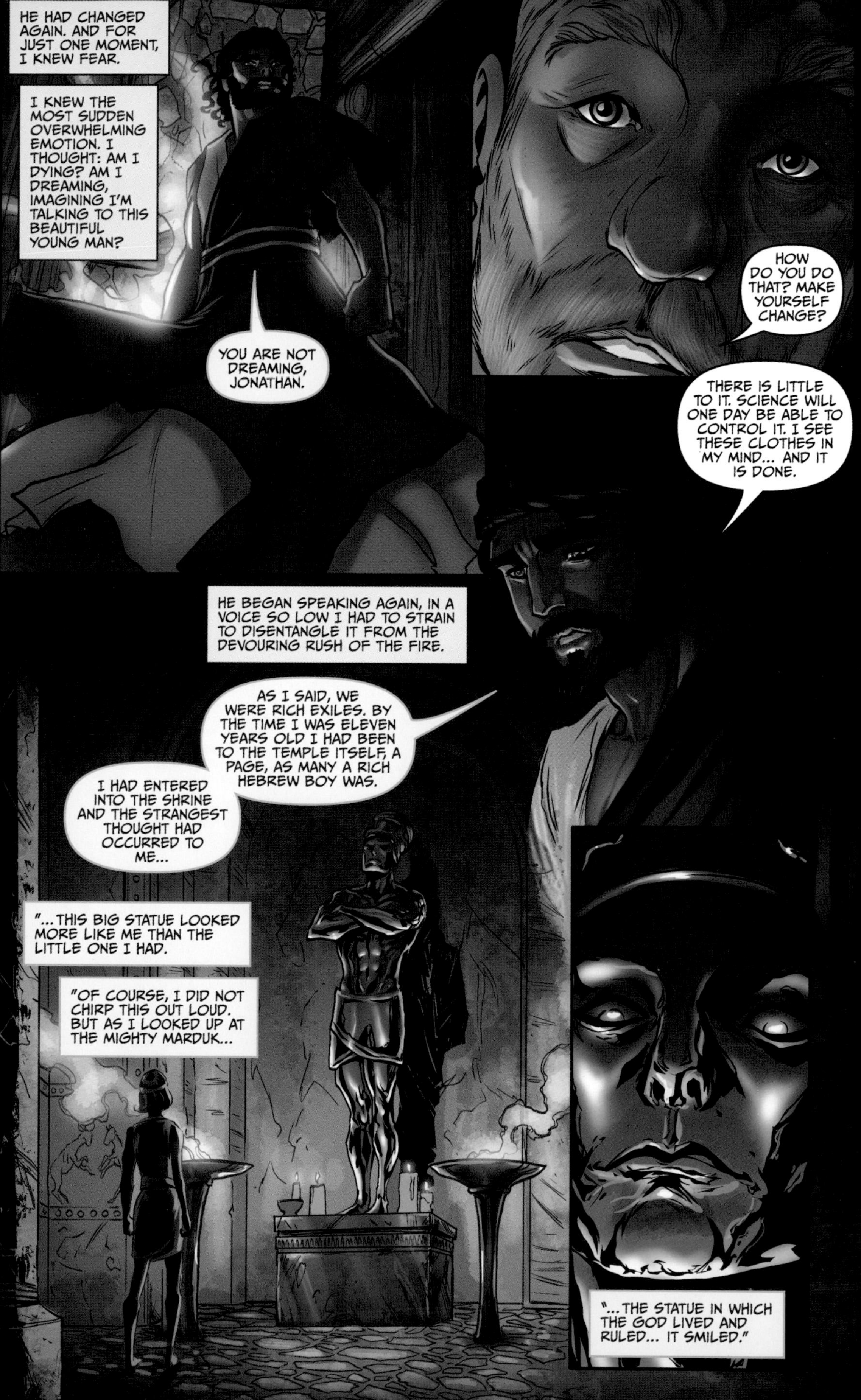
HE HAD CHANGED AGAIN. AND FOR JUST ONE MOMENT, I KNEW FEAR.
I KNEW THE MOST SUDDEN OVERWHELMING EMOTION. I THOUGHT: AM I DYING? AM I DREAMING, IMAGINING I'M TALKING TO THIS BEAUTIFUL YOUNG MAN?
YOU ARE NOT DREAMING, JONATHAN.
HOW DO YOU DO THAT? MAKE YOURSELF CHANGE?
THERE IS LITTLE TO IT. SCIENCE WILL ONE DAY BE ABLE TO CONTROL IT. I SEE THESE CLOTHES IN MY MIND... AND IT IS DONE.
HE BEGAN SPEAKING AGAIN, IN A VOICE SO LOW I HAD TO STRAIN TO DISENTANGLE IT FROM THE DEVOURING RUSH OF THE FIRE.
AS I SAID, WE WERE RICH EXILES. BY THE TIME I WAS ELEVEN YEARS OLD I HAD BEEN TO THE TEMPLE ITSELF, A PAGE, AS MANY A RICH HEBREW BOY WAS.
I HAD ENTERED INTO THE SHRINE AND THE STRANGEST THOUGHT HAD OCCURRED TO ME...
"...THIS BIG STATUE LOOKED MORE LIKE ME THAN THE LITTLE ONE I HAD.
"OF COURSE, I DID NOT CHIRP THIS OUT LOUD. BUT AS I LOOKED UP AT THE MIGHTY MARDUK...
"...THE STATUE IN WHICH THE GOD LIVED AND RULED... IT SMILED."

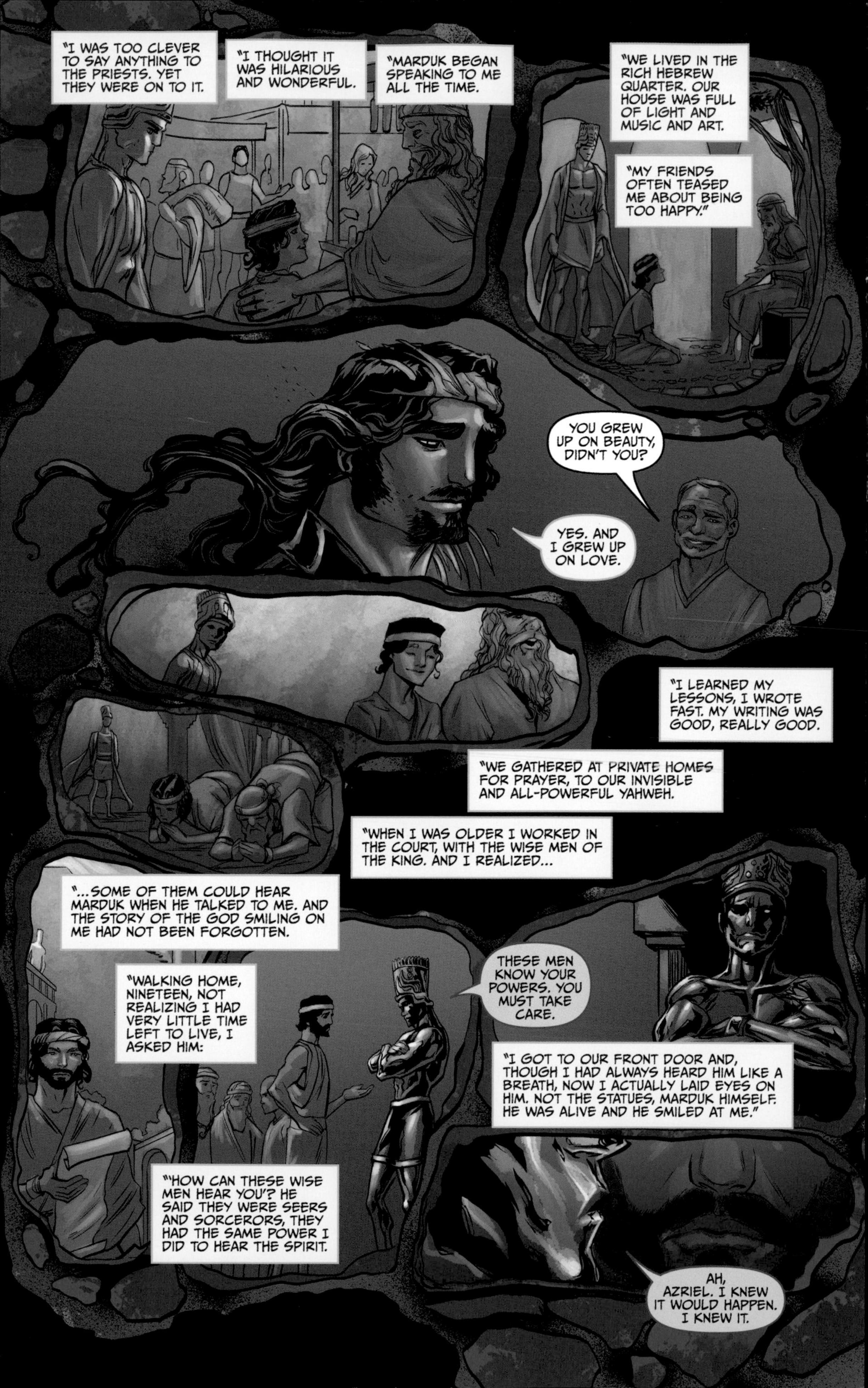
"I WAS TOO CLEVER TO SAY ANYTHING TO THE PRIESTS. YET THEY WERE ON TO IT.
"I THOUGHT IT WAS HILARIOUS AND WONDERFUL.
"MARDUK BEGAN SPEAKING TO ME ALL THE TIME.
"WE LIVED IN THE RICH HEBREW QUARTER. OUR HOUSE WAS FULL OF LIGHT AND MUSIC AND ART.
"MY FRIENDS OFTEN TEASED ME ABOUT BEING TOO HAPPY."
YOU GREW UP ON BEAUTY, DIDN'T YOU?
YES. AND I GREW UP ON LOVE.
"I LEARNED MY LESSONS, I WROTE FAST. MY WRITING WAS GOOD, REALLY GOOD.
"WE GATHERED AT PRIVATE HOMES FOR PRAYER, TO OUR INVISIBLE AND ALL-POWERFUL YAHWEH.
"WHEN I WAS OLDER I WORKED IN THE COURT, WITH THE WISE MEN OF THE KING. AND I REALIZED...
"...SOME OF THEM COULD HEAR MARDUK WHEN HE TALKED TO ME. AND THE STORY OF THE GOD SMILING ON ME HAD NOT BEEN FORGOTTEN.
THESE MEN KNOW YOUR POWERS. YOU MUST TAKE CARE.
"WALKING HOME, NINETEEN, NOT REALIZING I HAD VERY LITTLE TIME LEFT TO LIVE, I ASKED HIM:
"'HOW CAN THESE WISE MEN HEAR YOU'? HE SAID THEY WERE SEERS AND SORCERORS, THEY HAD THE SAME POWER I DID TO HEAR THE SPIRIT.
"I GOT TO OUR FRONT DOOR AND, THOUGH I HAD ALWAYS HEARD HIM LIKE A BREATH, NOW I ACTUALLY LAID EYES ON HIM. NOT THE STATUES, MARDUK HIMSELF. HE WAS ALIVE AND HE SMILED AT ME."
AH, AZRIEL. I KNEW IT WOULD HAPPEN. I KNEW IT.

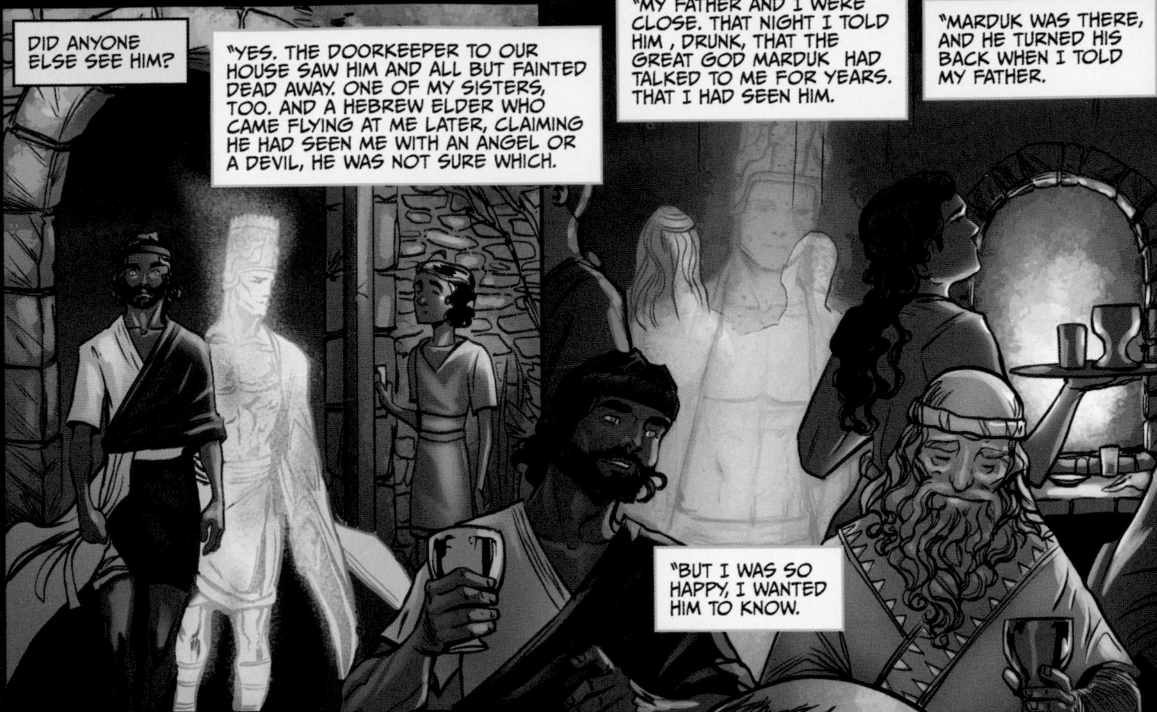
DID ANYONE ELSE SEE HIM?
"YES. THE DOORKEEPER TO OUR HOUSE SAW HIM AND ALL BUT FAINTED DEAD AWAY. ONE OF MY SISTERS, TOO. AND A HEBREW ELDER WHO CAME FLYING AT ME LATER, CLAIMING HE HAD SEEN ME WITH AN ANGEL OR A DEVIL, HE WAS NOT SURE WHICH.
"MY FATHER AND I WERE CLOSE. THAT NIGHT I TOLD HIM , DRUNK, THAT THE GREAT GOD MARDUK HAD TALKED TO ME FOR YEARS. THAT I HAD SEEN HIM.
"MARDUK WAS THERE, AND HE TURNED HIS BACK WHEN I TOLD MY FATHER.
"BUT I WAS SO HAPPY, I WANTED HIM TO KNOW.
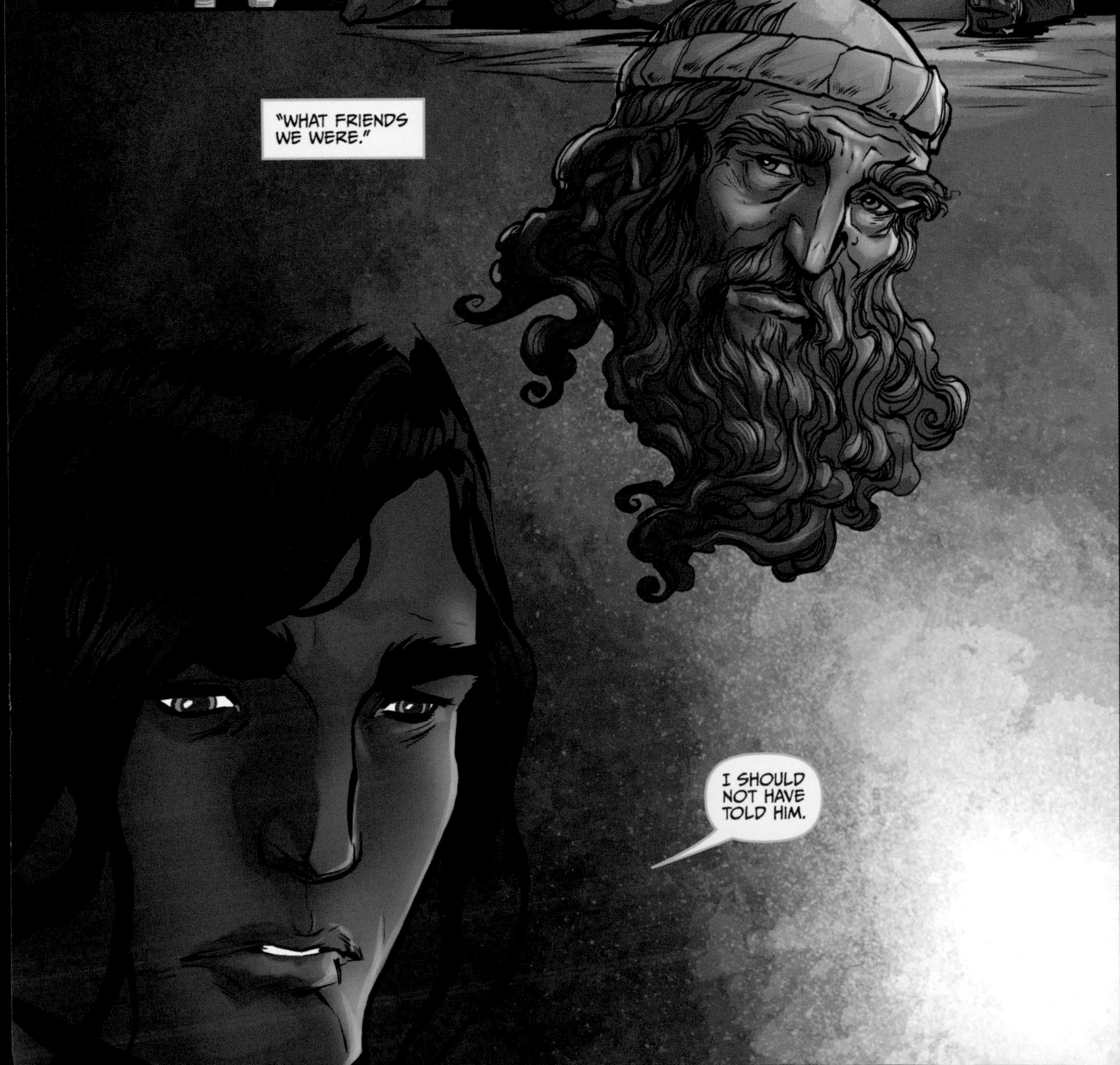
"WHAT FRIENDS WE WERE."
I SHOULD NOT HAVE TOLD HIM.

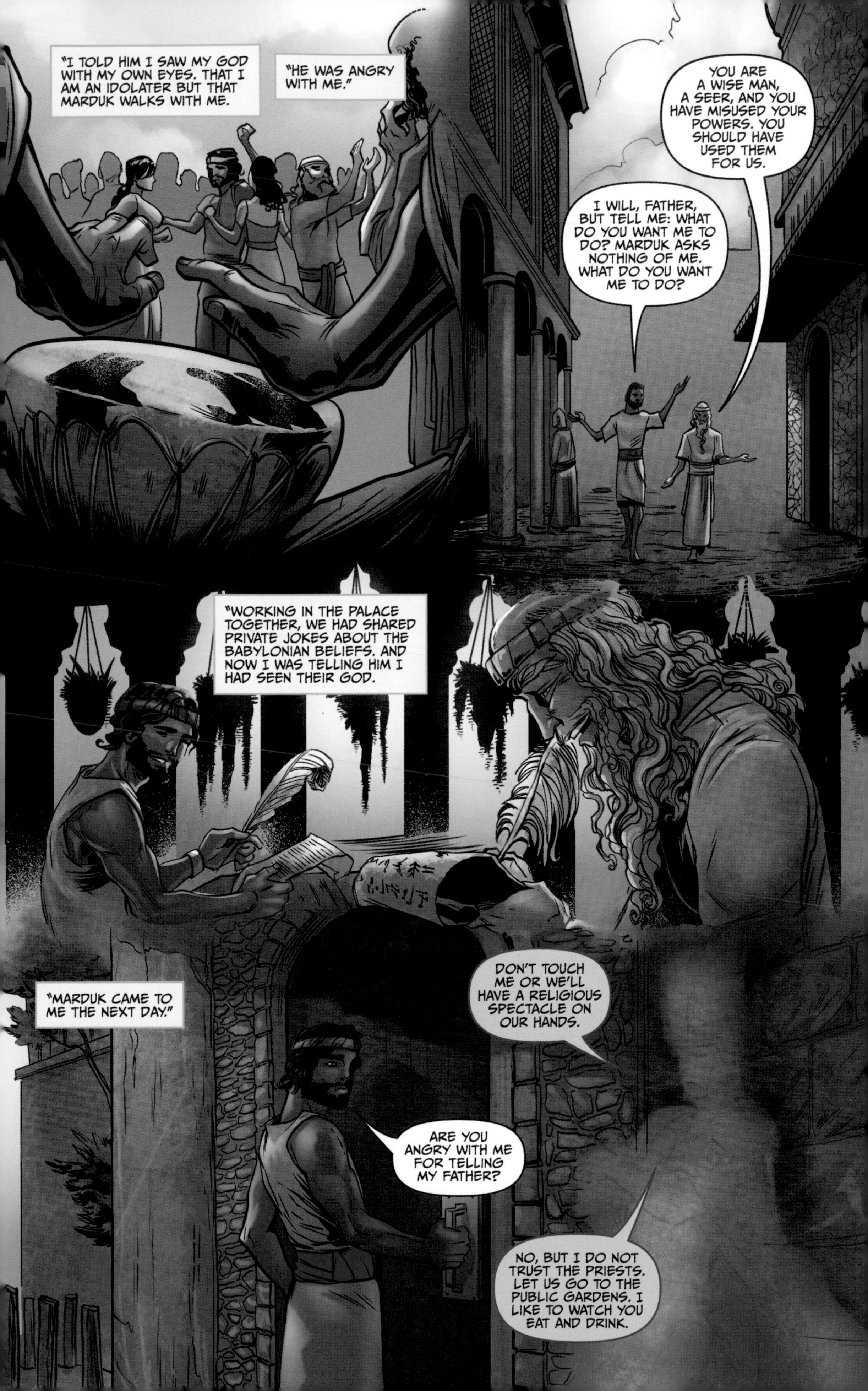
"I TOLD HIM I SAW MY GOD WITH MY OWN EYES. THAT I AM AN IDOLATER BUT THAT MARDUK WALKS WITH ME.
"HE WAS ANGRY WITH ME."
YOU ARE A WISE MAN, A SEER, AND YOU HAVE MISUSED YOUR POWERS. YOU SHOULD HAVE USED THEM FOR US.
I WILL, FATHER, BUT TELL ME: WHAT DO YOU WANT ME TO DO? MARDUK ASKS NOTHING OF ME. WHAT DO YOU WANT ME TO DO?
"WORKING IN THE PALACE TOGETHER, WE HAD SHARED PRIVATE JOKES ABOUT THE BABYLONIAN BELIEFS. AND NOW I WAS TELLING HIM I HAD SEEN THEIR GOD.
"MARDUK CAME TO ME THE NEXT DAY."
DON'T TOUCH ME OR WE'LL HAVE A RELIGIOUS SPECTACLE ON OUR HANDS.
ARE YOU ANGRY WITH ME FOR TELLING MY FATHER?
NO, BUT I DO NOT TRUST THE PRIESTS. LET US GO TO THE PUBLIC GARDENS. I LIKE TO WATCH YOU EAT AND DRINK.

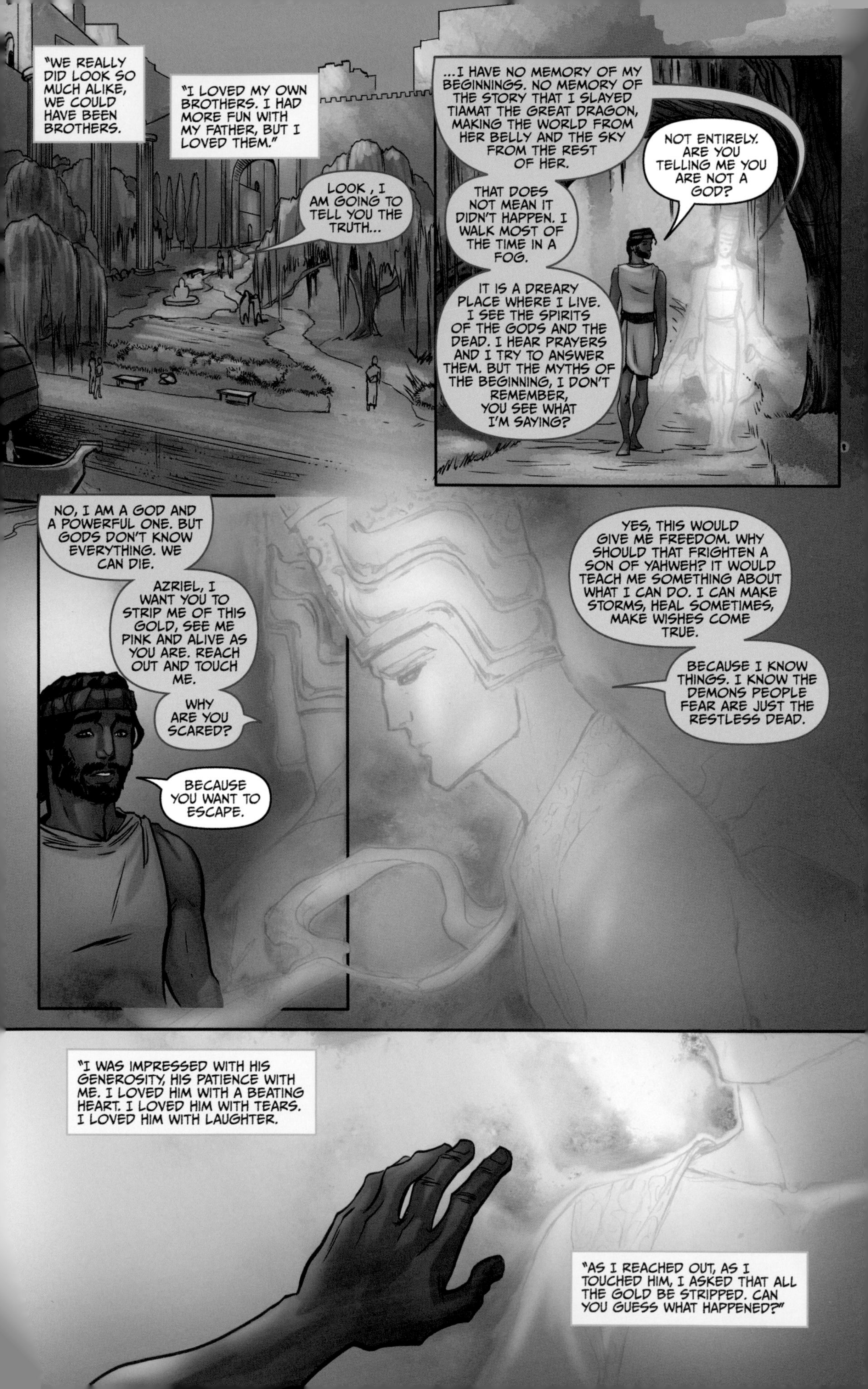
"WE REALLY DID LOOK SO MUCH ALIKE, WE COULD HAVE BEEN BROTHERS.
"I LOVED MY OWN BROTHERS. I HAD MORE FUN WITH MY FATHER, BUT I LOVED THEM."
LOOK , I AM GOING TO TELL YOU THE TRUTH...
...I HAVE NO MEMORY OF MY BEGINNINGS. NO MEMORY OF THE STORY THAT I SLAYED TIAMAT THE GREAT DRAGON, MAKING THE WORLD FROM HER BELLY AND THE SKY FROM THE REST OF HER.
NOT ENTIRELY. ARE YOU TELLING ME YOU ARE NOT A GOD?
THAT DOES NOT MEAN IT DIDN'T HAPPEN. I WALK MOST OF THE TIME IN A FOG.
IT IS A DREARY PLACE WHERE I LIVE. I SEE THE SPIRITS OF THE GODS AND THE DEAD. I HEAR PRAYERS AND I TRY TO ANSWER THEM. BUT THE MYTHS OF THE BEGINNING, I DON'T REMEMBER, YOU SEE WHAT I'M SAYING?
NO, I AM A GOD AND A POWERFUL ONE. BUT GODS DON'T KNOW EVERYTHING. WE CAN DIE.
AZRIEL, I WANT YOU TO STRIP ME OF THIS GOLD, SEE ME PINK AND ALIVE AS YOU ARE. REACH OUT AND TOUCH ME.
WHY ARE YOU SCARED?
BECAUSE YOU WANT TO ESCAPE.
YES, THIS WOULD GIVE ME FREEDOM. WHY SHOULD THAT FRIGHTEN A SON OF YAHWEH? IT WOULD TEACH ME SOMETHING ABOUT WHAT I CAN DO. I CAN MAKE STORMS, HEAL SOMETIMES, MAKE WISHES COME TRUE.
BECAUSE I KNOW THINGS. I KNOW THE DEMONS PEOPLE FEAR ARE JUST THE RESTLESS DEAD.
"I WAS IMPRESSED WITH HIS GENEROSITY, HIS PATIENCE WITH ME. I LOVED HIM WITH A BEATING HEART. I LOVED HIM WITH TEARS. I LOVED HIM WITH LAUGHTER.
"AS I REACHED OUT, AS I TOUCHED HIM, I ASKED THAT ALL THE GOLD BE STRIPPED. CAN YOU GUESS WHAT HAPPENED?"

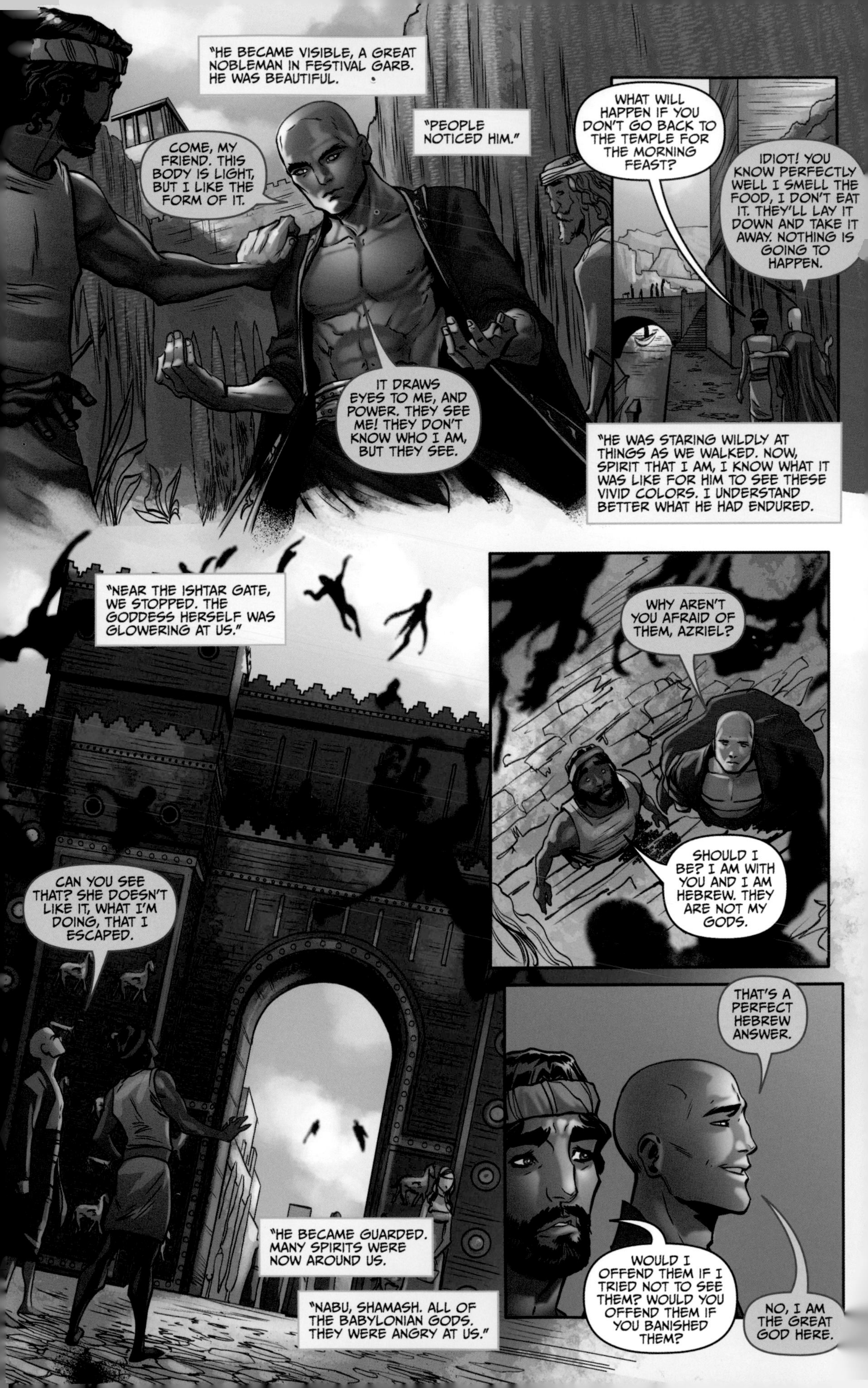
"HE BECAME VISIBLE, A GREAT NOBLEMAN IN FESTIVAL GARB. HE WAS BEAUTIFUL.
"PEOPLE NOTICED HIM."
COME, MY FRIEND. THIS BODY IS LIGHT, BUT I LIKE THE FORM OF IT.
IT DRAWS EYES TO ME, AND POWER. THEY SEE ME! THEY DON'T KNOW WHO I AM, BUT THEY SEE.
WHAT WILL HAPPEN IF YOU DON'T GO BACK TO THE TEMPLE FOR THE MORNING FEAST?
IDIOT! YOU KNOW PERFECTLY WELL I SMELL THE FOOD, I DON'T EAT IT. THEY'LL LAY IT DOWN AND TAKE IT AWAY. NOTHING IS GOING TO HAPPEN.
"HE WAS STARING WILDLY AT THINGS AS WE WALKED. NOW, SPIRIT THAT I AM, I KNOW WHAT IT WAS LIKE FOR HIM TO SEE THESE VIVID COLORS. I UNDERSTAND BETTER WHAT HE HAD ENDURED.
"NEAR THE ISHTAR GATE, WE STOPPED. THE GODDESS HERSELF WAS GLOWERING AT US."
CAN YOU SEE THAT? SHE DOESN'T LIKE IT, WHAT I'M DOING, THAT I ESCAPED.
"HE BECAME GUARDED. MANY SPIRITS WERE NOW AROUND US.
"NABU, SHAMASH. ALL OF THE BABYLONIAN GODS. THEY WERE ANGRY AT US."
WHY AREN'T YOU AFRAID OF THEM, AZRIEL?
SHOULD I BE? I AM WITH YOU AND I AM HEBREW. THEY ARE NOT MY GODS.
THAT'S A PERFECT HEBREW ANSWER.
WOULD I OFFEND THEM IF I TRIED NOT TO SEE THEM? WOULD YOU OFFEND THEM IF YOU BANISHED THEM?
NO, I AM THE GREAT GOD HERE.

"THE SPIRITS VANISHED. WHAT LINGERED WAS THE RESTLESS DEAD, EVERYWHERE THE RESTLESS DEAD."
RETURN TO YOUR SLUMBER, RETURN TO YOUR REST, RETURN TO YOUR GRAVES. TO THE SAFETY OF THE MEMORIES OF YOU IN THE HEARTS AND MINDS OF YOUR CHILDREN. RETURN TO MOTHER EARTH.
"AND THANK GOD, THEY WENT AWAY.
"MY HEART SANK. WE WERE ATTRACTING MUCH ATTENTION.
"I WAS CONFUSED. WHY DID MARDUK NOT LET THE PRIESTS BRING HIM TO LIFE IN GOLD AND WALK IN GOLD, THE GOD HIMSELF, ABOUT THE CITY?"
AZRIEL, THE PRIESTS ARE NOT STRONG ENOUGH TO MAKE ME SOLID, VISIBLE. THEY DON'T HAVE THE POWER. THEY DON'T HAVE YOUR GIFT.
I WOULD ONLY DO SUCH A THING IF BABYLON NEEDED IT OF ME. AND IT DOES NOT. BUT BABYLON NEEDS SOMETHING, AND SOON. AND YOU KNOW WHY.

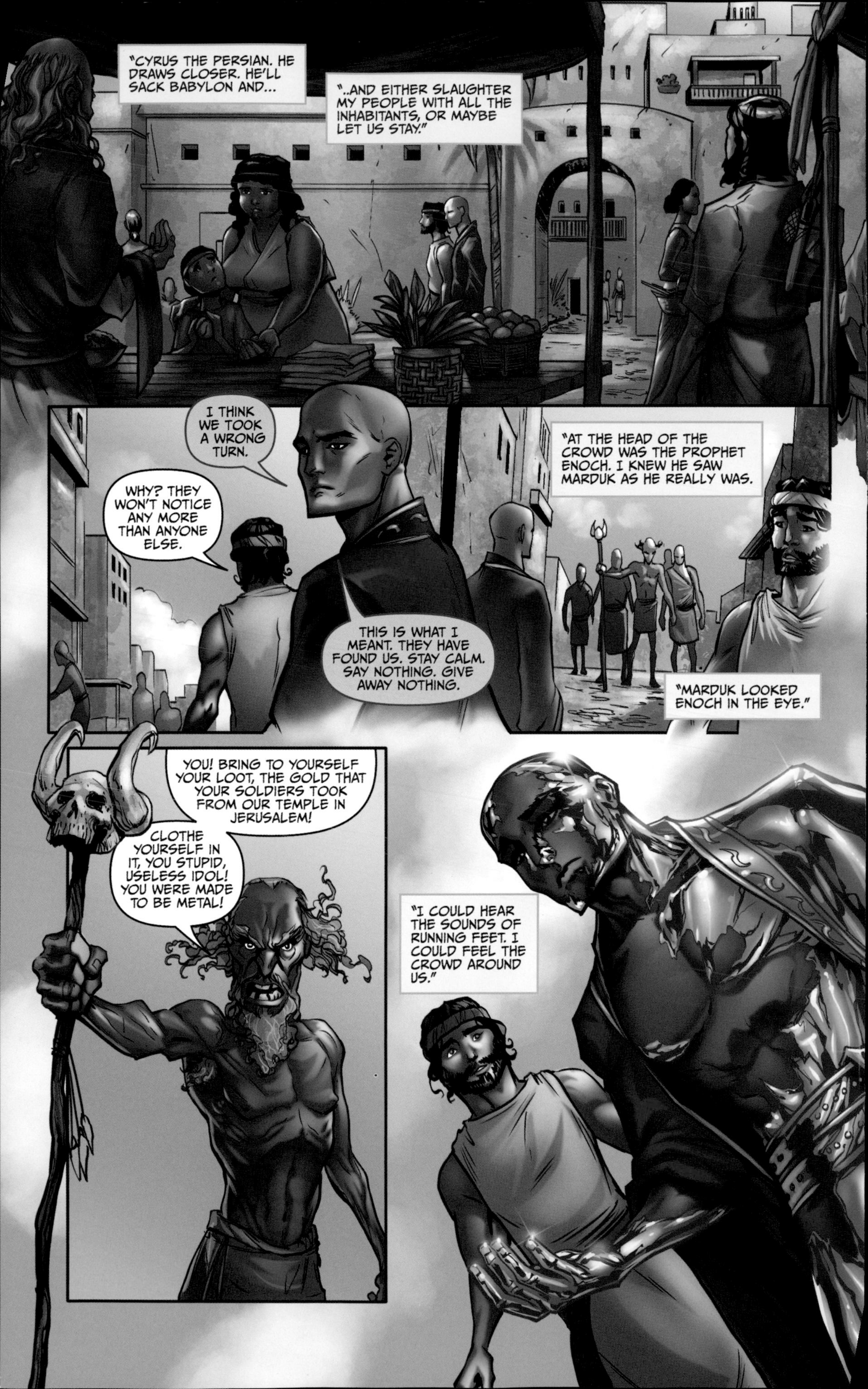
"CYRUS THE PERSIAN. HE DRAWS CLOSER. HE'LL SACK BABYLON AND...
"..AND EITHER SLAUGHTER MY PEOPLE WITH ALL THE INHABITANTS, OR MAYBE LET US STAY."
I THINK WE TOOK A WRONG TURN.
WHY? THEY WON'T NOTICE ANY MORE THAN ANYONE ELSE.
THIS IS WHAT I MEANT. THEY HAVE FOUND US. STAY CALM. SAY NOTHING. GIVE AWAY NOTHING.
"AT THE HEAD OF THE CROWD WAS THE PROPHET ENOCH. I KNEW HE SAW MARDUK AS HE REALLY WAS.
"MARDUK LOOKED ENOCH IN THE EYE."
YOU! BRING TO YOURSELF YOUR LOOT, THE GOLD THAT YOUR SOLDIERS TOOK FROM OUR TEMPLE IN JERUSALEM!
CLOTHE YOURSELF IN IT, YOU STUPID, USELESS IDOL! YOU WERE MADE TO BE METAL!
"I COULD HEAR THE SOUNDS OF RUNNING FEET. I COULD FEEL THE CROWD AROUND US."

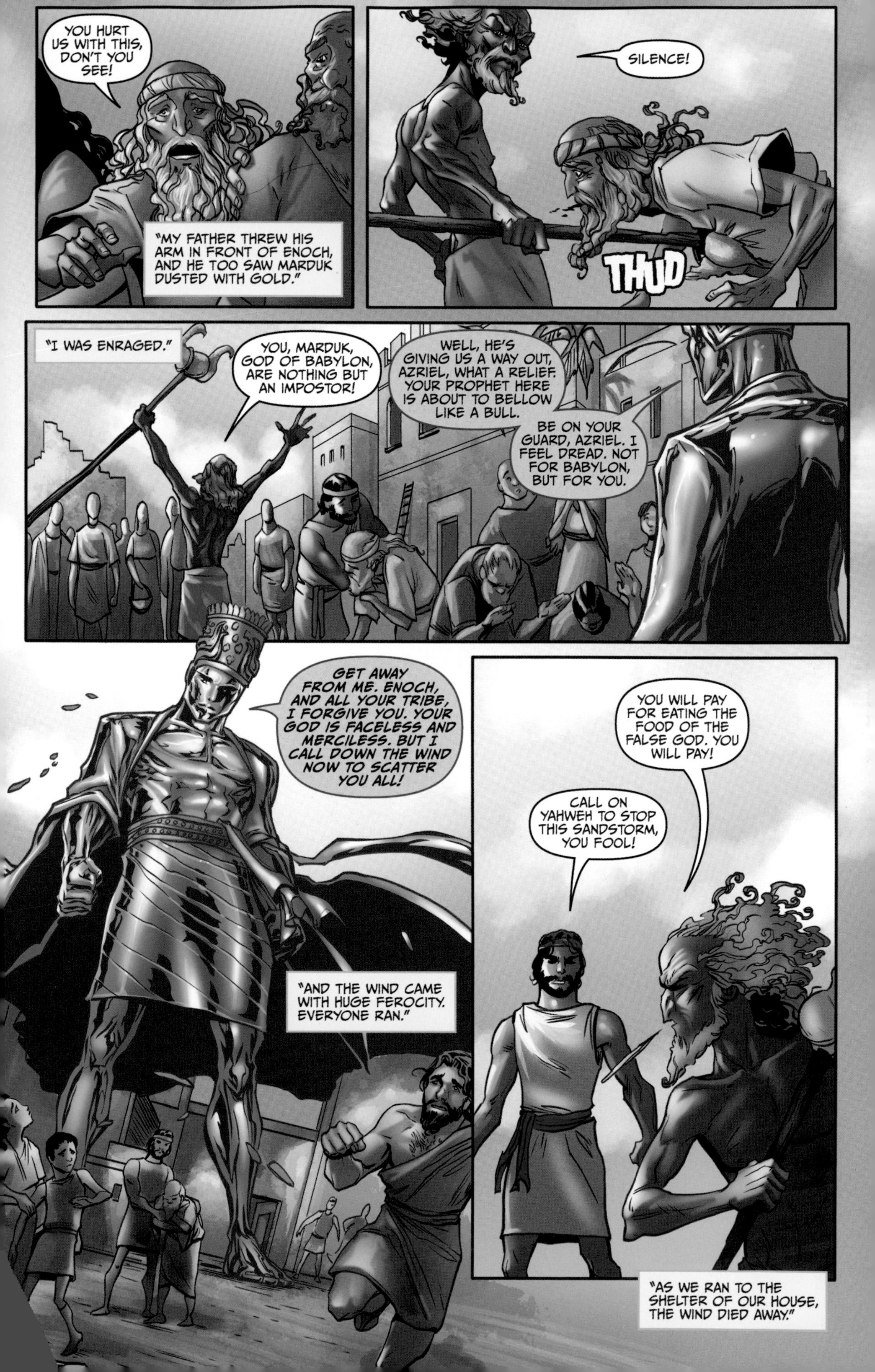
YOU HURT US WITH THIS, DON'T YOU SEE!
"MY FATHER THREW HIS ARM IN FRONT OF ENOCH, AND HE TOO SAW MARDUK DUSTED WITH GOLD."
SILENCE!
THUD
"I WAS ENRAGED."
YOU, MARDUK, GOD OF BABYLON, ARE NOTHING BUT AN IMPOSTOR!
WELL, HE'S GIVING US A WAY OUT, AZRIEL, WHAT A RELIEF. YOUR PROPHET HERE IS ABOUT TO BELLOW LIKE A BULL.
BE ON YOUR GUARD, AZRIEL. I FEEL DREAD. NOT FOR BABYLON, BUT FOR YOU.
GET AWAY FROM ME. ENOCH, AND ALL YOUR TRIBE, I FORGIVE YOU. YOUR GOD IS FACELESS AND MERCILESS. BUT I CALL DOWN THE WIND NOW TO SCATTER YOU ALL!
"AND THE WIND CAME WITH HUGE FEROCITY. EVERYONE RAN."
YOU WILL PAY FOR EATING THE FOOD OF THE FALSE GOD. YOU WILL PAY!
CALL ON YAHWEH TO STOP THIS SANDSTORM, YOU FOOL!
"AS WE RAN TO THE SHELTER OF OUR HOUSE, THE WIND DIED AWAY."

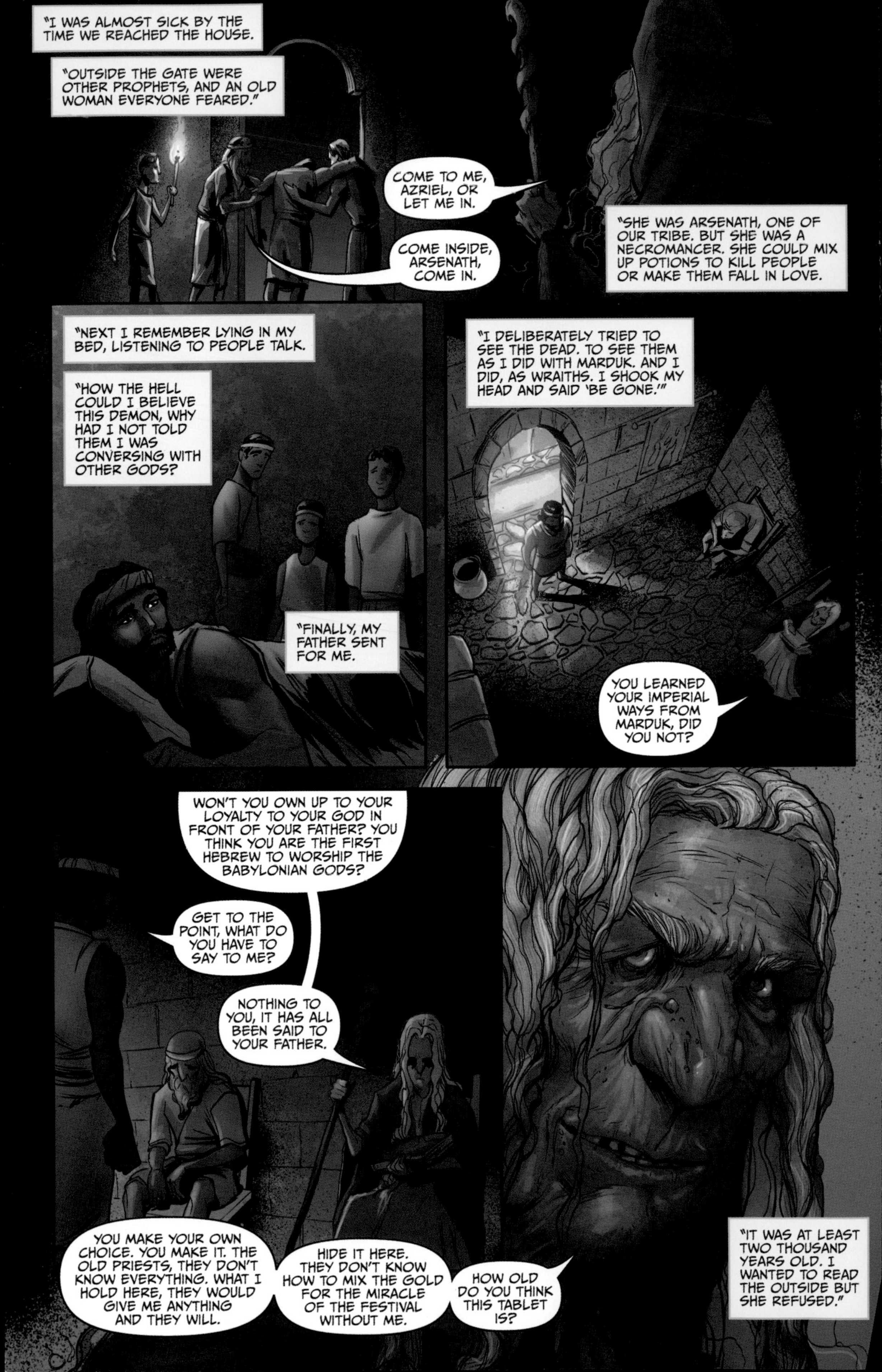
"I WAS ALMOST SICK BY THE TIME WE REACHED THE HOUSE.
"OUTSIDE THE GATE WERE OTHER PROPHETS, AND AN OLD WOMAN EVERYONE FEARED."
COME TO ME, AZRIEL, OR LET ME IN.
COME INSIDE, ARSENATH, COME IN.
"SHE WAS ARSENATH, ONE OF OUR TRIBE. BUT SHE WAS A NECROMANCER. SHE COULD MIX UP POTIONS TO KILL PEOPLE OR MAKE THEM FALL IN LOVE.
"NEXT I REMEMBER LYING IN MY BED, LISTENING TO PEOPLE TALK.
"HOW THE HELL COULD I BELIEVE THIS DEMON, WHY HAD I NOT TOLD THEM I WAS CONVERSING WITH OTHER GODS?
"FINALLY, MY FATHER SENT FOR ME.
"I DELIBERATELY TRIED TO SEE THE DEAD. TO SEE THEM AS I DID WITH MARDUK. AND I DID, AS WRAITHS. I SHOOK MY HEAD AND SAID 'BE GONE.'"
YOU LEARNED YOUR IMPERIAL WAYS FROM MARDUK, DID YOU NOT?
WON'T YOU OWN UP TO YOUR LOYALTY TO YOUR GOD IN FRONT OF YOUR FATHER? YOU THINK YOU ARE THE FIRST HEBREW TO WORSHIP THE BABYLONIAN GODS?
GET TO THE POINT, WHAT DO YOU HAVE TO SAY TO ME?
NOTHING TO YOU, IT HAS ALL BEEN SAID TO YOUR FATHER.
YOU MAKE YOUR OWN CHOICE. YOU MAKE IT. THE OLD PRIESTS, THEY DON'T KNOW EVERYTHING. WHAT I HOLD HERE, THEY WOULD GIVE ME ANYTHING AND THEY WILL.
HIDE IT HERE. THEY DON'T KNOW HOW TO MIX THE GOLD FOR THE MIRACLE OF THE FESTIVAL WITHOUT ME.
HOW OLD DO YOU THINK THIS TABLET IS?
"IT WAS AT LEAST TWO THOUSAND YEARS OLD. I WANTED TO READ THE OUTSIDE BUT SHE REFUSED."

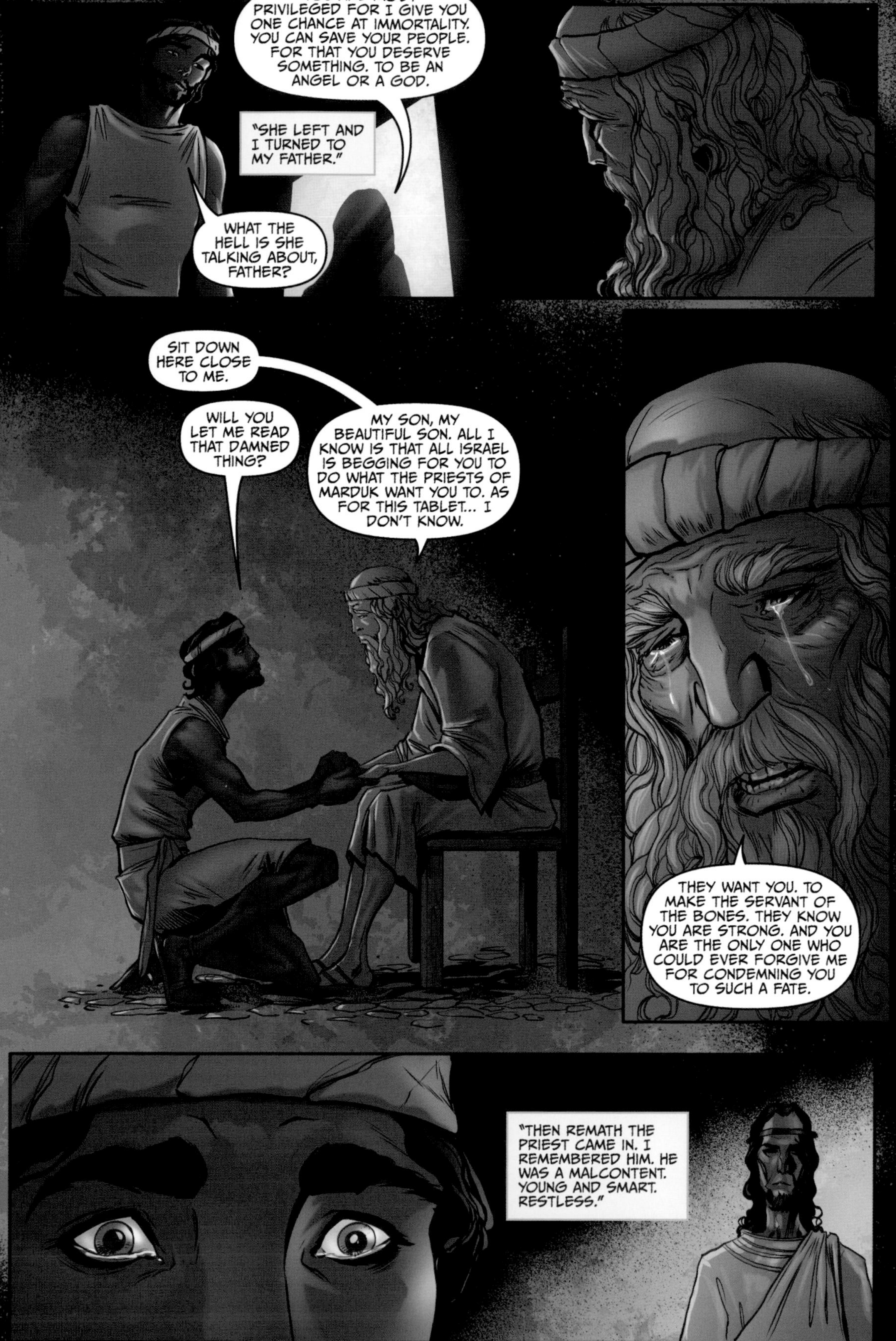
YOU ARE MOST PRIVILEGED FOR I GIVE YOU ONE CHANCE AT IMMORTALITY. YOU CAN SAVE YOUR PEOPLE. FOR THAT YOU DESERVE SOMETHING. TO BE AN ANGEL OR A GOD.
"SHE LEFT AND I TURNED TO MY FATHER."
WHAT THE HELL IS SHE TALKING ABOUT, FATHER?
SIT DOWN HERE CLOSE TO ME.
WILL YOU LET ME READ THAT DAMNED THING?
MY SON, MY BEAUTIFUL SON. ALL I KNOW IS THAT ALL ISRAEL IS BEGGING FOR YOU TO DO WHAT THE PRIESTS OF MARDUK WANT YOU TO. AS FOR THIS TABLET... I DON'T KNOW.
THEY WANT YOU. TO MAKE THE SERVANT OF THE BONES. THEY KNOW YOU ARE STRONG. AND YOU ARE THE ONLY ONE WHO COULD EVER FORGIVE ME FOR CONDEMNING YOU TO SUCH A FATE.
"THEN REMATH THE PRIEST CAME IN. I REMEMBERED HIM. HE WAS A MALCONTENT. YOUNG AND SMART. RESTLESS."

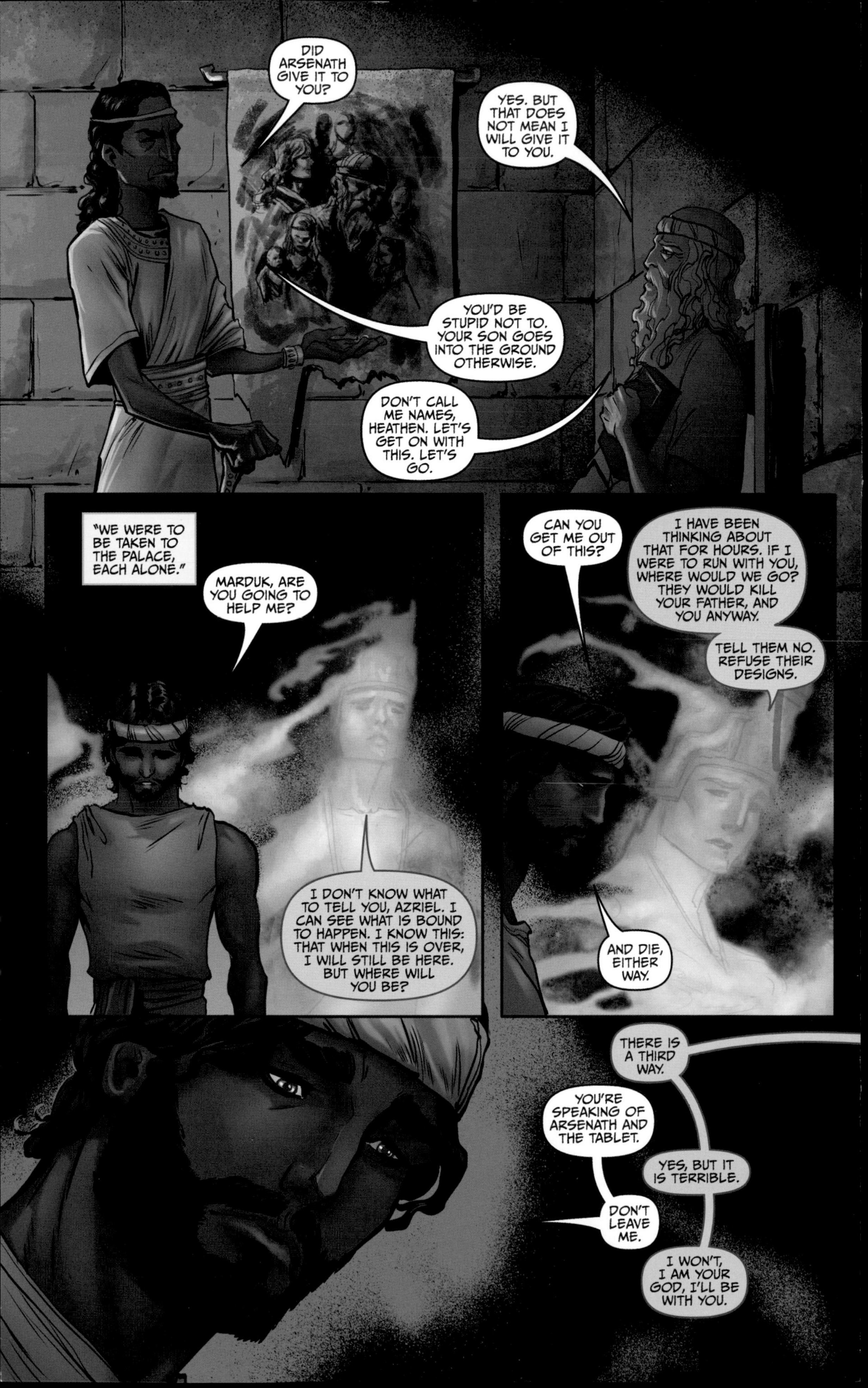
DID ARSENATH GIVE IT TO YOU?
YES. BUT THAT DOES NOT MEAN I WILL GIVE IT TO YOU.
YOU'D BE STUPID NOT TO. YOUR SON GOES INTO THE GROUND OTHERWISE.
DON'T CALL ME NAMES, HEATHEN. LET'S GET ON WITH THIS. LET'S GO.
"WE WERE TO BE TAKEN TO THE PALACE, EACH ALONE."
MARDUK, ARE YOU GOING TO HELP ME?
I DON'T KNOW WHAT TO TELL YOU, AZRIEL. I CAN SEE WHAT IS BOUND TO HAPPEN. I KNOW THIS: THAT WHEN THIS IS OVER, I WILL STILL BE HERE. BUT WHERE WILL YOU BE?
CAN YOU GET ME OUT OF THIS?
I HAVE BEEN THINKING ABOUT THAT FOR HOURS. IF I WERE TO RUN WITH YOU, WHERE WOULD WE GO? THEY WOULD KILL YOUR FATHER, AND YOU ANYWAY.
TELL THEM NO. REFUSE THEIR DESIGNS.
AND DIE, EITHER WAY.
THERE IS A THIRD WAY.
YOU'RE SPEAKING OF ARSENATH AND THE TABLET.
YES, BUT IT IS TERRIBLE.
DON'T LEAVE ME.
I WON'T, I AM YOUR GOD, I'LL BE WITH YOU.

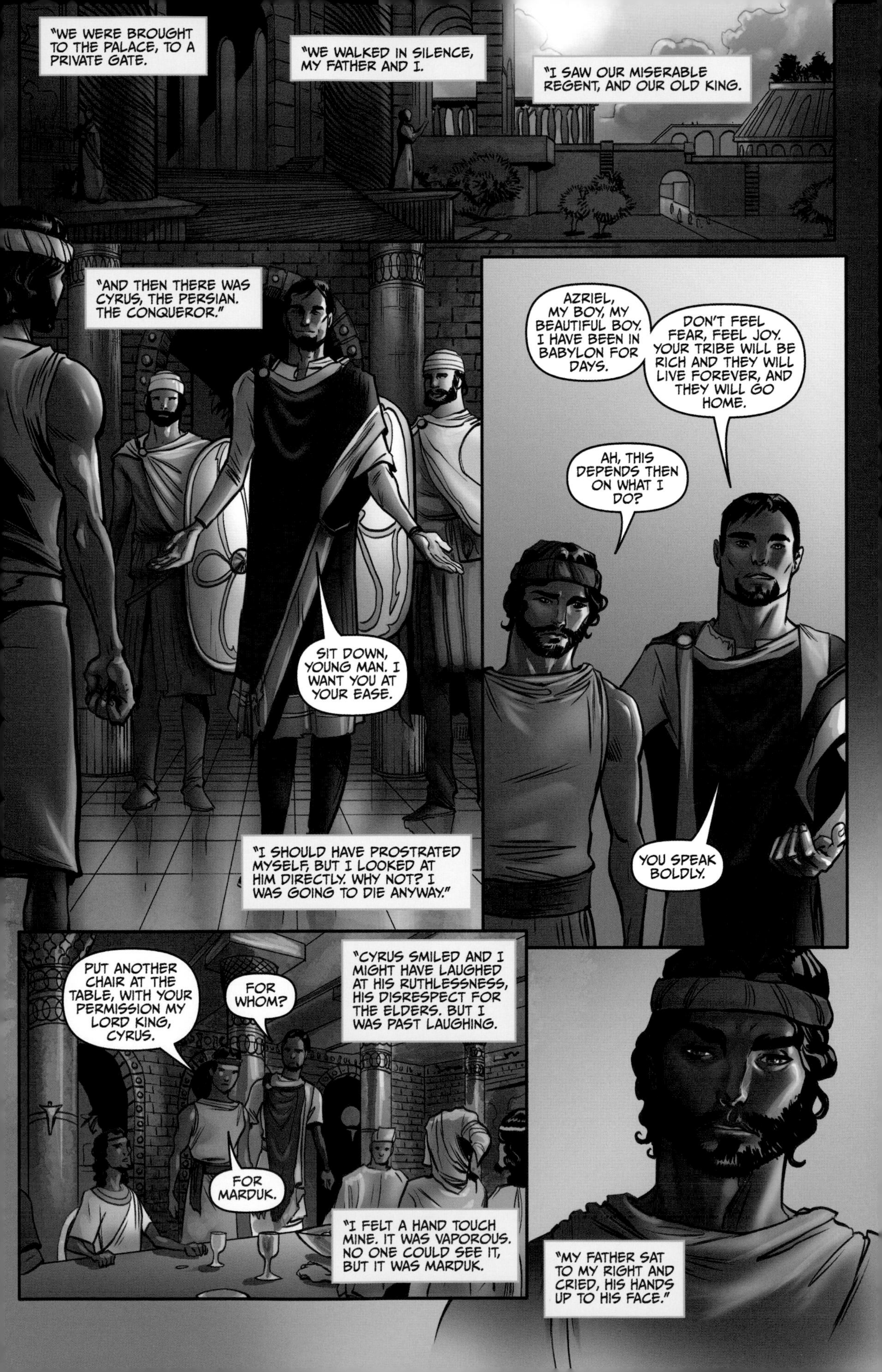
"WE WERE BROUGHT TO THE PALACE, TO A PRIVATE GATE.
"WE WALKED IN SILENCE, MY FATHER AND I.
"I SAW OUR MISERABLE REGENT, AND OUR OLD KING.
"AND THEN THERE WAS CYRUS, THE PERSIAN. THE CONQUEROR."
SIT DOWN, YOUNG MAN. I WANT YOU AT YOUR EASE.
"I SHOULD HAVE PROSTRATED MYSELF, BUT I LOOKED AT HIM DIRECTLY. WHY NOT? I WAS GOING TO DIE ANYWAY."
AZRIEL, MY BOY, MY BEAUTIFUL BOY. I HAVE BEEN IN BABYLON FOR DAYS.
DON'T FEEL FEAR, FEEL JOY. YOUR TRIBE WILL BE RICH AND THEY WILL LIVE FOREVER, AND THEY WILL GO HOME.
AH, THIS DEPENDS THEN ON WHAT I DO?
YOU SPEAK BOLDLY.
PUT ANOTHER CHAIR AT THE TABLE, WITH YOUR PERMISSION MY LORD KING, CYRUS.
FOR WHOM?
"CYRUS SMILED AND I MIGHT HAVE LAUGHED AT HIS RUTHLESSNESS, HIS DISRESPECT FOR THE ELDERS. BUT I WAS PAST LAUGHING.
FOR MARDUK.
"I FELT A HAND TOUCH MINE. IT WAS VAPOROUS. NO ONE COULD SEE IT, BUT IT WAS MARDUK.
"MY FATHER SAT TO MY RIGHT AND CRIED, HIS HANDS UP TO HIS FACE."

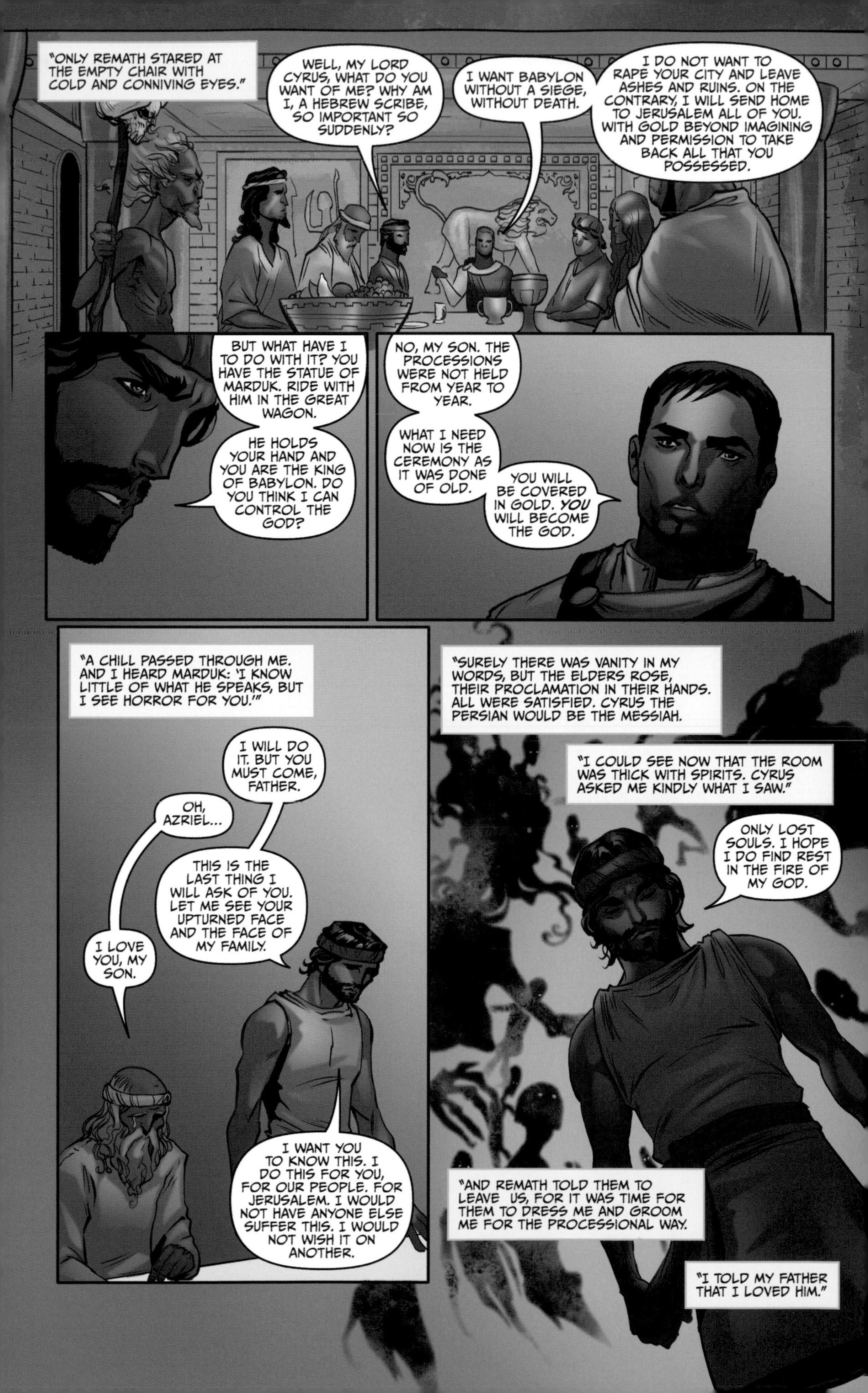
"ONLY REMATH STARED AT THE EMPTY CHAIR WITH COLD AND CONNIVING EYES."
WELL, MY LORD CYRUS, WHAT DO YOU WANT OF ME? WHY AM I, A HEBREW SCRIBE, SO IMPORTANT SO SUDDENLY?
I WANT BABYLON WITHOUT A SIEGE, WITHOUT DEATH.
I DO NOT WANT TO RAPE YOUR CITY AND LEAVE ASHES AND RUINS. ON THE CONTRARY, I WILL SEND HOME TO JERUSALEM ALL OF YOU. WITH GOLD BEYOND IMAGINING AND PERMISSION TO TAKE BACK ALL THAT YOU POSSESSED.
BUT WHAT HAVE I TO DO WITH IT? YOU HAVE THE STATUE OF MARDUK. RIDE WITH HIM IN THE GREAT WAGON.
HE HOLDS YOUR HAND AND YOU ARE THE KING OF BABYLON. DO YOU THINK I CAN CONTROL THE GOD?
NO, MY SON. THE PROCESSIONS WERE NOT HELD FROM YEAR TO YEAR.
WHAT I NEED NOW IS THE CEREMONY AS IT WAS DONE OF OLD.
YOU WILL BE COVERED IN GOLD. YOU WILL BECOME THE GOD.
"A CHILL PASSED THROUGH ME. AND I HEARD MARDUK: 'I KNOW LITTLE OF WHAT HE SPEAKS, BUT I SEE HORROR FOR YOU.'"
I WILL DO IT. BUT YOU MUST COME, FATHER.
OH, AZRIEL...
THIS IS THE LAST THING I WILL ASK OF YOU. LET ME SEE YOUR UPTURNED FACE AND THE FACE OF MY FAMILY.
I LOVE YOU, MY SON.
I WANT YOU TO KNOW THIS. I DO THIS FOR YOU, FOR OUR PEOPLE. FOR JERUSALEM. I WOULD NOT HAVE ANYONE ELSE SUFFER THIS. I WOULD NOT WISH IT ON ANOTHER.
"SURELY THERE WAS VANITY IN MY WORDS, BUT THE ELDERS ROSE, THEIR PROCLAMATION IN THEIR HANDS. ALL WERE SATISFIED. CYRUS THE PERSIAN WOULD BE THE MESSIAH.
"I COULD SEE NOW THAT THE ROOM WAS THICK WITH SPIRITS. CYRUS ASKED ME KINDLY WHAT I SAW."
ONLY LOST SOULS. I HOPE I DO FIND REST IN THE FIRE OF MY GOD.
"AND REMATH TOLD THEM TO LEAVE US, FOR IT WAS TIME FOR THEM TO DRESS ME AND GROOM ME FOR THE PROCESSIONAL WAY.
"I TOLD MY FATHER THAT I LOVED HIM."

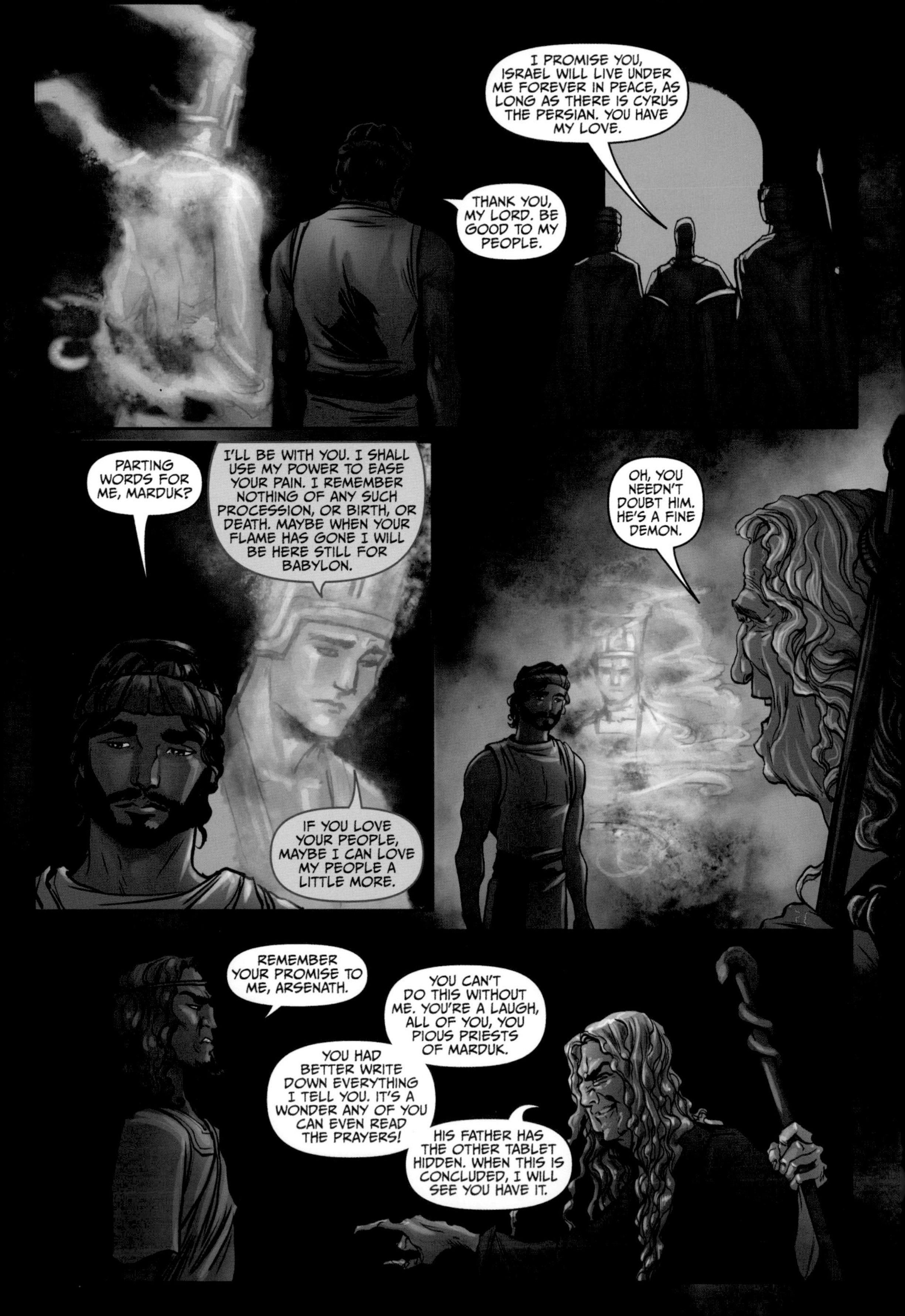
I PROMISE YOU, ISRAEL WILL LIVE UNDER ME FOREVER IN PEACE, AS LONG AS THERE IS CYRUS THE PERSIAN. YOU HAVE MY LOVE.
THANK YOU, MY LORD. BE GOOD TO MY PEOPLE.
PARTING WORDS FOR ME, MARDUK?
I'LL BE WITH YOU. I SHALL USE MY POWER TO EASE YOUR PAIN. I REMEMBER NOTHING OF ANY SUCH PROCESSION, OR BIRTH, OR DEATH. MAYBE WHEN YOUR FLAME HAS GONE I WILL BE HERE STILL FOR BABYLON.
IF YOU LOVE YOUR PEOPLE, MAYBE I CAN LOVE MY PEOPLE A LITTLE MORE.
OH, YOU NEEDN'T DOUBT HIM. HE'S A FINE DEMON.
REMEMBER YOUR PROMISE TO ME, ARSENATH.
YOU CAN'T DO THIS WITHOUT ME. YOU'RE A LAUGH, ALL OF YOU, YOU PIOUS PRIESTS OF MARDUK.
YOU HAD BETTER WRITE DOWN EVERYTHING I TELL YOU. IT'S A WONDER ANY OF YOU CAN EVEN READ THE PRAYERS!
HIS FATHER HAS THE OTHER TABLET HIDDEN. WHEN THIS IS CONCLUDED, I WILL SEE YOU HAVE IT.

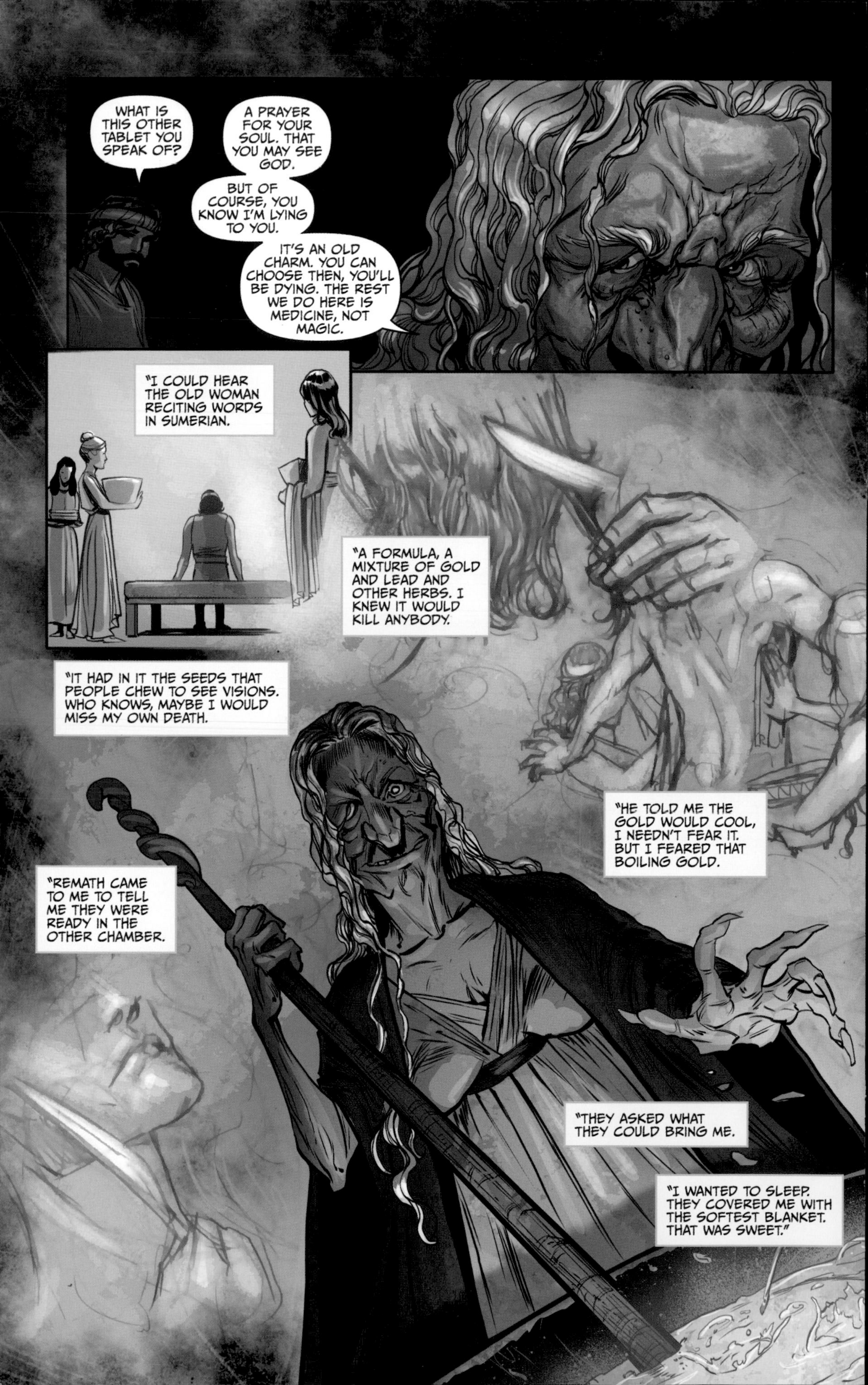
WHAT IS THIS OTHER TABLET YOU SPEAK OF?
A PRAYER FOR YOUR SOUL. THAT YOU MAY SEE GOD.
BUT OF COURSE, YOU KNOW I'M LYING TO YOU.
IT'S AN OLD CHARM. YOU CAN CHOOSE THEN, YOU'LL BE DYING. THE REST WE DO HERE IS MEDICINE, NOT MAGIC.
"I COULD HEAR THE OLD WOMAN RECITING WORDS IN SUMERIAN.
"A FORMULA, A MIXTURE OF GOLD AND LEAD AND OTHER HERBS. I KNEW IT WOULD KILL ANYBODY.
"IT HAD IN IT THE SEEDS THAT PEOPLE CHEW TO SEE VISIONS. WHO KNOWS, MAYBE I WOULD MISS MY OWN DEATH.
"HE TOLD ME THE GOLD WOULD COOL, I NEEDN'T FEAR IT. BUT I FEARED THAT BOILING GOLD.
"REMATH CAME TO ME TO TELL ME THEY WERE READY IN THE OTHER CHAMBER.
"THEY ASKED WHAT THEY COULD BRING ME.
"I WANTED TO SLEEP. THEY COVERED ME WITH THE SOFTEST BLANKET. THAT WAS SWEET."

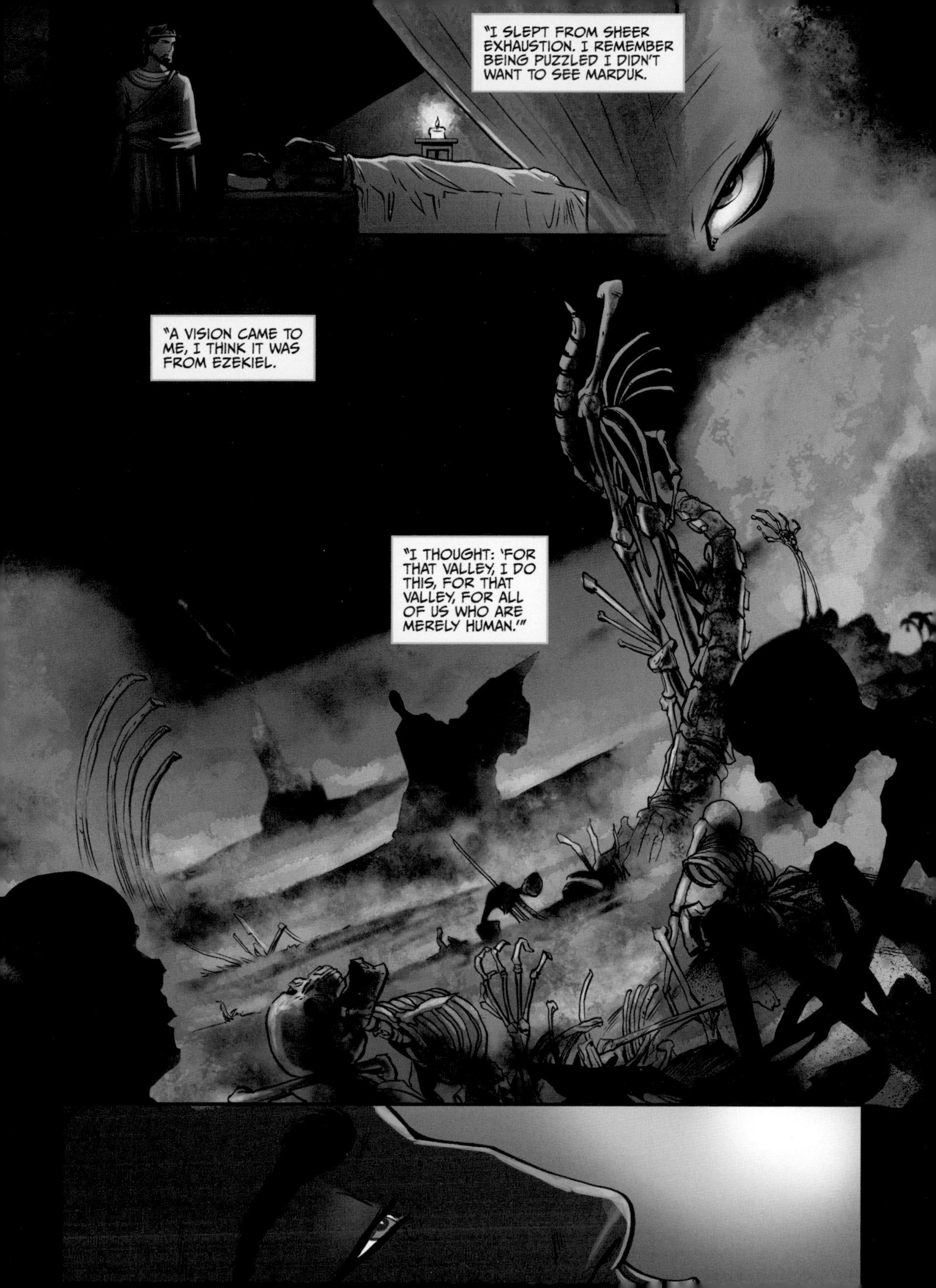
"I SLEPT FROM SHEER EXHAUSTION. I REMEMBER BEING PUZZLED I DIDN'T WANT TO SEE MARDUK.
"A VISION CAME TO ME, I THINK IT WAS FROM EZEKIEL.
"I THOUGHT: 'FOR THAT VALLEY, I DO THIS, FOR THAT VALLEY, FOR ALL OF US WHO ARE MERELY HUMAN.'"

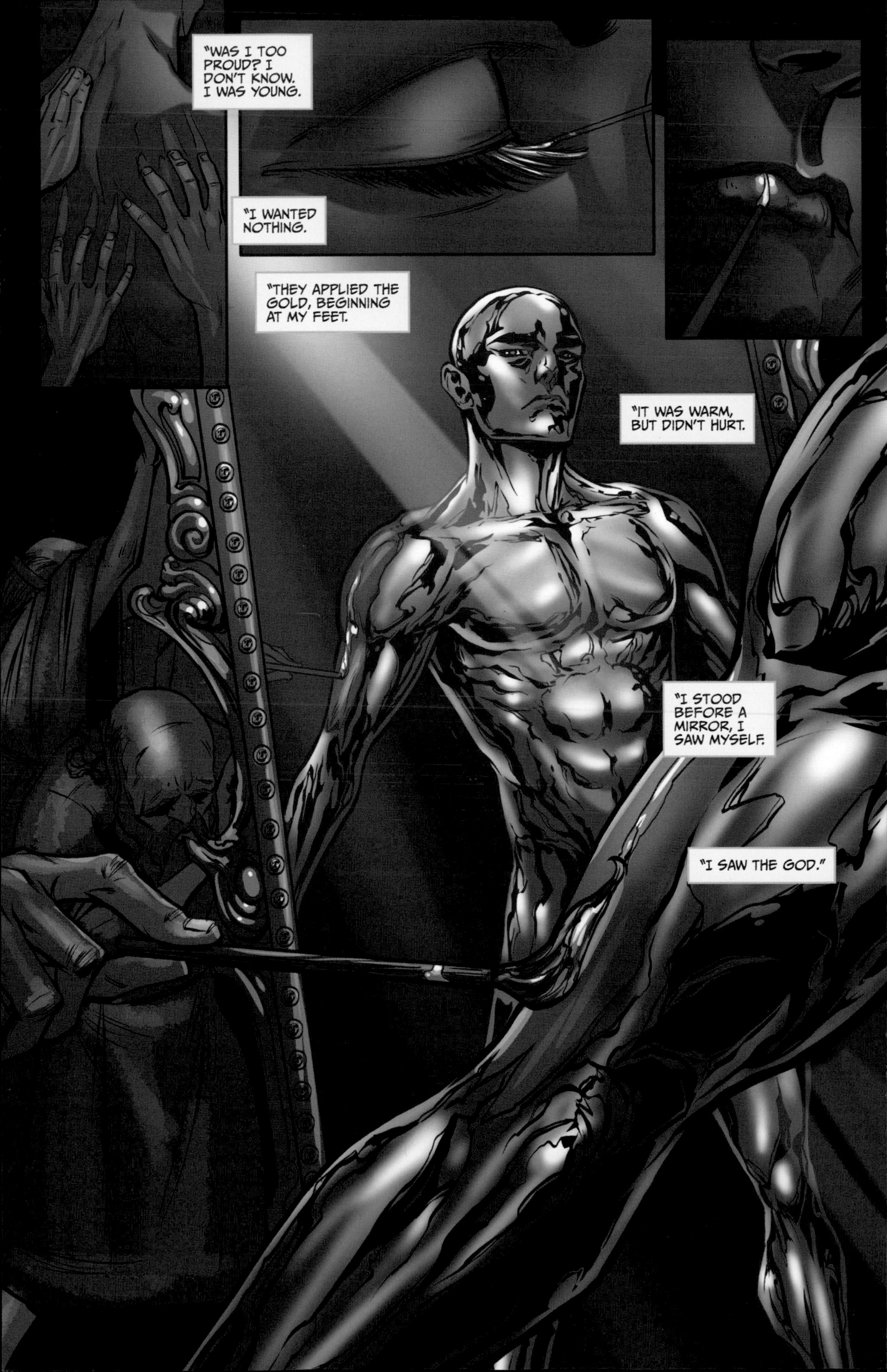
"WAS I TOO PROUD? I DON'T KNOW. I WAS YOUNG.
"I WANTED NOTHING.
"THEY APPLIED THE GOLD, BEGINNING AT MY FEET.
"IT WAS WARM, BUT DIDN'T HURT.
"I STOOD BEFORE A MIRROR, I SAW MYSELF.
"I SAW THE GOD."

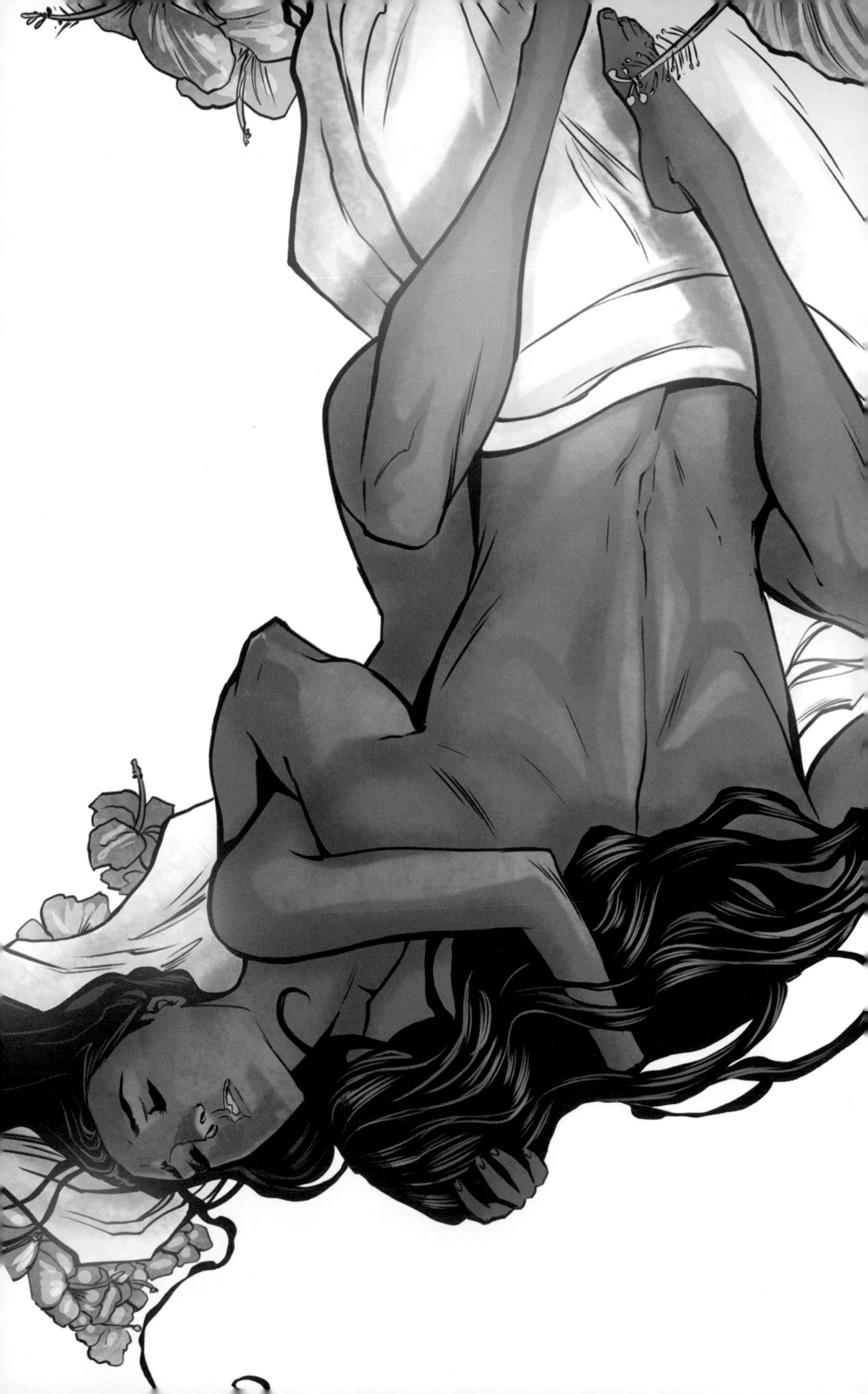

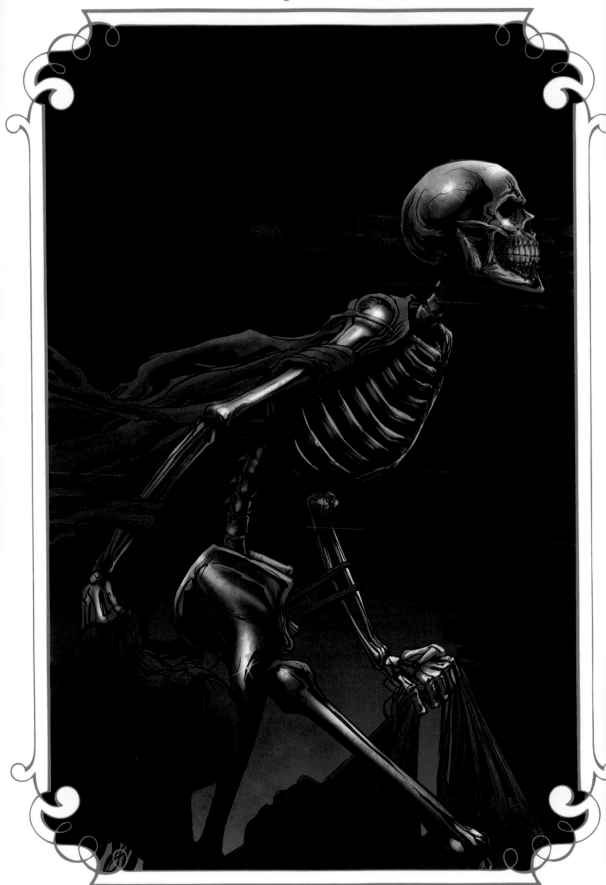

Art by Renae De Liz • Colors by Ray Dillon

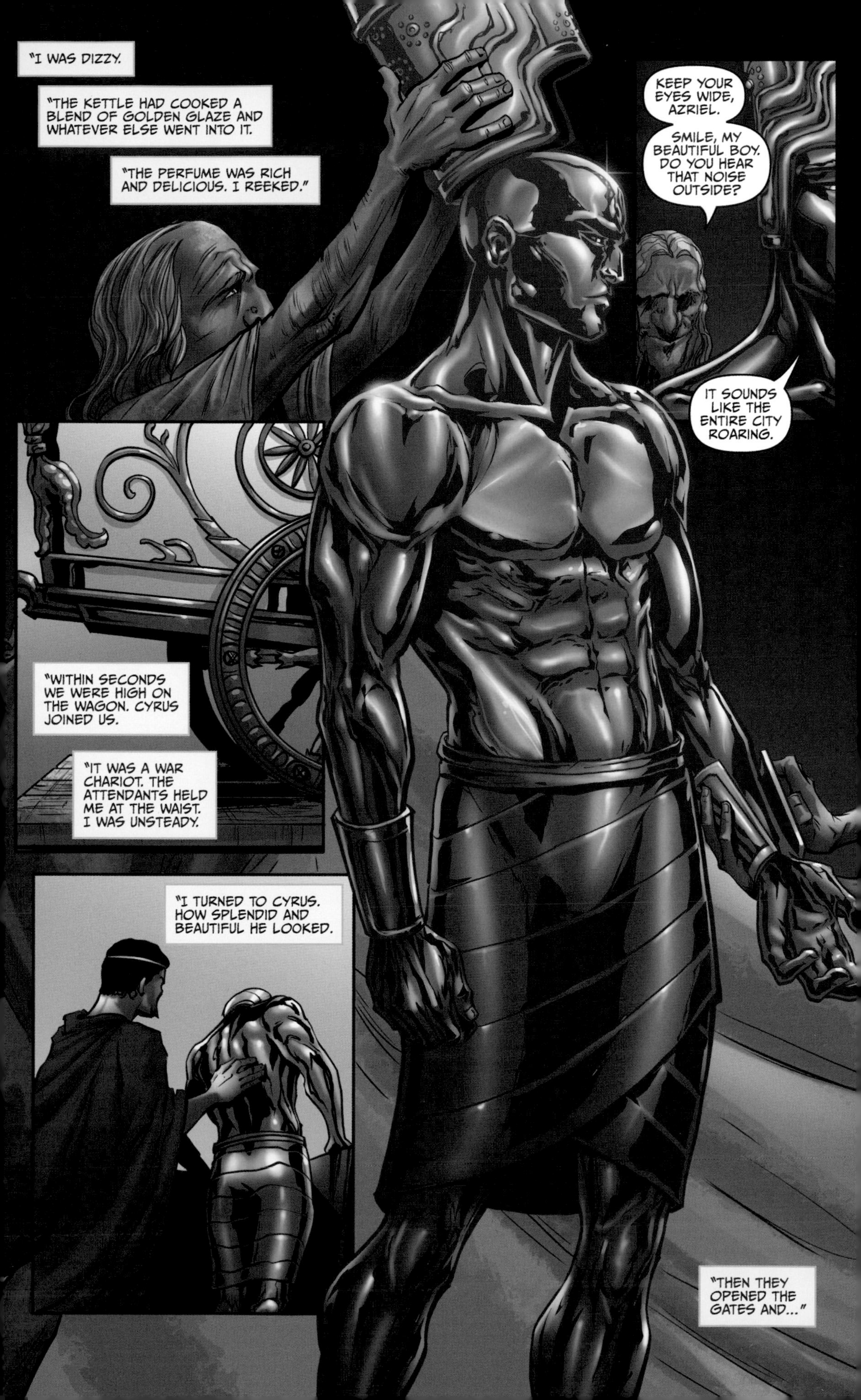
"I WAS DIZZY.
"THE KETTLE HAD COOKED A BLEND OF GOLDEN GLAZE AND WHATEVER ELSE WENT INTO IT.
"THE PERFUME WAS RICH AND DELICIOUS. I REEKED."
KEEP YOUR EYES WIDE, AZRIEL.
SMILE, MY BEAUTIFUL BOY. DO YOU HEAR THAT NOISE OUTSIDE?
IT SOUNDS LIKE THE ENTIRE CITY ROARING.
"WITHIN SECONDS WE WERE HIGH ON THE WAGON. CYRUS JOINED US.
"IT WAS A WAR CHARIOT. THE ATTENDANTS HELD ME AT THE WAIST. I WAS UNSTEADY.
"I TURNED TO CYRUS. HOW SPLENDID AND BEAUTIFUL HE LOOKED.
"THEN THEY OPENED THE GATES AND..."

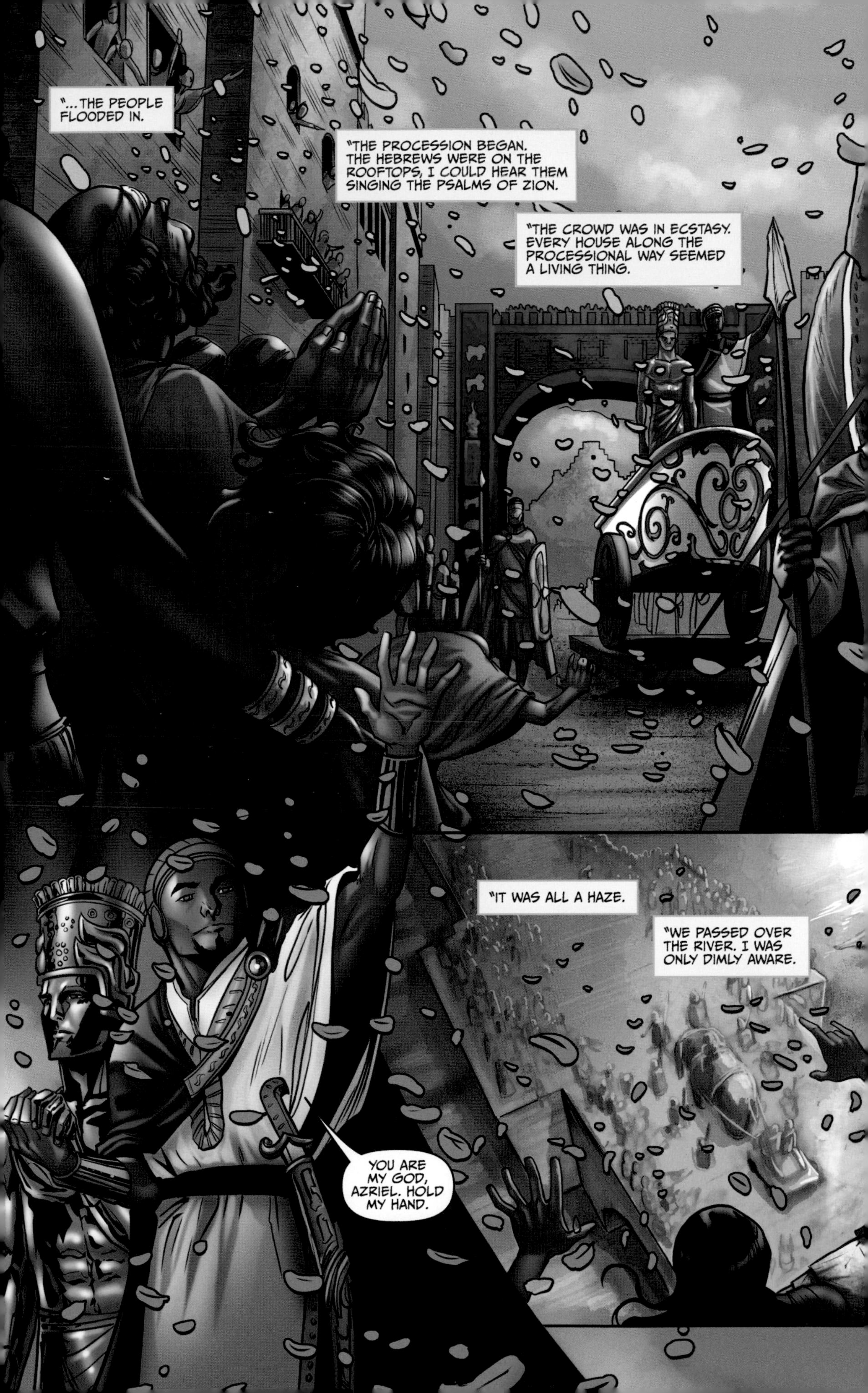
"...THE PEOPLE FLOODED IN.
"THE PROCESSION BEGAN. THE HEBREWS WERE ON THE ROOFTOPS, I COULD HEAR THEM SINGING THE PSALMS OF ZION.
"THE CROWD WAS IN ECSTASY. EVERY HOUSE ALONG THE PROCESSIONAL WAY SEEMED A LIVING THING.
YOU ARE MY GOD, AZRIEL. HOLD MY HAND.
"IT WAS ALL A HAZE.
"WE PASSED OVER THE RIVER. I WAS ONLY DIMLY AWARE.

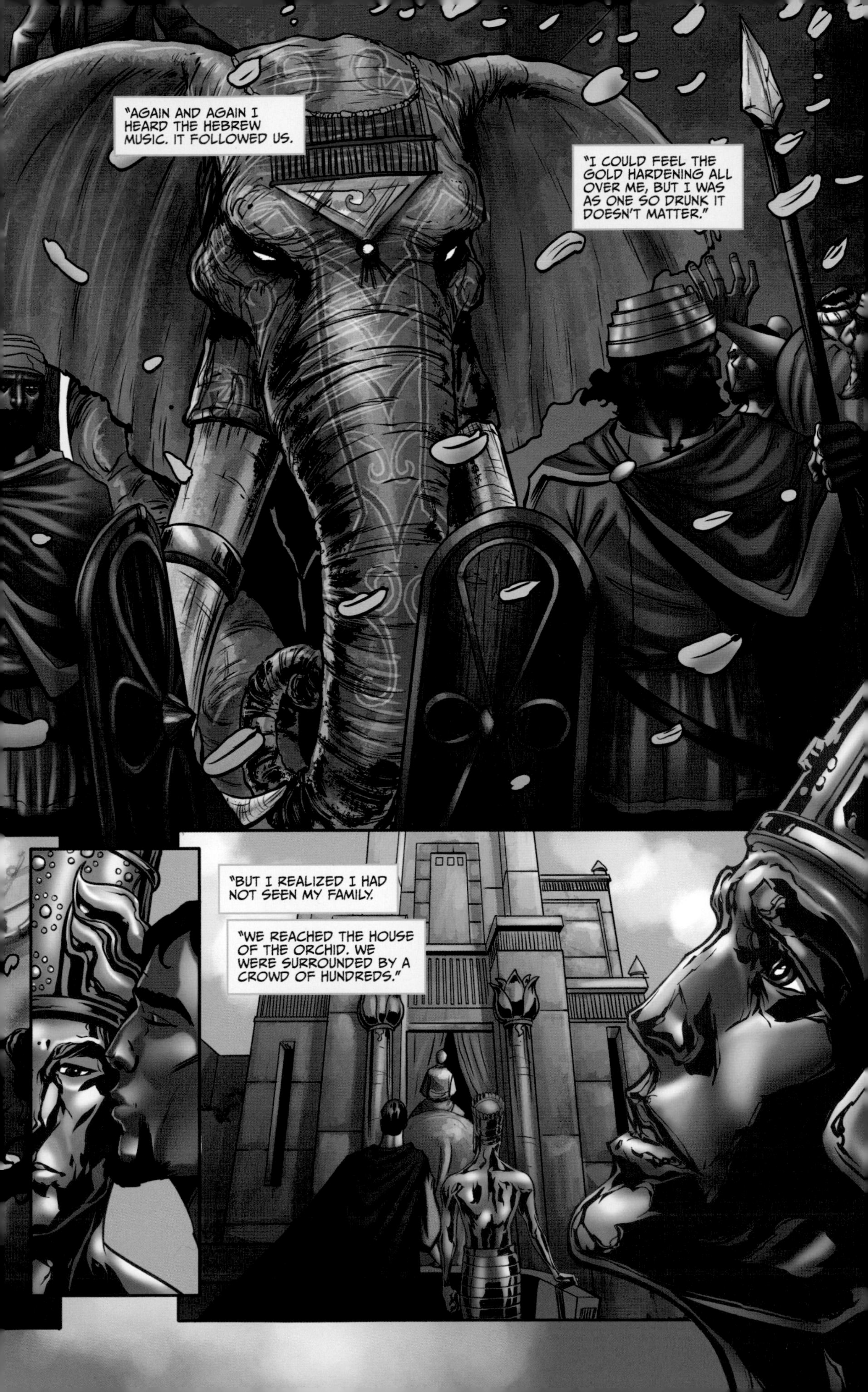
"AGAIN AND AGAIN I HEARD THE HEBREW MUSIC. IT FOLLOWED US.
"I COULD FEEL THE GOLD HARDENING ALL OVER ME, BUT I WAS AS ONE SO DRUNK IT DOESN'T MATTER."
"BUT I REALIZED I HAD NOT SEEN MY FAMILY.
"WE REACHED THE HOUSE OF THE ORCHID. WE WERE SURROUNDED BY A CROWD OF HUNDREDS."

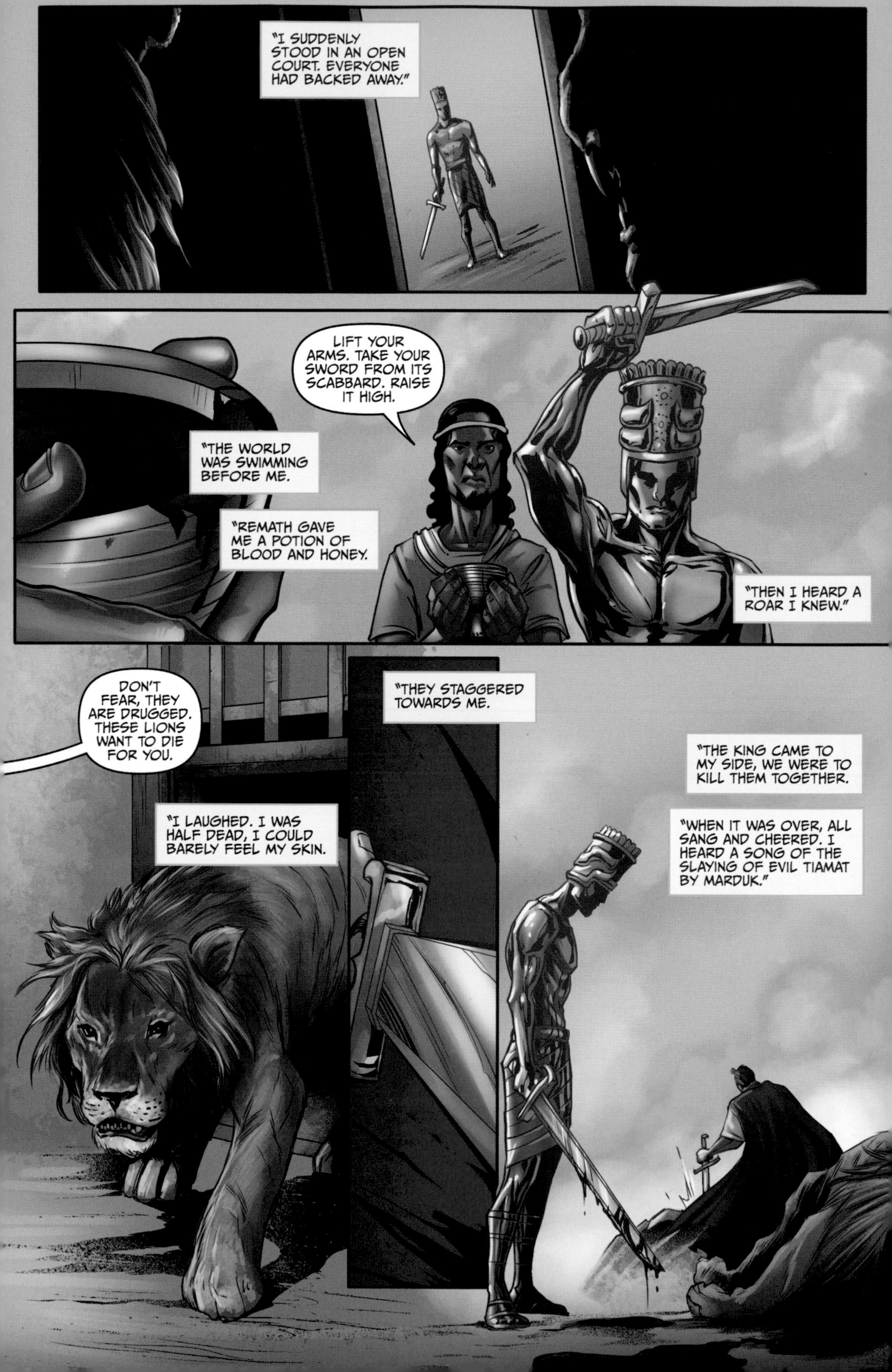
"I SUDDENLY STOOD IN AN OPEN COURT. EVERYONE HAD BACKED AWAY."
LIFT YOUR ARMS. TAKE YOUR SWORD FROM ITS SCABBARD. RAISE IT HIGH.
"THE WORLD WAS SWIMMING BEFORE ME.
"REMATH GAVE ME A POTION OF BLOOD AND HONEY.
"THEN I HEARD A ROAR I KNEW."
DON'T FEAR, THEY ARE DRUGGED. THESE LIONS WANT TO DIE FOR YOU.
"THEY STAGGERED TOWARDS ME.
"I LAUGHED. I WAS HALF DEAD, I COULD BARELY FEEL MY SKIN.
"THE KING CAME TO MY SIDE, WE WERE TO KILL THEM TOGETHER.
"WHEN IT WAS OVER, ALL SANG AND CHEERED. I HEARD A SONG OF THE SLAYING OF EVIL TIAMAT BY MARDUK."

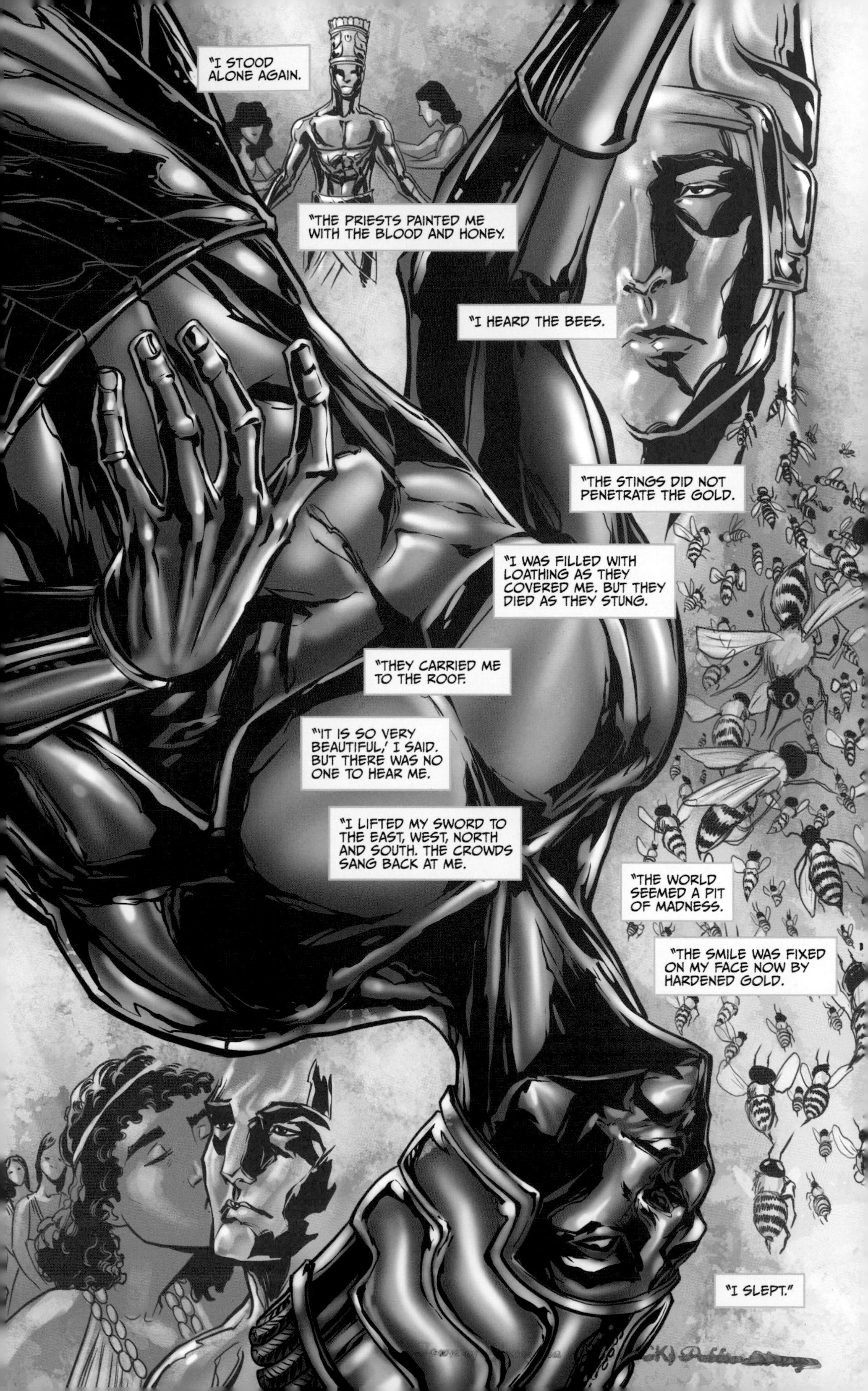
"I STOOD ALONE AGAIN.
"THE PRIESTS PAINTED ME WITH THE BLOOD AND HONEY.
"I HEARD THE BEES.
"THE STINGS DID NOT PENETRATE THE GOLD.
"I WAS FILLED WITH LOATHING AS THEY COVERED ME. BUT THEY DIED AS THEY STUNG.
"THEY CARRIED ME TO THE ROOF.
"'IT IS SO VERY BEAUTIFUL,' I SAID. BUT THERE WAS NO ONE TO HEAR ME.
"I LIFTED MY SWORD TO THE EAST, WEST, NORTH AND SOUTH. THE CROWDS SANG BACK AT ME.
"THE WORLD SEEMED A PIT OF MADNESS.
"THE SMILE WAS FIXED ON MY FACE NOW BY HARDENED GOLD.
"I SLEPT."

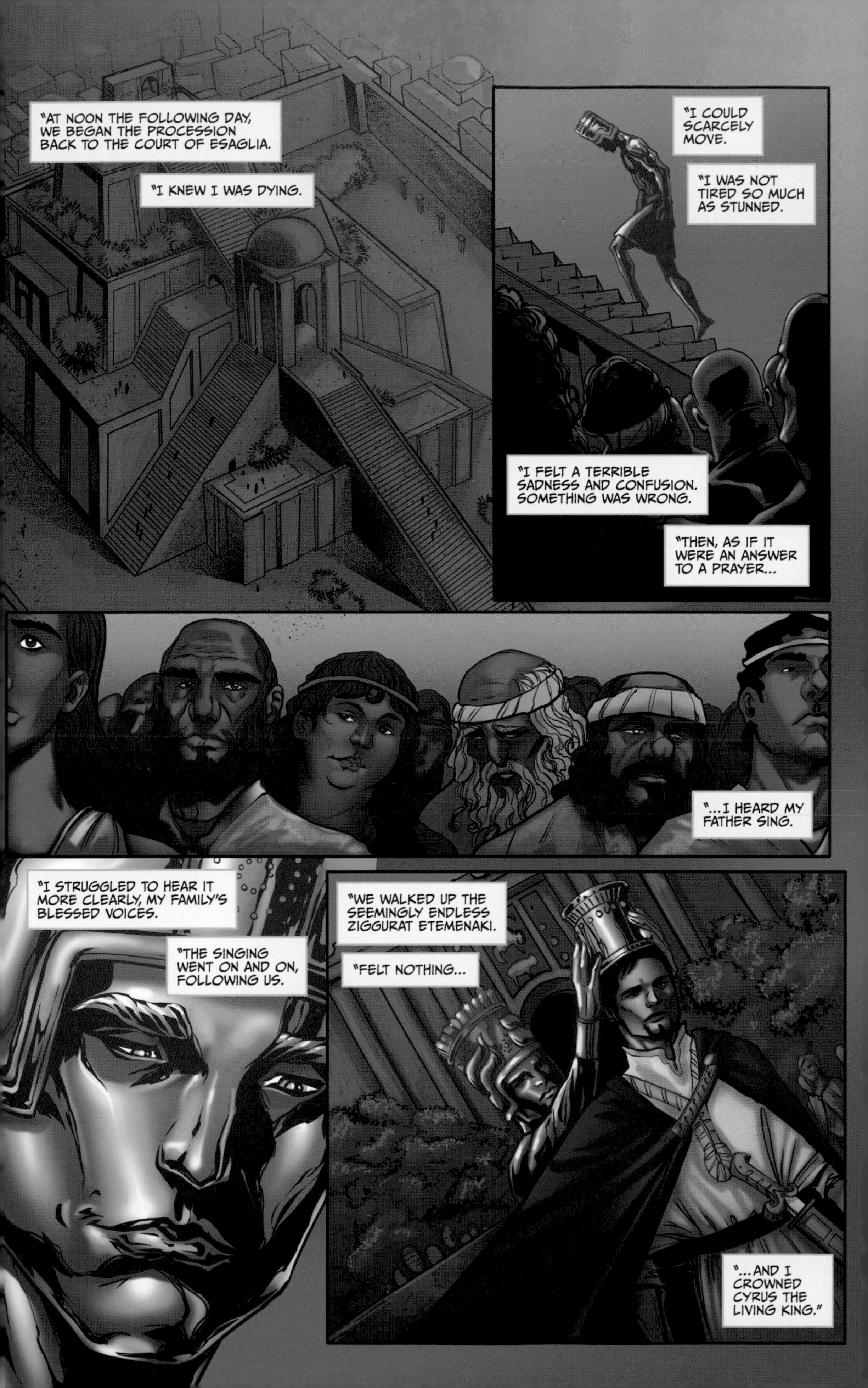
"AT NOON THE FOLLOWING DAY, WE BEGAN THE PROCESSION BACK TO THE COURT OF ESAGLIA.
"I KNEW I WAS DYING.
"I COULD SCARCELY MOVE.
"I WAS NOT TIRED SO MUCH AS STUNNED.
"I FELT A TERRIBLE SADNESS AND CONFUSION. SOMETHING WAS WRONG.
"THEN, AS IF IT WERE AN ANSWER TO A PRAYER...
"...I HEARD MY FATHER SING.
"I STRUGGLED TO HEAR IT MORE CLEARLY, MY FAMILY'S BLESSED VOICES.
"THE SINGING WENT ON AND ON, FOLLOWING US.
"WE WALKED UP THE SEEMINGLY ENDLESS ZIGGURAT ETEMENAKI.
"FELT NOTHING...
"...AND I CROWNED CYRUS THE LIVING KING."

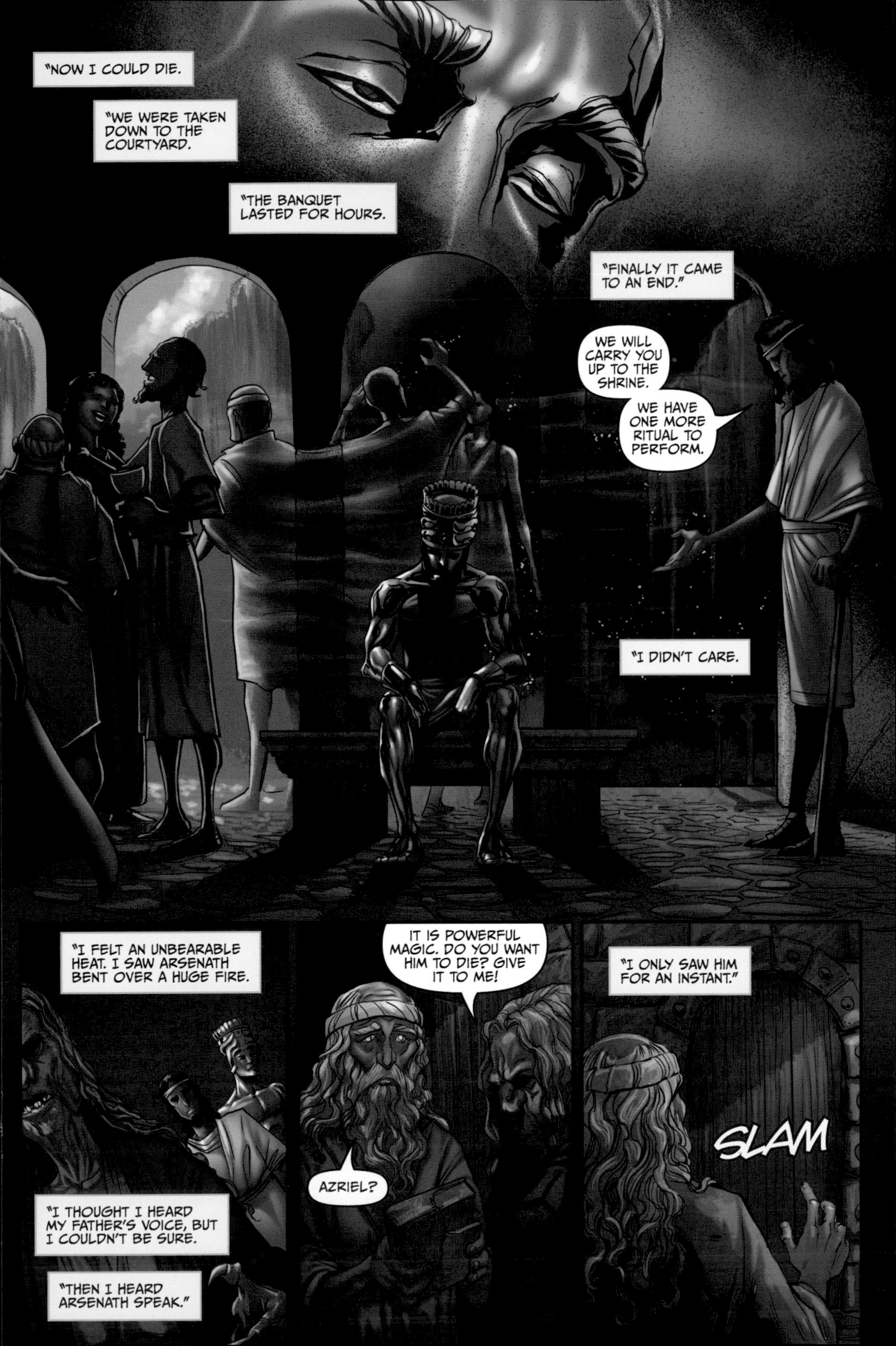
"NOW I COULD DIE.
"WE WERE TAKEN DOWN TO THE COURTYARD.
"THE BANQUET LASTED FOR HOURS.
"FINALLY IT CAME TO AN END."
WE WILL CARRY YOU UP TO THE SHRINE.
WE HAVE ONE MORE RITUAL TO PERFORM.
"I DIDN'T CARE.
"I FELT AN UNBEARABLE HEAT. I SAW ARSENATH BENT OVER A HUGE FIRE.
"I THOUGHT I HEARD MY FATHER'S VOICE, BUT I COULDN'T BE SURE.
"THEN I HEARD ARSENATH SPEAK."
IT IS POWERFUL MAGIC. DO YOU WANT HIM TO DIE? GIVE IT TO ME!
AZRIEL?
"I ONLY SAW HIM FOR AN INSTANT."
SLAM

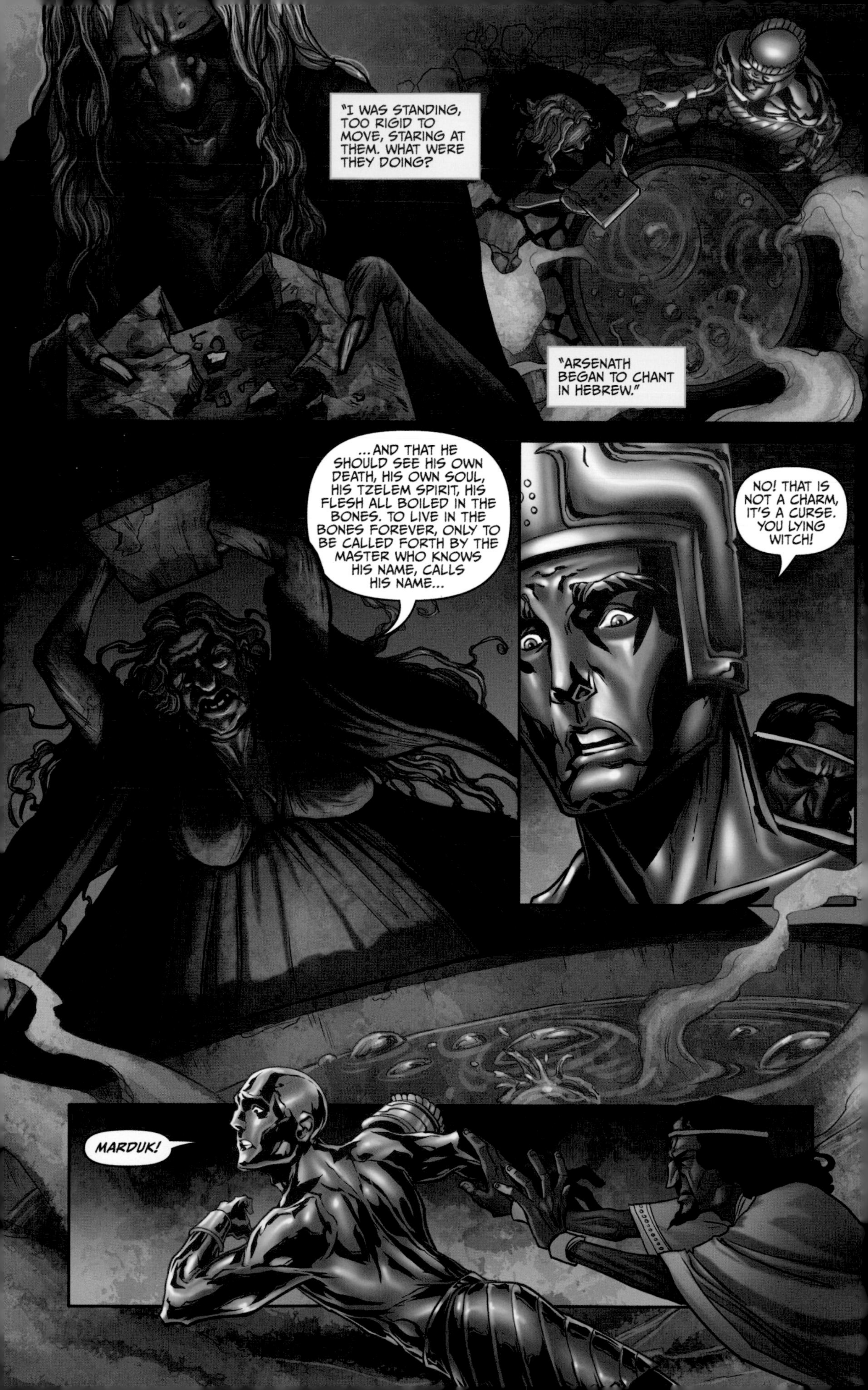
"I WAS STANDING, TOO RIGID TO MOVE, STARING AT THEM. WHAT WERE THEY DOING?
"ARSENATH BEGAN TO CHANT IN HEBREW."
...AND THAT HE SHOULD SEE HIS OWN DEATH, HIS OWN SOUL, HIS TZELEM SPIRIT, HIS FLESH ALL BOILED IN THE BONES. TO LIVE IN THE BONES FOREVER, ONLY TO BE CALLED FORTH BY THE MASTER WHO KNOWS HIS NAME, CALLS HIS NAME...
NO! THAT IS NOT A CHARM, IT'S A CURSE. YOU LYING WITCH!
MARDUK!

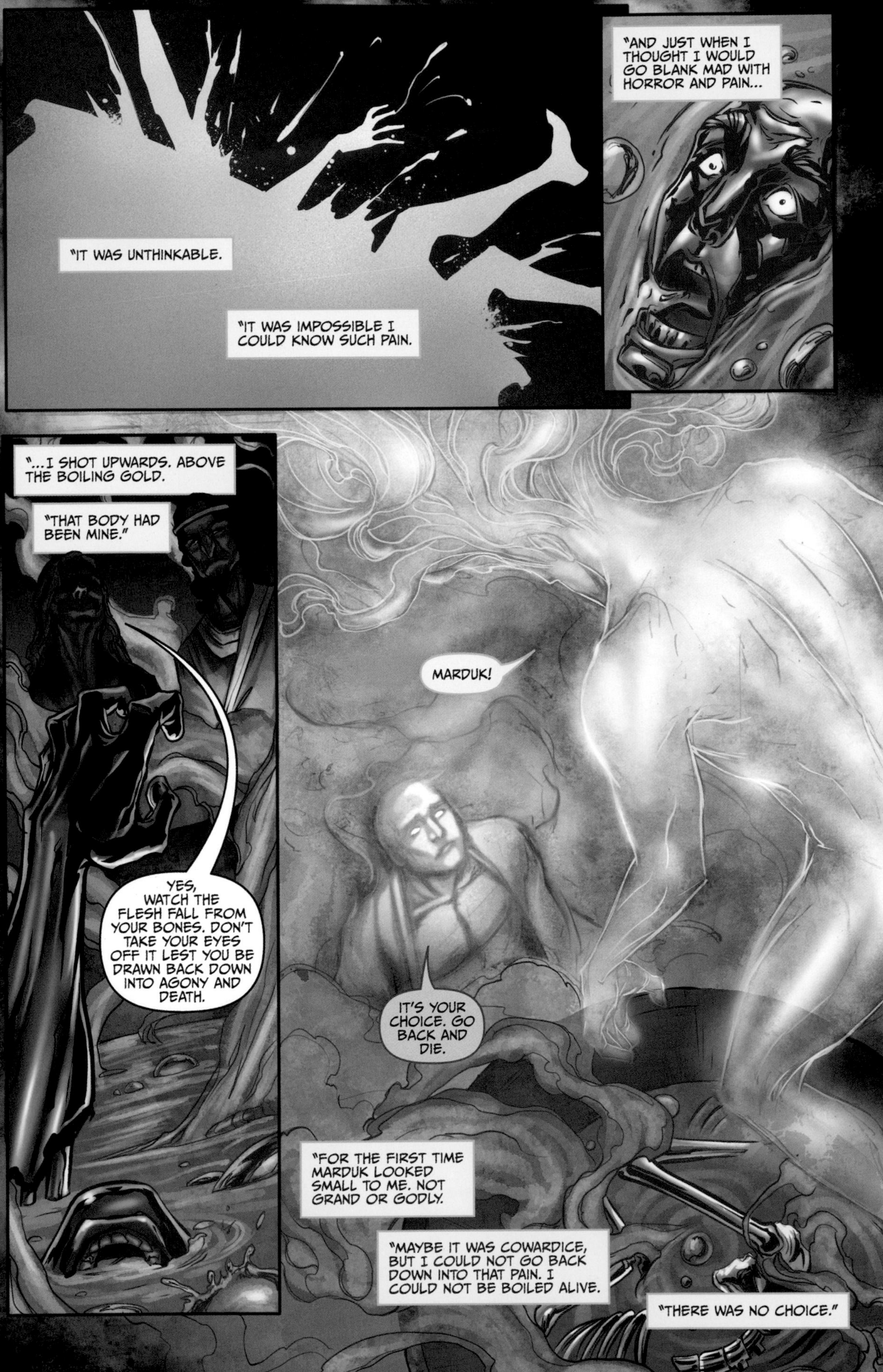
"IT WAS UNTHINKABLE.
"IT WAS IMPOSSIBLE I COULD KNOW SUCH PAIN.
"AND JUST WHEN I THOUGHT I WOULD GO BLANK MAD WITH HORROR AND PAIN...
"...I SHOT UPWARDS. ABOVE THE BOILING GOLD.
"THAT BODY HAD BEEN MINE."
YES, WATCH THE FLESH FALL FROM YOUR BONES. DON'T TAKE YOUR EYES OFF IT LEST YOU BE DRAWN BACK DOWN INTO AGONY AND DEATH.
MARDUK!
IT'S YOUR CHOICE. GO BACK AND DIE.
"FOR THE FIRST TIME MARDUK LOOKED SMALL TO ME. NOT GRAND OR GODLY.
"MAYBE IT WAS COWARDICE, BUT I COULD NOT GO BACK DOWN INTO THAT PAIN. I COULD NOT BE BOILED ALIVE.
"THERE WAS NO CHOICE."

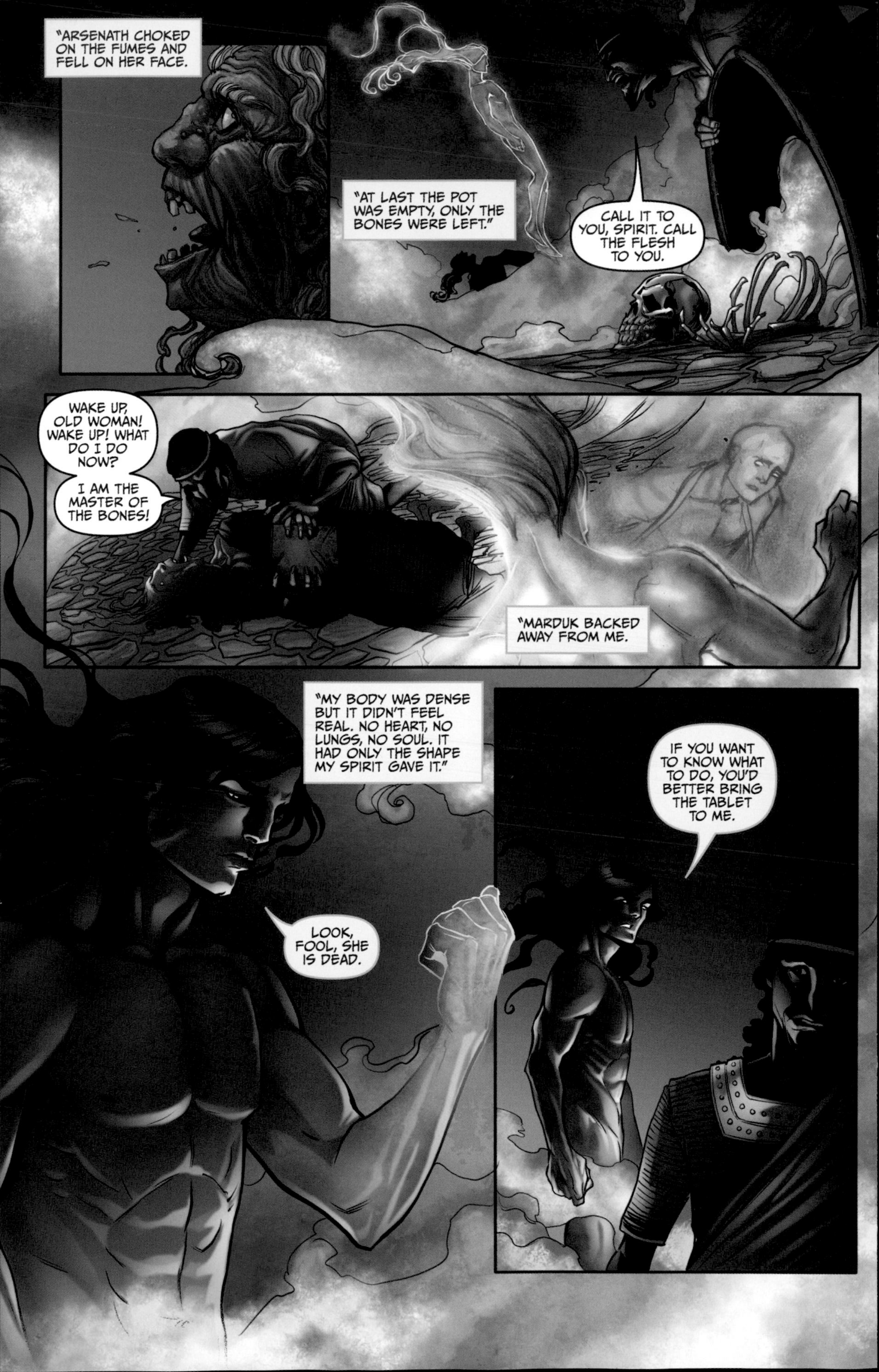
"ARSENATH CHOKED ON THE FUMES AND FELL ON HER FACE.
"AT LAST THE POT WAS EMPTY, ONLY THE BONES WERE LEFT."
CALL IT TO YOU, SPIRIT. CALL THE FLESH TO YOU.
WAKE UP, OLD WOMAN! WAKE UP! WHAT DO I DO NOW?
I AM THE MASTER OF THE BONES!
"MARDUK BACKED AWAY FROM ME.
"MY BODY WAS DENSE BUT IT DIDN'T FEEL REAL. NO HEART, NO LUNGS, NO SOUL. IT HAD ONLY THE SHAPE MY SPIRIT GAVE IT."
LOOK, FOOL, SHE IS DEAD.
IF YOU WANT TO KNOW WHAT TO DO, YOU'D BETTER BRING THE TABLET TO ME.

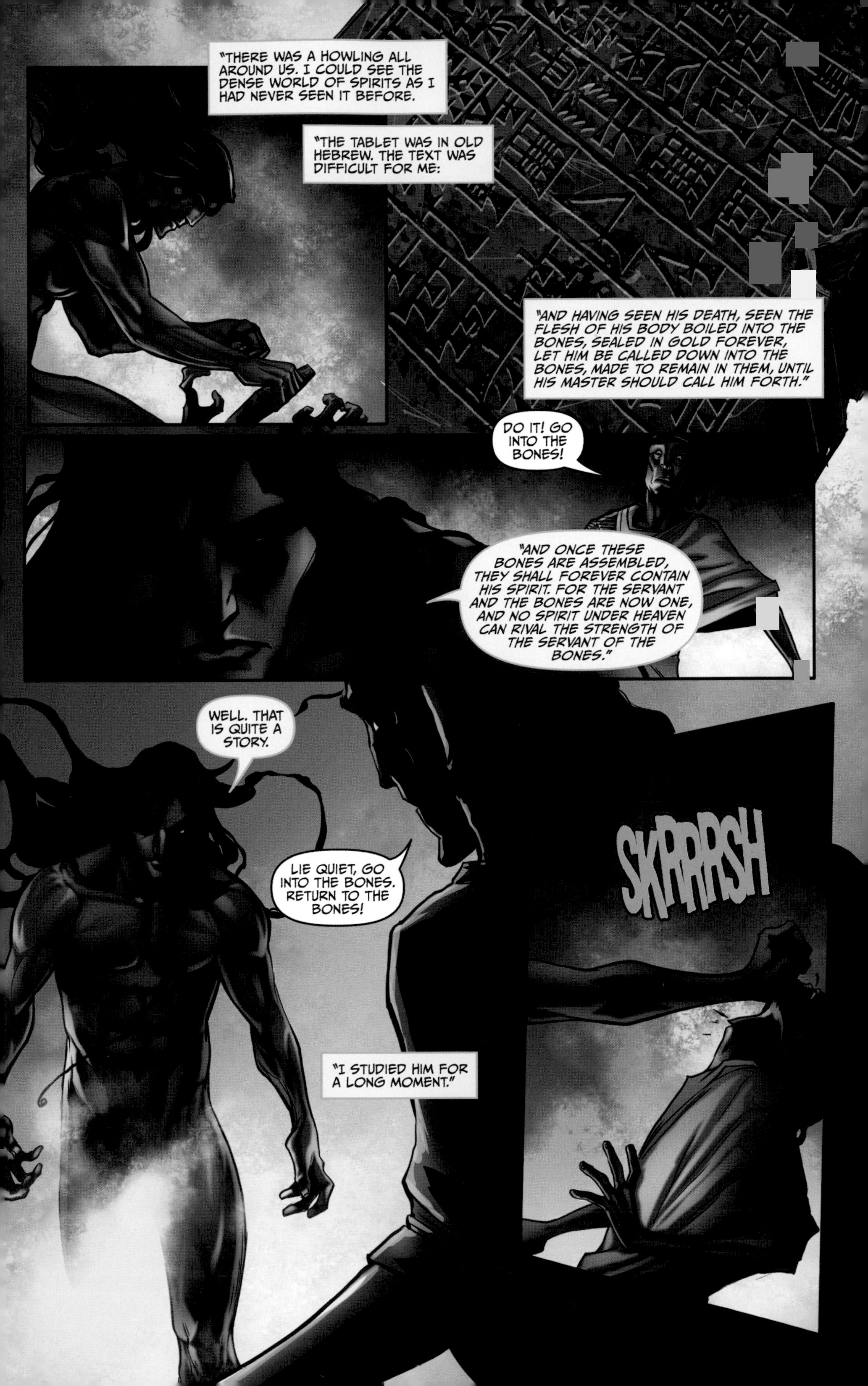
"THERE WAS A HOWLING ALL AROUND US. I COULD SEE THE DENSE WORLD OF SPIRITS AS I HAD NEVER SEEN IT BEFORE.
"THE TABLET WAS IN OLD HEBREW. THE TEXT WAS DIFFICULT FOR ME:
"AND HAVING SEEN HIS DEATH, SEEN THE FLESH OF HIS BODY BOILED INTO THE BONES, SEALED IN GOLD FOREVER, LET HIM BE CALLED DOWN INTO THE BONES, MADE TO REMAIN IN THEM, UNTIL HIS MASTER SHOULD CALL HIM FORTH."
DO IT! GO INTO THE BONES!
"AND ONCE THESE BONES ARE ASSEMBLED, THEY SHALL FOREVER CONTAIN HIS SPIRIT. FOR THE SERVANT AND THE BONES ARE NOW ONE, AND NO SPIRIT UNDER HEAVEN CAN RIVAL THE STRENGTH OF THE SERVANT OF THE BONES."
WELL. THAT IS QUITE A STORY.
LIE QUIET, GO INTO THE BONES. RETURN TO THE BONES!
SKRRRSH
"I STUDIED HIM FOR A LONG MOMENT."

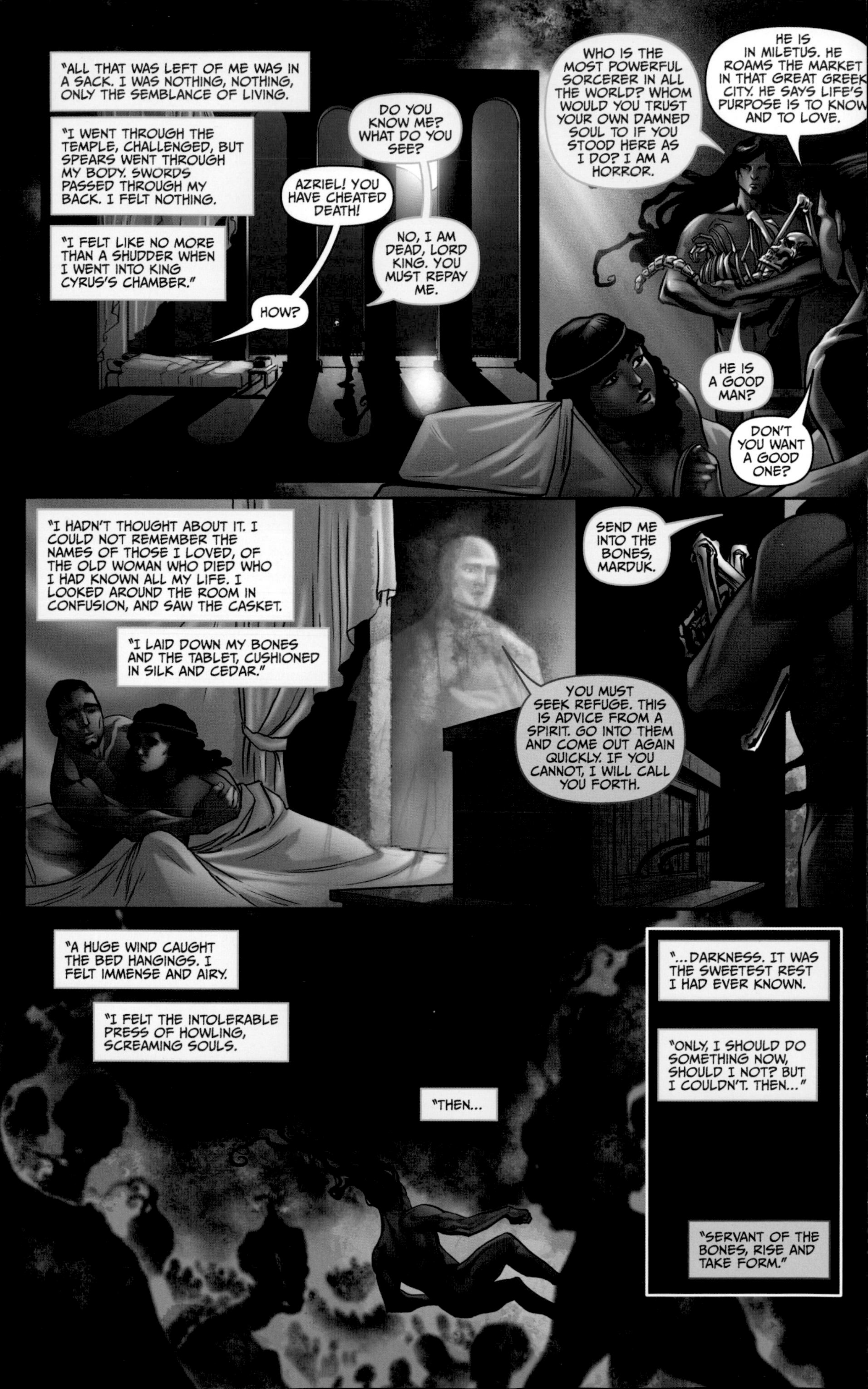
"ALL THAT WAS LEFT OF ME WAS IN A SACK. I WAS NOTHING, NOTHING, ONLY THE SEMBLANCE OF LIVING.
"I WENT THROUGH THE TEMPLE, CHALLENGED, BUT SPEARS WENT THROUGH MY BODY. SWORDS PASSED THROUGH MY BACK. I FELT NOTHING.
"I FELT LIKE NO MORE THAN A SHUDDER WHEN I WENT INTO KING CYRUS'S CHAMBER."
AZRIEL! YOU HAVE CHEATED DEATH!
DO YOU KNOW ME? WHAT DO YOU SEE?
HOW?
NO, I AM DEAD, LORD KING. YOU MUST REPAY ME.
WHO IS THE MOST POWERFUL SORCERER IN ALL THE WORLD? WHOM WOULD YOU TRUST YOUR OWN DAMNED SOUL TO IF YOU STOOD HERE AS I DO? I AM A HORROR.
HE IS IN MILETUS. HE ROAMS THE MARKET IN THAT GREAT GREEK CITY. HE SAYS LIFE'S PURPOSE IS TO KNOW AND TO LOVE.
HE IS A GOOD MAN?
DON'T YOU WANT A GOOD ONE?
"I HADN'T THOUGHT ABOUT IT. I COULD NOT REMEMBER THE NAMES OF THOSE I LOVED, OF THE OLD WOMAN WHO DIED WHO I HAD KNOWN ALL MY LIFE. I LOOKED AROUND THE ROOM IN CONFUSION, AND SAW THE CASKET.
"I LAID DOWN MY BONES AND THE TABLET, CUSHIONED IN SILK AND CEDAR."
SEND ME INTO THE BONES, MARDUK.
YOU MUST SEEK REFUGE. THIS IS ADVICE FROM A SPIRIT. GO INTO THEM AND COME OUT AGAIN QUICKLY. IF YOU CANNOT, I WILL CALL YOU FORTH.
"A HUGE WIND CAUGHT THE BED HANGINGS. I FELT IMMENSE AND AIRY.
"I FELT THE INTOLERABLE PRESS OF HOWLING, SCREAMING SOULS.
"THEN...
"...DARKNESS. IT WAS THE SWEETEST REST I HAD EVER KNOWN.
"ONLY, I SHOULD DO SOMETHING NOW, SHOULD I NOT? BUT I COULDN'T. THEN..."
"SERVANT OF THE BONES, RISE AND TAKE FORM."

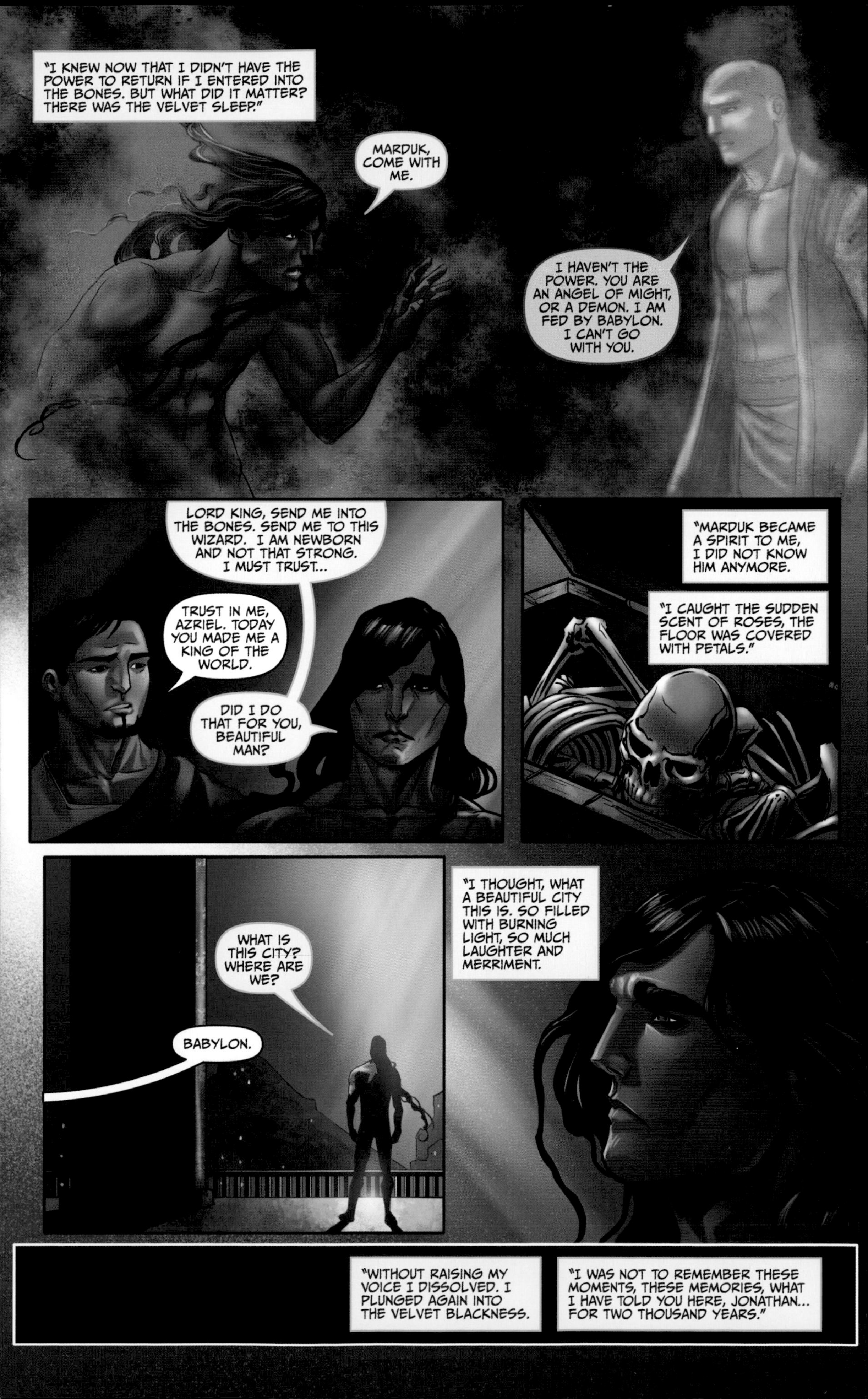
"I KNEW NOW THAT I DIDN'T HAVE THE POWER TO RETURN IF I ENTERED INTO THE BONES. BUT WHAT DID IT MATTER? THERE WAS THE VELVET SLEEP."
MARDUK, COME WITH ME.
I HAVEN'T THE POWER. YOU ARE AN ANGEL OF MIGHT, OR A DEMON. I AM FED BY BABYLON. I CAN'T GO WITH YOU.
LORD KING, SEND ME INTO THE BONES. SEND ME TO THIS WIZARD. I AM NEWBORN AND NOT THAT STRONG. I MUST TRUST...
TRUST IN ME, AZRIEL. TODAY YOU MADE ME A KING OF THE WORLD.
DID I DO THAT FOR YOU, BEAUTIFUL MAN?
"MARDUK BECAME A SPIRIT TO ME, I DID NOT KNOW HIM ANYMORE.
"I CAUGHT THE SUDDEN SCENT OF ROSES, THE FLOOR WAS COVERED WITH PETALS."
WHAT IS THIS CITY? WHERE ARE WE?
BABYLON.
"I THOUGHT, WHAT A BEAUTIFUL CITY THIS IS. SO FILLED WITH BURNING LIGHT, SO MUCH LAUGHTER AND MERRIMENT.
"WITHOUT RAISING MY VOICE I DISSOLVED. I PLUNGED AGAIN INTO THE VELVET BLACKNESS.
"I WAS NOT TO REMEMBER THESE MOMENTS, THESE MEMORIES, WHAT I HAVE TOLD YOU HERE, JONATHAN... FOR TWO THOUSAND YEARS."

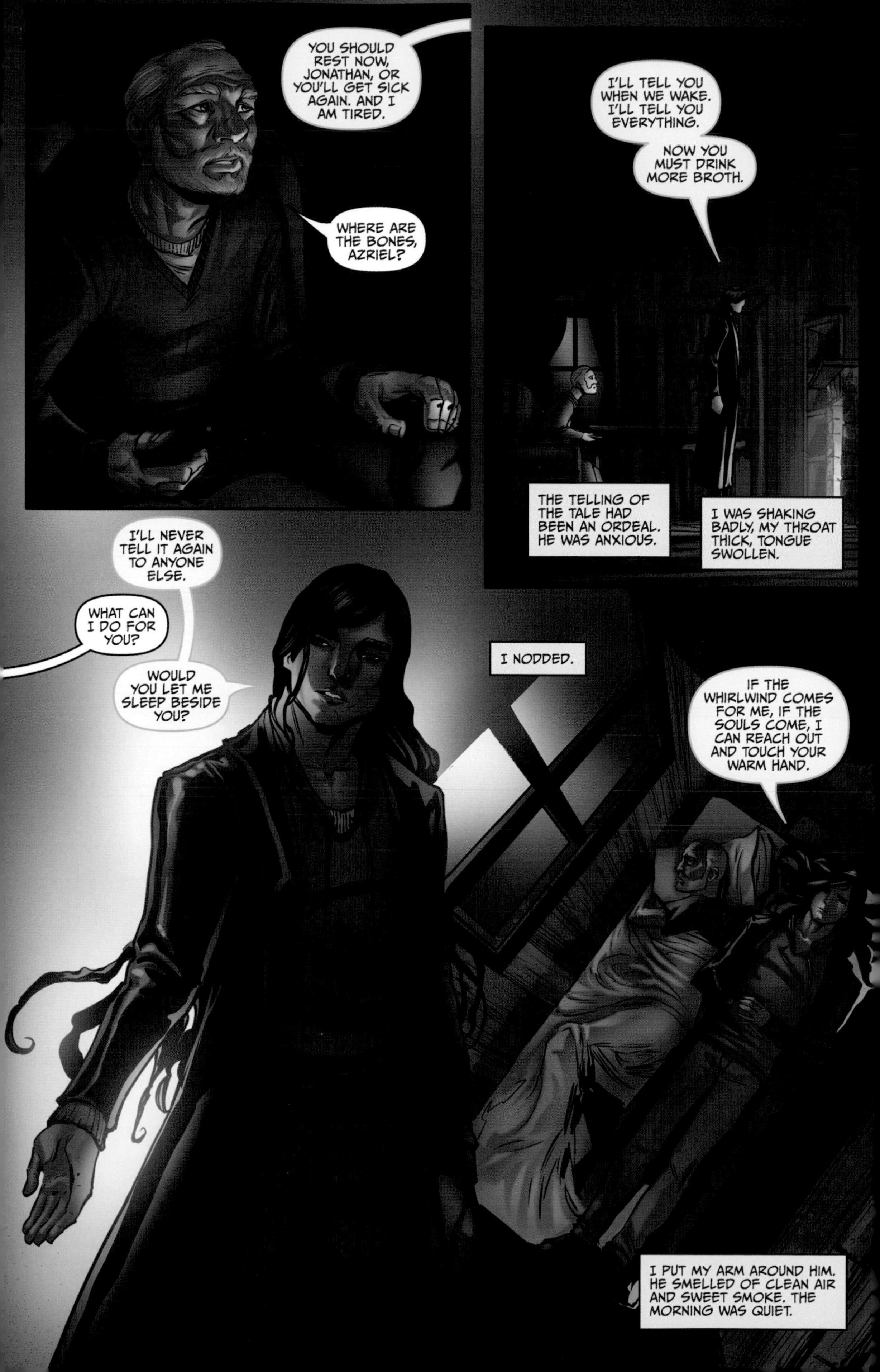

YOU SHOULD REST NOW, JONATHAN, OR YOU'LL GET SICK AGAIN. AND I AM TIRED.
WHERE ARE THE BONES, AZRIEL?
I'LL TELL YOU WHEN WE WAKE. I'LL TELL YOU EVERYTHING.
NOW YOU MUST DRINK MORE BROTH.
THE TELLING OF THE TALE HAD BEEN AN ORDEAL. HE WAS ANXIOUS.
I WAS SHAKING BADLY, MY THROAT THICK, TONGUE SWOLLEN.
I'LL NEVER TELL IT AGAIN TO ANYONE ELSE.
WHAT CAN I DO FOR YOU?
WOULD YOU LET ME SLEEP BESIDE YOU?
I NODDED.
IF THE WHIRLWIND COMES FOR ME, IF THE SOULS COME, I CAN REACH OUT AND TOUCH YOUR WARM HAND.
I PUT MY ARM AROUND HIM. HE SMELLED OF CLEAN AIR AND SWEET SMOKE. THE MORNING WAS QUIET.

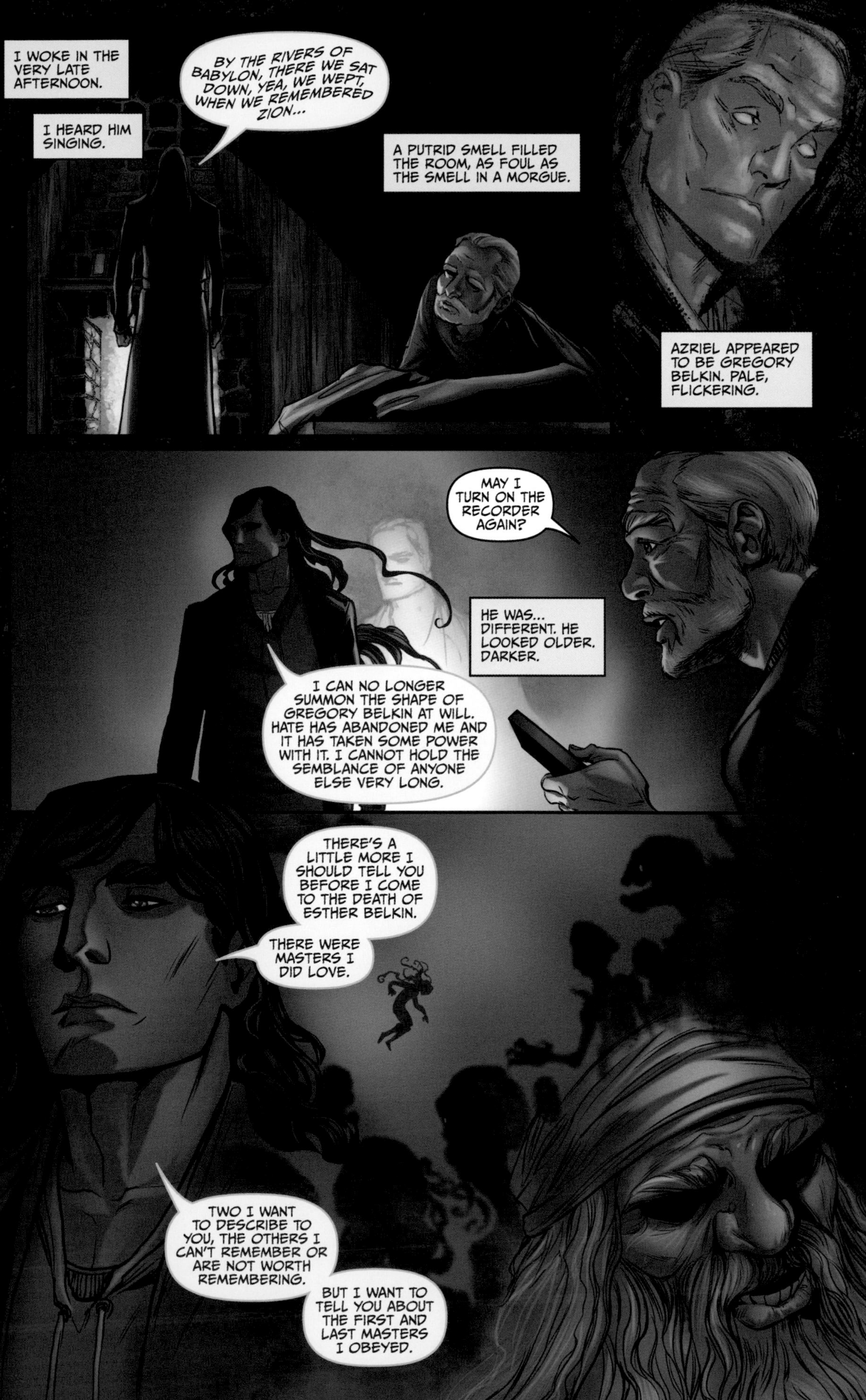

I WOKE IN THE VERY LATE AFTERNOON.
I HEARD HIM SINGING.
BY THE RIVERS OF BABYLON, THERE WE SAT DOWN, YEA, WE WEPT, WHEN WE REMEMBERED ZION...
A PUTRID SMELL FILLED THE ROOM, AS FOUL AS THE SMELL IN A MORGUE.
AZRIEL APPEARED TO BE GREGORY BELKIN. PALE, FLICKERING.
MAY I TURN ON THE RECORDER AGAIN?
HE WAS... DIFFERENT. HE LOOKED OLDER. DARKER.
I CAN NO LONGER SUMMON THE SHAPE OF GREGORY BELKIN AT WILL. HATE HAS ABANDONED ME AND IT HAS TAKEN SOME POWER WITH IT. I CANNOT HOLD THE SEMBLANCE OF ANYONE ELSE VERY LONG.
THERE'S A LITTLE MORE I SHOULD TELL YOU BEFORE I COME TO THE DEATH OF ESTHER BELKIN.
THERE WERE MASTERS I DID LOVE.
TWO I WANT TO DESCRIBE TO YOU, THE OTHERS I CAN'T REMEMBER OR ARE NOT WORTH REMEMBERING.
BUT I WANT TO TELL YOU ABOUT THE FIRST AND LAST MASTERS I OBEYED.

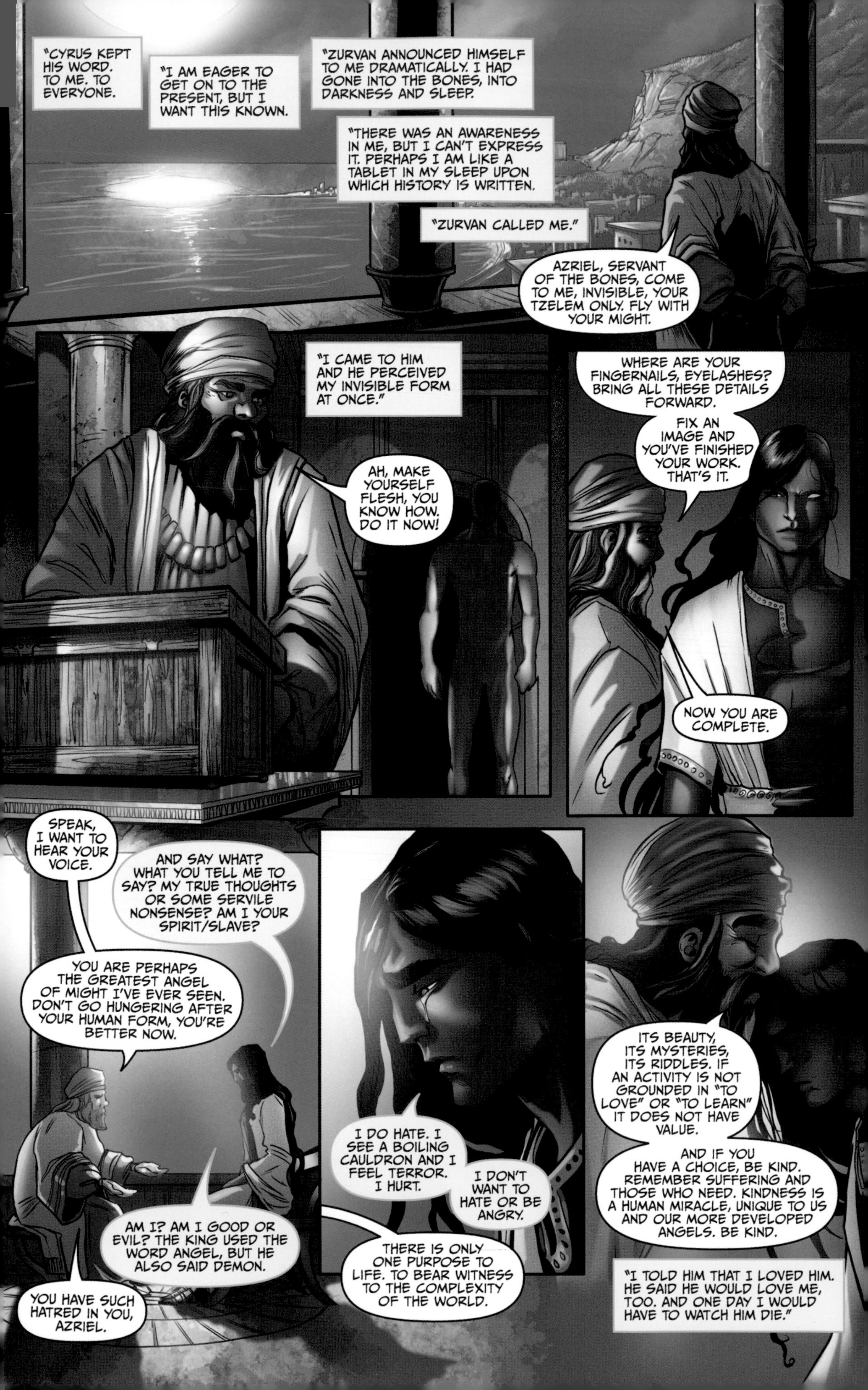
"CYRUS KEPT HIS WORD. TO ME. TO EVERYONE.
"I AM EAGER TO GET ON TO THE PRESENT, BUT I WANT THIS KNOWN.
"ZURVAN ANNOUNCED HIMSELF TO ME DRAMATICALLY. I HAD GONE INTO THE BONES, INTO DARKNESS AND SLEEP.
"THERE WAS AN AWARENESS IN ME, BUT I CAN'T EXPRESS IT. PERHAPS I AM LIKE A TABLET IN MY SLEEP UPON WHICH HISTORY IS WRITTEN.
"ZURVAN CALLED ME."
AZRIEL, SERVANT OF THE BONES, COME TO ME, INVISIBLE, YOUR TZELEM ONLY. FLY WITH YOUR MIGHT.
"I CAME TO HIM AND HE PERCEIVED MY INVISIBLE FORM AT ONCE."
AH, MAKE YOURSELF FLESH, YOU KNOW HOW. DO IT NOW!
WHERE ARE YOUR FINGERNAILS, EYELASHES? BRING ALL THESE DETAILS FORWARD.
FIX AN IMAGE AND YOU'VE FINISHED YOUR WORK. THAT'S IT.
NOW YOU ARE COMPLETE.
SPEAK, I WANT TO HEAR YOUR VOICE.
AND SAY WHAT? WHAT YOU TELL ME TO SAY? MY TRUE THOUGHTS OR SOME SERVILE NONSENSE? AM I YOUR SPIRIT/SLAVE?
YOU ARE PERHAPS THE GREATEST ANGEL OF MIGHT I'VE EVER SEEN. DON'T GO HUNGERING AFTER YOUR HUMAN FORM, YOU'RE BETTER NOW.
AM I? AM I GOOD OR EVIL? THE KING USED THE WORD ANGEL, BUT HE ALSO SAID DEMON.
YOU HAVE SUCH HATRED IN YOU, AZRIEL.
I DO HATE. I SEE A BOILING CAULDRON AND I FEEL TERROR. I HURT.
I DON'T WANT TO HATE OR BE ANGRY.
THERE IS ONLY ONE PURPOSE TO LIFE. TO BEAR WITNESS TO THE COMPLEXITY OF THE WORLD.
ITS BEAUTY, ITS MYSTERIES, ITS RIDDLES. IF AN ACTIVITY IS NOT GROUNDED IN "TO LOVE" OR "TO LEARN" IT DOES NOT HAVE VALUE.
AND IF YOU HAVE A CHOICE, BE KIND. REMEMBER SUFFERING AND THOSE WHO NEED. KINDNESS IS A HUMAN MIRACLE, UNIQUE TO US AND OUR MORE DEVELOPED ANGELS. BE KIND.
"I TOLD HIM THAT I LOVED HIM. HE SAID HE WOULD LOVE ME, TOO. AND ONE DAY I WOULD HAVE TO WATCH HIM DIE."

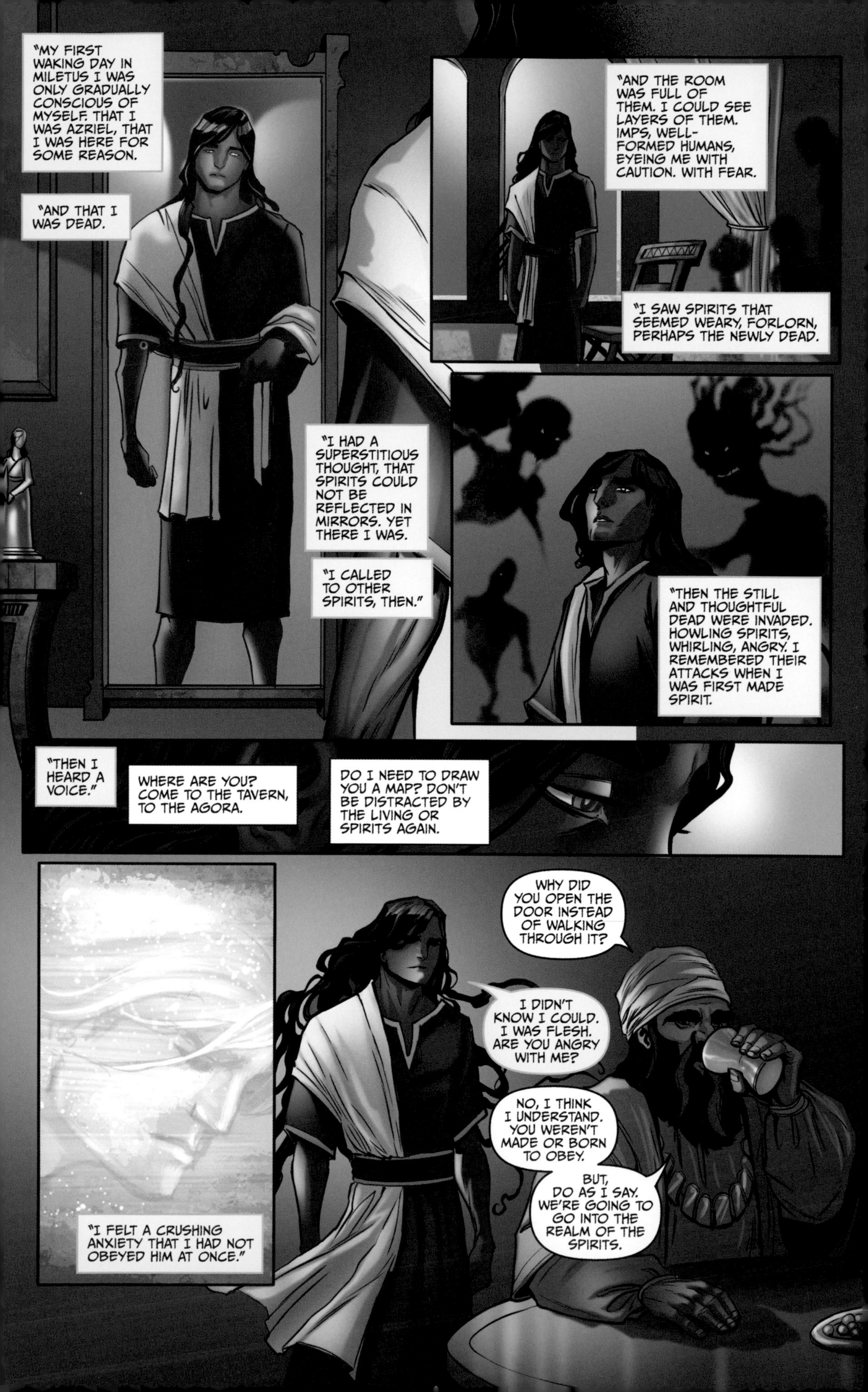
"MY FIRST WAKING DAY IN MILETUS I WAS ONLY GRADUALLY CONSCIOUS OF MYSELF. THAT I WAS AZRIEL, THAT I WAS HERE FOR SOME REASON.
"AND THAT I WAS DEAD.
"AND THE ROOM WAS FULL OF THEM. I COULD SEE LAYERS OF THEM. IMPS, WELL-FORMED HUMANS, EYEING ME WITH CAUTION. WITH FEAR.
"I SAW SPIRITS THAT SEEMED WEARY, FORLORN, PERHAPS THE NEWLY DEAD.
"I HAD A SUPERSTITIOUS THOUGHT, THAT SPIRITS COULD NOT BE REFLECTED IN MIRRORS. YET THERE I WAS.
"I CALLED TO OTHER SPIRITS, THEN."
"THEN THE STILL AND THOUGHTFUL DEAD WERE INVADED. HOWLING SPIRITS, WHIRLING, ANGRY. I REMEMBERED THEIR ATTACKS WHEN I WAS FIRST MADE SPIRIT.
"THEN I HEARD A VOICE."
WHERE ARE YOU? COME TO THE TAVERN, TO THE AGORA.
DO I NEED TO DRAW YOU A MAP? DON'T BE DISTRACTED BY THE LIVING OR SPIRITS AGAIN.
"I FELT A CRUSHING ANXIETY THAT I HAD NOT OBEYED HIM AT ONCE."
WHY DID YOU OPEN THE DOOR INSTEAD OF WALKING THROUGH IT?
I DIDN'T KNOW I COULD. I WAS FLESH. ARE YOU ANGRY WITH ME?
NO, I THINK I UNDERSTAND. YOU WEREN'T MADE OR BORN TO OBEY.
BUT, DO AS I SAY. WE'RE GOING TO GO INTO THE REALM OF THE SPIRITS.

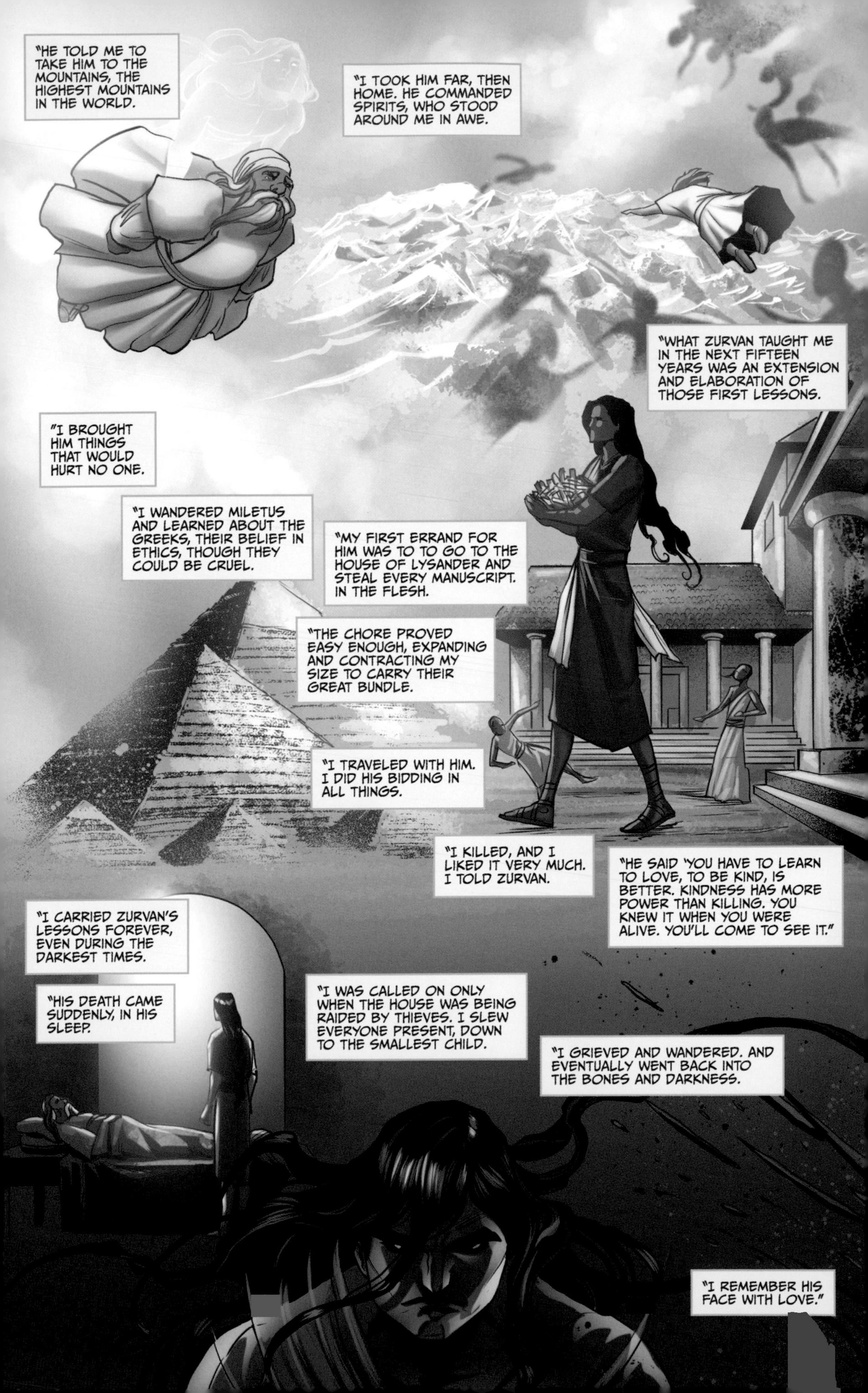
"HE TOLD ME TO TAKE HIM TO THE MOUNTAINS, THE HIGHEST MOUNTAINS IN THE WORLD.
"I TOOK HIM FAR, THEN HOME. HE COMMANDED SPIRITS, WHO STOOD AROUND ME IN AWE.
"WHAT ZURVAN TAUGHT ME IN THE NEXT FIFTEEN YEARS WAS AN EXTENSION AND ELABORATION OF THOSE FIRST LESSONS.
"I BROUGHT HIM THINGS THAT WOULD HURT NO ONE.
"I WANDERED MILETUS AND LEARNED ABOUT THE GREEKS, THEIR BELIEF IN ETHICS, THOUGH THEY COULD BE CRUEL.
"MY FIRST ERRAND FOR HIM WAS TO TO GO TO THE HOUSE OF LYSANDER AND STEAL EVERY MANUSCRIPT. IN THE FLESH.
"THE CHORE PROVED EASY ENOUGH, EXPANDING AND CONTRACTING MY SIZE TO CARRY THEIR GREAT BUNDLE.
"I TRAVELED WITH HIM. I DID HIS BIDDING IN ALL THINGS.
"I KILLED, AND I LIKED IT VERY MUCH. I TOLD ZURVAN.
"HE SAID 'YOU HAVE TO LEARN TO LOVE, TO BE KIND, IS BETTER. KINDNESS HAS MORE POWER THAN KILLING. YOU KNEW IT WHEN YOU WERE ALIVE. YOU'LL COME TO SEE IT."
"I CARRIED ZURVAN'S LESSONS FOREVER, EVEN DURING THE DARKEST TIMES.
"HIS DEATH CAME SUDDENLY, IN HIS SLEEP.
"I WAS CALLED ON ONLY WHEN THE HOUSE WAS BEING RAIDED BY THIEVES. I SLEW EVERYONE PRESENT, DOWN TO THE SMALLEST CHILD.
"I GRIEVED AND WANDERED. AND EVENTUALLY WENT BACK INTO THE BONES AND DARKNESS.
"I REMEMBER HIS FACE WITH LOVE."

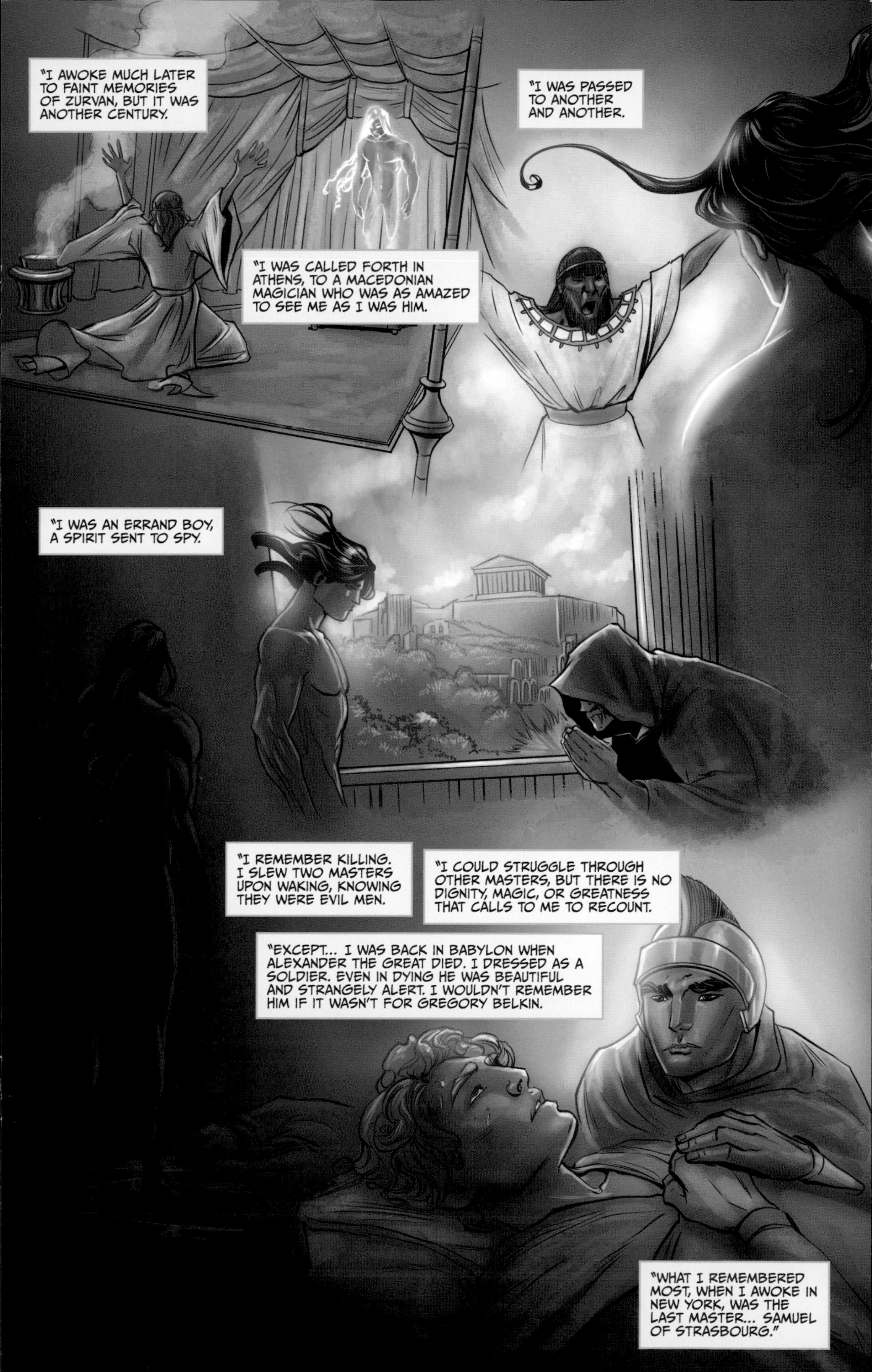
"I AWOKE MUCH LATER TO FAINT MEMORIES OF ZURVAN, BUT IT WAS ANOTHER CENTURY.
"I WAS PASSED TO ANOTHER AND ANOTHER.
"I WAS CALLED FORTH IN ATHENS, TO A MACEDONIAN MAGICIAN WHO WAS AS AMAZED TO SEE ME AS I WAS HIM.
"I WAS AN ERRAND BOY, A SPIRIT SENT TO SPY.
"I REMEMBER KILLING. I SLEW TWO MASTERS UPON WAKING, KNOWING THEY WERE EVIL MEN.
"I COULD STRUGGLE THROUGH OTHER MASTERS, BUT THERE IS NO DIGNITY, MAGIC, OR GREATNESS THAT CALLS TO ME TO RECOUNT.
"EXCEPT... I WAS BACK IN BABYLON WHEN ALEXANDER THE GREAT DIED. I DRESSED AS A SOLDIER. EVEN IN DYING HE WAS BEAUTIFUL AND STRANGELY ALERT. I WOULDN'T REMEMBER HIM IF IT WASN'T FOR GREGORY BELKIN.
"WHAT I REMEMBERED MOST, WHEN I AWOKE IN NEW YORK, WAS THE LAST MASTER... SAMUEL OF STRASBOURG."

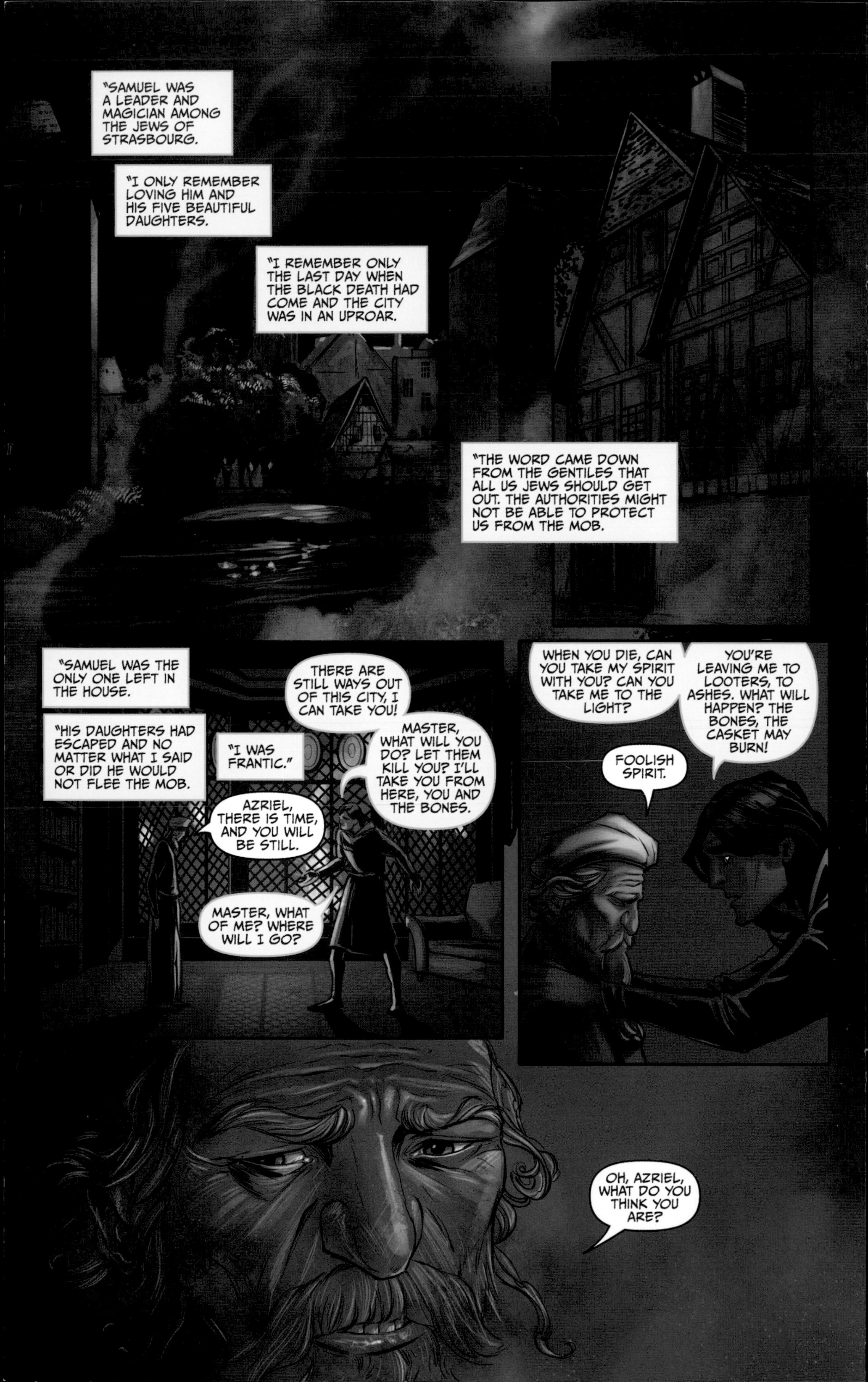
"SAMUEL WAS A LEADER AND MAGICIAN AMONG THE JEWS OF STRASBOURG.
"I ONLY REMEMBER LOVING HIM AND HIS FIVE BEAUTIFUL DAUGHTERS.
"I REMEMBER ONLY THE LAST DAY WHEN THE BLACK DEATH HAD COME AND THE CITY WAS IN AN UPROAR.
"THE WORD CAME DOWN FROM THE GENTILES THAT ALL US JEWS SHOULD GET OUT. THE AUTHORITIES MIGHT NOT BE ABLE TO PROTECT US FROM THE MOB.
"SAMUEL WAS THE ONLY ONE LEFT IN THE HOUSE.
"HIS DAUGHTERS HAD ESCAPED AND NO MATTER WHAT I SAID OR DID HE WOULD NOT FLEE THE MOB.
"I WAS FRANTIC."
THERE ARE STILL WAYS OUT OF THIS CITY, I CAN TAKE YOU!
MASTER, WHAT WILL YOU DO? LET THEM KILL YOU? I'LL TAKE YOU FROM HERE, YOU AND THE BONES.
AZRIEL, THERE IS TIME, AND YOU WILL BE STILL.
MASTER, WHAT OF ME? WHERE WILL I GO?
WHEN YOU DIE, CAN YOU TAKE MY SPIRIT WITH YOU? CAN YOU TAKE ME TO THE LIGHT?
YOU'RE LEAVING ME TO LOOTERS, TO ASHES. WHAT WILL HAPPEN? THE BONES, THE CASKET MAY BURN!
FOOLISH SPIRIT.
OH, AZRIEL, WHAT DO YOU THINK YOU ARE?

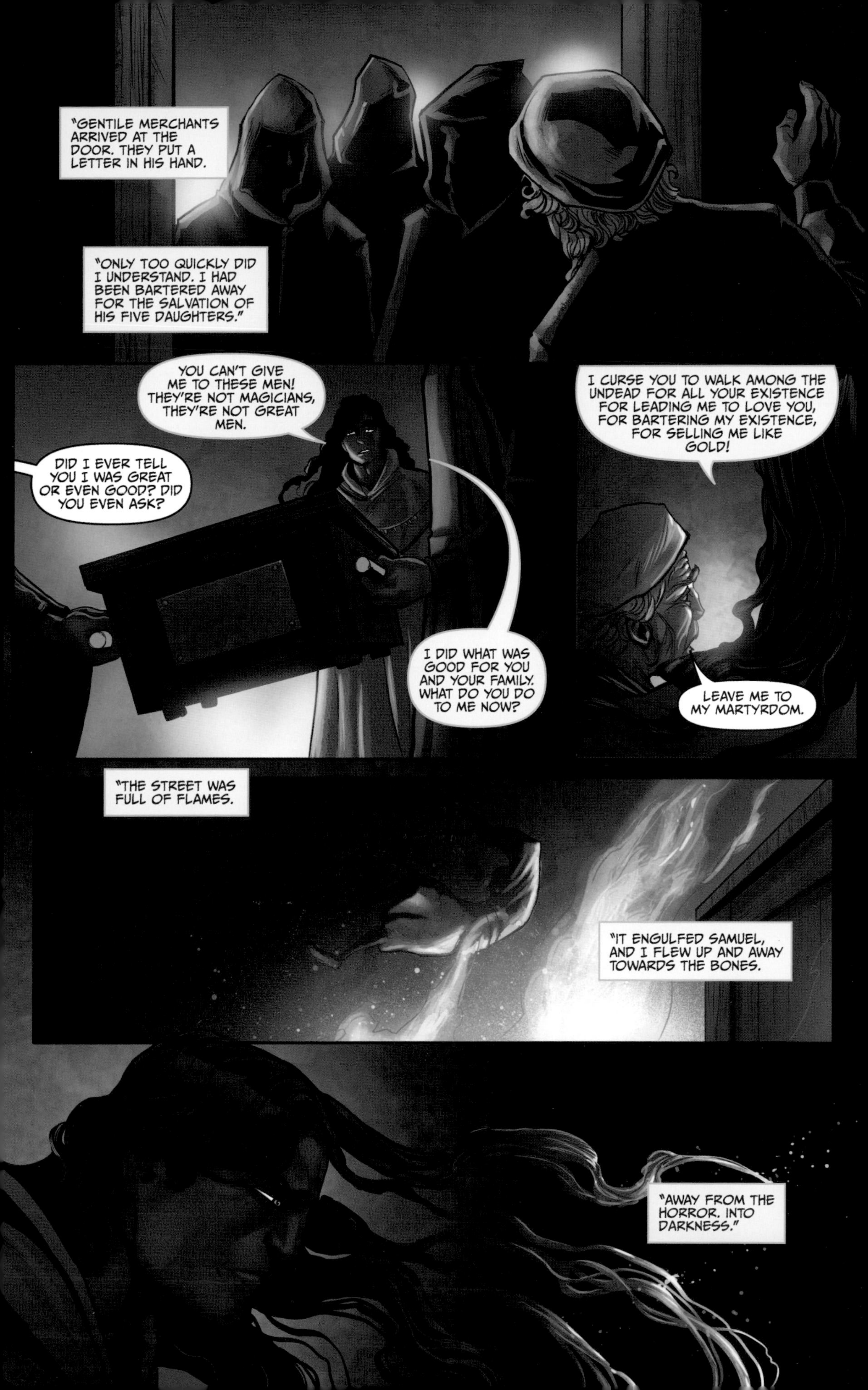
"GENTILE MERCHANTS ARRIVED AT THE DOOR. THEY PUT A LETTER IN HIS HAND.
"ONLY TOO QUICKLY DID I UNDERSTAND. I HAD BEEN BARTERED AWAY FOR THE SALVATION OF HIS FIVE DAUGHTERS."
YOU CAN'T GIVE ME TO THESE MEN! THEY'RE NOT MAGICIANS, THEY'RE NOT GREAT MEN.
DID I EVER TELL YOU I WAS GREAT OR EVEN GOOD? DID YOU EVEN ASK?
I DID WHAT WAS GOOD FOR YOU AND YOUR FAMILY. WHAT DO YOU DO TO ME NOW?
I CURSE YOU TO WALK AMONG THE UNDEAD FOR ALL YOUR EXISTENCE FOR LEADING ME TO LOVE YOU, FOR BARTERING MY EXISTENCE, FOR SELLING ME LIKE GOLD!
LEAVE ME TO MY MARTYRDOM.
"THE STREET WAS FULL OF FLAMES.
"IT ENGULFED SAMUEL, AND I FLEW UP AND AWAY TOWARDS THE BONES.
"AWAY FROM THE HORROR. INTO DARKNESS."

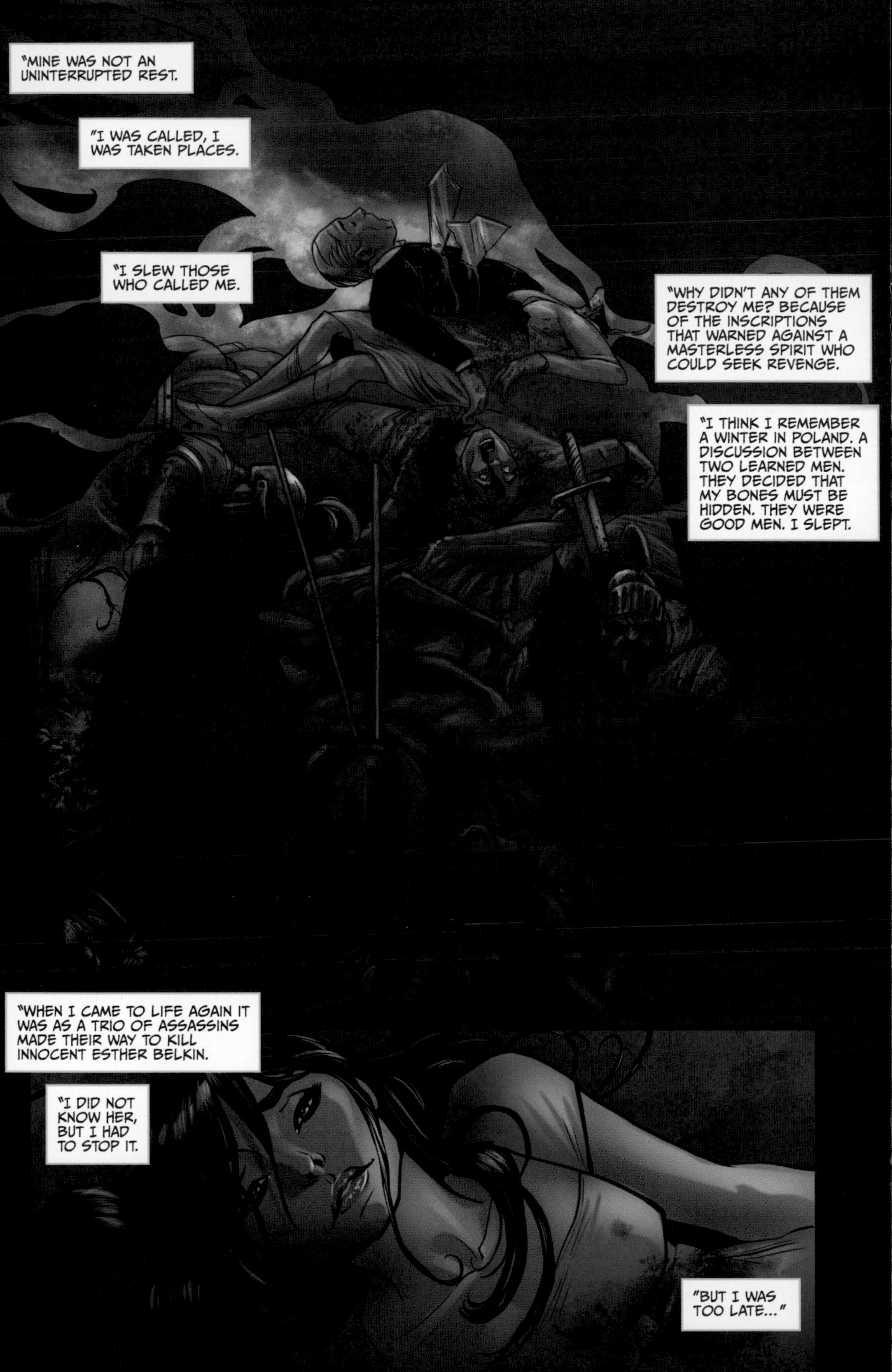
"MINE WAS NOT AN UNINTERRUPTED REST.
"I WAS CALLED, I WAS TAKEN PLACES.
"I SLEW THOSE WHO CALLED ME.
"WHY DIDN'T ANY OF THEM DESTROY ME? BECAUSE OF THE INSCRIPTIONS THAT WARNED AGAINST A MASTERLESS SPIRIT WHO COULD SEEK REVENGE.
"I THINK I REMEMBER A WINTER IN POLAND. A DISCUSSION BETWEEN TWO LEARNED MEN. THEY DECIDED THAT MY BONES MUST BE HIDDEN. THEY WERE GOOD MEN. I SLEPT.
"WHEN I CAME TO LIFE AGAIN IT WAS AS A TRIO OF ASSASSINS MADE THEIR WAY TO KILL INNOCENT ESTHER BELKIN.
"I DID NOT KNOW HER, BUT I HAD TO STOP IT.
"BUT I WAS TOO LATE..."

Aesthetic Theory

Contrive a poem out of ears.
Tell it
so that its petals unchocolate
like a brain in a jar.
Wax walnut, melting with thought.
Make it a poem almost
lewdly knowledgeable
and make its knowledge
ooze, syrup from the punched trunk.
Make it snake up to the molecule whorey
and put its mouth
atomic against the mouth of its core.
Pull on its stem
To expose its foetus. Make it
Have children with sleek ginger jaws,
Make the dogs moan when it passes,
let it out of its jar,
make it lie with our corpse, our chaos.
Make it hungry, evil, enemy of Death.
Put it on paper. Read it. Make surgery
its sigh, and of such sting
the scorpions call it Jehovah & Who.
Make it now before you crap out.
Contrive it, sperm it, stroke it,
make it efficient, make it fit,
make it more poem than Poem can survie.

❧ Stan Rice, *Some Lamb* 1975 ☙

Chapter Four

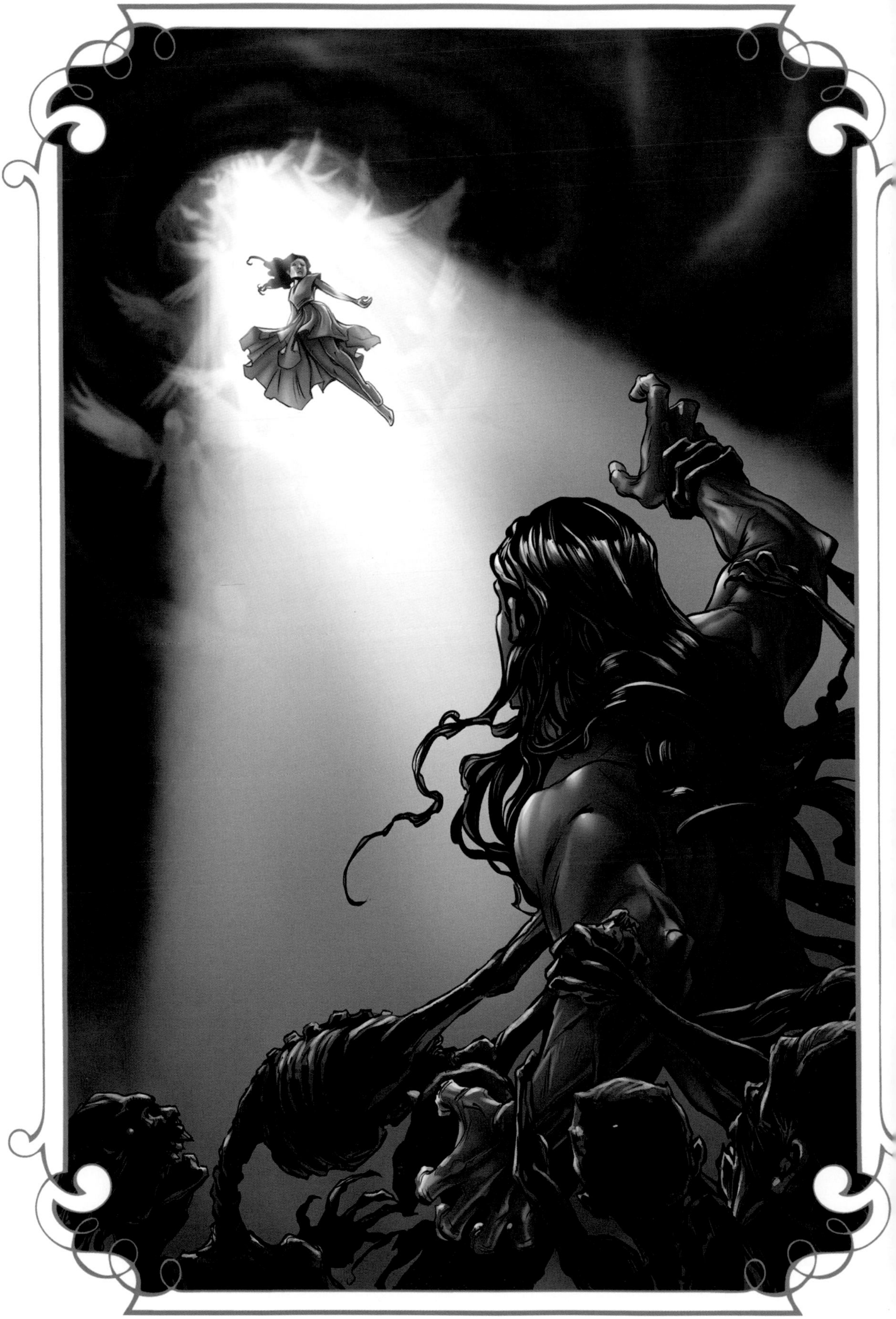

Art by Renae De Liz • Colors by Ray Dillon

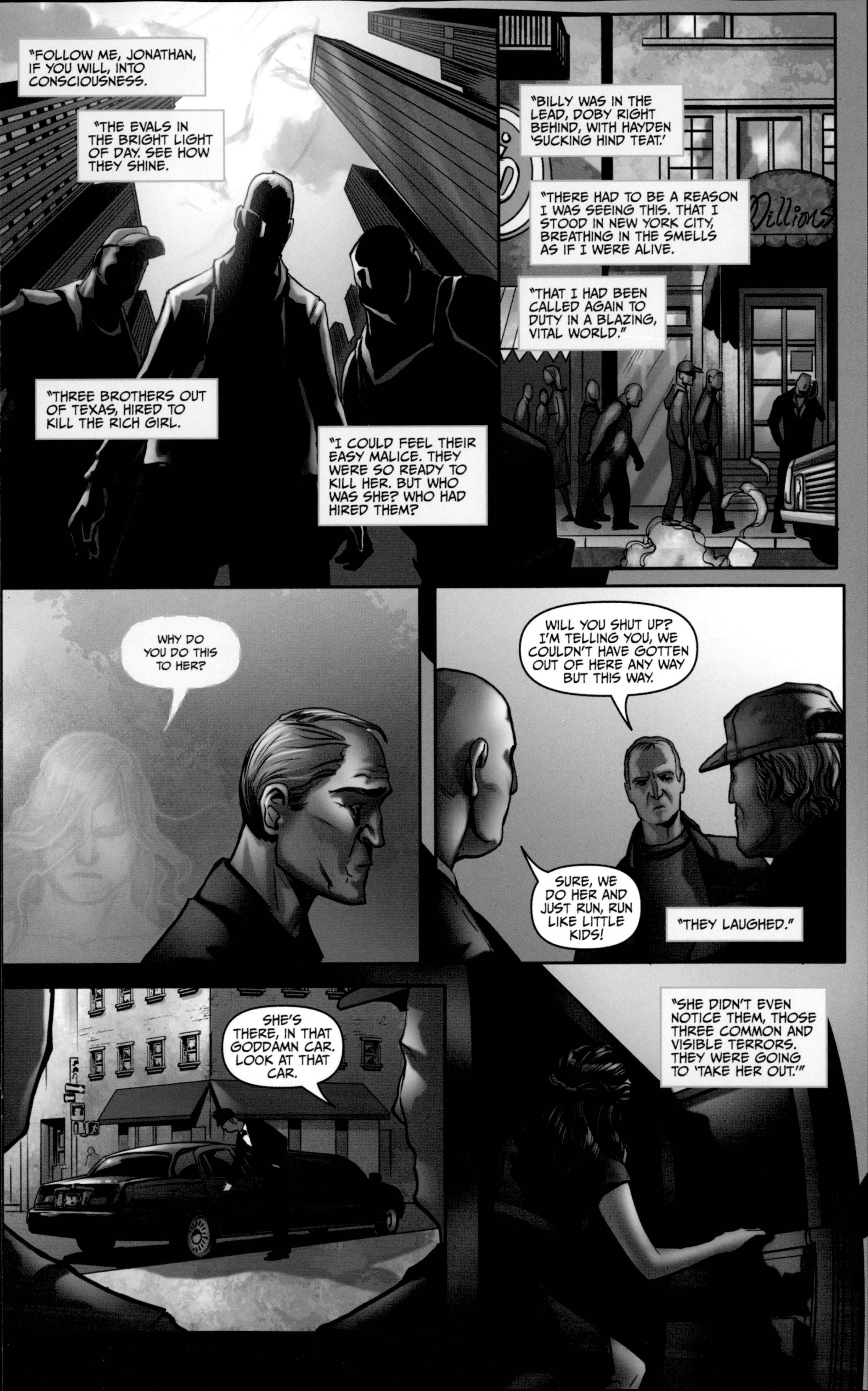
"FOLLOW ME, JONATHAN, IF YOU WILL, INTO CONSCIOUSNESS.
"THE EVALS IN THE BRIGHT LIGHT OF DAY. SEE HOW THEY SHINE.
"THREE BROTHERS OUT OF TEXAS, HIRED TO KILL THE RICH GIRL.
"I COULD FEEL THEIR EASY MALICE. THEY WERE SO READY TO KILL HER. BUT WHO WAS SHE? WHO HAD HIRED THEM?
"BILLY WAS IN THE LEAD, DOBY RIGHT BEHIND, WITH HAYDEN 'SUCKING HIND TEAT.'
"THERE HAD TO BE A REASON I WAS SEEING THIS. THAT I STOOD IN NEW YORK CITY, BREATHING IN THE SMELLS AS IF I WERE ALIVE.
"THAT I HAD BEEN CALLED AGAIN TO DUTY IN A BLAZING, VITAL WORLD."
Dillions
WHY DO YOU DO THIS TO HER?
WILL YOU SHUT UP? I'M TELLING YOU, WE COULDN'T HAVE GOTTEN OUT OF HERE ANY WAY BUT THIS WAY.
SURE, WE DO HER AND JUST RUN, RUN LIKE LITTLE KIDS!
"THEY LAUGHED."
SHE'S THERE, IN THAT GODDAMN CAR. LOOK AT THAT CAR.
"SHE DIDN'T EVEN NOTICE THEM, THOSE THREE COMMON AND VISIBLE TERRORS. THEY WERE GOING TO 'TAKE HER OUT.'"

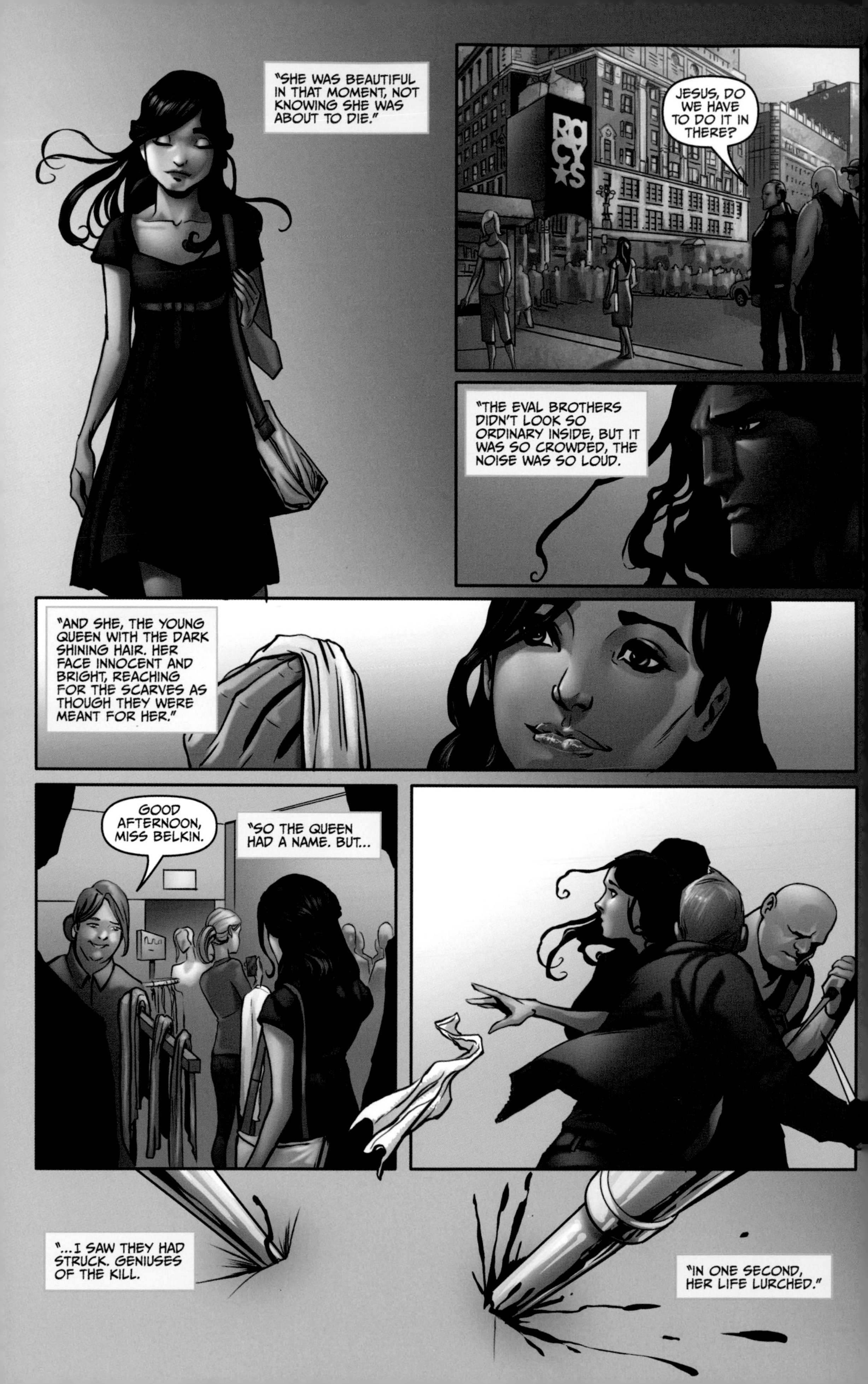
"SHE WAS BEAUTIFUL IN THAT MOMENT, NOT KNOWING SHE WAS ABOUT TO DIE."
JESUS, DO WE HAVE TO DO IT IN THERE?
"THE EVAL BROTHERS DIDN'T LOOK SO ORDINARY INSIDE, BUT IT WAS SO CROWDED, THE NOISE WAS SO LOUD.
"AND SHE, THE YOUNG QUEEN WITH THE DARK SHINING HAIR. HER FACE INNOCENT AND BRIGHT, REACHING FOR THE SCARVES AS THOUGH THEY WERE MEANT FOR HER."
GOOD AFTERNOON, MISS BELKIN.
"SO THE QUEEN HAD A NAME. BUT...
"...I SAW THEY HAD STRUCK. GENIUSES OF THE KILL.
"IN ONE SECOND, HER LIFE LURCHED."

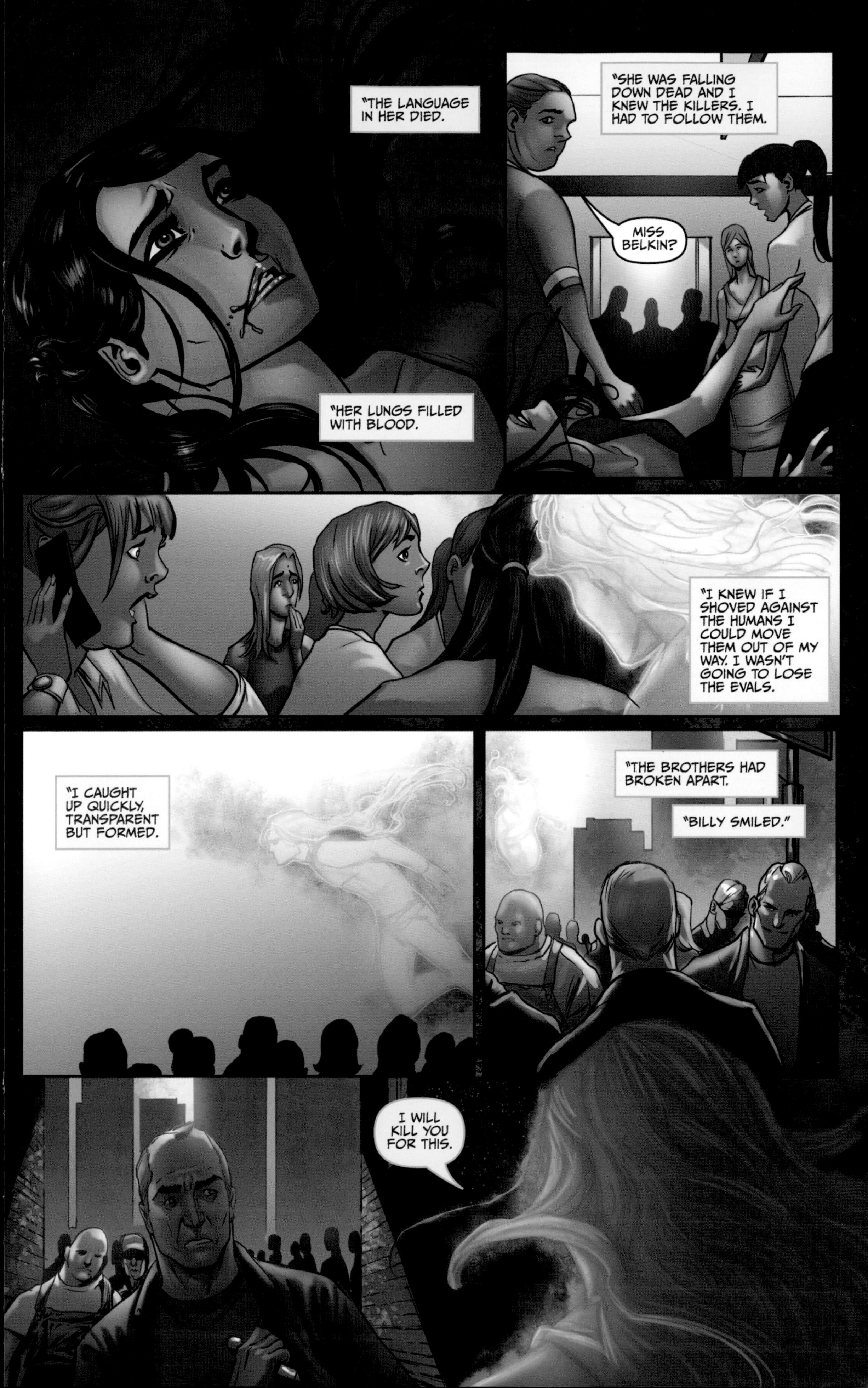
"THE LANGUAGE IN HER DIED.
"HER LUNGS FILLED WITH BLOOD.
"SHE WAS FALLING DOWN DEAD AND I KNEW THE KILLERS. I HAD TO FOLLOW THEM.
MISS BELKIN?
"I KNEW IF I SHOVED AGAINST THE HUMANS I COULD MOVE THEM OUT OF MY WAY. I WASN'T GOING TO LOSE THE EVALS.
"I CAUGHT UP QUICKLY, TRANSPARENT BUT FORMED.
"THE BROTHERS HAD BROKEN APART.
"BILLY SMILED."
I WILL KILL YOU FOR THIS.

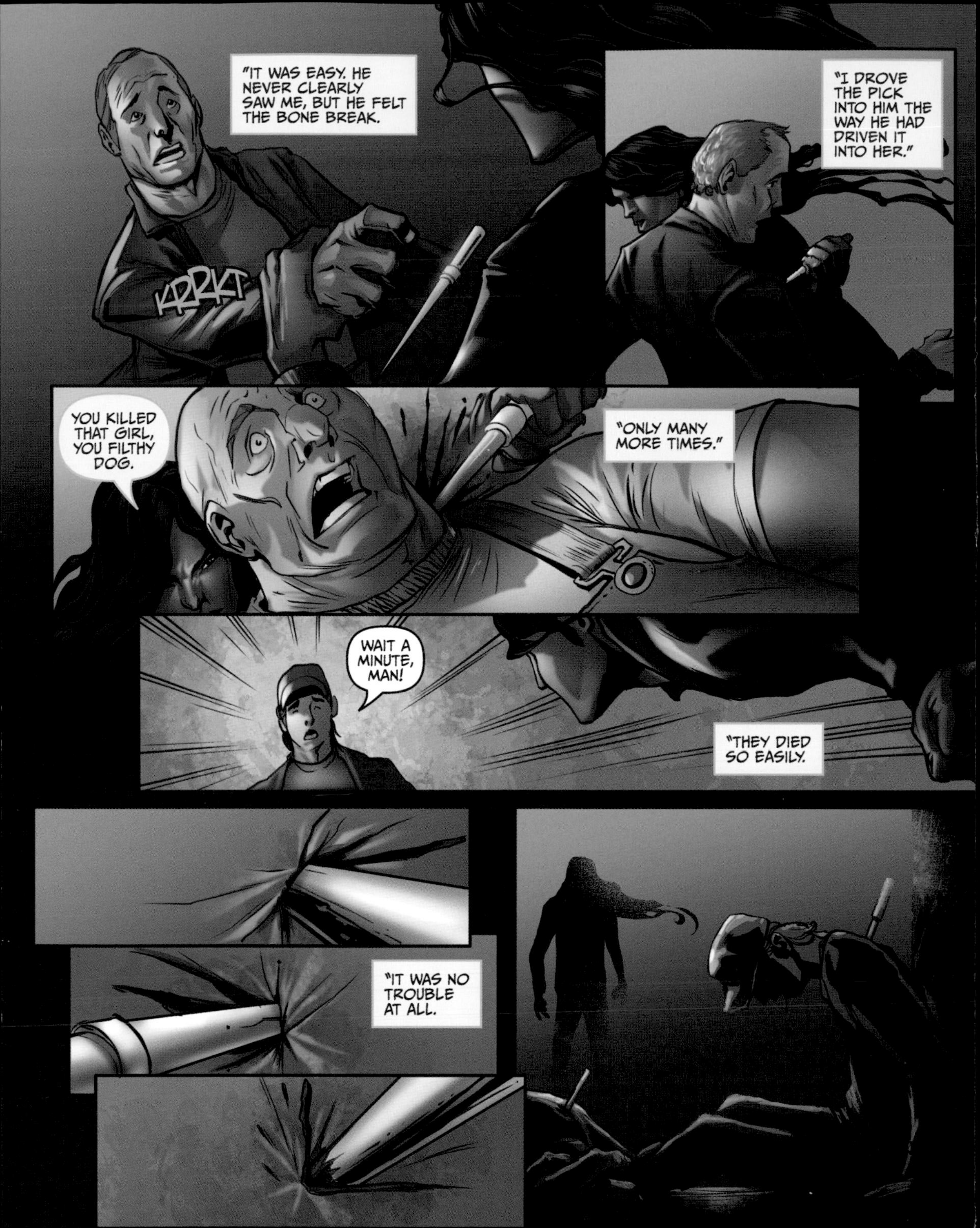
"IT WAS EASY. HE NEVER CLEARLY SAW ME, BUT HE FELT THE BONE BREAK.
KRRKT
"I DROVE THE PICK INTO HIM THE WAY HE HAD DRIVEN IT INTO HER."
YOU KILLED THAT GIRL, YOU FILTHY DOG.
"ONLY MANY MORE TIMES."
WAIT A MINUTE, MAN!
"THEY DIED SO EASILY.
"IT WAS NO TROUBLE AT ALL.

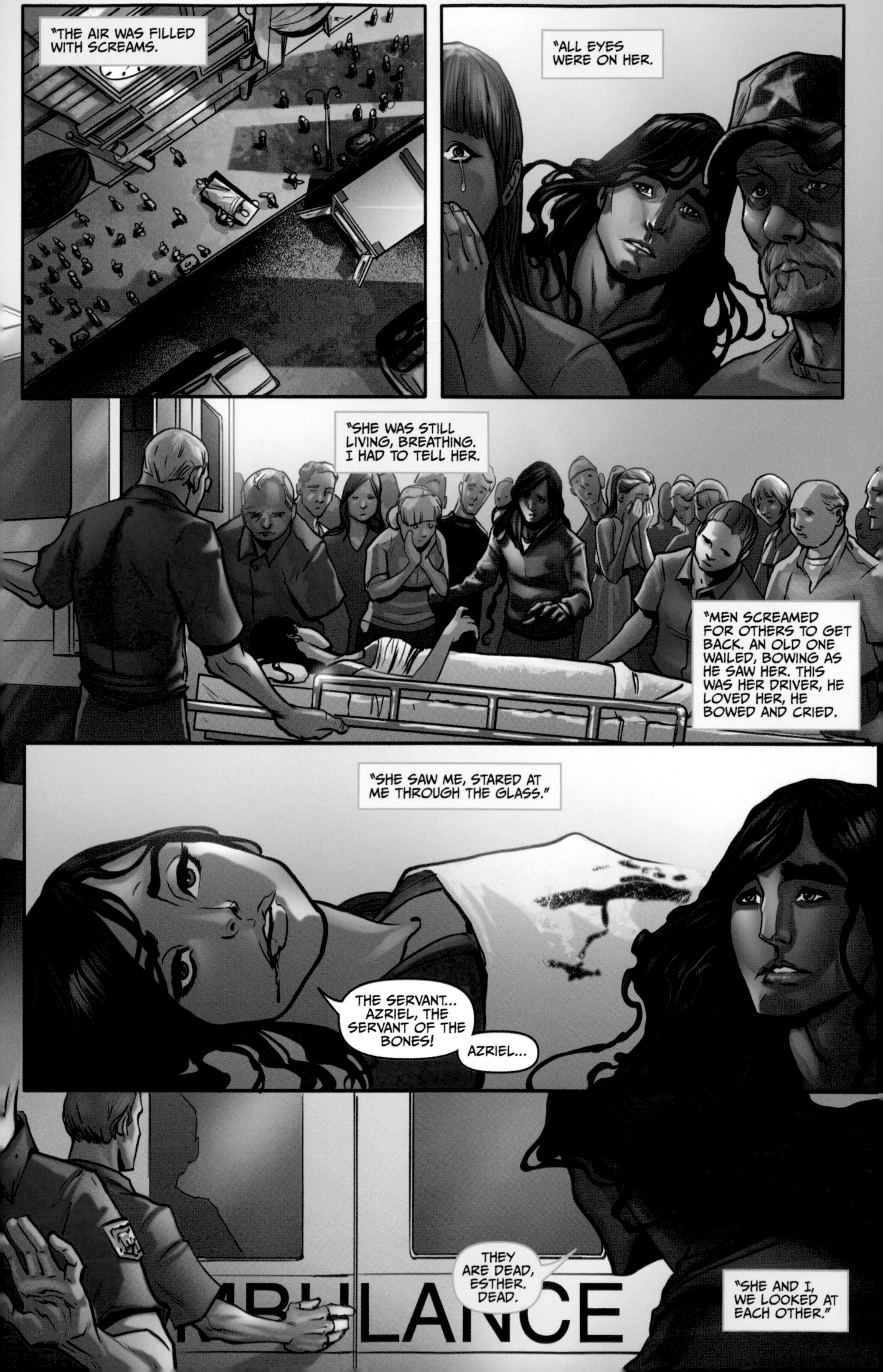
"THE AIR WAS FILLED WITH SCREAMS.
"ALL EYES WERE ON HER.
"SHE WAS STILL LIVING, BREATHING. I HAD TO TELL HER.
"MEN SCREAMED FOR OTHERS TO GET BACK. AN OLD ONE WAILED, BOWING AS HE SAW HER. THIS WAS HER DRIVER, HE LOVED HER, HE BOWED AND CRIED.
"SHE SAW ME, STARED AT ME THROUGH THE GLASS."
THE SERVANT... AZRIEL, THE SERVANT OF THE BONES!
AZRIEL...
THEY ARE DEAD, ESTHER. DEAD.
"SHE AND I, WE LOOKED AT EACH OTHER."
AMBULANCE

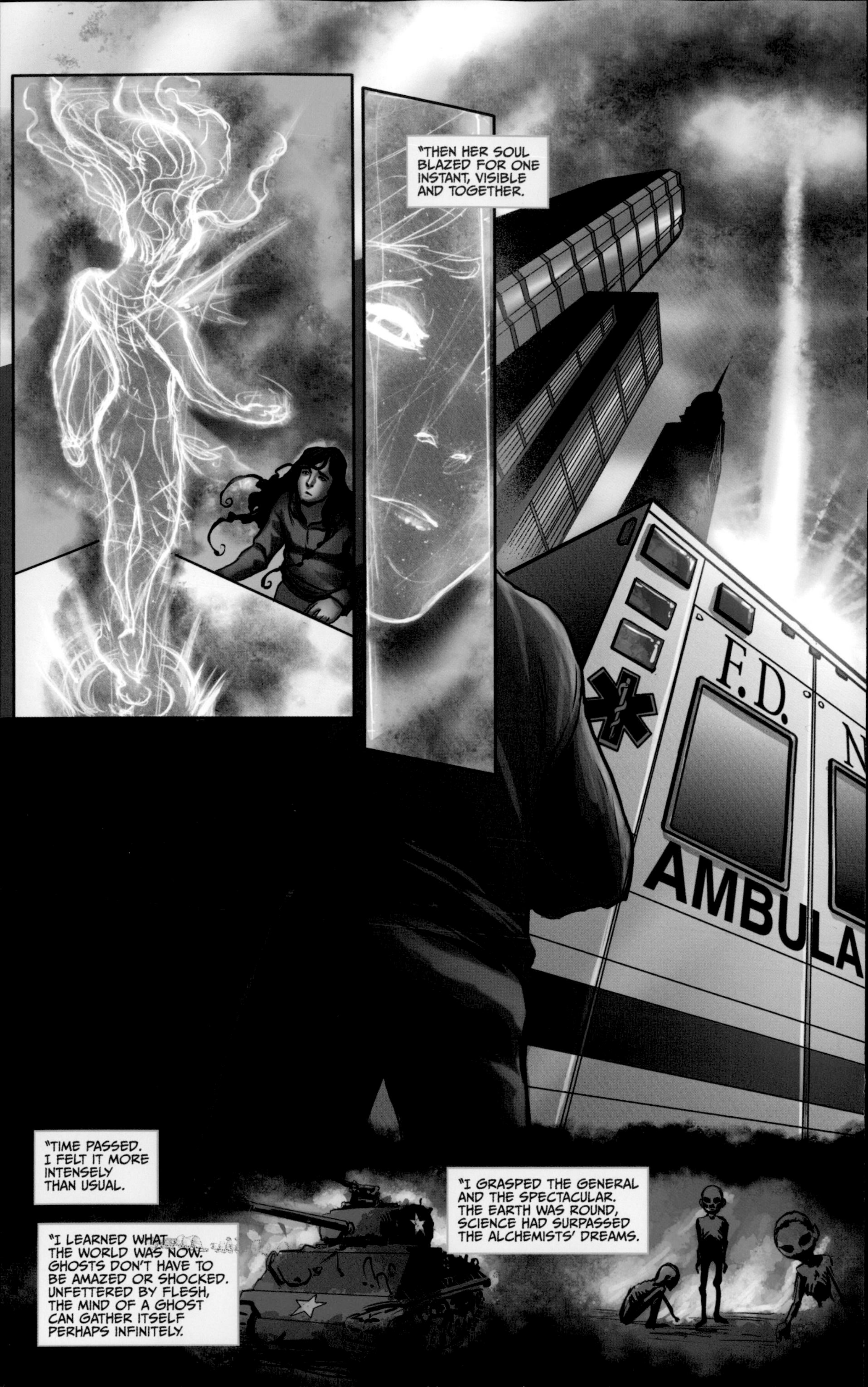
"THEN HER SOUL BLAZED FOR ONE INSTANT, VISIBLE AND TOGETHER.
F.D. N
AMBULA
"TIME PASSED. I FELT IT MORE INTENSELY THAN USUAL.
"I LEARNED WHAT THE WORLD WAS NOW. GHOSTS DON'T HAVE TO BE AMAZED OR SHOCKED. UNFETTERED BY FLESH, THE MIND OF A GHOST CAN GATHER ITSELF PERHAPS INFINITELY.
"I GRASPED THE GENERAL AND THE SPECTACULAR. THE EARTH WAS ROUND, SCIENCE HAD SURPASSED THE ALCHEMISTS' DREAMS.

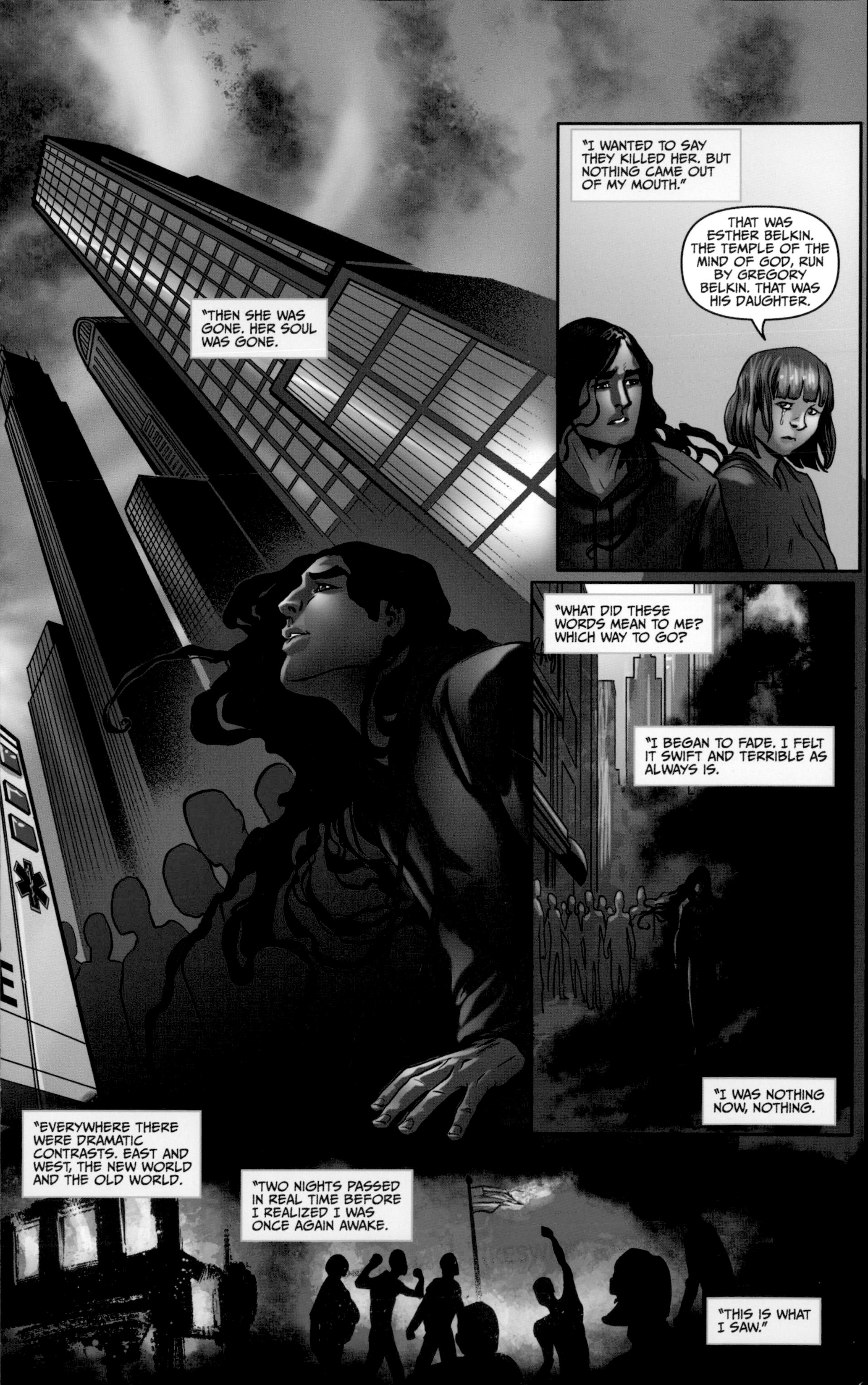
"THEN SHE WAS GONE. HER SOUL WAS GONE.
"I WANTED TO SAY THEY KILLED HER. BUT NOTHING CAME OUT OF MY MOUTH."
THAT WAS ESTHER BELKIN. THE TEMPLE OF THE MIND OF GOD, RUN BY GREGORY BELKIN. THAT WAS HIS DAUGHTER.
"WHAT DID THESE WORDS MEAN TO ME? WHICH WAY TO GO?
"I BEGAN TO FADE. I FELT IT SWIFT AND TERRIBLE AS ALWAYS IS.
"I WAS NOTHING NOW, NOTHING.
"EVERYWHERE THERE WERE DRAMATIC CONTRASTS. EAST AND WEST, THE NEW WORLD AND THE OLD WORLD.
"TWO NIGHTS PASSED IN REAL TIME BEFORE I REALIZED I WAS ONCE AGAIN AWAKE.
"THIS IS WHAT I SAW."

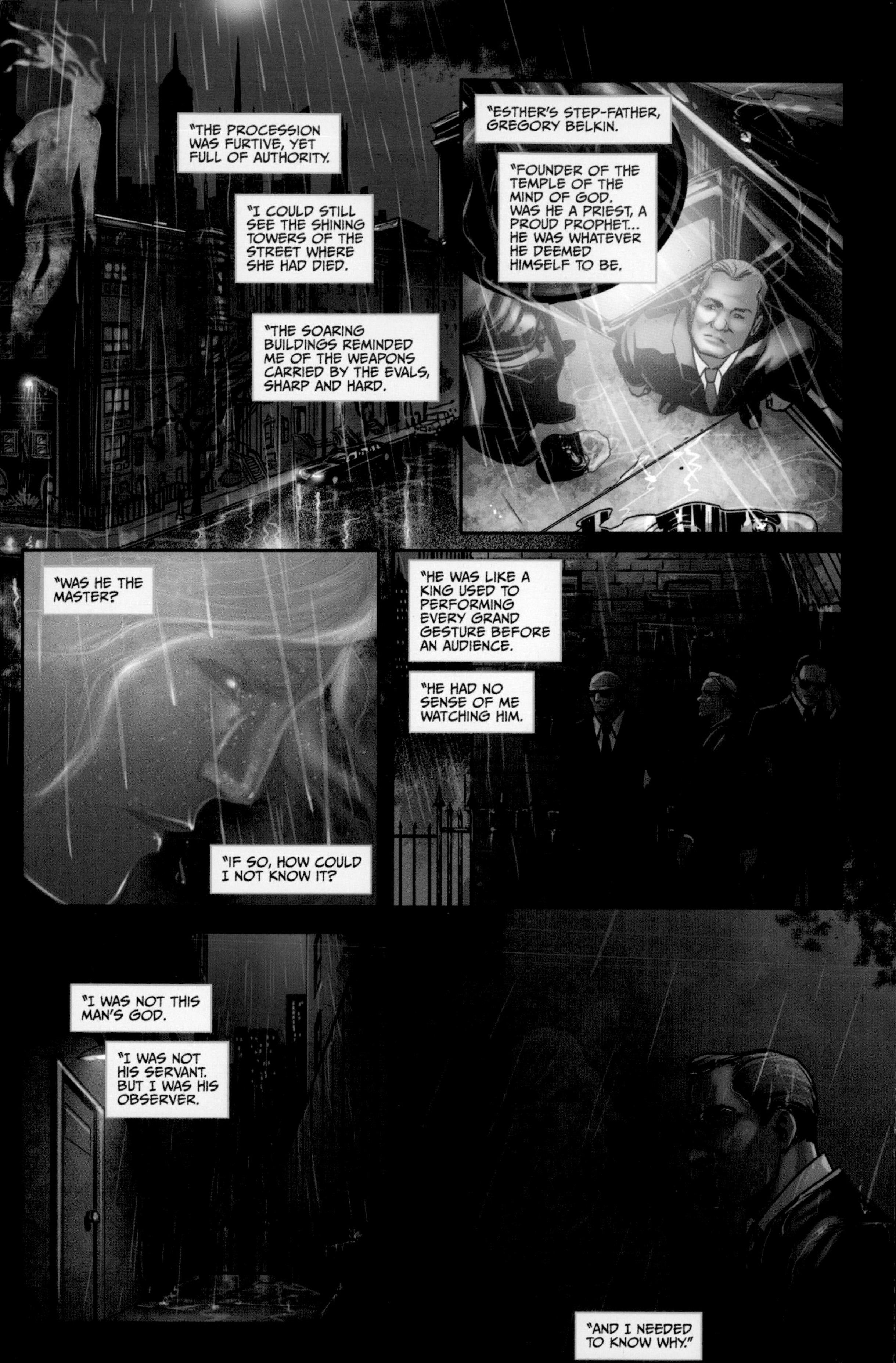
"THE PROCESSION WAS FURTIVE, YET FULL OF AUTHORITY.
"I COULD STILL SEE THE SHINING TOWERS OF THE STREET WHERE SHE HAD DIED.
"THE SOARING BUILDINGS REMINDED ME OF THE WEAPONS CARRIED BY THE EVALS, SHARP AND HARD.
"ESTHER'S STEP-FATHER, GREGORY BELKIN.
"FOUNDER OF THE TEMPLE OF THE MIND OF GOD. WAS HE A PRIEST, A PROUD PROPHET... HE WAS WHATEVER HE DEEMED HIMSELF TO BE.
"WAS HE THE MASTER?
"IF SO, HOW COULD I NOT KNOW IT?
"HE WAS LIKE A KING USED TO PERFORMING EVERY GRAND GESTURE BEFORE AN AUDIENCE.
"HE HAD NO SENSE OF ME WATCHING HIM.
"I WAS NOT THIS MAN'S GOD.
"I WAS NOT HIS SERVANT. BUT I WAS HIS OBSERVER.
"AND I NEEDED TO KNOW WHY."

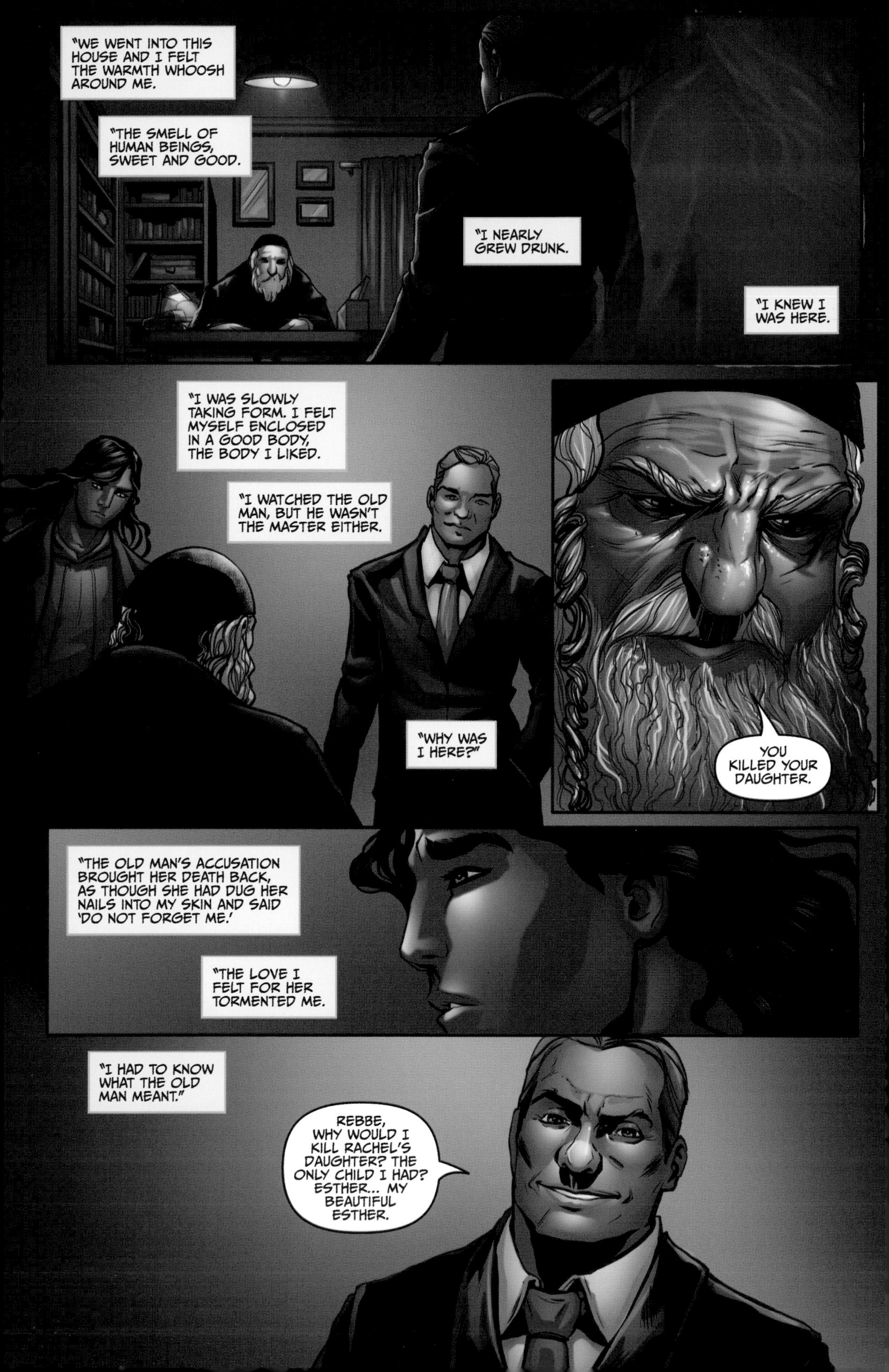
"WE WENT INTO THIS HOUSE AND I FELT THE WARMTH WHOOSH AROUND ME.
"THE SMELL OF HUMAN BEINGS, SWEET AND GOOD.
"I NEARLY GREW DRUNK.
"I KNEW I WAS HERE.
"I WAS SLOWLY TAKING FORM. I FELT MYSELF ENCLOSED IN A GOOD BODY, THE BODY I LIKED.
"I WATCHED THE OLD MAN, BUT HE WASN'T THE MASTER EITHER.
"WHY WAS I HERE?"
YOU KILLED YOUR DAUGHTER.
"THE OLD MAN'S ACCUSATION BROUGHT HER DEATH BACK, AS THOUGH SHE HAD DUG HER NAILS INTO MY SKIN AND SAID 'DO NOT FORGET ME.'
"THE LOVE I FELT FOR HER TORMENTED ME.
"I HAD TO KNOW WHAT THE OLD MAN MEANT."
REBBE, WHY WOULD I KILL RACHEL'S DAUGHTER? THE ONLY CHILD I HAD? ESTHER... MY BEAUTIFUL ESTHER.

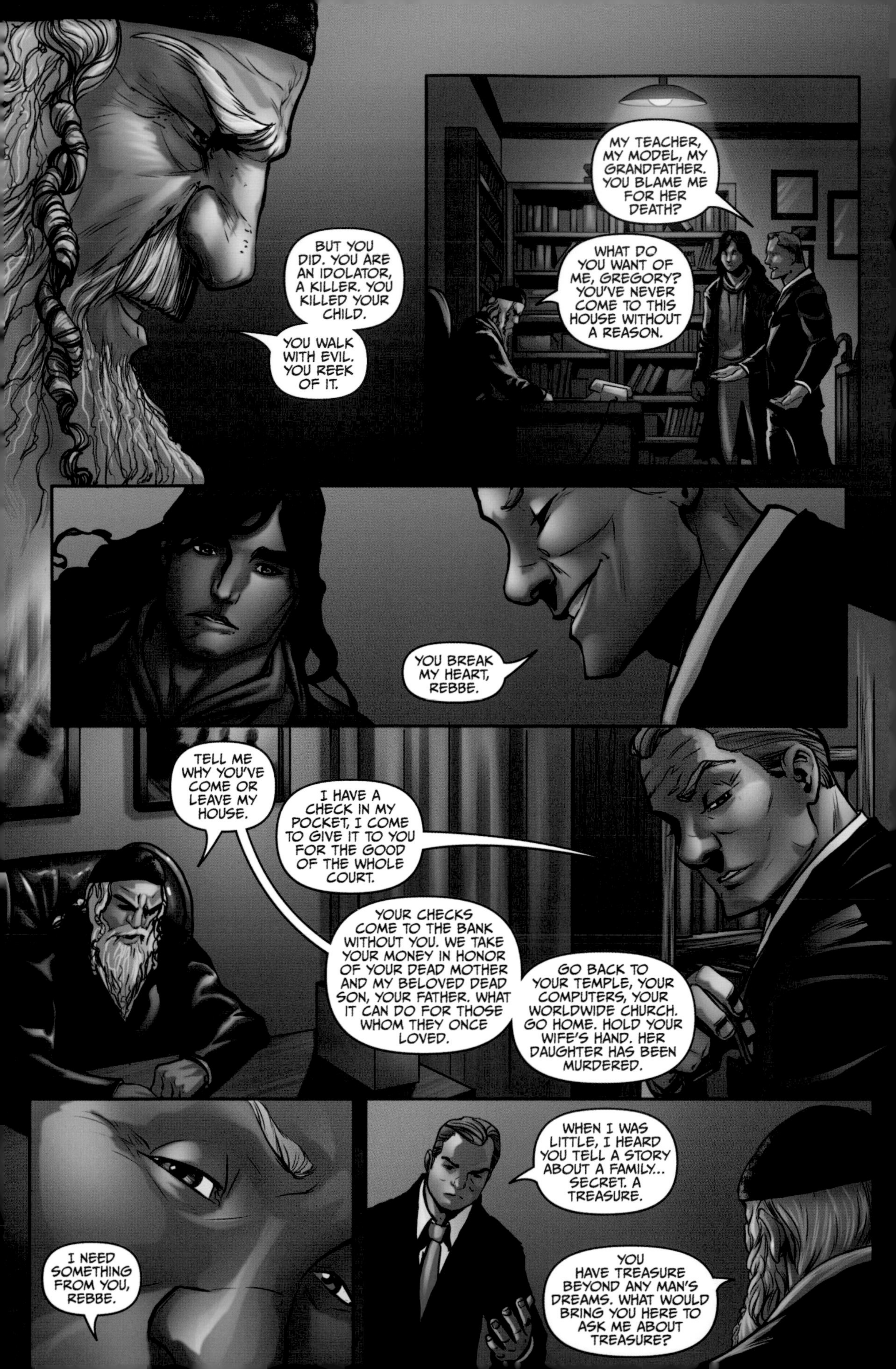

BUT YOU DID. YOU ARE AN IDOLATOR, A KILLER. YOU KILLED YOUR CHILD.
YOU WALK WITH EVIL. YOU REEK OF IT.
MY TEACHER, MY MODEL, MY GRANDFATHER. YOU BLAME ME FOR HER DEATH?
WHAT DO YOU WANT OF ME, GREGORY? YOU'VE NEVER COME TO THIS HOUSE WITHOUT A REASON.
YOU BREAK MY HEART, REBBE.
TELL ME WHY YOU'VE COME OR LEAVE MY HOUSE.
I HAVE A CHECK IN MY POCKET, I COME TO GIVE IT TO YOU FOR THE GOOD OF THE WHOLE COURT.
YOUR CHECKS COME TO THE BANK WITHOUT YOU. WE TAKE YOUR MONEY IN HONOR OF YOUR DEAD MOTHER AND MY BELOVED DEAD SON, YOUR FATHER. WHAT IT CAN DO FOR THOSE WHOM THEY ONCE LOVED.
GO BACK TO YOUR TEMPLE, YOUR COMPUTERS, YOUR WORLDWIDE CHURCH. GO HOME. HOLD YOUR WIFE'S HAND. HER DAUGHTER HAS BEEN MURDERED.
I NEED SOMETHING FROM YOU, REBBE.
WHEN I WAS LITTLE, I HEARD YOU TELL A STORY ABOUT A FAMILY... SECRET. A TREASURE.
YOU HAVE TREASURE BEYOND ANY MAN'S DREAMS. WHAT WOULD BRING YOU HERE TO ASK ME ABOUT TREASURE?

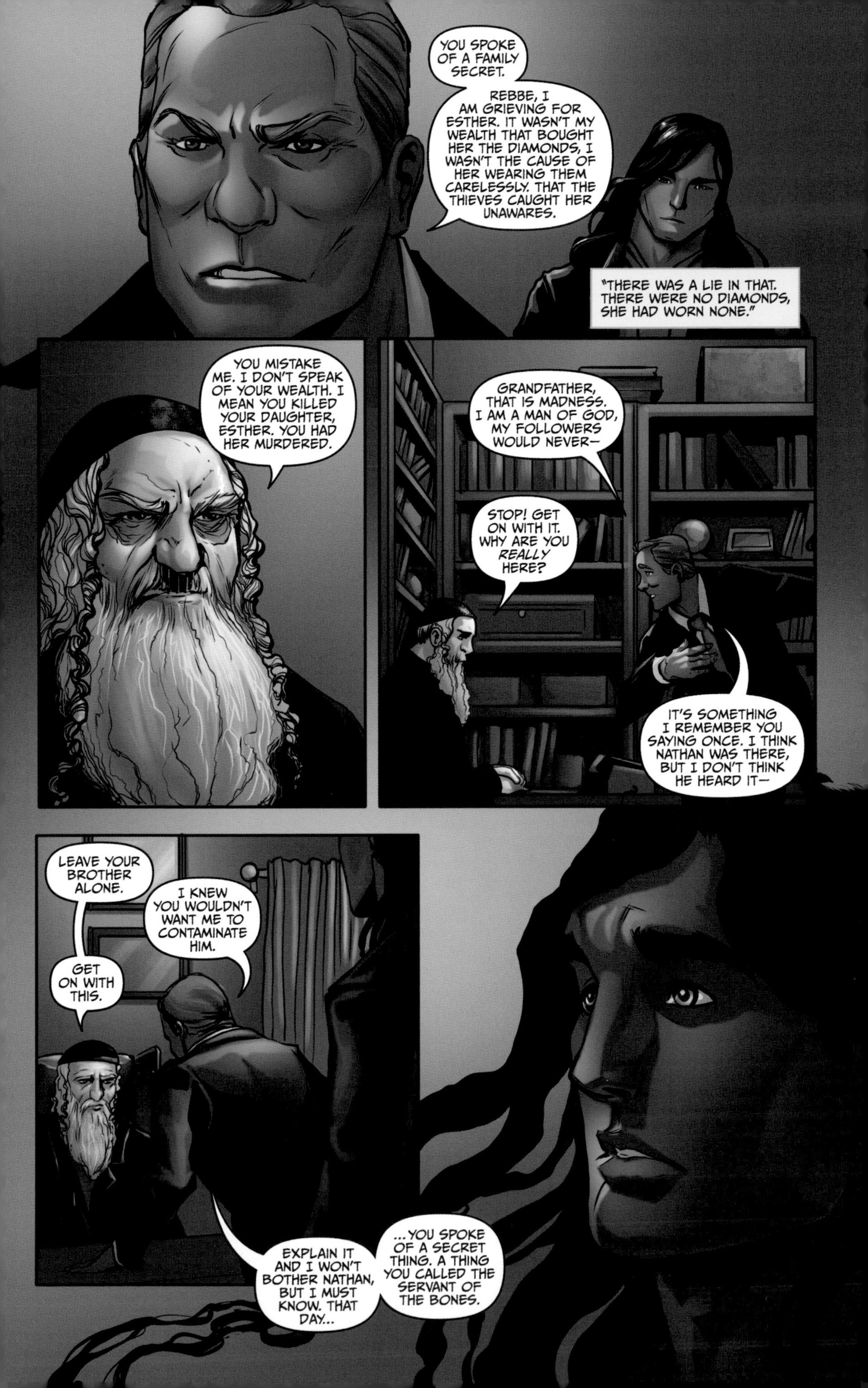
YOU SPOKE OF A FAMILY SECRET.
REBBE, I AM GRIEVING FOR ESTHER. IT WASN'T MY WEALTH THAT BOUGHT HER THE DIAMONDS, I WASN'T THE CAUSE OF HER WEARING THEM CARELESSLY. THAT THE THIEVES CAUGHT HER UNAWARES.
"THERE WAS A LIE IN THAT. THERE WERE NO DIAMONDS, SHE HAD WORN NONE."
YOU MISTAKE ME. I DON'T SPEAK OF YOUR WEALTH. I MEAN YOU KILLED YOUR DAUGHTER, ESTHER. YOU HAD HER MURDERED.
GRANDFATHER, THAT IS MADNESS. I AM A MAN OF GOD, MY FOLLOWERS WOULD NEVER—
STOP! GET ON WITH IT. WHY ARE YOU *REALLY* HERE?
IT'S SOMETHING I REMEMBER YOU SAYING ONCE. I THINK NATHAN WAS THERE, BUT I DON'T THINK HE HEARD IT—
LEAVE YOUR BROTHER ALONE.
I KNEW YOU WOULDN'T WANT ME TO CONTAMINATE HIM.
GET ON WITH THIS.
EXPLAIN IT AND I WON'T BOTHER NATHAN, BUT I MUST KNOW. THAT DAY...
...YOU SPOKE OF A SECRET THING. A THING YOU CALLED THE SERVANT OF THE BONES.

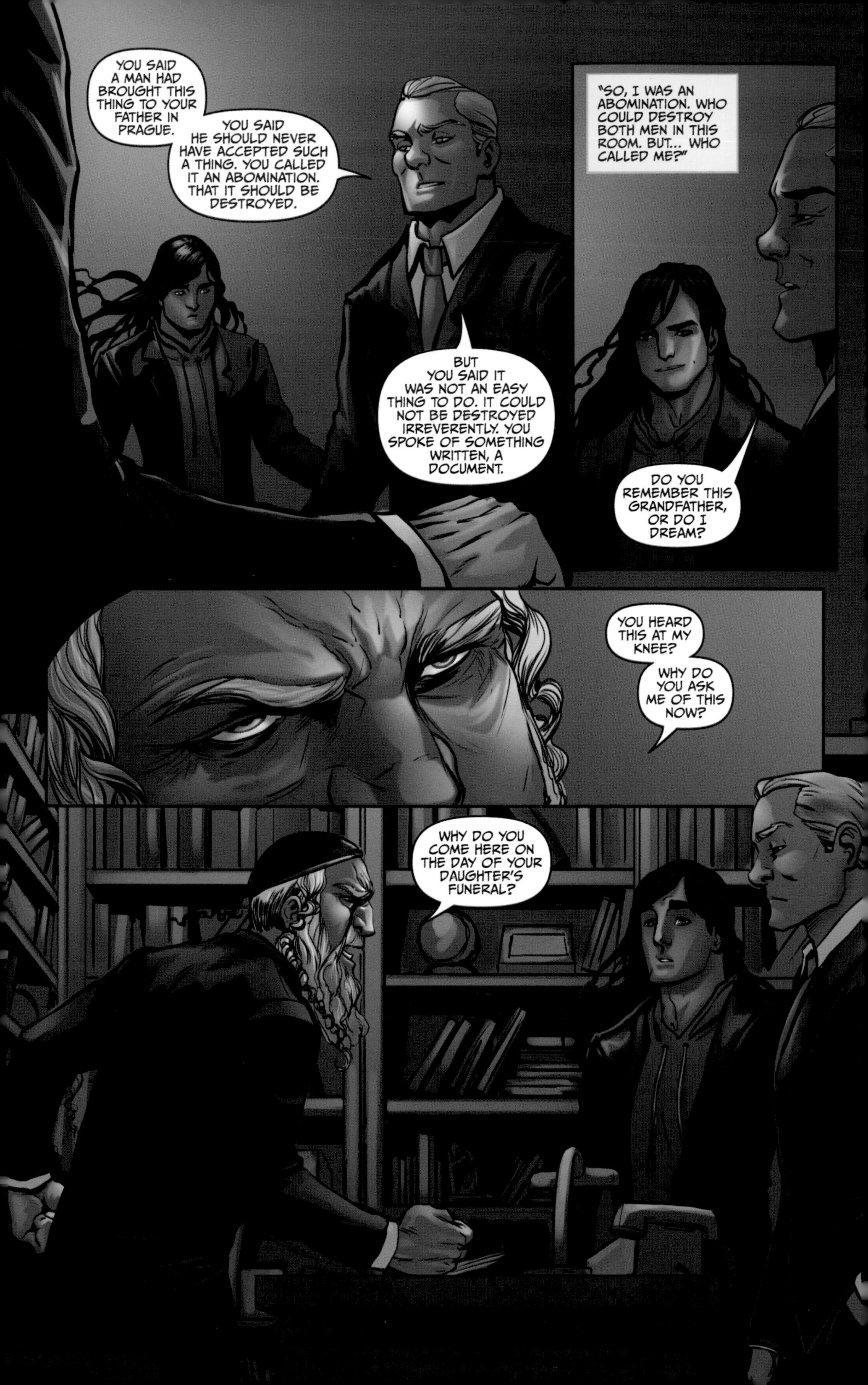
YOU SAID A MAN HAD BROUGHT THIS THING TO YOUR FATHER IN PRAGUE.
YOU SAID HE SHOULD NEVER HAVE ACCEPTED SUCH A THING. YOU CALLED IT AN ABOMINATION. THAT IT SHOULD BE DESTROYED.
BUT YOU SAID IT WAS NOT AN EASY THING TO DO. IT COULD NOT BE DESTROYED IRREVERENTLY. YOU SPOKE OF SOMETHING WRITTEN, A DOCUMENT.
"SO, I WAS AN ABOMINATION. WHO COULD DESTROY BOTH MEN IN THIS ROOM. BUT... WHO CALLED ME?"
DO YOU REMEMBER THIS GRANDFATHER, OR DO I DREAM?
YOU HEARD THIS AT MY KNEE?
WHY DO YOU ASK ME OF THIS NOW?
WHY DO YOU COME HERE ON THE DAY OF YOUR DAUGHTER'S FUNERAL?

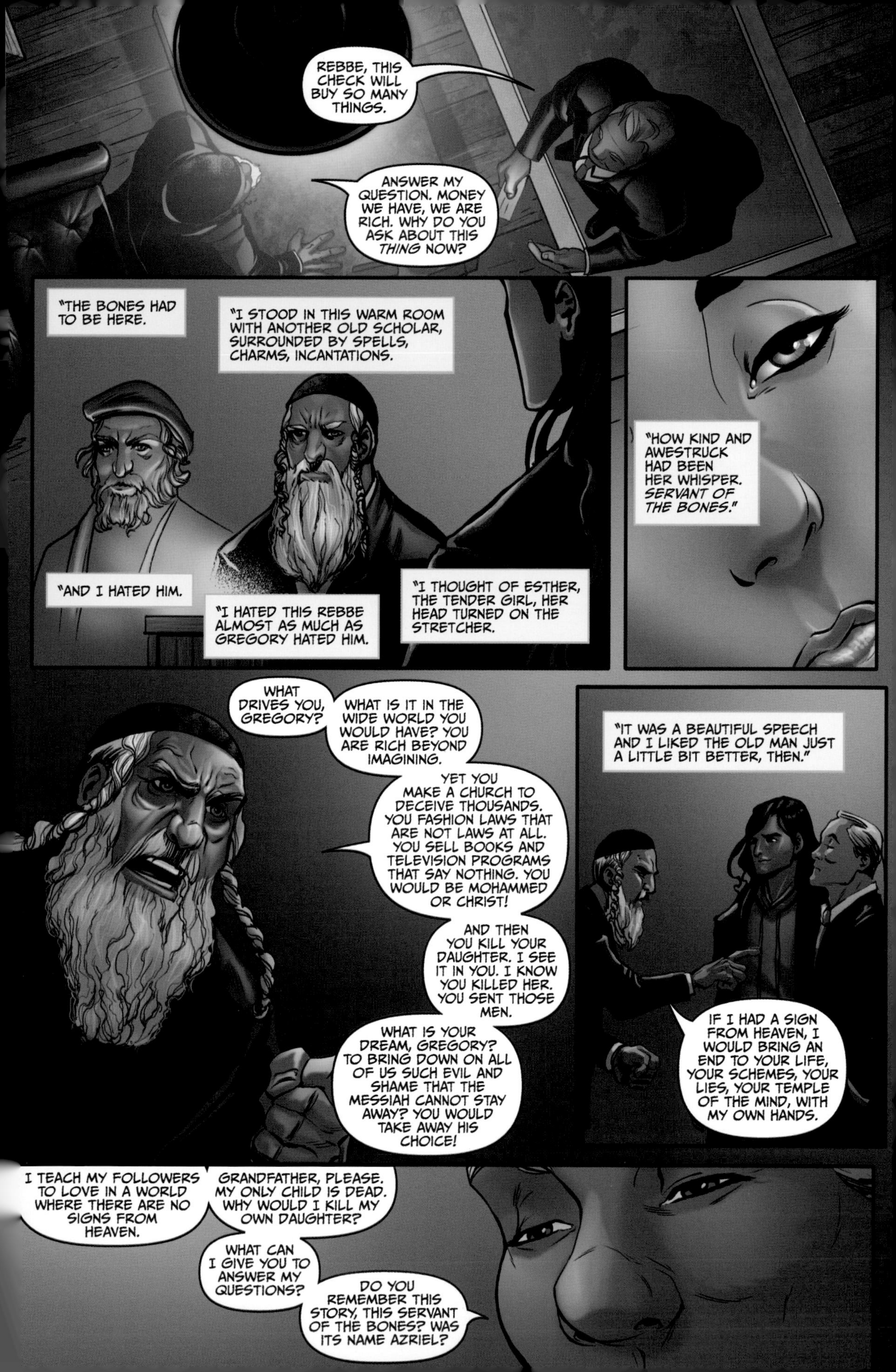

REBBE, THIS CHECK WILL BUY SO MANY THINGS.
ANSWER MY QUESTION. MONEY WE HAVE, WE ARE RICH. WHY DO YOU ASK ABOUT THIS *THING* NOW?
"THE BONES HAD TO BE HERE.
"I STOOD IN THIS WARM ROOM WITH ANOTHER OLD SCHOLAR, SURROUNDED BY SPELLS, CHARMS, INCANTATIONS.
"AND I HATED HIM.
"I HATED THIS REBBE ALMOST AS MUCH AS GREGORY HATED HIM.
"I THOUGHT OF ESTHER, THE TENDER GIRL, HER HEAD TURNED ON THE STRETCHER.
"HOW KIND AND AWESTRUCK HAD BEEN HER WHISPER. *SERVANT OF THE BONES."*
WHAT DRIVES YOU, GREGORY?
WHAT IS IT IN THE WIDE WORLD YOU WOULD HAVE? YOU ARE RICH BEYOND IMAGINING.
YET YOU MAKE A CHURCH TO DECEIVE THOUSANDS. YOU FASHION LAWS THAT ARE NOT LAWS AT ALL. YOU SELL BOOKS AND TELEVISION PROGRAMS THAT SAY NOTHING. YOU WOULD BE MOHAMMED OR CHRIST!
AND THEN YOU KILL YOUR DAUGHTER. I SEE IT IN YOU. I KNOW YOU KILLED HER. YOU SENT THOSE MEN.
WHAT IS YOUR DREAM, GREGORY? TO BRING DOWN ON ALL OF US SUCH EVIL AND SHAME THAT THE MESSIAH CANNOT STAY AWAY? YOU WOULD TAKE AWAY HIS CHOICE!
"IT WAS A BEAUTIFUL SPEECH AND I LIKED THE OLD MAN JUST A LITTLE BIT BETTER, THEN."
IF I HAD A SIGN FROM HEAVEN, I WOULD BRING AN END TO YOUR LIFE, YOUR SCHEMES, YOUR LIES, YOUR TEMPLE OF THE MIND, WITH MY OWN HANDS.
I TEACH MY FOLLOWERS TO LOVE IN A WORLD WHERE THERE ARE NO SIGNS FROM HEAVEN.
GRANDFATHER, PLEASE. MY ONLY CHILD IS DEAD. WHY WOULD I KILL MY OWN DAUGHTER?
WHAT CAN I GIVE YOU TO ANSWER MY QUESTIONS?
DO YOU REMEMBER THIS STORY, THIS SERVANT OF THE BONES? WAS ITS NAME AZRIEL?

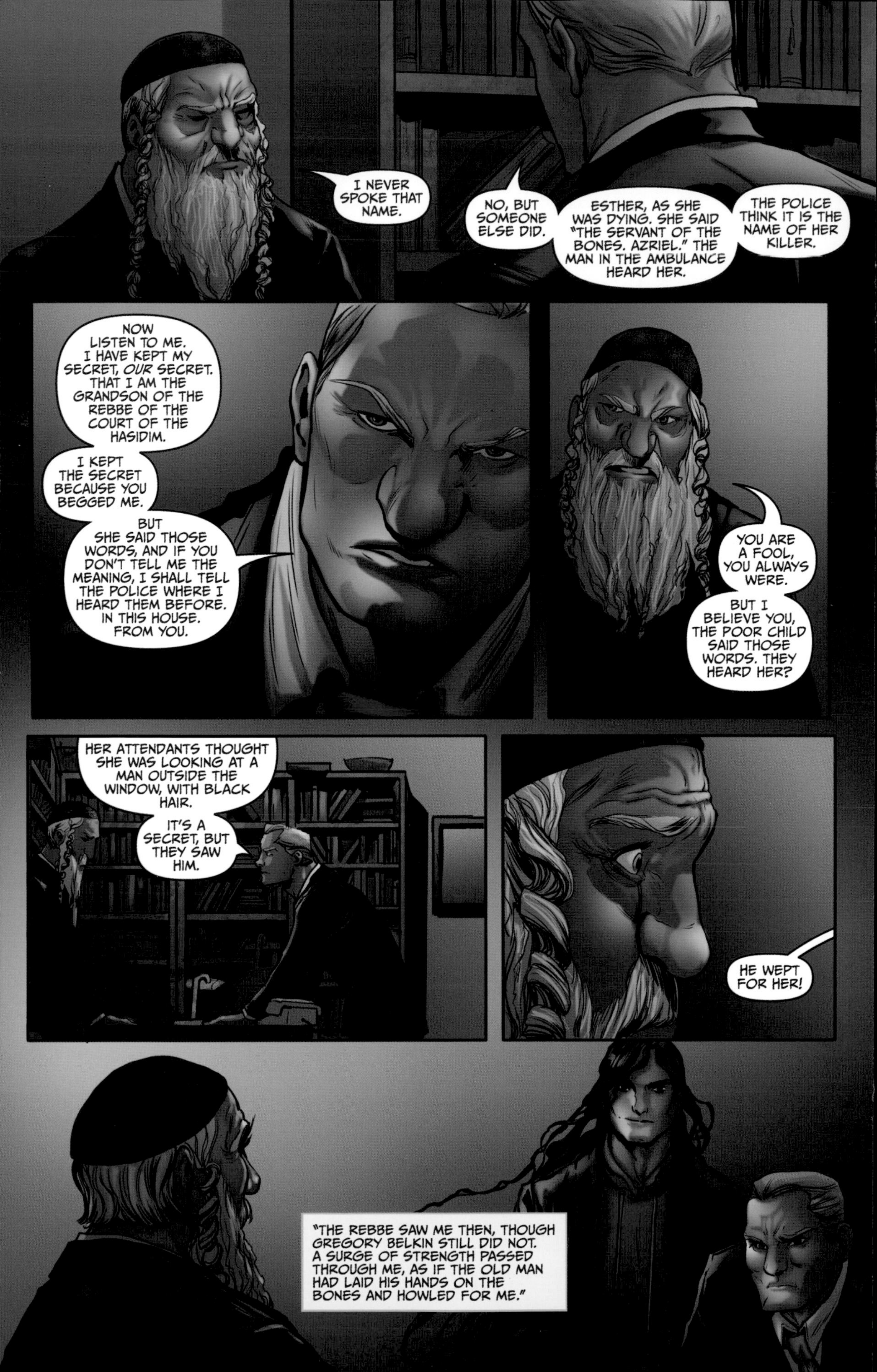
I NEVER SPOKE THAT NAME.
NO, BUT SOMEONE ELSE DID.
ESTHER, AS SHE WAS DYING. SHE SAID "THE SERVANT OF THE BONES. AZRIEL." THE MAN IN THE AMBULANCE HEARD HER.
THE POLICE THINK IT IS THE NAME OF HER KILLER.
NOW LISTEN TO ME. I HAVE KEPT MY SECRET, *OUR* SECRET. THAT I AM THE GRANDSON OF THE REBBE OF THE COURT OF THE HASIDIM.
I KEPT THE SECRET BECAUSE YOU BEGGED ME.
BUT SHE SAID THOSE WORDS, AND IF YOU DON'T TELL ME THE MEANING, I SHALL TELL THE POLICE WHERE I HEARD THEM BEFORE. IN THIS HOUSE. FROM YOU.
YOU ARE A FOOL, YOU ALWAYS WERE.
BUT I BELIEVE YOU, THE POOR CHILD SAID THOSE WORDS. THEY HEARD HER?
HER ATTENDANTS THOUGHT SHE WAS LOOKING AT A MAN OUTSIDE THE WINDOW, WITH BLACK HAIR.
IT'S A SECRET, BUT THEY SAW HIM.
HE WEPT FOR HER!
"THE REBBE SAW ME THEN, THOUGH GREGORY BELKIN STILL DID NOT. A SURGE OF STRENGTH PASSED THROUGH ME, AS IF THE OLD MAN HAD LAID HIS HANDS ON THE BONES AND HOWLED FOR ME."

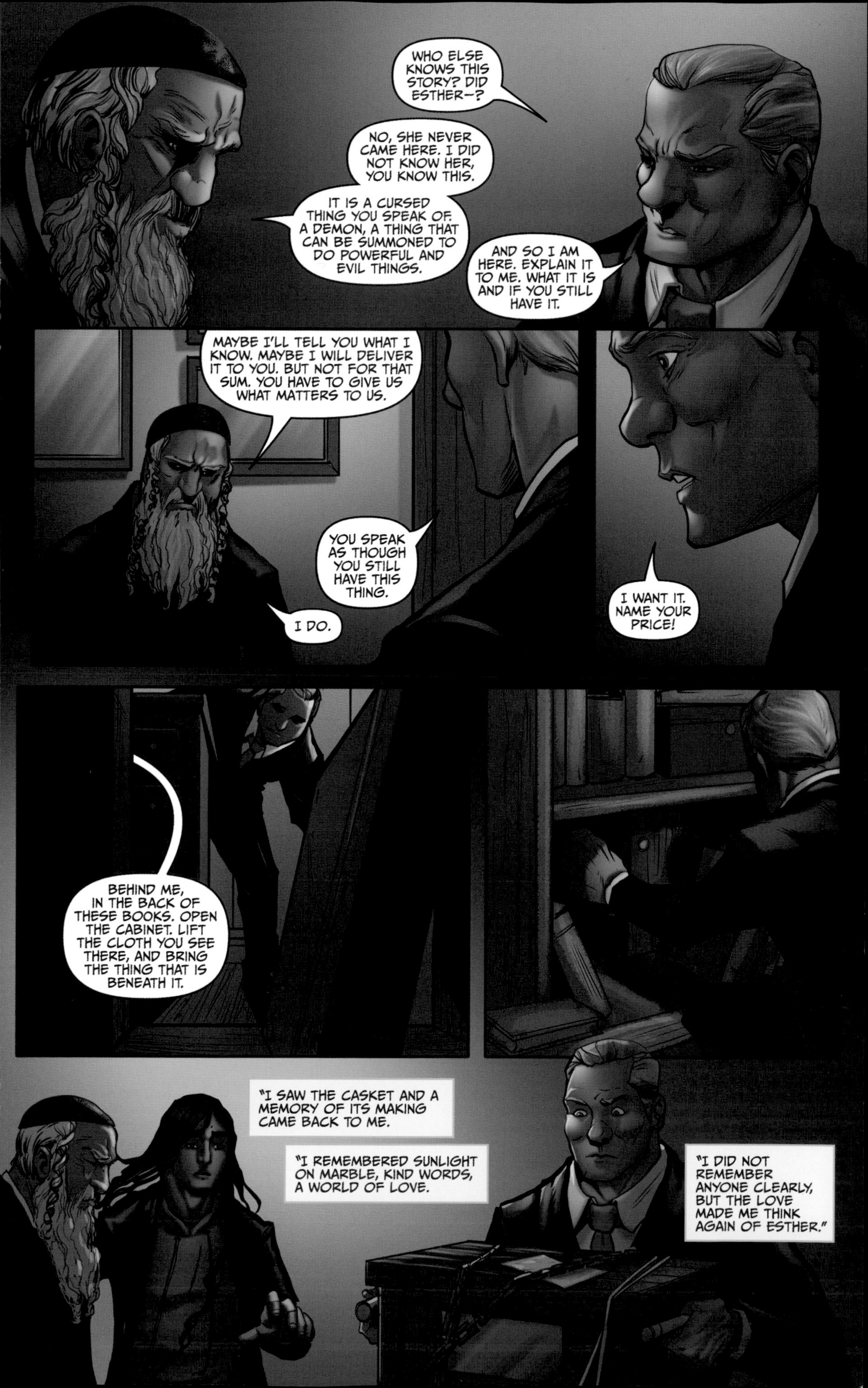
WHO ELSE KNOWS THIS STORY? DID ESTHER--?
NO, SHE NEVER CAME HERE. I DID NOT KNOW HER, YOU KNOW THIS.
IT IS A CURSED THING YOU SPEAK OF. A DEMON, A THING THAT CAN BE SUMMONED TO DO POWERFUL AND EVIL THINGS.
AND SO I AM HERE. EXPLAIN IT TO ME. WHAT IT IS AND IF YOU STILL HAVE IT.
MAYBE I'LL TELL YOU WHAT I KNOW. MAYBE I WILL DELIVER IT TO YOU. BUT NOT FOR THAT SUM. YOU HAVE TO GIVE US WHAT MATTERS TO US.
YOU SPEAK AS THOUGH YOU STILL HAVE THIS THING.
I DO.
I WANT IT. NAME YOUR PRICE!
BEHIND ME, IN THE BACK OF THESE BOOKS. OPEN THE CABINET. LIFT THE CLOTH YOU SEE THERE, AND BRING THE THING THAT IS BENEATH IT.
"I SAW THE CASKET AND A MEMORY OF ITS MAKING CAME BACK TO ME.
"I REMEMBERED SUNLIGHT ON MARBLE, KIND WORDS, A WORLD OF LOVE.
"I DID NOT REMEMBER ANYONE CLEARLY, BUT THE LOVE MADE ME THINK AGAIN OF ESTHER."

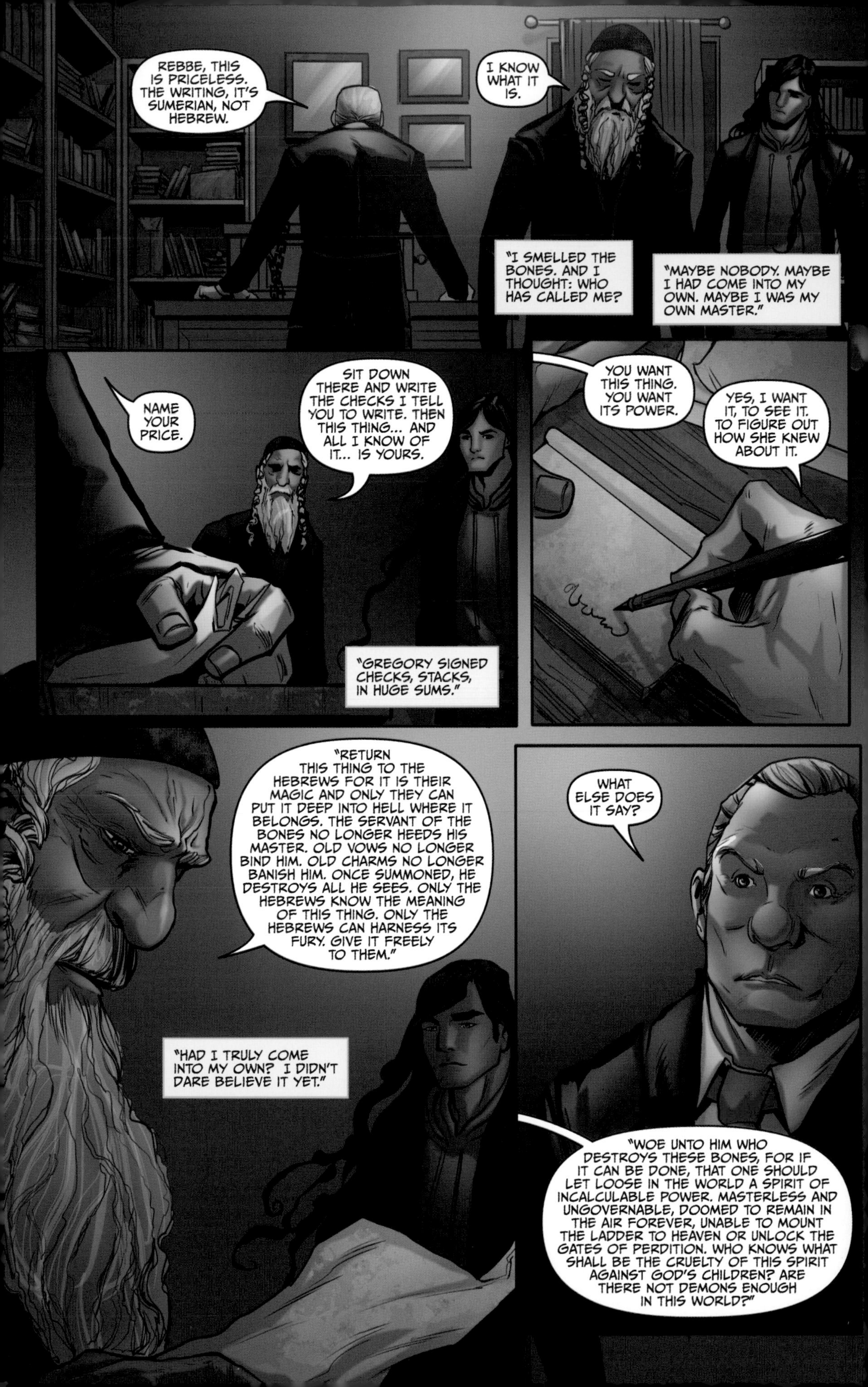
REBBE, THIS IS PRICELESS. THE WRITING, IT'S SUMERIAN, NOT HEBREW.
I KNOW WHAT IT IS.
"I SMELLED THE BONES. AND I THOUGHT: WHO HAS CALLED ME?
"MAYBE NOBODY. MAYBE I HAD COME INTO MY OWN. MAYBE I WAS MY OWN MASTER."
NAME YOUR PRICE.
SIT DOWN THERE AND WRITE THE CHECKS I TELL YOU TO WRITE. THEN THIS THING... AND ALL I KNOW OF IT... IS YOURS.
"GREGORY SIGNED CHECKS, STACKS, IN HUGE SUMS."
YOU WANT THIS THING. YOU WANT ITS POWER.
YES, I WANT IT, TO SEE IT. TO FIGURE OUT HOW SHE KNEW ABOUT IT.
"RETURN THIS THING TO THE HEBREWS FOR IT IS THEIR MAGIC AND ONLY THEY CAN PUT IT DEEP INTO HELL WHERE IT BELONGS. THE SERVANT OF THE BONES NO LONGER HEEDS HIS MASTER. OLD VOWS NO LONGER BIND HIM. OLD CHARMS NO LONGER BANISH HIM. ONCE SUMMONED, HE DESTROYS ALL HE SEES. ONLY THE HEBREWS KNOW THE MEANING OF THIS THING. ONLY THE HEBREWS CAN HARNESS ITS FURY. GIVE IT FREELY TO THEM."
WHAT ELSE DOES IT SAY?
"HAD I TRULY COME INTO MY OWN? I DIDN'T DARE BELIEVE IT YET."
"WOE UNTO HIM WHO DESTROYS THESE BONES, FOR IF IT CAN BE DONE, THAT ONE SHOULD LET LOOSE IN THE WORLD A SPIRIT OF INCALCULABLE POWER. MASTERLESS AND UNGOVERNABLE, DOOMED TO REMAIN IN THE AIR FOREVER, UNABLE TO MOUNT THE LADDER TO HEAVEN OR UNLOCK THE GATES OF PERDITION. WHO KNOWS WHAT SHALL BE THE CRUELTY OF THIS SPIRIT AGAINST GOD'S CHILDREN? ARE THERE NOT DEMONS ENOUGH IN THIS WORLD?"

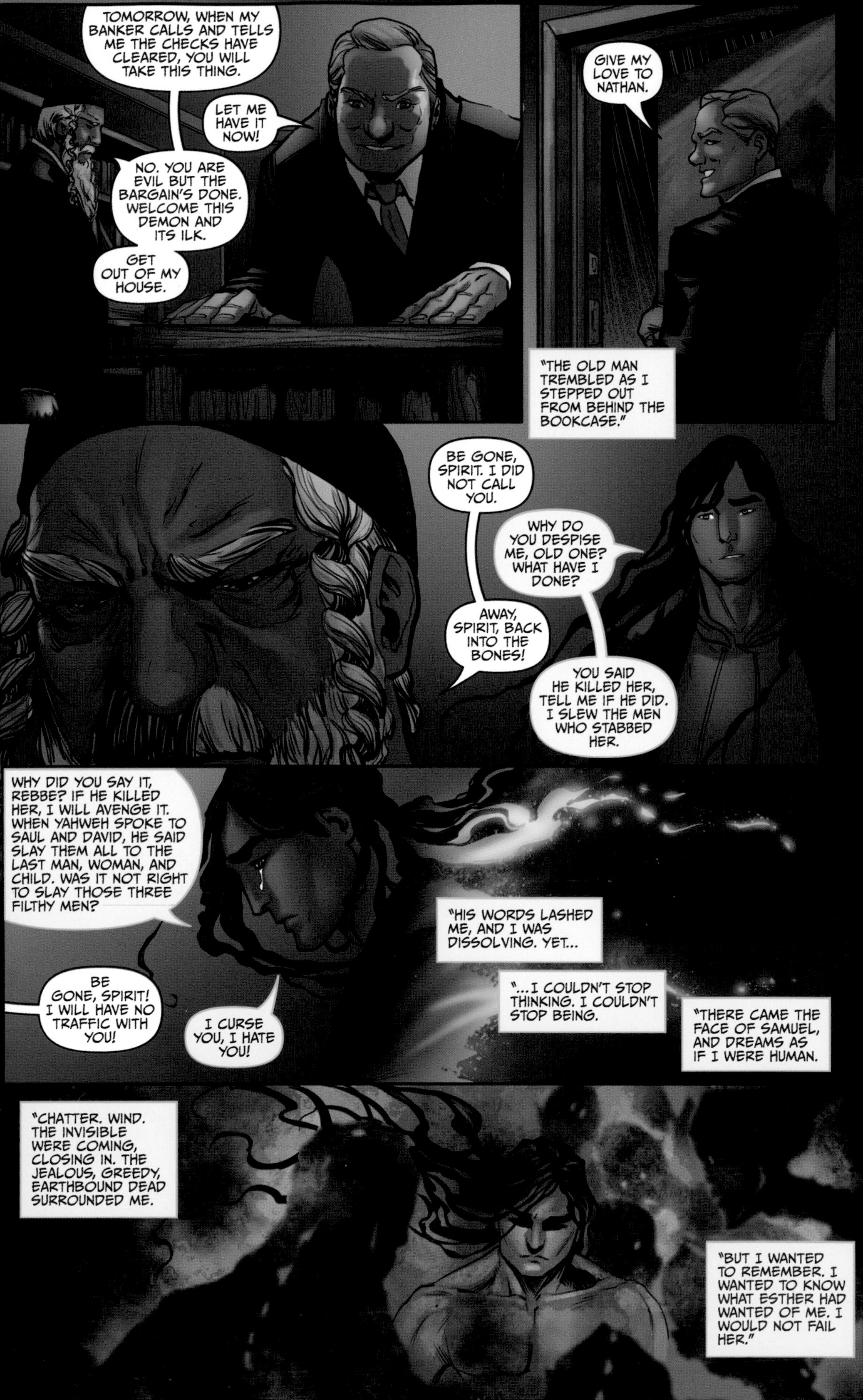

TOMORROW, WHEN MY BANKER CALLS AND TELLS ME THE CHECKS HAVE CLEARED, YOU WILL TAKE THIS THING.
LET ME HAVE IT NOW!
NO. YOU ARE EVIL BUT THE BARGAIN'S DONE. WELCOME THIS DEMON AND ITS ILK.
GET OUT OF MY HOUSE.
GIVE MY LOVE TO NATHAN.
"THE OLD MAN TREMBLED AS I STEPPED OUT FROM BEHIND THE BOOKCASE."
BE GONE, SPIRIT. I DID NOT CALL YOU.
WHY DO YOU DESPISE ME, OLD ONE? WHAT HAVE I DONE?
AWAY, SPIRIT, BACK INTO THE BONES!
YOU SAID HE KILLED HER, TELL ME IF HE DID. I SLEW THE MEN WHO STABBED HER.
WHY DID YOU SAY IT, REBBE? IF HE KILLED HER, I WILL AVENGE IT. WHEN YAHWEH SPOKE TO SAUL AND DAVID, HE SAID SLAY THEM ALL TO THE LAST MAN, WOMAN, AND CHILD. WAS IT NOT RIGHT TO SLAY THOSE THREE FILTHY MEN?
BE GONE, SPIRIT! I WILL HAVE NO TRAFFIC WITH YOU!
I CURSE YOU, I HATE YOU!
"HIS WORDS LASHED ME, AND I WAS DISSOLVING. YET...
"...I COULDN'T STOP THINKING. I COULDN'T STOP BEING.
"THERE CAME THE FACE OF SAMUEL, AND DREAMS AS IF I WERE HUMAN.
"CHATTER. WIND. THE INVISIBLE WERE COMING, CLOSING IN. THE JEALOUS, GREEDY, EARTHBOUND DEAD SURROUNDED ME.
"BUT I WANTED TO REMEMBER. I WANTED TO KNOW WHAT ESTHER HAD WANTED OF ME. I WOULD NOT FAIL HER."

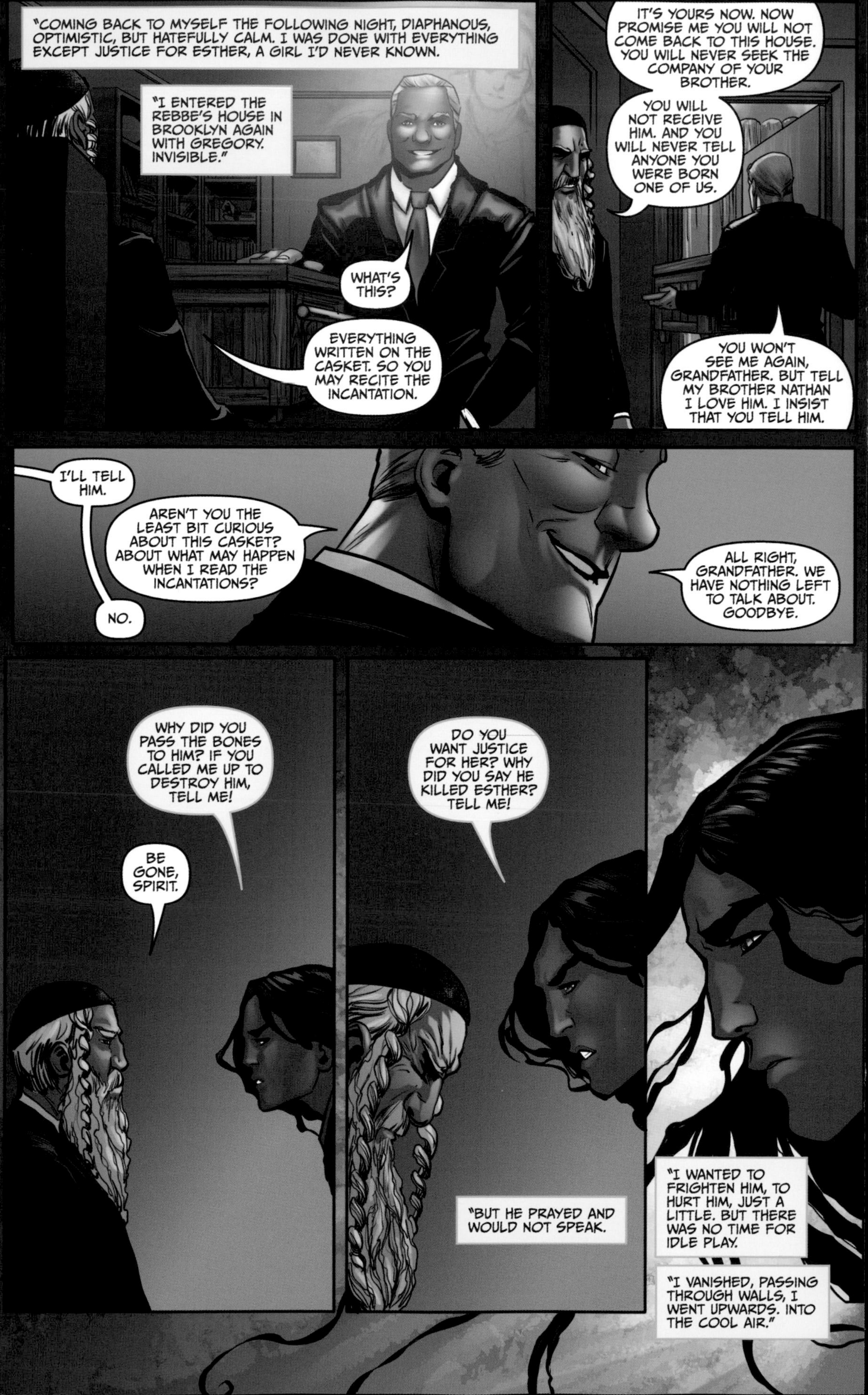
"COMING BACK TO MYSELF THE FOLLOWING NIGHT, DIAPHANOUS, OPTIMISTIC, BUT HATEFULLY CALM. I WAS DONE WITH EVERYTHING EXCEPT JUSTICE FOR ESTHER, A GIRL I'D NEVER KNOWN.
"I ENTERED THE REBBE'S HOUSE IN BROOKLYN AGAIN WITH GREGORY. INVISIBLE."
WHAT'S THIS?
EVERYTHING WRITTEN ON THE CASKET. SO YOU MAY RECITE THE INCANTATION.
IT'S YOURS NOW. NOW PROMISE ME YOU WILL NOT COME BACK TO THIS HOUSE. YOU WILL NEVER SEEK THE COMPANY OF YOUR BROTHER.
YOU WILL NOT RECEIVE HIM. AND YOU WILL NEVER TELL ANYONE YOU WERE BORN ONE OF US.
YOU WON'T SEE ME AGAIN, GRANDFATHER. BUT TELL MY BROTHER NATHAN I LOVE HIM. I INSIST THAT YOU TELL HIM.
I'LL TELL HIM.
AREN'T YOU THE LEAST BIT CURIOUS ABOUT THIS CASKET? ABOUT WHAT MAY HAPPEN WHEN I READ THE INCANTATIONS?
NO.
ALL RIGHT, GRANDFATHER. WE HAVE NOTHING LEFT TO TALK ABOUT. GOODBYE.
WHY DID YOU PASS THE BONES TO HIM? IF YOU CALLED ME UP TO DESTROY HIM, TELL ME!
BE GONE, SPIRIT.
DO YOU WANT JUSTICE FOR HER? WHY DID YOU SAY HE KILLED ESTHER? TELL ME!
"BUT HE PRAYED AND WOULD NOT SPEAK.
"I WANTED TO FRIGHTEN HIM, TO HURT HIM, JUST A LITTLE. BUT THERE WAS NO TIME FOR IDLE PLAY.
"I VANISHED, PASSING THROUGH WALLS, I WENT UPWARDS. INTO THE COOL AIR."

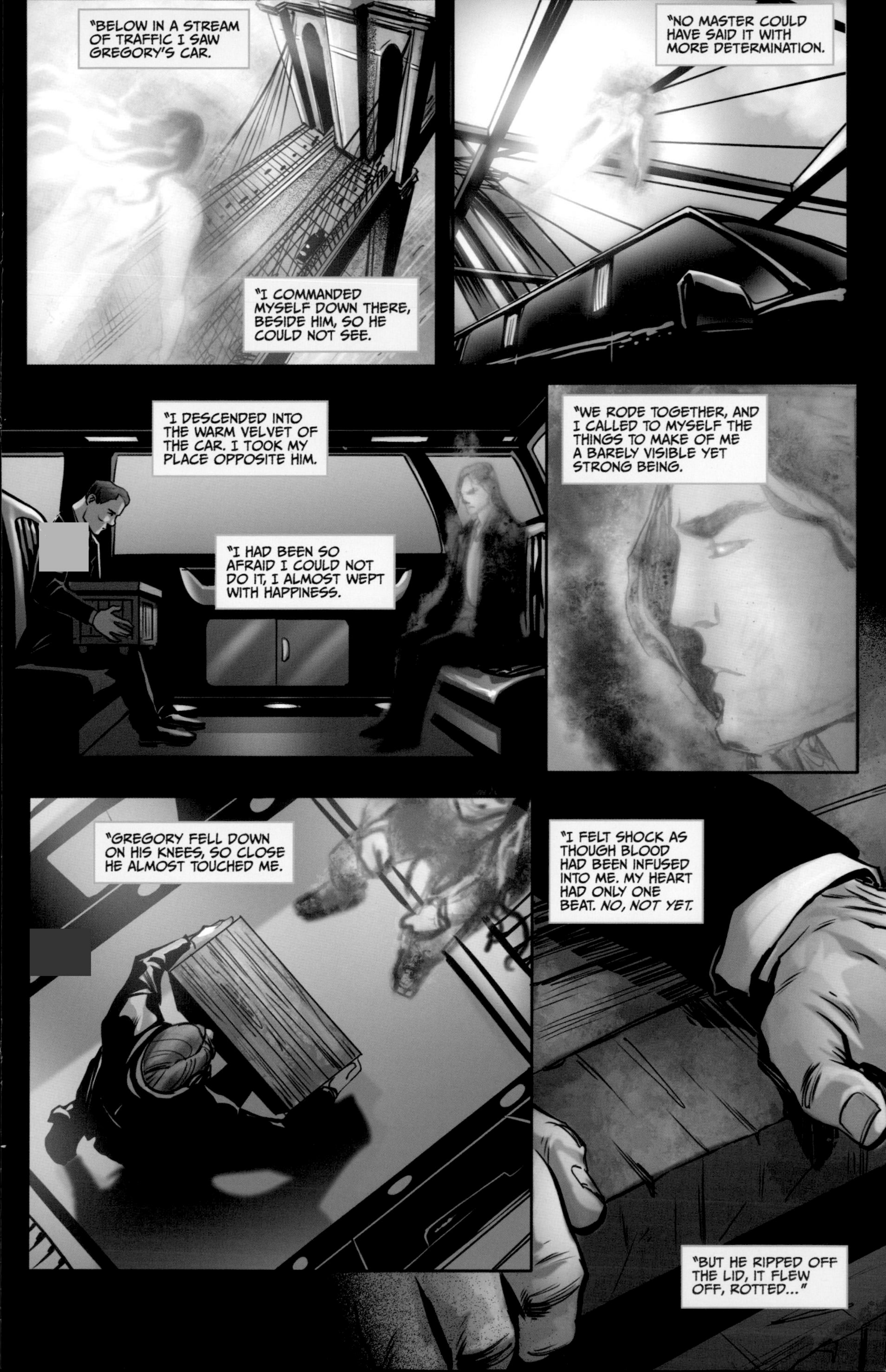
"BELOW IN A STREAM OF TRAFFIC I SAW GREGORY'S CAR.
"I COMMANDED MYSELF DOWN THERE, BESIDE HIM, SO HE COULD NOT SEE.
"NO MASTER COULD HAVE SAID IT WITH MORE DETERMINATION.
"I DESCENDED INTO THE WARM VELVET OF THE CAR. I TOOK MY PLACE OPPOSITE HIM.
"I HAD BEEN SO AFRAID I COULD NOT DO IT, I ALMOST WEPT WITH HAPPINESS.
"WE RODE TOGETHER, AND I CALLED TO MYSELF THE THINGS TO MAKE OF ME A BARELY VISIBLE YET STRONG BEING.
"GREGORY FELL DOWN ON HIS KNEES, SO CLOSE HE ALMOST TOUCHED ME.
"I FELT SHOCK AS THOUGH BLOOD HAD BEEN INFUSED INTO ME. MY HEART HAD ONLY ONE BEAT. *NO, NOT YET.*
"BUT HE RIPPED OFF THE LID, IT FLEW OFF, ROTTED..."

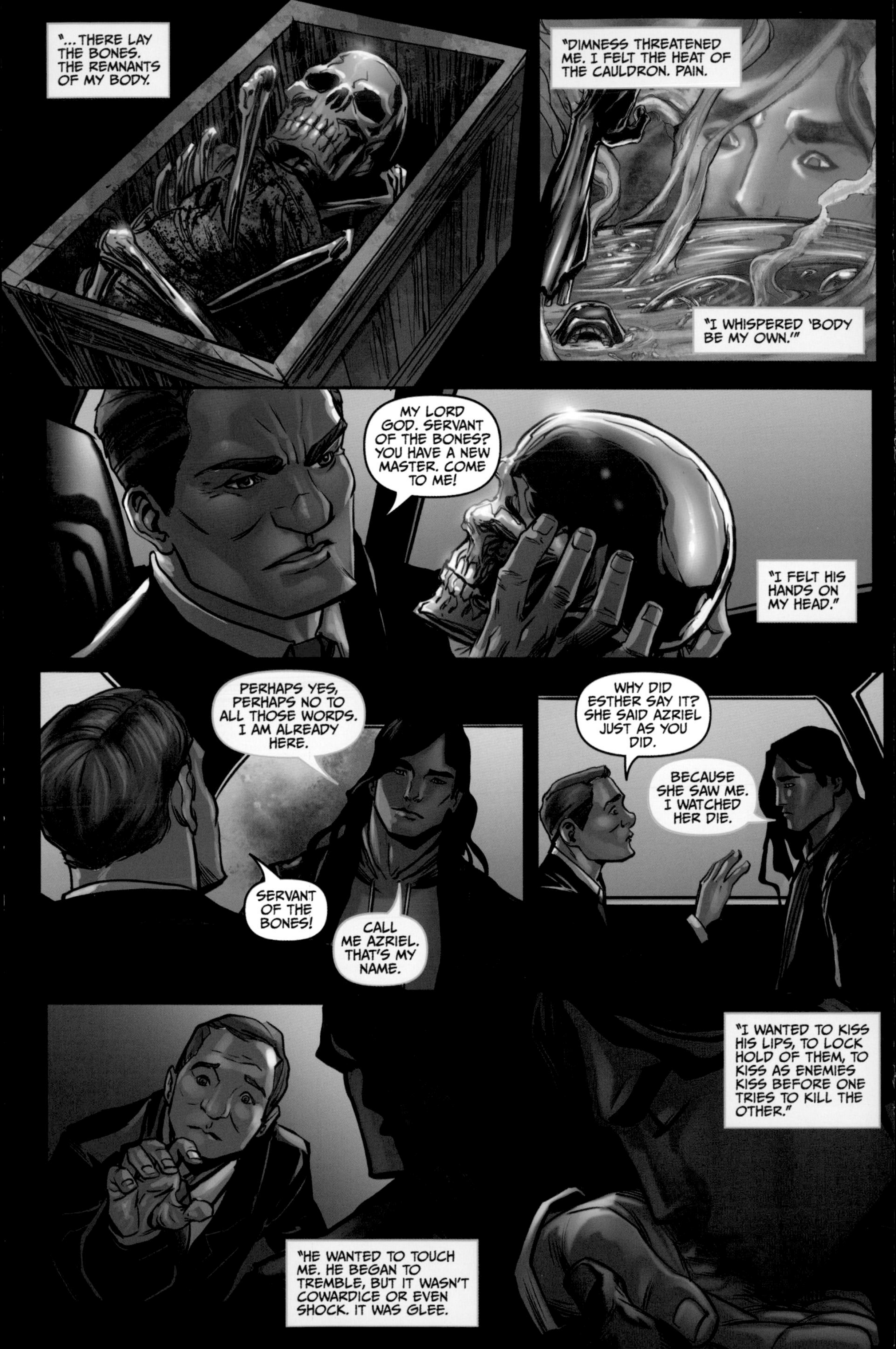
"...THERE LAY THE BONES. THE REMNANTS OF MY BODY.
"DIMNESS THREATENED ME. I FELT THE HEAT OF THE CAULDRON. PAIN.
"I WHISPERED 'BODY BE MY OWN.'"
MY LORD GOD. SERVANT OF THE BONES? YOU HAVE A NEW MASTER. COME TO ME!
"I FELT HIS HANDS ON MY HEAD."
PERHAPS YES, PERHAPS NO TO ALL THOSE WORDS. I AM ALREADY HERE.
SERVANT OF THE BONES!
CALL ME AZRIEL. THAT'S MY NAME.
WHY DID ESTHER SAY IT? SHE SAID AZRIEL JUST AS YOU DID.
BECAUSE SHE SAW ME. I WATCHED HER DIE.
"I WANTED TO KISS HIS LIPS, TO LOCK HOLD OF THEM, TO KISS AS ENEMIES KISS BEFORE ONE TRIES TO KILL THE OTHER."
"HE WANTED TO TOUCH ME. HE BEGAN TO TREMBLE, BUT IT WASN'T COWARDICE OR EVEN SHOCK. IT WAS GLEE.

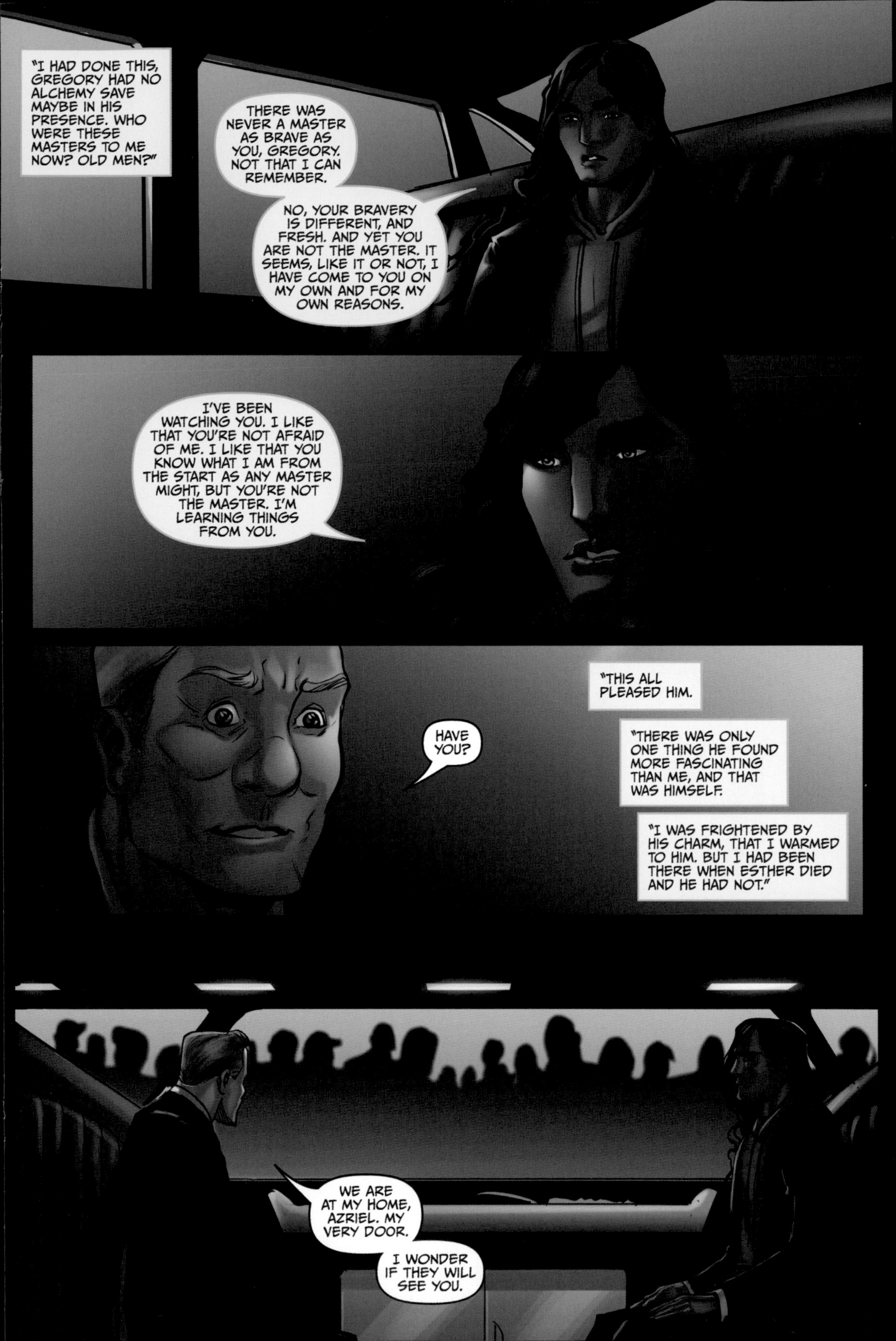
"I HAD DONE THIS, GREGORY HAD NO ALCHEMY SAVE MAYBE IN HIS PRESENCE. WHO WERE THESE MASTERS TO ME NOW? OLD MEN?"
THERE WAS NEVER A MASTER AS BRAVE AS YOU, GREGORY. NOT THAT I CAN REMEMBER.
NO, YOUR BRAVERY IS DIFFERENT, AND FRESH. AND YET YOU ARE NOT THE MASTER. IT SEEMS, LIKE IT OR NOT, I HAVE COME TO YOU ON MY OWN AND FOR MY OWN REASONS.
I'VE BEEN WATCHING YOU. I LIKE THAT YOU'RE NOT AFRAID OF ME. I LIKE THAT YOU KNOW WHAT I AM FROM THE START AS ANY MASTER MIGHT, BUT YOU'RE NOT THE MASTER. I'M LEARNING THINGS FROM YOU.
HAVE YOU?
"THIS ALL PLEASED HIM.
"THERE WAS ONLY ONE THING HE FOUND MORE FASCINATING THAN ME, AND THAT WAS HIMSELF.
"I WAS FRIGHTENED BY HIS CHARM, THAT I WARMED TO HIM. BUT I HAD BEEN THERE WHEN ESTHER DIED AND HE HAD NOT."
WE ARE AT MY HOME, AZRIEL. MY VERY DOOR.
I WONDER IF THEY WILL SEE YOU.

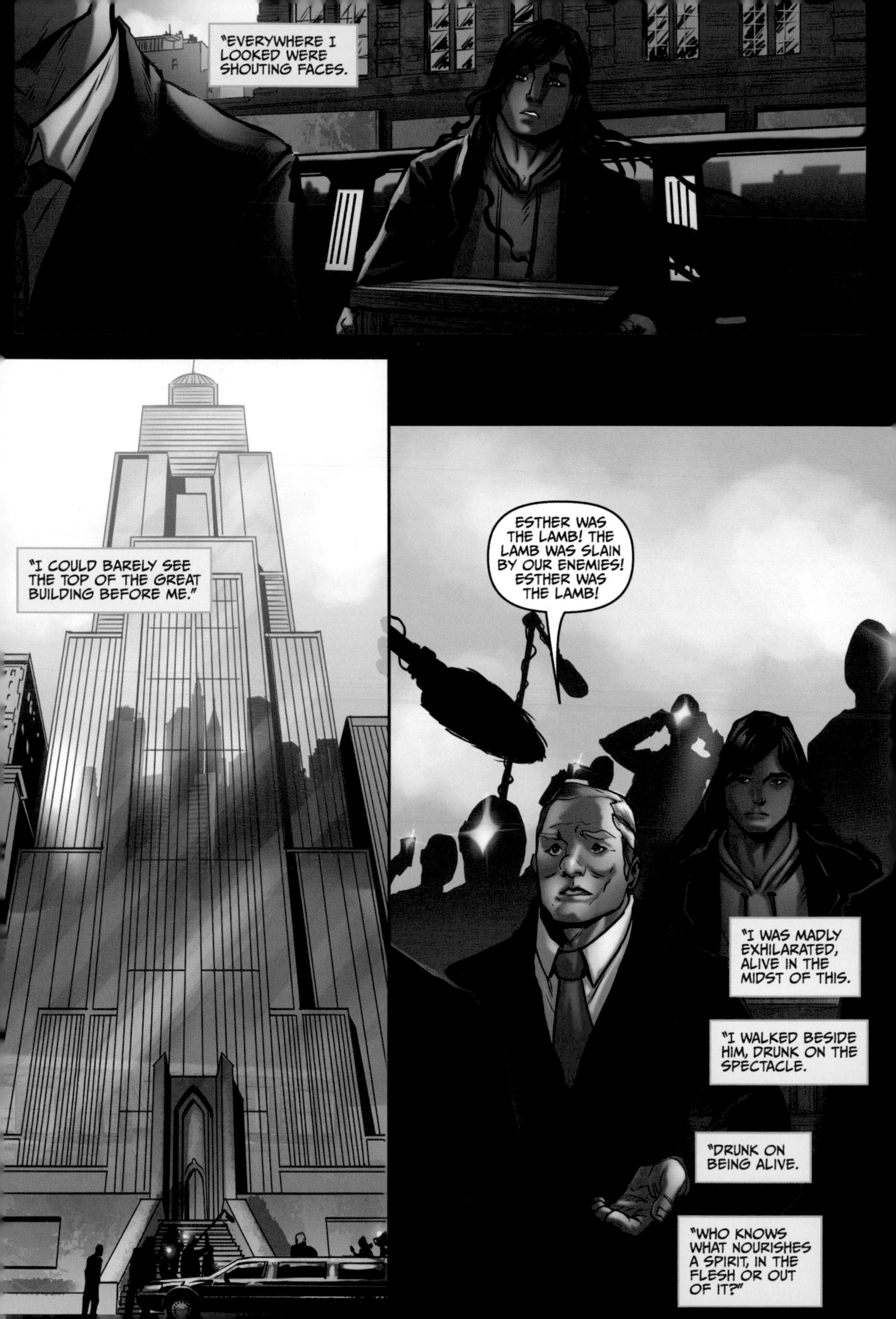
"EVERYWHERE I LOOKED WERE SHOUTING FACES.
"I COULD BARELY SEE THE TOP OF THE GREAT BUILDING BEFORE ME."
ESTHER WAS THE LAMB! THE LAMB WAS SLAIN BY OUR ENEMIES! ESTHER WAS THE LAMB!
"I WAS MADLY EXHILARATED, ALIVE IN THE MIDST OF THIS.
"I WALKED BESIDE HIM, DRUNK ON THE SPECTACLE.
"DRUNK ON BEING ALIVE.
"WHO KNOWS WHAT NOURISHES A SPIRIT, IN THE FLESH OR OUT OF IT?"

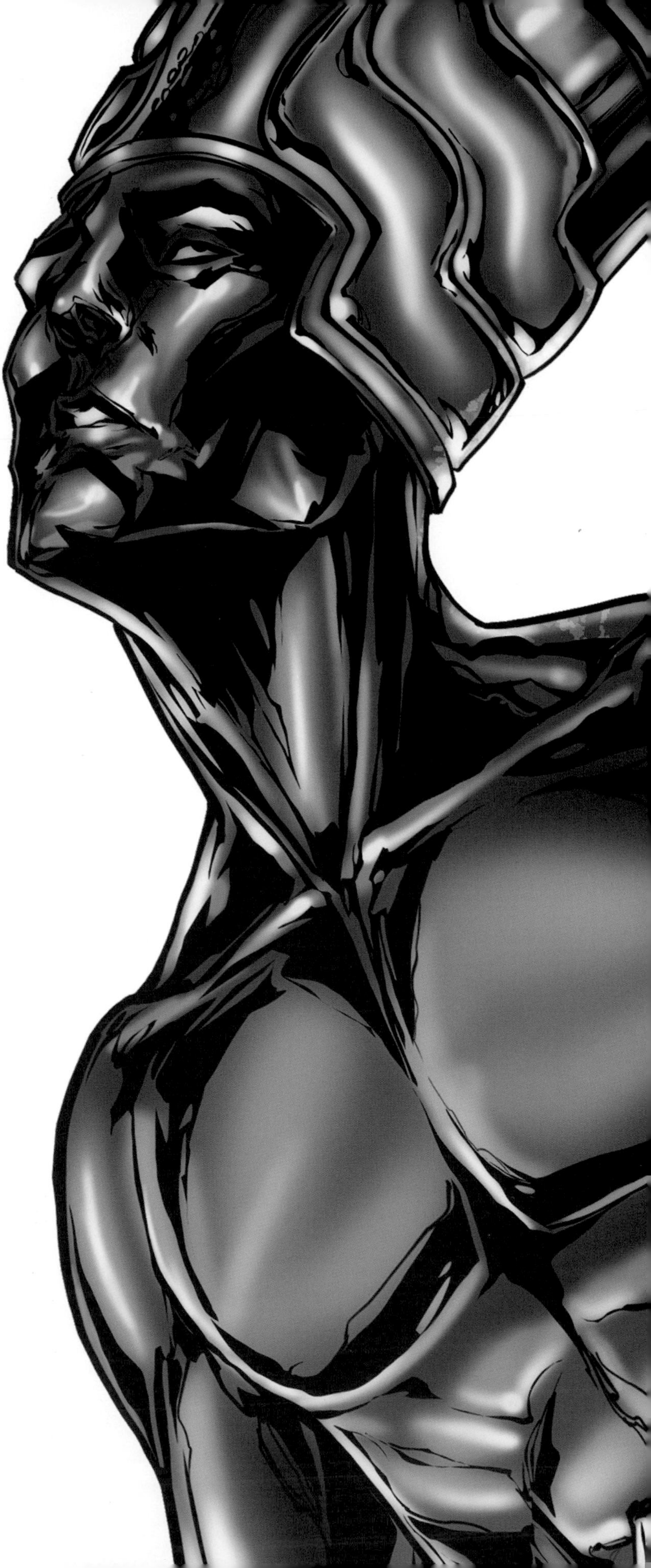

Chapter Five

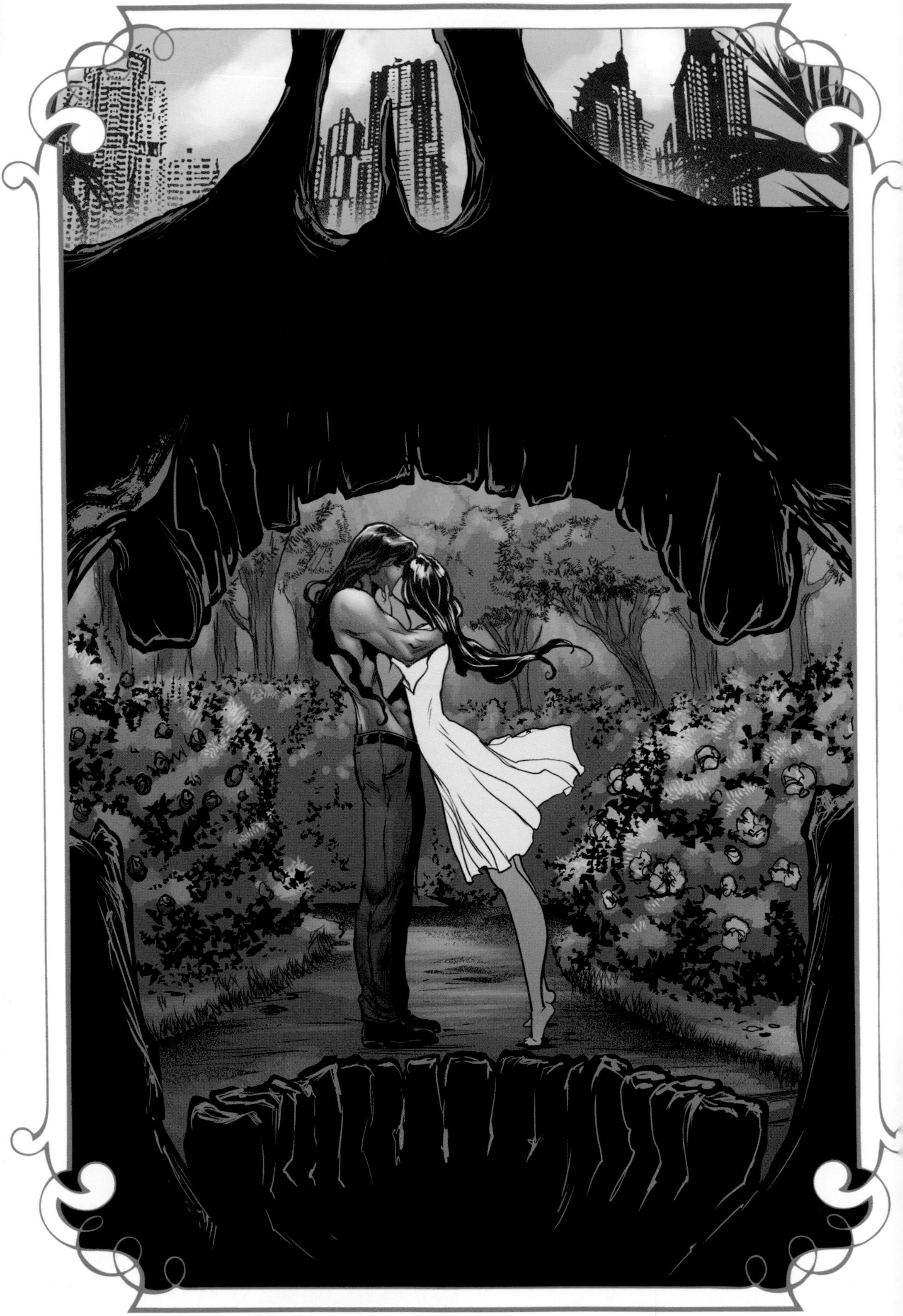

Art by Renae De Liz • Colors by Ray Dillon

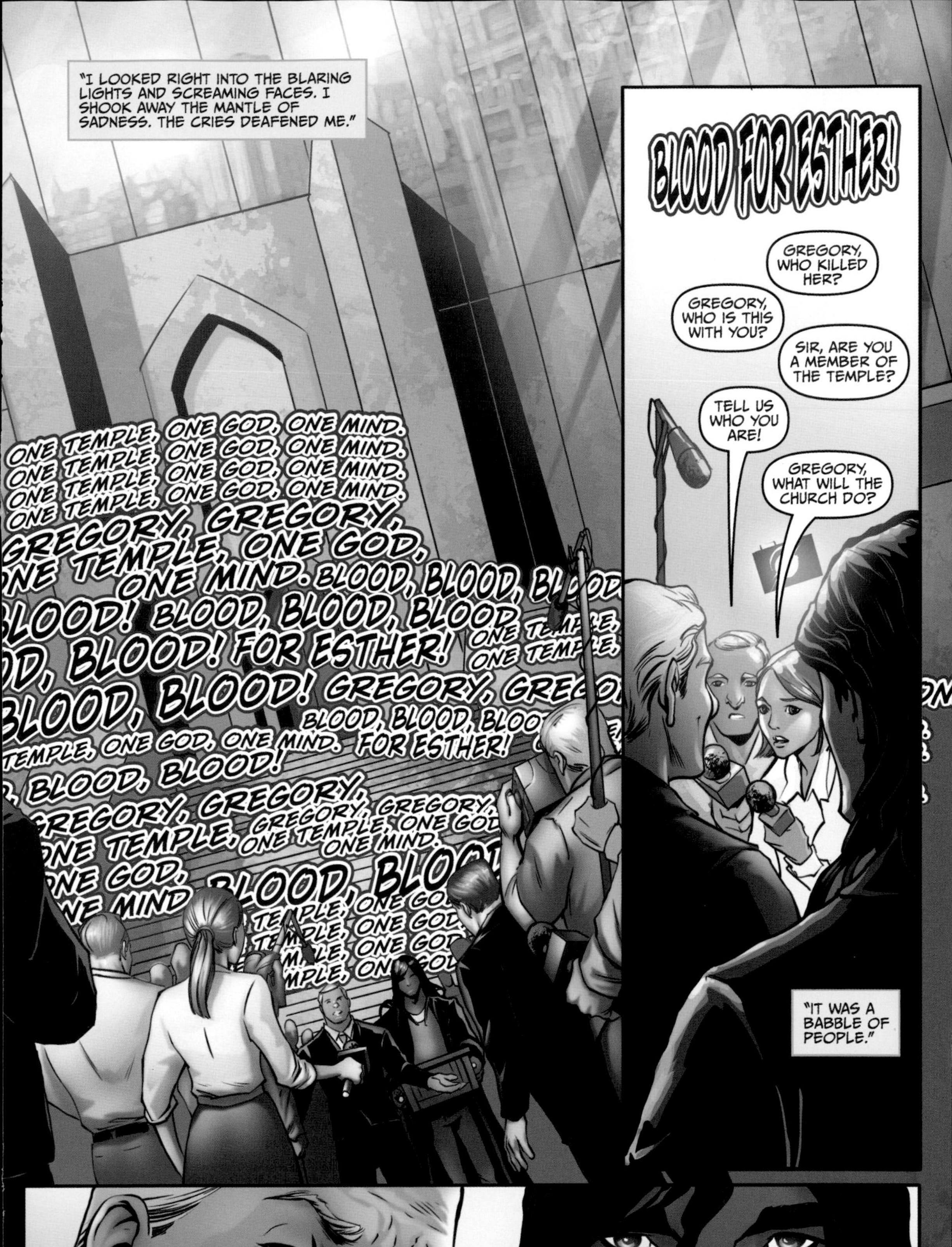

"I LOOKED RIGHT INTO THE BLARING LIGHTS AND SCREAMING FACES. I SHOOK AWAY THE MANTLE OF SADNESS. THE CRIES DEAFENED ME."
ONE TEMPLE, ONE GOD, ONE MIND.
ONE TEMPLE, ONE GOD, ONE MIND.
ONE TEMPLE, ONE GOD, ONE MIND.
ONE TEMPLE, ONE GOD, ONE MIND.
GREGORY, GREGORY,
ONE TEMPLE, ONE GOD,
ONE MIND.
BLOOD, BLOOD, BLOOD!
BLOOD, BLOOD, BLOOD!
FOR ESTHER!
GREGORY,
FOR ESTHER!
BLOOD, BLOOD!
GREGORY, GREGORY,
ONE TEMPLE,
ONE GOD,
ONE MIND
BLOOD! FOR ESTHER!
GREGORY, WHO KILLED HER?
GREGORY, WHO IS THIS WITH YOU?
SIR, ARE YOU A MEMBER OF THE TEMPLE?
TELL US WHO YOU ARE!
GREGORY, WHAT WILL THE CHURCH DO?
"IT WAS A BABBLE OF PEOPLE."
INDEED, THEY DO SEE YOU.

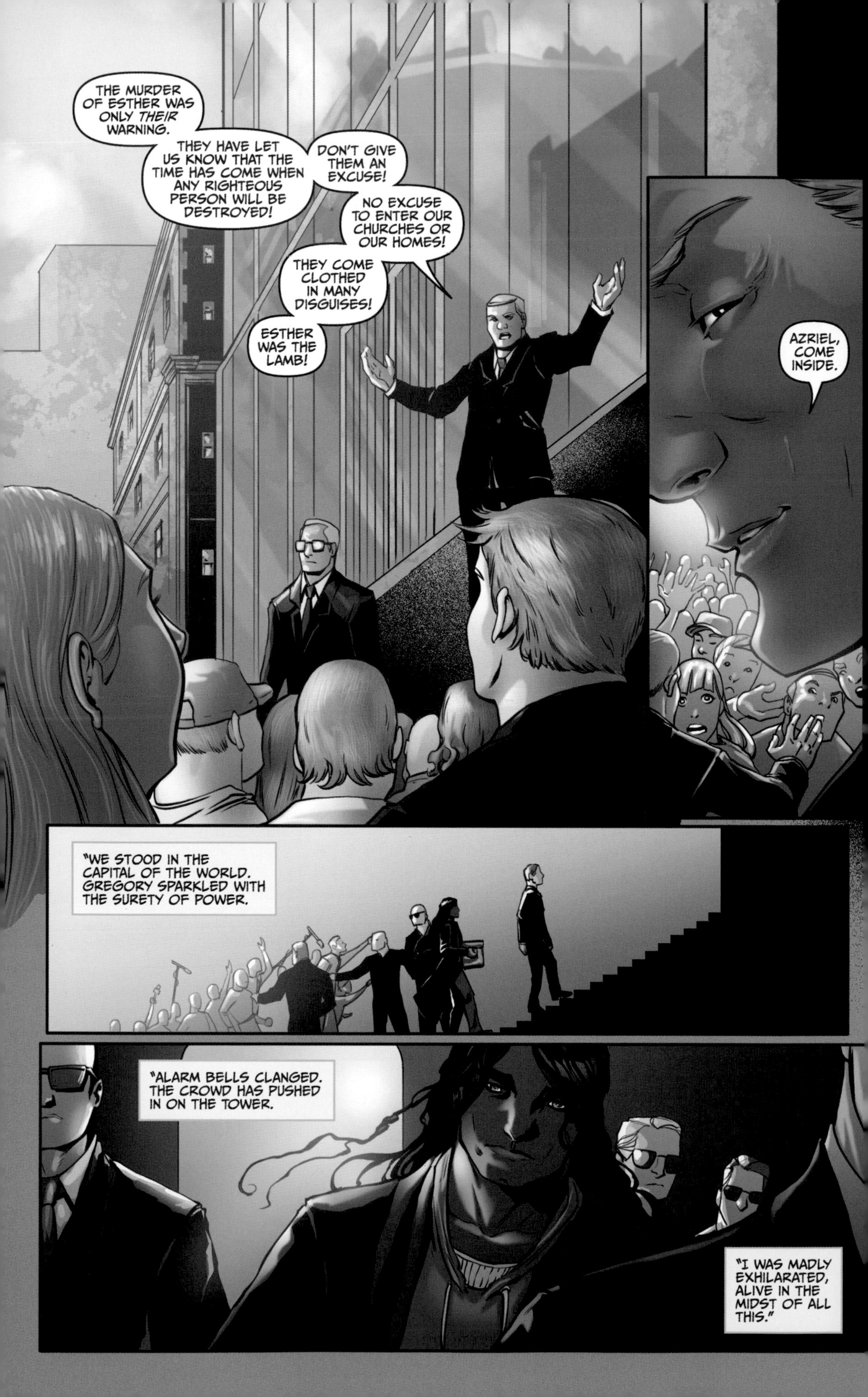
THE MURDER OF ESTHER WAS ONLY *THEIR* WARNING.
THEY HAVE LET US KNOW THAT THE TIME HAS COME WHEN ANY RIGHTEOUS PERSON WILL BE DESTROYED!
DON'T GIVE THEM AN EXCUSE!
NO EXCUSE TO ENTER OUR CHURCHES OR OUR HOMES!
THEY COME CLOTHED IN MANY DISGUISES!
ESTHER WAS THE LAMB!
AZRIEL, COME INSIDE.
"WE STOOD IN THE CAPITAL OF THE WORLD. GREGORY SPARKLED WITH THE SURETY OF POWER.
"ALARM BELLS CLANGED. THE CROWD HAS PUSHED IN ON THE TOWER.
"I WAS MADLY EXHILARATED, ALIVE IN THE MIDST OF ALL THIS."

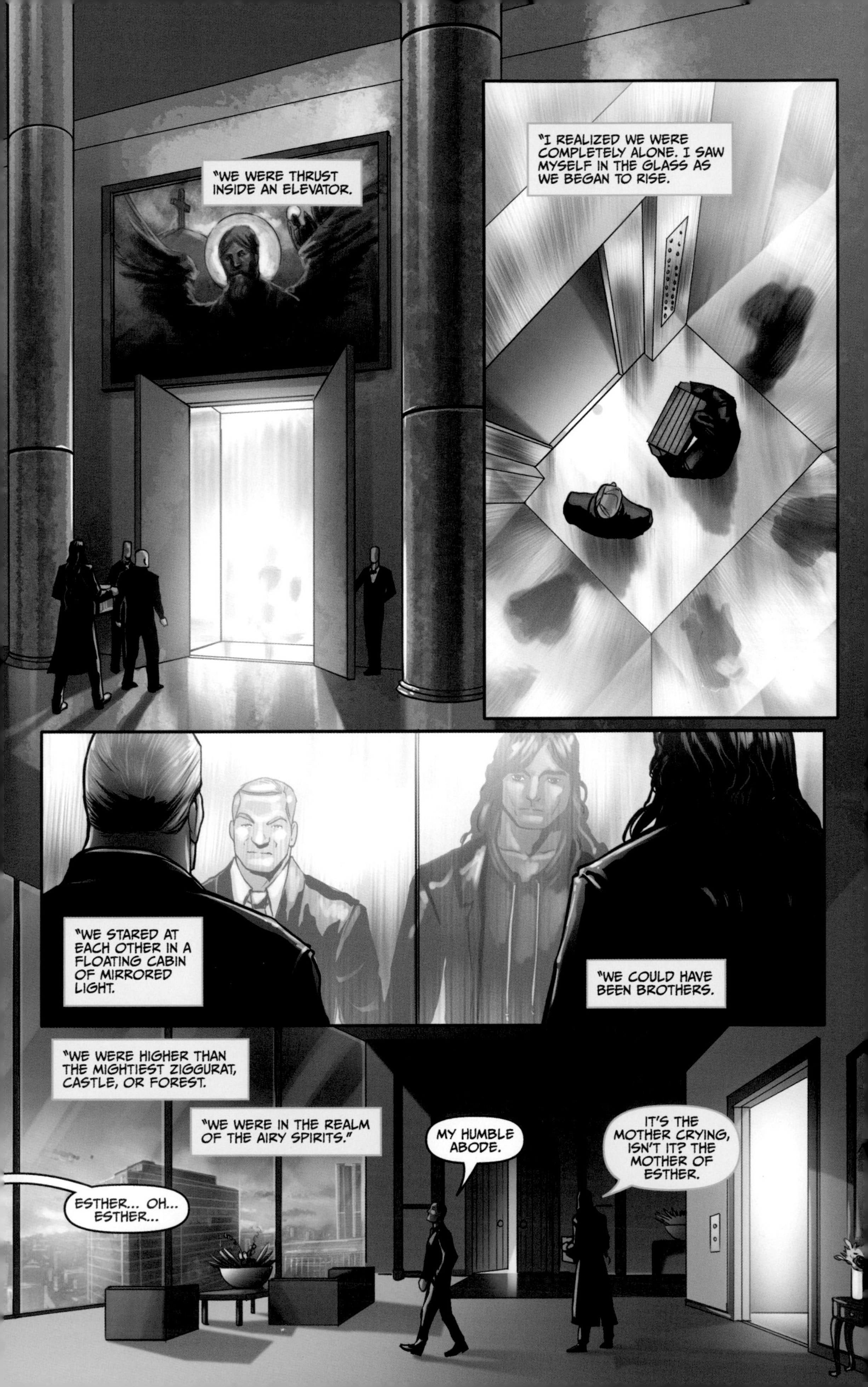
"WE WERE THRUST INSIDE AN ELEVATOR.
"I REALIZED WE WERE COMPLETELY ALONE. I SAW MYSELF IN THE GLASS AS WE BEGAN TO RISE.
"WE STARED AT EACH OTHER IN A FLOATING CABIN OF MIRRORED LIGHT.
"WE COULD HAVE BEEN BROTHERS.
"WE WERE HIGHER THAN THE MIGHTIEST ZIGGURAT, CASTLE, OR FOREST.
"WE WERE IN THE REALM OF THE AIRY SPIRITS."
MY HUMBLE ABODE.
IT'S THE MOTHER CRYING, ISN'T IT? THE MOTHER OF ESTHER.
ESTHER... OH... ESTHER...

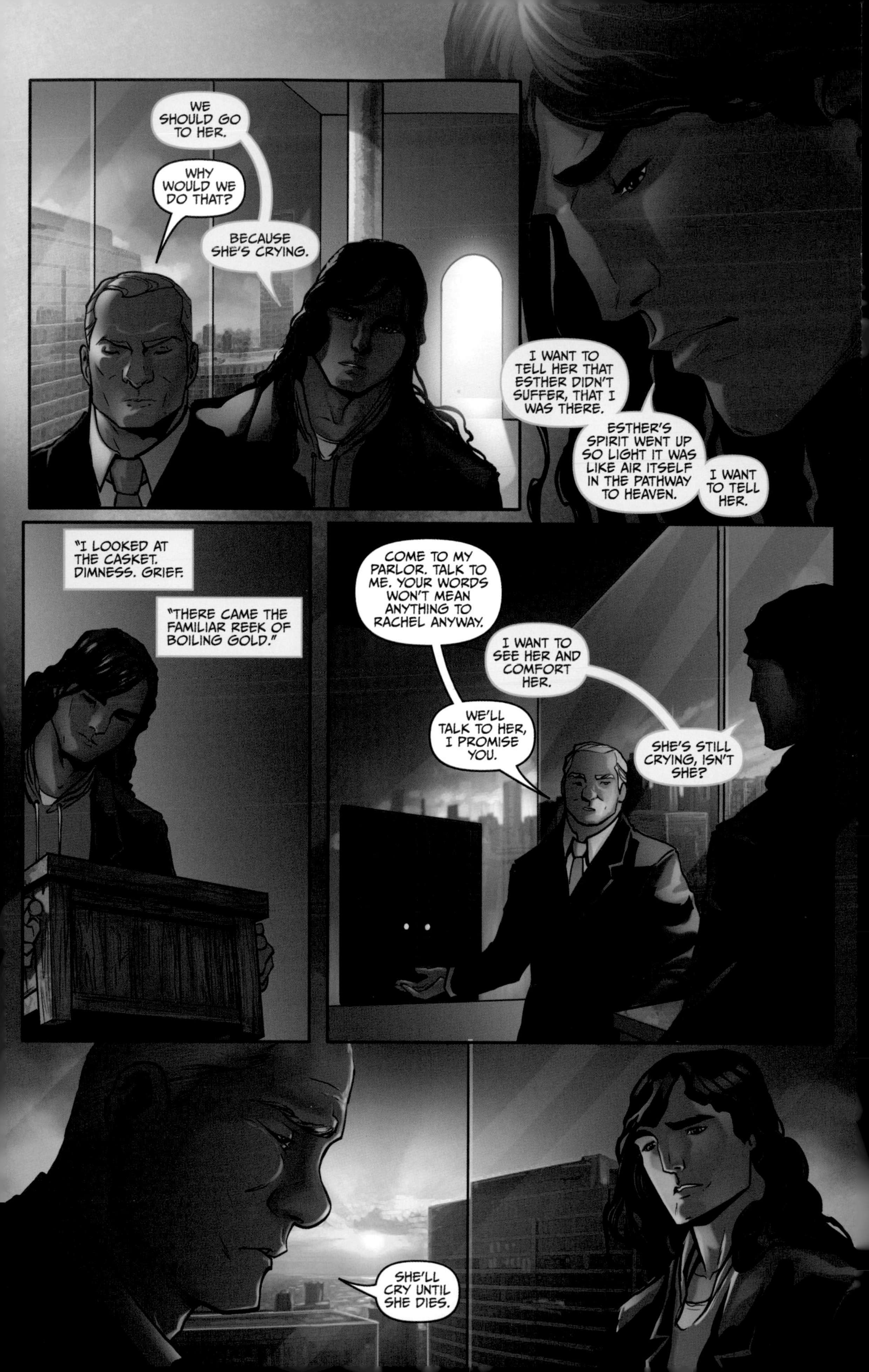
WE SHOULD GO TO HER.
WHY WOULD WE DO THAT?
BECAUSE SHE'S CRYING.
I WANT TO TELL HER THAT ESTHER DIDN'T SUFFER, THAT I WAS THERE.
ESTHER'S SPIRIT WENT UP SO LIGHT IT WAS LIKE AIR ITSELF IN THE PATHWAY TO HEAVEN.
I WANT TO TELL HER.
"I LOOKED AT THE CASKET. DIMNESS. GRIEF.
"THERE CAME THE FAMILIAR REEK OF BOILING GOLD."
COME TO MY PARLOR. TALK TO ME. YOUR WORDS WON'T MEAN ANYTHING TO RACHEL ANYWAY.
I WANT TO SEE HER AND COMFORT HER.
WE'LL TALK TO HER, I PROMISE YOU.
SHE'S STILL CRYING, ISN'T SHE?
SHE'LL CRY UNTIL SHE DIES.

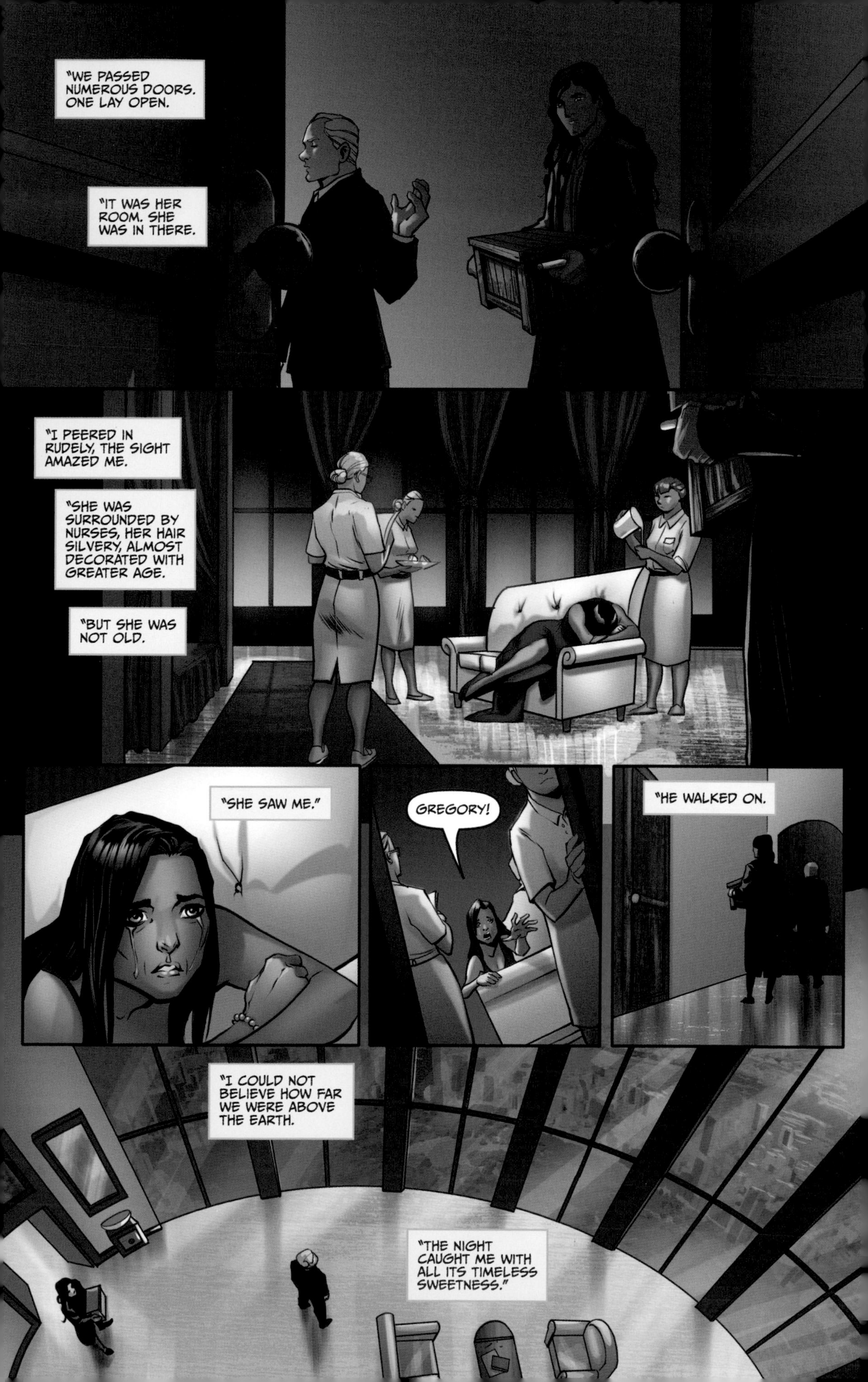

"WE PASSED NUMEROUS DOORS. ONE LAY OPEN.
"IT WAS HER ROOM. SHE WAS IN THERE.
"I PEERED IN RUDELY, THE SIGHT AMAZED ME.
"SHE WAS SURROUNDED BY NURSES, HER HAIR SILVERY, ALMOST DECORATED WITH GREATER AGE.
"BUT SHE WAS NOT OLD.
"SHE SAW ME."
GREGORY!
"HE WALKED ON.
"I COULD NOT BELIEVE HOW FAR WE WERE ABOVE THE EARTH.
"THE NIGHT CAUGHT ME WITH ALL ITS TIMELESS SWEETNESS."

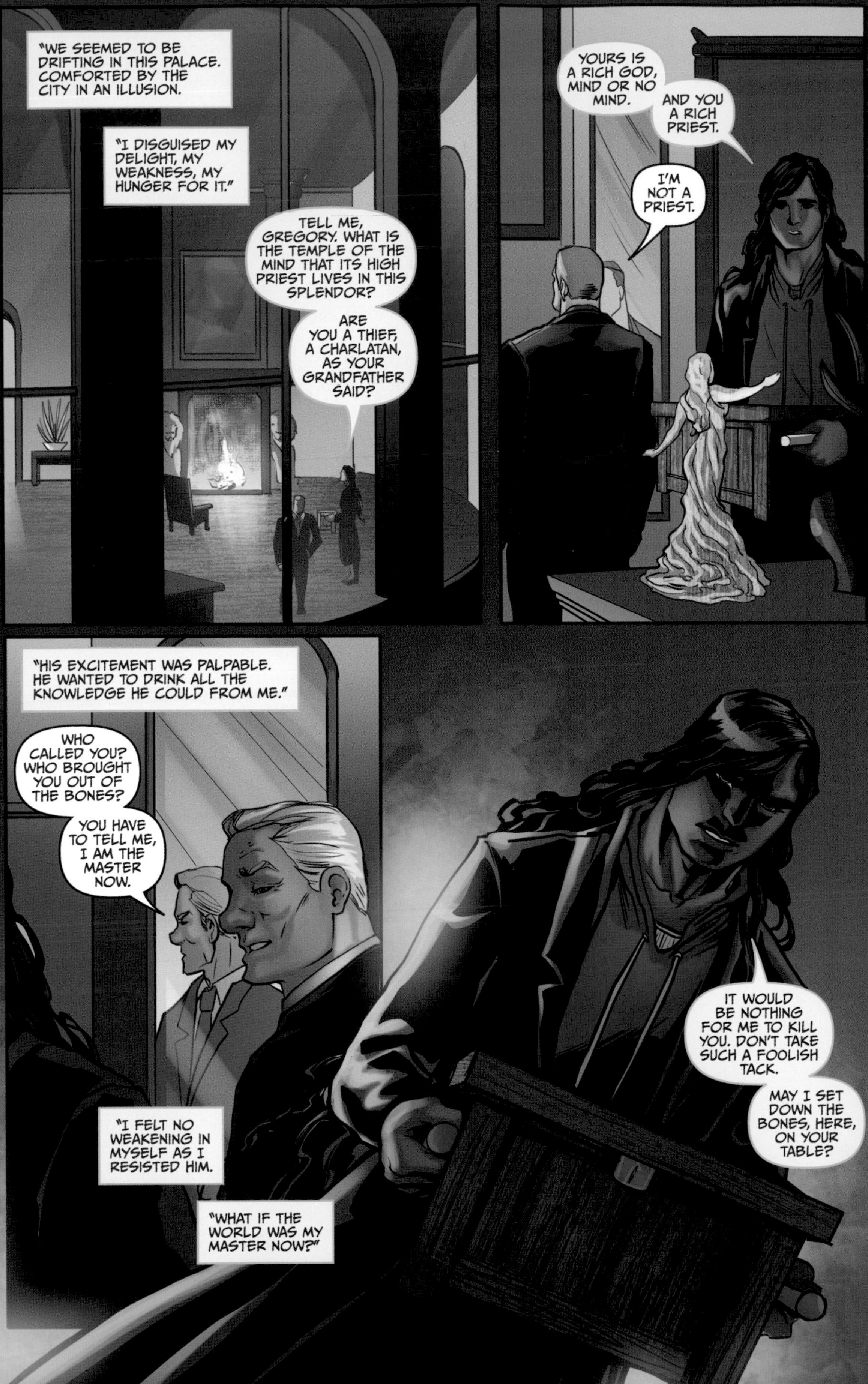
"WE SEEMED TO BE DRIFTING IN THIS PALACE. COMFORTED BY THE CITY IN AN ILLUSION.
"I DISGUISED MY DELIGHT, MY WEAKNESS, MY HUNGER FOR IT."
TELL ME, GREGORY. WHAT IS THE TEMPLE OF THE MIND THAT ITS HIGH PRIEST LIVES IN THIS SPLENDOR?
ARE YOU A THIEF, A CHARLATAN, AS YOUR GRANDFATHER SAID?
YOURS IS A RICH GOD, MIND OR NO MIND.
AND YOU A RICH PRIEST.
I'M NOT A PRIEST.
"HIS EXCITEMENT WAS PALPABLE. HE WANTED TO DRINK ALL THE KNOWLEDGE HE COULD FROM ME."
WHO CALLED YOU? WHO BROUGHT YOU OUT OF THE BONES?
YOU HAVE TO TELL ME, I AM THE MASTER NOW.
IT WOULD BE NOTHING FOR ME TO KILL YOU. DON'T TAKE SUCH A FOOLISH TACK.
MAY I SET DOWN THE BONES, HERE, ON YOUR TABLE?
"I FELT NO WEAKENING IN MYSELF AS I RESISTED HIM.
"WHAT IF THE WORLD WAS MY MASTER NOW?"

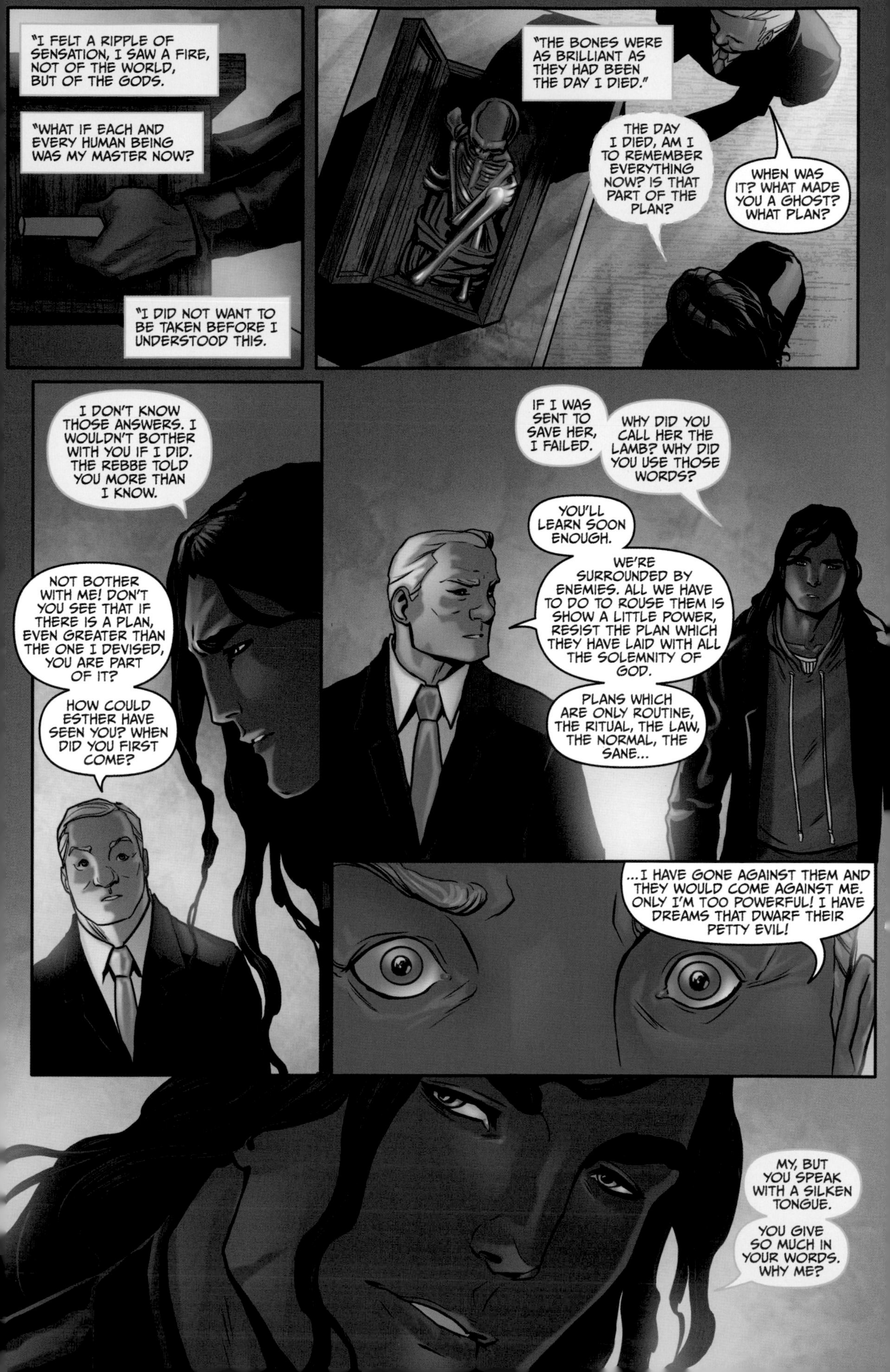

"I FELT A RIPPLE OF SENSATION, I SAW A FIRE, NOT OF THE WORLD, BUT OF THE GODS.
"WHAT IF EACH AND EVERY HUMAN BEING WAS MY MASTER NOW?
"I DID NOT WANT TO BE TAKEN BEFORE I UNDERSTOOD THIS.
"THE BONES WERE AS BRILLIANT AS THEY HAD BEEN THE DAY I DIED."
THE DAY I DIED, AM I TO REMEMBER EVERYTHING NOW? IS THAT PART OF THE PLAN?
WHEN WAS IT? WHAT MADE YOU A GHOST? WHAT PLAN?
I DON'T KNOW THOSE ANSWERS. I WOULDN'T BOTHER WITH YOU IF I DID. THE REBBE TOLD YOU MORE THAN I KNOW.
IF I WAS SENT TO SAVE HER, I FAILED.
WHY DID YOU CALL HER THE LAMB? WHY DID YOU USE THOSE WORDS?
YOU'LL LEARN SOON ENOUGH.
WE'RE SURROUNDED BY ENEMIES. ALL WE HAVE TO DO TO ROUSE THEM IS SHOW A LITTLE POWER, RESIST THE PLAN WHICH THEY HAVE LAID WITH ALL THE SOLEMNITY OF GOD.
PLANS WHICH ARE ONLY ROUTINE, THE RITUAL, THE LAW, THE NORMAL, THE SANE...
NOT BOTHER WITH ME! DON'T YOU SEE THAT IF THERE IS A PLAN, EVEN GREATER THAN THE ONE I DEVISED, YOU ARE PART OF IT?
HOW COULD ESTHER HAVE SEEN YOU? WHEN DID YOU FIRST COME?
...I HAVE GONE AGAINST THEM AND THEY WOULD COME AGAINST ME. ONLY I'M TOO POWERFUL! I HAVE DREAMS THAT DWARF THEIR PETTY EVIL!
MY, BUT YOU SPEAK WITH A SILKEN TONGUE.
YOU GIVE SO MUCH IN YOUR WORDS. WHY ME?

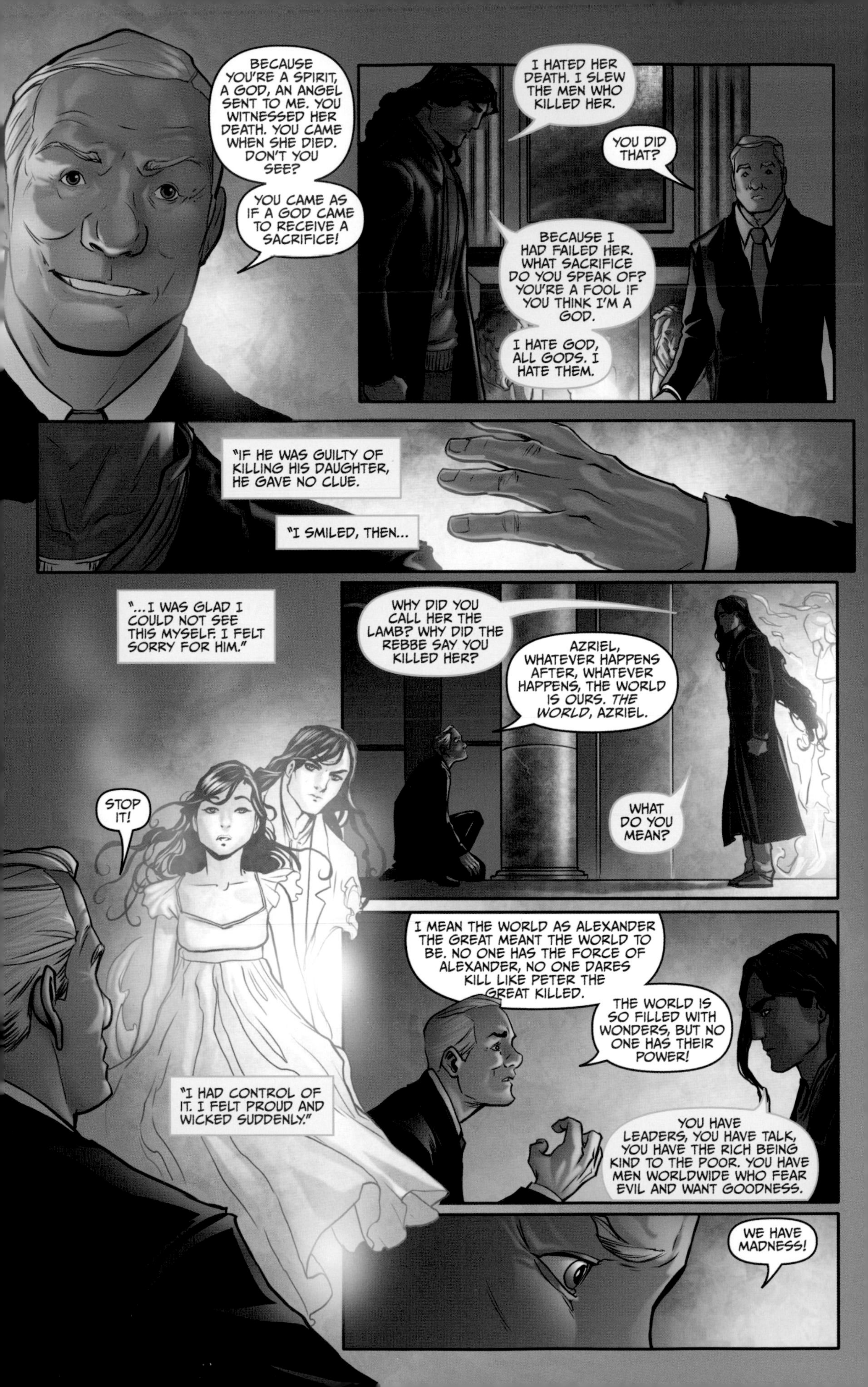
BECAUSE YOU'RE A SPIRIT, A GOD, AN ANGEL SENT TO ME. YOU WITNESSED HER DEATH. YOU CAME WHEN SHE DIED. DON'T YOU SEE?
YOU CAME AS IF A GOD CAME TO RECEIVE A SACRIFICE!
I HATED HER DEATH. I SLEW THE MEN WHO KILLED HER.
YOU DID THAT?
BECAUSE I HAD FAILED HER. WHAT SACRIFICE DO YOU SPEAK OF? YOU'RE A FOOL IF YOU THINK I'M A GOD.
I HATE GOD, ALL GODS. I HATE THEM.
"IF HE WAS GUILTY OF KILLING HIS DAUGHTER, HE GAVE NO CLUE.
"I SMILED, THEN...
"...I WAS GLAD I COULD NOT SEE THIS MYSELF. I FELT SORRY FOR HIM."
WHY DID YOU CALL HER THE LAMB? WHY DID THE REBBE SAY YOU KILLED HER?
AZRIEL, WHATEVER HAPPENS AFTER, WHATEVER HAPPENS, THE WORLD IS OURS. *THE WORLD*, AZRIEL.
STOP IT!
WHAT DO YOU MEAN?
I MEAN THE WORLD AS ALEXANDER THE GREAT MEANT THE WORLD TO BE. NO ONE HAS THE FORCE OF ALEXANDER, NO ONE DARES KILL LIKE PETER THE GREAT KILLED.
THE WORLD IS SO FILLED WITH WONDERS, BUT NO ONE HAS THEIR POWER!
"I HAD CONTROL OF IT. I FELT PROUD AND WICKED SUDDENLY."
YOU HAVE LEADERS, YOU HAVE TALK, YOU HAVE THE RICH BEING KIND TO THE POOR. YOU HAVE MEN WORLDWIDE WHO FEAR EVIL AND WANT GOODNESS.
WE HAVE MADNESS!

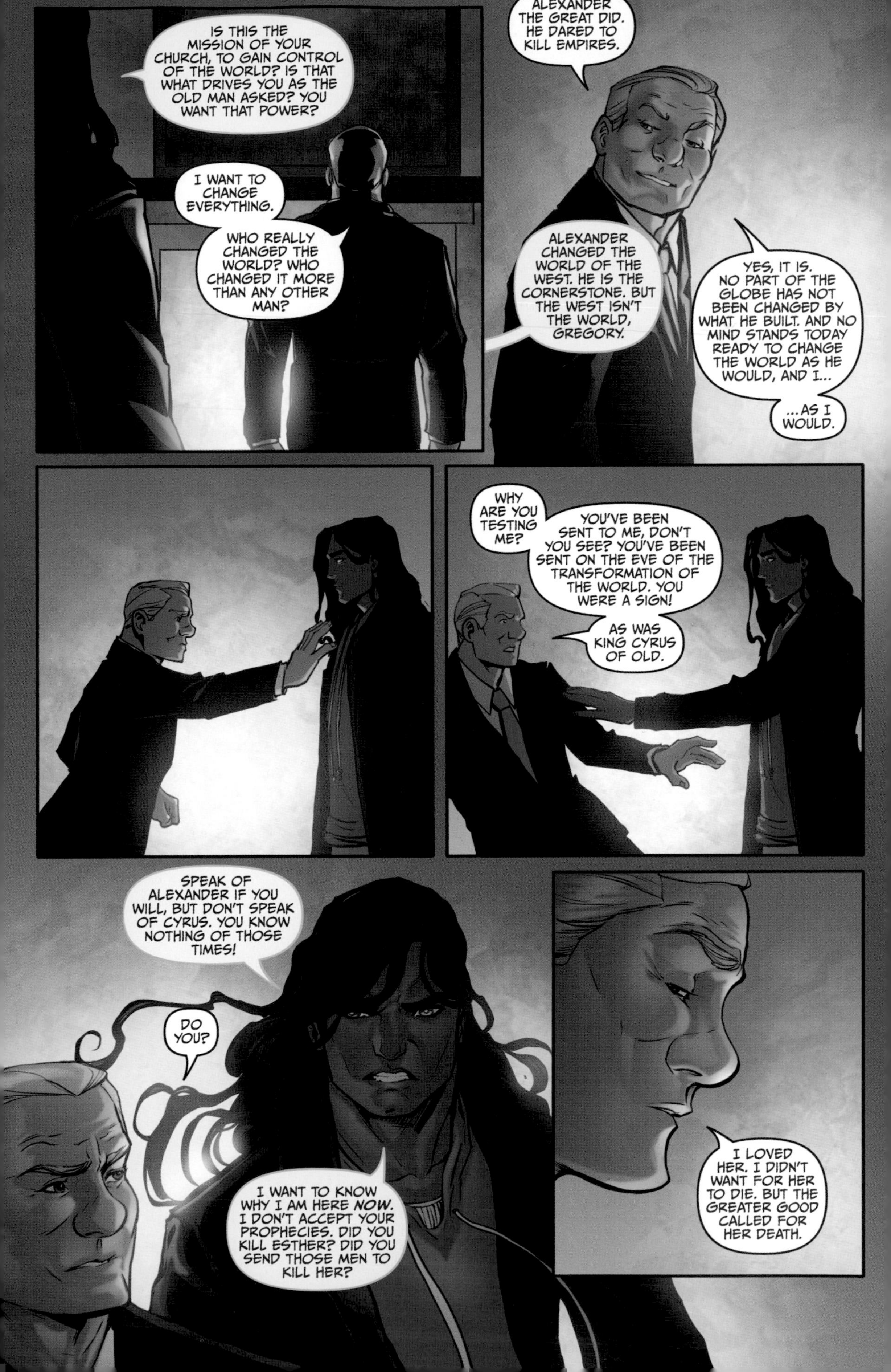
IS THIS THE MISSION OF YOUR CHURCH, TO GAIN CONTROL OF THE WORLD? IS THAT WHAT DRIVES YOU AS THE OLD MAN ASKED? YOU WANT THAT POWER?
I WANT TO CHANGE EVERYTHING.
WHO REALLY CHANGED THE WORLD? WHO CHANGED IT MORE THAN ANY OTHER MAN?
ALEXANDER THE GREAT DID. HE DARED TO KILL EMPIRES.
ALEXANDER CHANGED THE WORLD OF THE WEST. HE IS THE CORNERSTONE. BUT THE WEST ISN'T THE WORLD, GREGORY.
YES, IT IS. NO PART OF THE GLOBE HAS NOT BEEN CHANGED BY WHAT HE BUILT. AND NO MIND STANDS TODAY READY TO CHANGE THE WORLD AS HE WOULD, AND I...
...AS I WOULD.
WHY ARE YOU TESTING ME?
YOU'VE BEEN SENT TO ME, DON'T YOU SEE? YOU'VE BEEN SENT ON THE EVE OF THE TRANSFORMATION OF THE WORLD. YOU WERE A SIGN!
AS WAS KING CYRUS OF OLD.
SPEAK OF ALEXANDER IF YOU WILL, BUT DON'T SPEAK OF CYRUS. YOU KNOW NOTHING OF THOSE TIMES!
DO YOU?
I WANT TO KNOW WHY I AM HERE *NOW*. I DON'T ACCEPT YOUR PROPHECIES. DID YOU KILL ESTHER? DID YOU SEND THOSE MEN TO KILL HER?
I LOVED HER. I DIDN'T WANT FOR HER TO DIE. BUT THE GREATER GOOD CALLED FOR HER DEATH.

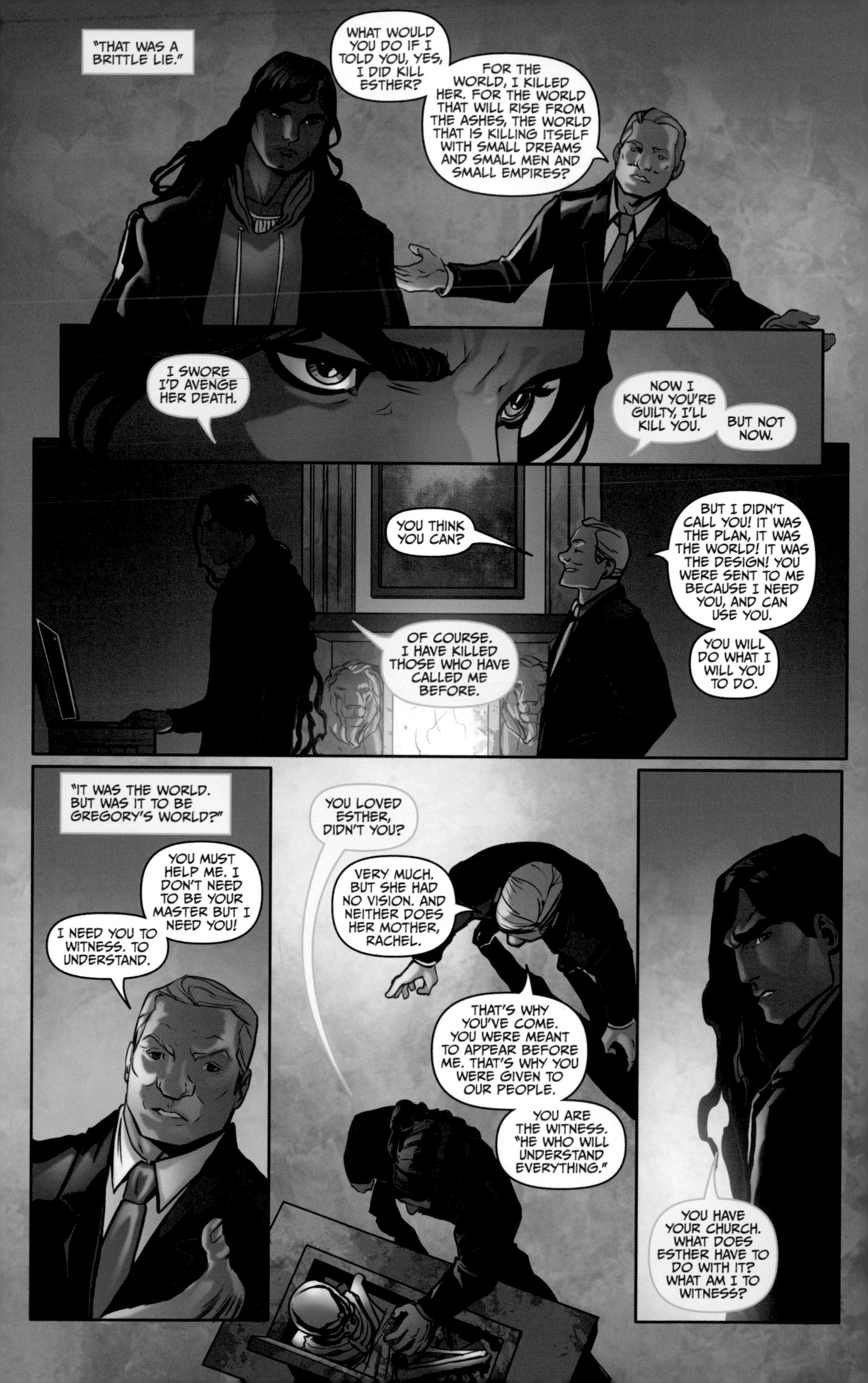

"THAT WAS A BRITTLE LIE."
WHAT WOULD YOU DO IF I TOLD YOU, YES, I DID KILL ESTHER?
FOR THE WORLD, I KILLED HER. FOR THE WORLD THAT WILL RISE FROM THE ASHES, THE WORLD THAT IS KILLING ITSELF WITH SMALL DREAMS AND SMALL MEN AND SMALL EMPIRES?
I SWORE I'D AVENGE HER DEATH.
NOW I KNOW YOU'RE GUILTY, I'LL KILL YOU.
BUT NOT NOW.
YOU THINK YOU CAN?
OF COURSE. I HAVE KILLED THOSE WHO HAVE CALLED ME BEFORE.
BUT I DIDN'T CALL YOU! IT WAS THE PLAN, IT WAS THE WORLD! IT WAS THE DESIGN! YOU WERE SENT TO ME BECAUSE I NEED YOU, AND CAN USE YOU.
YOU WILL DO WHAT I WILL YOU TO DO.
"IT WAS THE WORLD. BUT WAS IT TO BE GREGORY'S WORLD?"
YOU MUST HELP ME. I DON'T NEED TO BE YOUR MASTER BUT I NEED YOU!
I NEED YOU TO WITNESS. TO UNDERSTAND.
YOU LOVED ESTHER, DIDN'T YOU?
VERY MUCH. BUT SHE HAD NO VISION. AND NEITHER DOES HER MOTHER, RACHEL.
THAT'S WHY YOU'VE COME. YOU WERE MEANT TO APPEAR BEFORE ME. THAT'S WHY YOU WERE GIVEN TO OUR PEOPLE.
YOU ARE THE WITNESS. "HE WHO WILL UNDERSTAND EVERYTHING."
YOU HAVE YOUR CHURCH. WHAT DOES ESTHER HAVE TO DO WITH IT? WHAT AM I TO WITNESS?

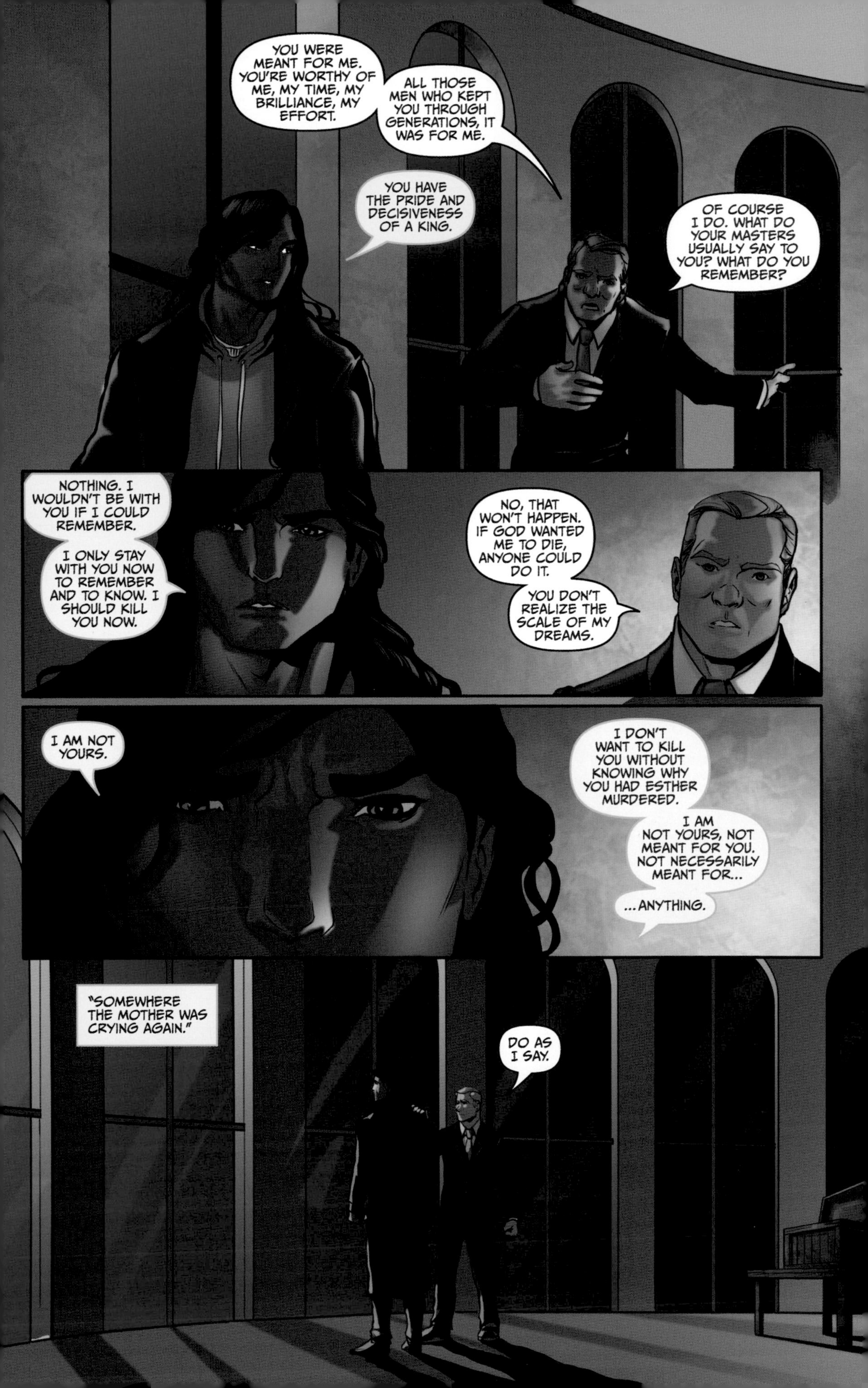
YOU WERE MEANT FOR ME. YOU'RE WORTHY OF ME, MY TIME, MY BRILLIANCE, MY EFFORT.
ALL THOSE MEN WHO KEPT YOU THROUGH GENERATIONS, IT WAS FOR ME.
YOU HAVE THE PRIDE AND DECISIVENESS OF A KING.
OF COURSE I DO. WHAT DO YOUR MASTERS USUALLY SAY TO YOU? WHAT DO YOU REMEMBER?
NOTHING. I WOULDN'T BE WITH YOU IF I COULD REMEMBER.
I ONLY STAY WITH YOU NOW TO REMEMBER AND TO KNOW. I SHOULD KILL YOU NOW.
NO, THAT WON'T HAPPEN. IF GOD WANTED ME TO DIE, ANYONE COULD DO IT.
YOU DON'T REALIZE THE SCALE OF MY DREAMS.
I AM NOT YOURS.
I DON'T WANT TO KILL YOU WITHOUT KNOWING WHY YOU HAD ESTHER MURDERED.
I AM NOT YOURS, NOT MEANT FOR YOU. NOT NECESSARILY MEANT FOR...
...ANYTHING.
"SOMEWHERE THE MOTHER WAS CRYING AGAIN."
DO AS I SAY.

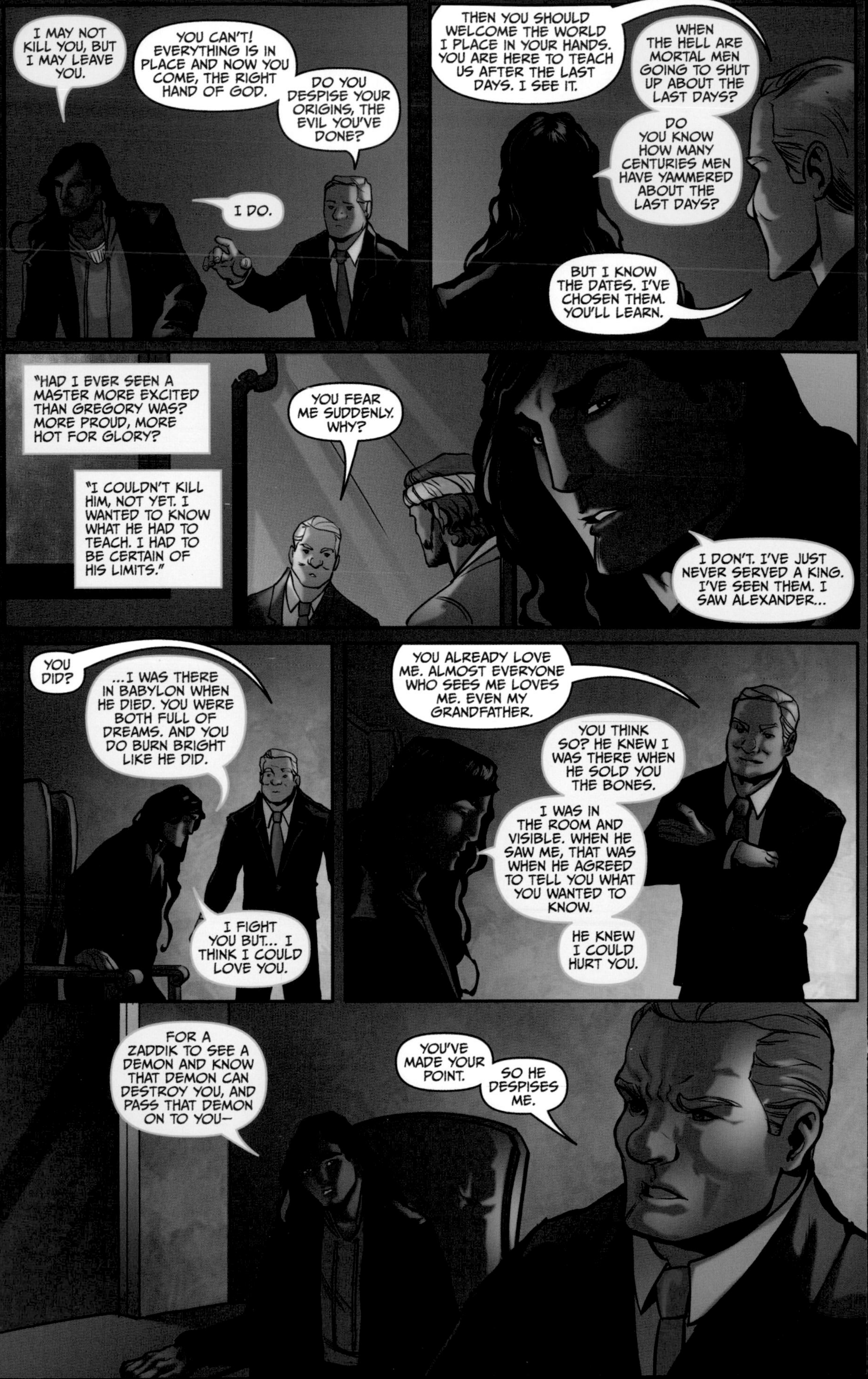
I MAY NOT KILL YOU, BUT I MAY LEAVE YOU.
YOU CAN'T! EVERYTHING IS IN PLACE AND NOW YOU COME, THE RIGHT HAND OF GOD.
DO YOU DESPISE YOUR ORIGINS, THE EVIL YOU'VE DONE?
I DO.
THEN YOU SHOULD WELCOME THE WORLD I PLACE IN YOUR HANDS. YOU ARE HERE TO TEACH US AFTER THE LAST DAYS. I SEE IT.
WHEN THE HELL ARE MORTAL MEN GOING TO SHUT UP ABOUT THE LAST DAYS?
DO YOU KNOW HOW MANY CENTURIES MEN HAVE YAMMERED ABOUT THE LAST DAYS?
BUT I KNOW THE DATES. I'VE CHOSEN THEM. YOU'LL LEARN.
"HAD I EVER SEEN A MASTER MORE EXCITED THAN GREGORY WAS? MORE PROUD, MORE HOT FOR GLORY?
"I COULDN'T KILL HIM, NOT YET. I WANTED TO KNOW WHAT HE HAD TO TEACH. I HAD TO BE CERTAIN OF HIS LIMITS."
YOU FEAR ME SUDDENLY. WHY?
I DON'T. I'VE JUST NEVER SERVED A KING. I'VE SEEN THEM. I SAW ALEXANDER...
YOU DID?
...I WAS THERE IN BABYLON WHEN HE DIED. YOU WERE BOTH FULL OF DREAMS. AND YOU DO BURN BRIGHT LIKE HE DID.
I FIGHT YOU BUT... I THINK I COULD LOVE YOU.
YOU ALREADY LOVE ME. ALMOST EVERYONE WHO SEES ME LOVES ME. EVEN MY GRANDFATHER.
YOU THINK SO? HE KNEW I WAS THERE WHEN HE SOLD YOU THE BONES.
I WAS IN THE ROOM AND VISIBLE. WHEN HE SAW ME, THAT WAS WHEN HE AGREED TO TELL YOU WHAT YOU WANTED TO KNOW.
HE KNEW I COULD HURT YOU.
FOR A ZADDIK TO SEE A DEMON AND KNOW THAT DEMON CAN DESTROY YOU, AND PASS THAT DEMON ON TO YOU—
YOU'VE MADE YOUR POINT.
SO HE DESPISES ME.

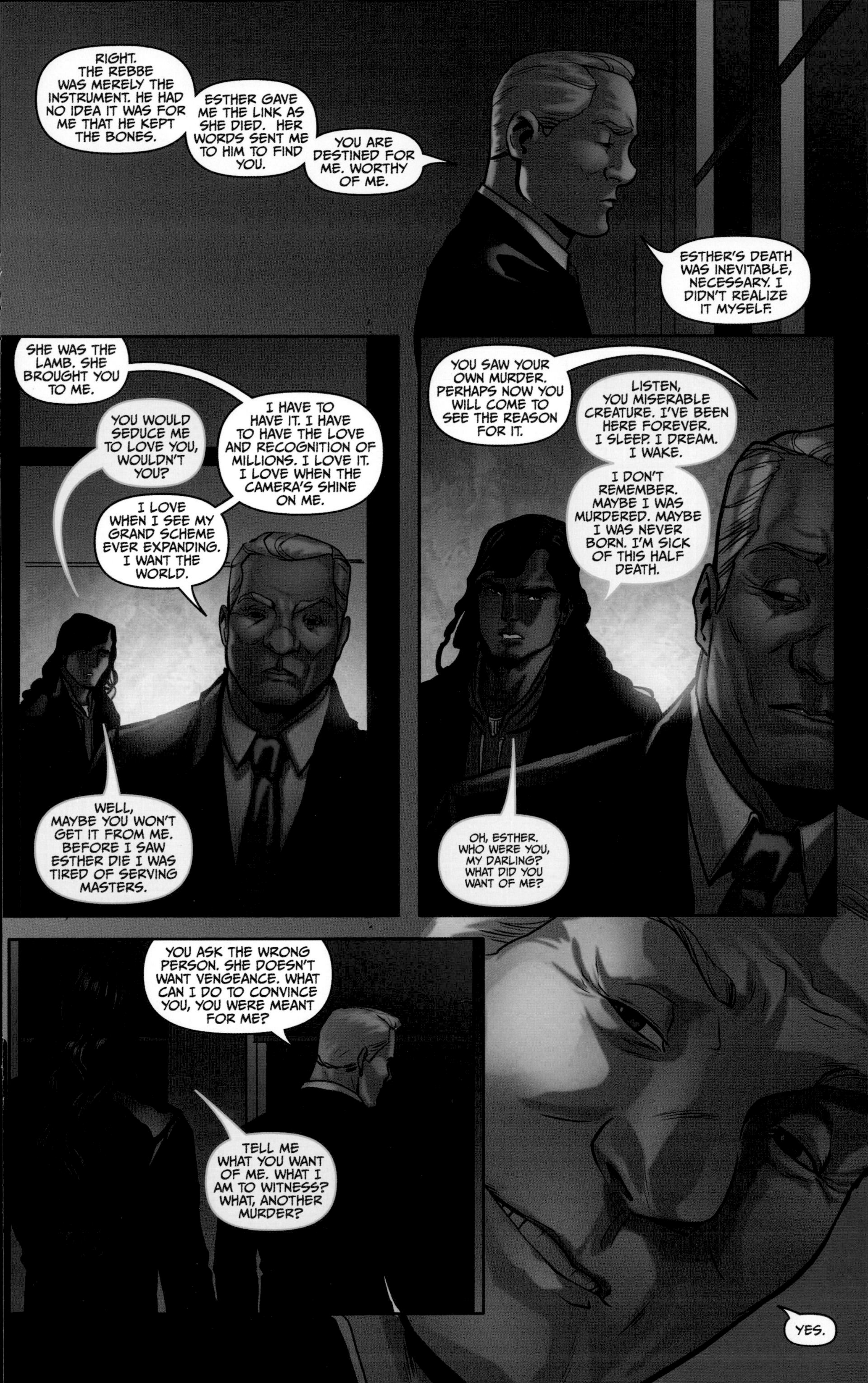
RIGHT. THE REBBE WAS MERELY THE INSTRUMENT. HE HAD NO IDEA IT WAS FOR ME THAT HE KEPT THE BONES.
ESTHER GAVE ME THE LINK AS SHE DIED. HER WORDS SENT ME TO HIM TO FIND YOU.
YOU ARE DESTINED FOR ME. WORTHY OF ME.
ESTHER'S DEATH WAS INEVITABLE, NECESSARY. I DIDN'T REALIZE IT MYSELF.
SHE WAS THE LAMB. SHE BROUGHT YOU TO ME.
YOU WOULD SEDUCE ME TO LOVE YOU, WOULDN'T YOU?
I HAVE TO HAVE IT. I HAVE TO HAVE THE LOVE AND RECOGNITION OF MILLIONS. I LOVE IT. I LOVE WHEN THE CAMERA'S SHINE ON ME.
I LOVE WHEN I SEE MY GRAND SCHEME EVER EXPANDING. I WANT THE WORLD.
WELL, MAYBE YOU WON'T GET IT FROM ME. BEFORE I SAW ESTHER DIE I WAS TIRED OF SERVING MASTERS.
YOU SAW YOUR OWN MURDER. PERHAPS NOW YOU WILL COME TO SEE THE REASON FOR IT.
LISTEN, YOU MISERABLE CREATURE. I'VE BEEN HERE FOREVER. I SLEEP. I DREAM. I WAKE.
I DON'T REMEMBER. MAYBE I WAS MURDERED. MAYBE I WAS NEVER BORN. I'M SICK OF THIS HALF DEATH.
OH, ESTHER. WHO WERE YOU, MY DARLING? WHAT DID YOU WANT OF ME?
YOU ASK THE WRONG PERSON. SHE DOESN'T WANT VENGEANCE. WHAT CAN I DO TO CONVINCE YOU, YOU WERE MEANT FOR ME?
TELL ME WHAT YOU WANT OF ME. WHAT I AM TO WITNESS? WHAT, ANOTHER MURDER?
YES.

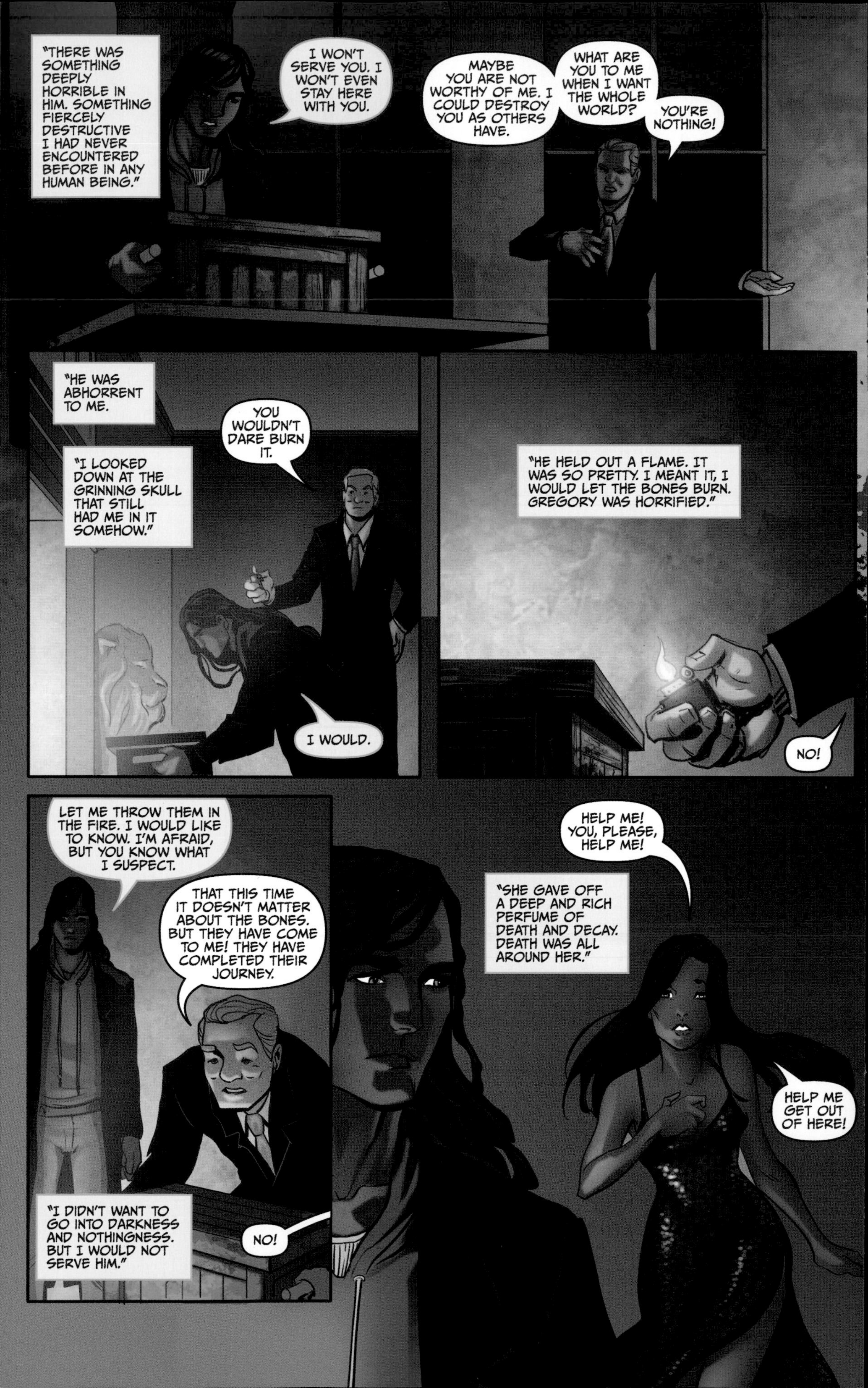
"THERE WAS SOMETHING DEEPLY HORRIBLE IN HIM. SOMETHING FIERCELY DESTRUCTIVE I HAD NEVER ENCOUNTERED BEFORE IN ANY HUMAN BEING."
I WON'T SERVE YOU. I WON'T EVEN STAY HERE WITH YOU.
MAYBE YOU ARE NOT WORTHY OF ME. I COULD DESTROY YOU AS OTHERS HAVE.
WHAT ARE YOU TO ME WHEN I WANT THE WHOLE WORLD?
YOU'RE NOTHING!
"HE WAS ABHORRENT TO ME.
"I LOOKED DOWN AT THE GRINNING SKULL THAT STILL HAD ME IN IT SOMEHOW."
YOU WOULDN'T DARE BURN IT.
I WOULD.
"HE HELD OUT A FLAME. IT WAS SO PRETTY. I MEANT IT, I WOULD LET THE BONES BURN. GREGORY WAS HORRIFIED."
NO!
LET ME THROW THEM IN THE FIRE. I WOULD LIKE TO KNOW. I'M AFRAID, BUT YOU KNOW WHAT I SUSPECT.
THAT THIS TIME IT DOESN'T MATTER ABOUT THE BONES. BUT THEY HAVE COME TO ME! THEY HAVE COMPLETED THEIR JOURNEY.
"I DIDN'T WANT TO GO INTO DARKNESS AND NOTHINGNESS. BUT I WOULD NOT SERVE HIM."
NO!
HELP ME! YOU, PLEASE, HELP ME!
"SHE GAVE OFF A DEEP AND RICH PERFUME OF DEATH AND DECAY. DEATH WAS ALL AROUND HER."
HELP ME GET OUT OF HERE!

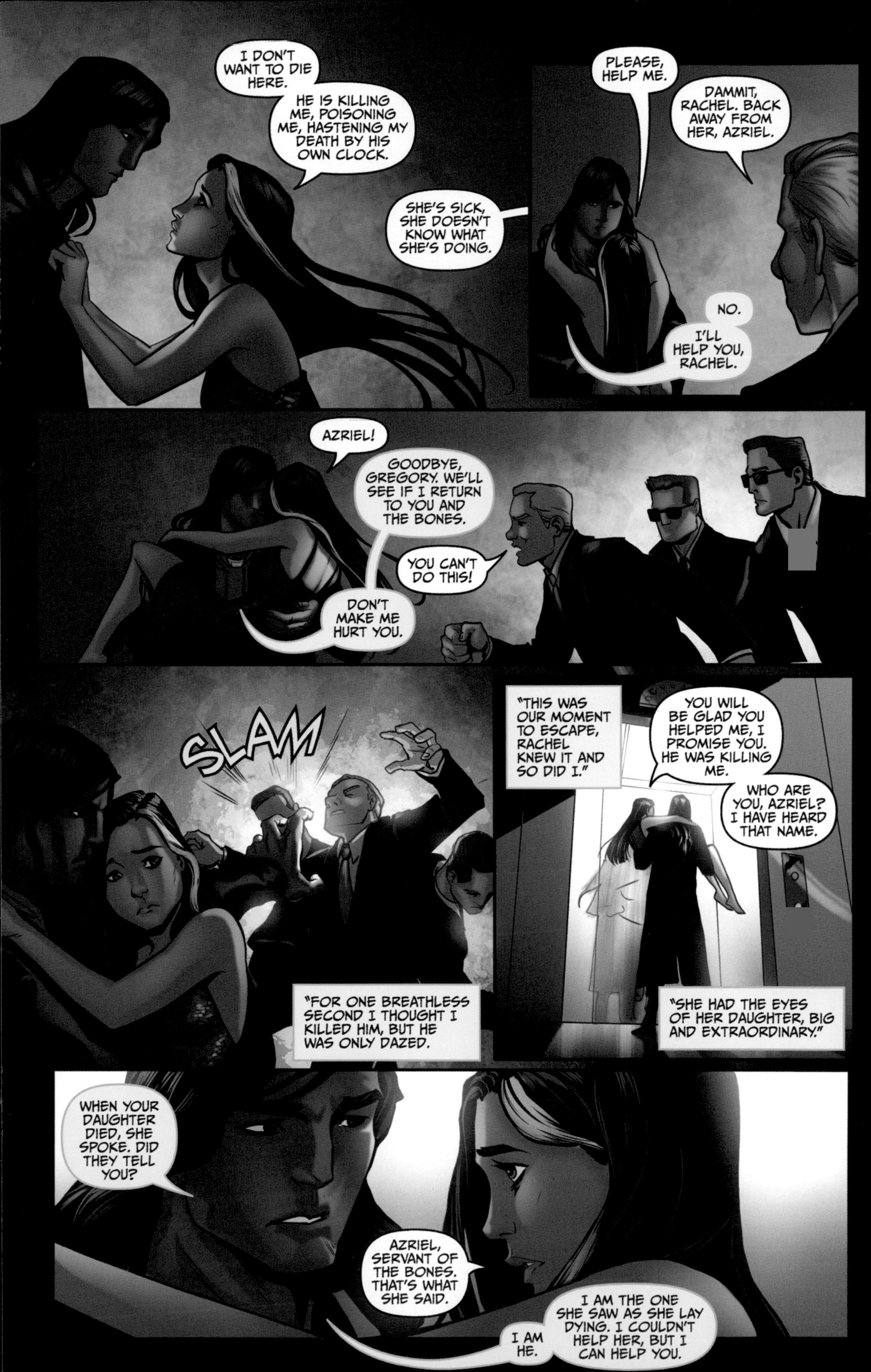
I DON'T WANT TO DIE HERE.
HE IS KILLING ME, POISONING ME, HASTENING MY DEATH BY HIS OWN CLOCK.
SHE'S SICK, SHE DOESN'T KNOW WHAT SHE'S DOING.
PLEASE, HELP ME.
DAMMIT, RACHEL. BACK AWAY FROM HER, AZRIEL.
NO.
I'LL HELP YOU, RACHEL.
AZRIEL!
GOODBYE, GREGORY. WE'LL SEE IF I RETURN TO YOU AND THE BONES.
YOU CAN'T DO THIS!
DON'T MAKE ME HURT YOU.
SLAM
"FOR ONE BREATHLESS SECOND I THOUGHT I KILLED HIM, BUT HE WAS ONLY DAZED.
"THIS WAS OUR MOMENT TO ESCAPE, RACHEL KNEW IT AND SO DID I."
YOU WILL BE GLAD YOU HELPED ME, I PROMISE YOU. HE WAS KILLING ME.
WHO ARE YOU, AZRIEL? I HAVE HEARD THAT NAME.
"SHE HAD THE EYES OF HER DAUGHTER, BIG AND EXTRAORDINARY."
WHEN YOUR DAUGHTER DIED, SHE SPOKE. DID THEY TELL YOU?
AZRIEL, SERVANT OF THE BONES. THAT'S WHAT SHE SAID.
I AM HE.
I AM THE ONE SHE SAW AS SHE LAY DYING. I COULDN'T HELP HER, BUT I CAN HELP YOU.

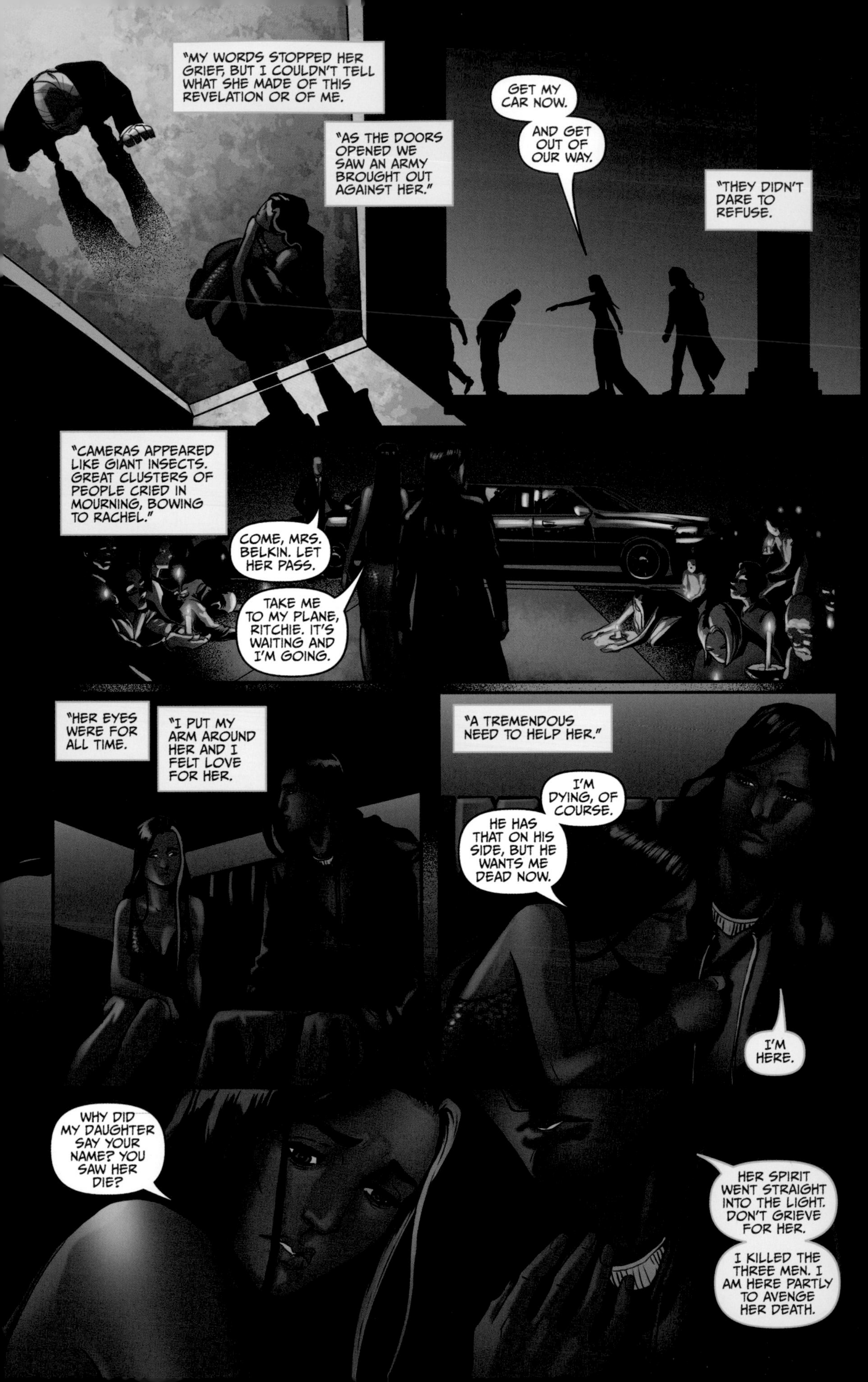
"MY WORDS STOPPED HER GRIEF, BUT I COULDN'T TELL WHAT SHE MADE OF THIS REVELATION OR OF ME.
"AS THE DOORS OPENED WE SAW AN ARMY BROUGHT OUT AGAINST HER."
GET MY CAR NOW.
AND GET OUT OF OUR WAY.
"THEY DIDN'T DARE TO REFUSE.
"CAMERAS APPEARED LIKE GIANT INSECTS. GREAT CLUSTERS OF PEOPLE CRIED IN MOURNING, BOWING TO RACHEL."
COME, MRS. BELKIN. LET HER PASS.
TAKE ME TO MY PLANE, RITCHIE. IT'S WAITING AND I'M GOING.
"HER EYES WERE FOR ALL TIME.
"I PUT MY ARM AROUND HER AND I FELT LOVE FOR HER.
"A TREMENDOUS NEED TO HELP HER."
I'M DYING, OF COURSE.
HE HAS THAT ON HIS SIDE, BUT HE WANTS ME DEAD NOW.
I'M HERE.
WHY DID MY DAUGHTER SAY YOUR NAME? YOU SAW HER DIE?
HER SPIRIT WENT STRAIGHT INTO THE LIGHT. DON'T GRIEVE FOR HER.
I KILLED THE THREE MEN. I AM HERE PARTLY TO AVENGE HER DEATH.

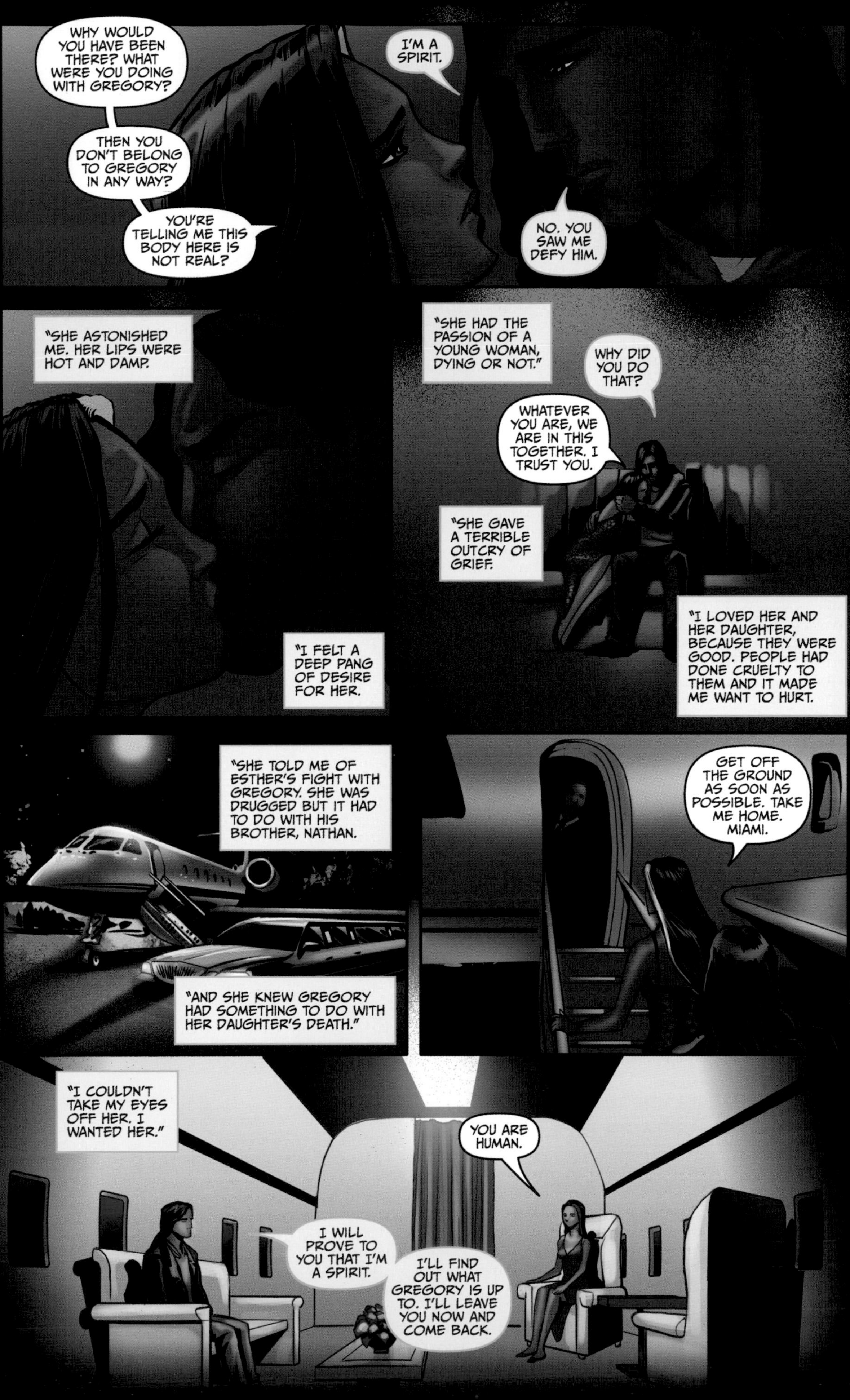
WHY WOULD YOU HAVE BEEN THERE? WHAT WERE YOU DOING WITH GREGORY?
I'M A SPIRIT.
THEN YOU DON'T BELONG TO GREGORY IN ANY WAY?
NO. YOU SAW ME DEFY HIM.
YOU'RE TELLING ME THIS BODY HERE IS NOT REAL?
"SHE ASTONISHED ME. HER LIPS WERE HOT AND DAMP.
"I FELT A DEEP PANG OF DESIRE FOR HER.
"SHE HAD THE PASSION OF A YOUNG WOMAN, DYING OR NOT."
WHY DID YOU DO THAT?
WHATEVER YOU ARE, WE ARE IN THIS TOGETHER. I TRUST YOU.
"SHE GAVE A TERRIBLE OUTCRY OF GRIEF.
"I LOVED HER AND HER DAUGHTER, BECAUSE THEY WERE GOOD. PEOPLE HAD DONE CRUELTY TO THEM AND IT MADE ME WANT TO HURT.
"SHE TOLD ME OF ESTHER'S FIGHT WITH GREGORY. SHE WAS DRUGGED BUT IT HAD TO DO WITH HIS BROTHER, NATHAN.
"AND SHE KNEW GREGORY HAD SOMETHING TO DO WITH HER DAUGHTER'S DEATH."
GET OFF THE GROUND AS SOON AS POSSIBLE. TAKE ME HOME. MIAMI.
"I COULDN'T TAKE MY EYES OFF HER. I WANTED HER."
YOU ARE HUMAN.
I WILL PROVE TO YOU THAT I'M A SPIRIT.
I'LL FIND OUT WHAT GREGORY IS UP TO. I'LL LEAVE YOU NOW AND COME BACK.

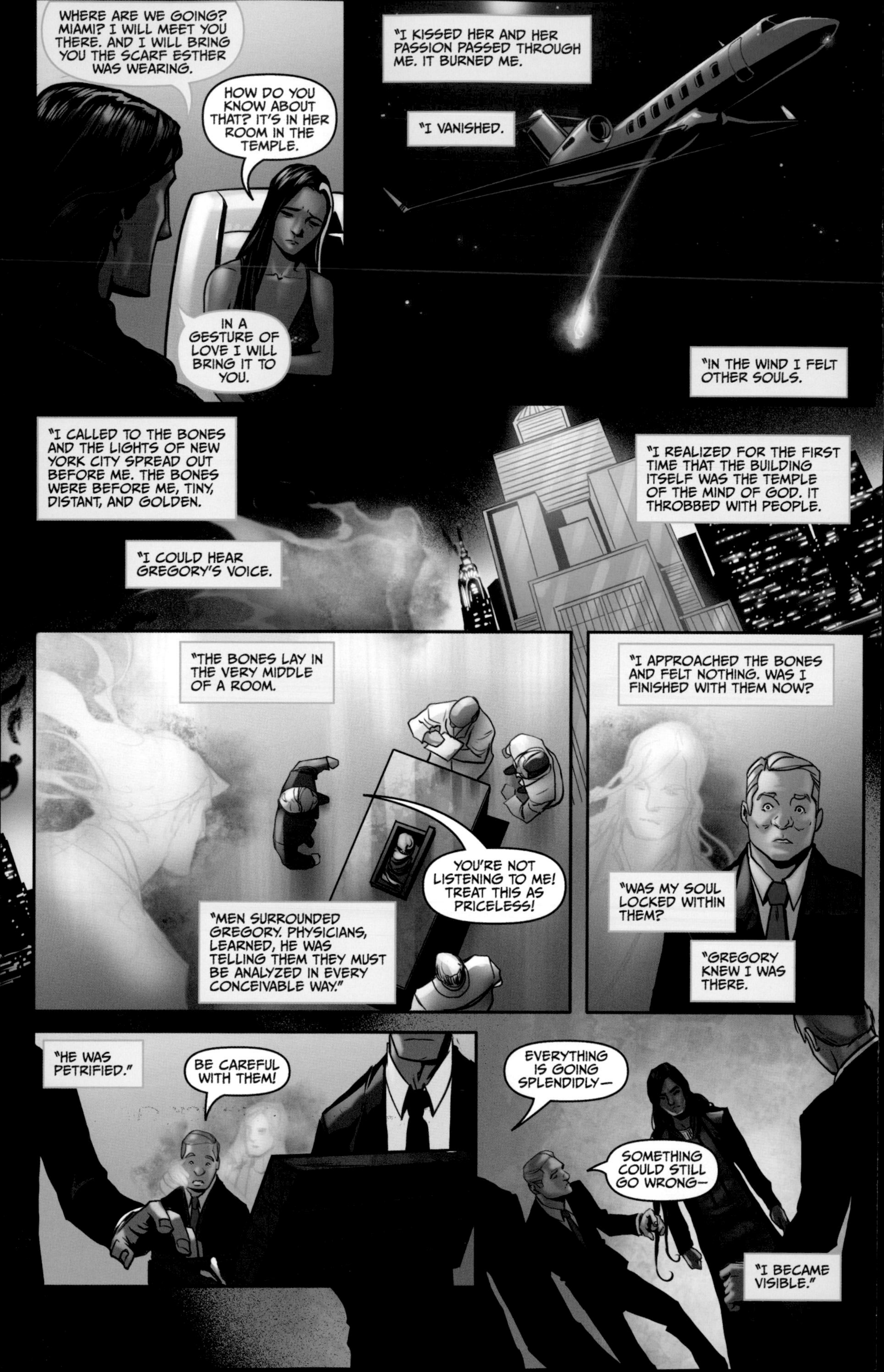
WHERE ARE WE GOING? MIAMI? I WILL MEET YOU THERE. AND I WILL BRING YOU THE SCARF ESTHER WAS WEARING.
HOW DO YOU KNOW ABOUT THAT? IT'S IN HER ROOM IN THE TEMPLE.
IN A GESTURE OF LOVE I WILL BRING IT TO YOU.
"I KISSED HER AND HER PASSION PASSED THROUGH ME. IT BURNED ME.
"I VANISHED.
"IN THE WIND I FELT OTHER SOULS.
"I CALLED TO THE BONES AND THE LIGHTS OF NEW YORK CITY SPREAD OUT BEFORE ME. THE BONES WERE BEFORE ME, TINY, DISTANT, AND GOLDEN.
"I COULD HEAR GREGORY'S VOICE.
"I REALIZED FOR THE FIRST TIME THAT THE BUILDING ITSELF WAS THE TEMPLE OF THE MIND OF GOD. IT THROBBED WITH PEOPLE.
"THE BONES LAY IN THE VERY MIDDLE OF A ROOM.
YOU'RE NOT LISTENING TO ME! TREAT THIS AS PRICELESS!
"MEN SURROUNDED GREGORY. PHYSICIANS, LEARNED, HE WAS TELLING THEM THEY MUST BE ANALYZED IN EVERY CONCEIVABLE WAY."
"I APPROACHED THE BONES AND FELT NOTHING. WAS I FINISHED WITH THEM NOW?
"WAS MY SOUL LOCKED WITHIN THEM?
"GREGORY KNEW I WAS THERE.
"HE WAS PETRIFIED."
BE CAREFUL WITH THEM!
EVERYTHING IS GOING SPLENDIDLY—
SOMETHING COULD STILL GO WRONG—
"I BECAME VISIBLE."

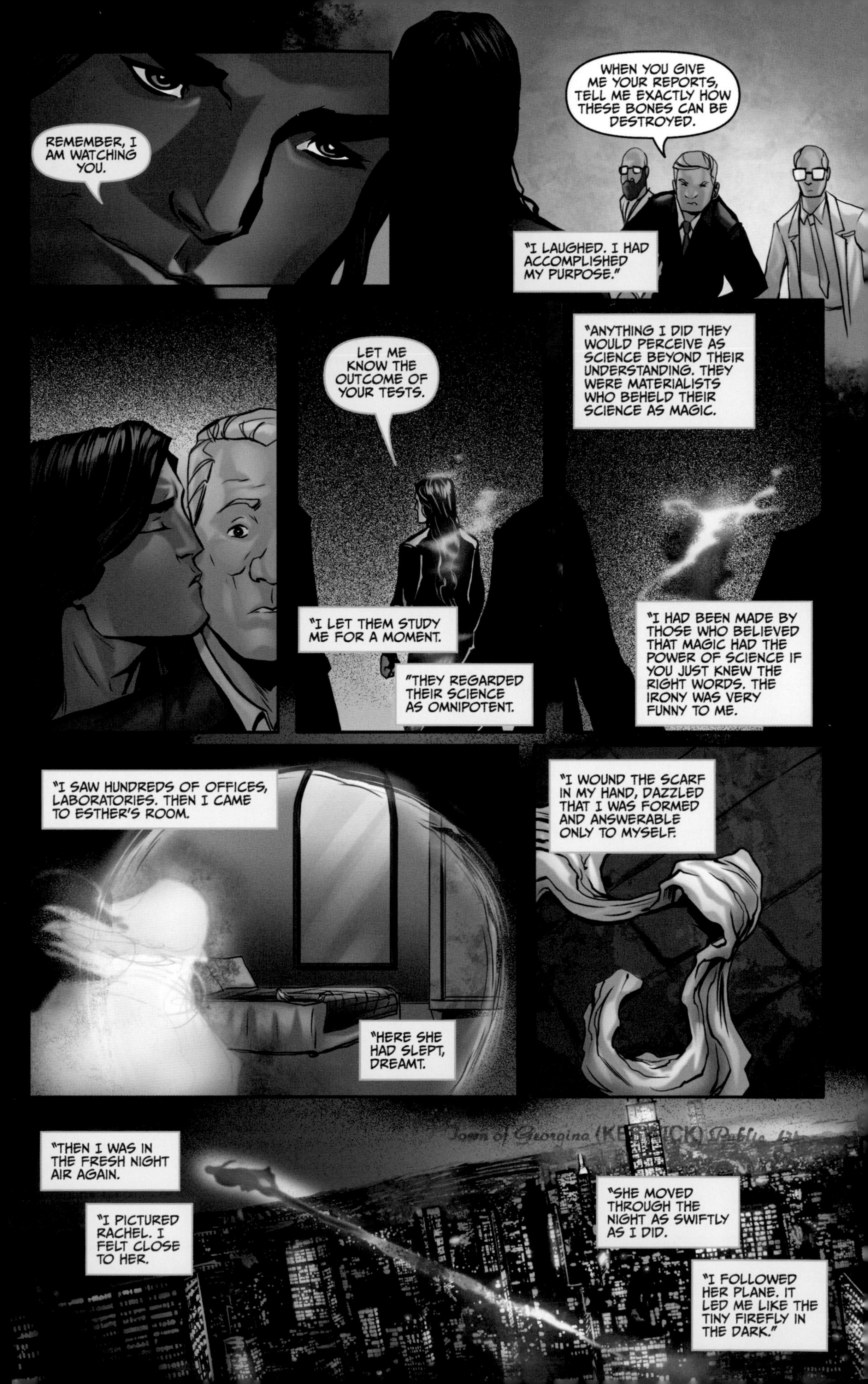
REMEMBER, I AM WATCHING YOU.
WHEN YOU GIVE ME YOUR REPORTS, TELL ME EXACTLY HOW THESE BONES CAN BE DESTROYED.
"I LAUGHED. I HAD ACCOMPLISHED MY PURPOSE."
LET ME KNOW THE OUTCOME OF YOUR TESTS.
"I LET THEM STUDY ME FOR A MOMENT.
"THEY REGARDED THEIR SCIENCE AS OMNIPOTENT.
"ANYTHING I DID THEY WOULD PERCEIVE AS SCIENCE BEYOND THEIR UNDERSTANDING. THEY WERE MATERIALISTS WHO BEHELD THEIR SCIENCE AS MAGIC.
"I HAD BEEN MADE BY THOSE WHO BELIEVED THAT MAGIC HAD THE POWER OF SCIENCE IF YOU JUST KNEW THE RIGHT WORDS. THE IRONY WAS VERY FUNNY TO ME.
"I SAW HUNDREDS OF OFFICES, LABORATORIES. THEN I CAME TO ESTHER'S ROOM.
"HERE SHE HAD SLEPT, DREAMT.
"I WOUND THE SCARF IN MY HAND, DAZZLED THAT I WAS FORMED AND ANSWERABLE ONLY TO MYSELF.
"THEN I WAS IN THE FRESH NIGHT AIR AGAIN.
"I PICTURED RACHEL. I FELT CLOSE TO HER.
"SHE MOVED THROUGH THE NIGHT AS SWIFTLY AS I DID.
"I FOLLOWED HER PLANE. IT LED ME LIKE THE TINY FIREFLY IN THE DARK."

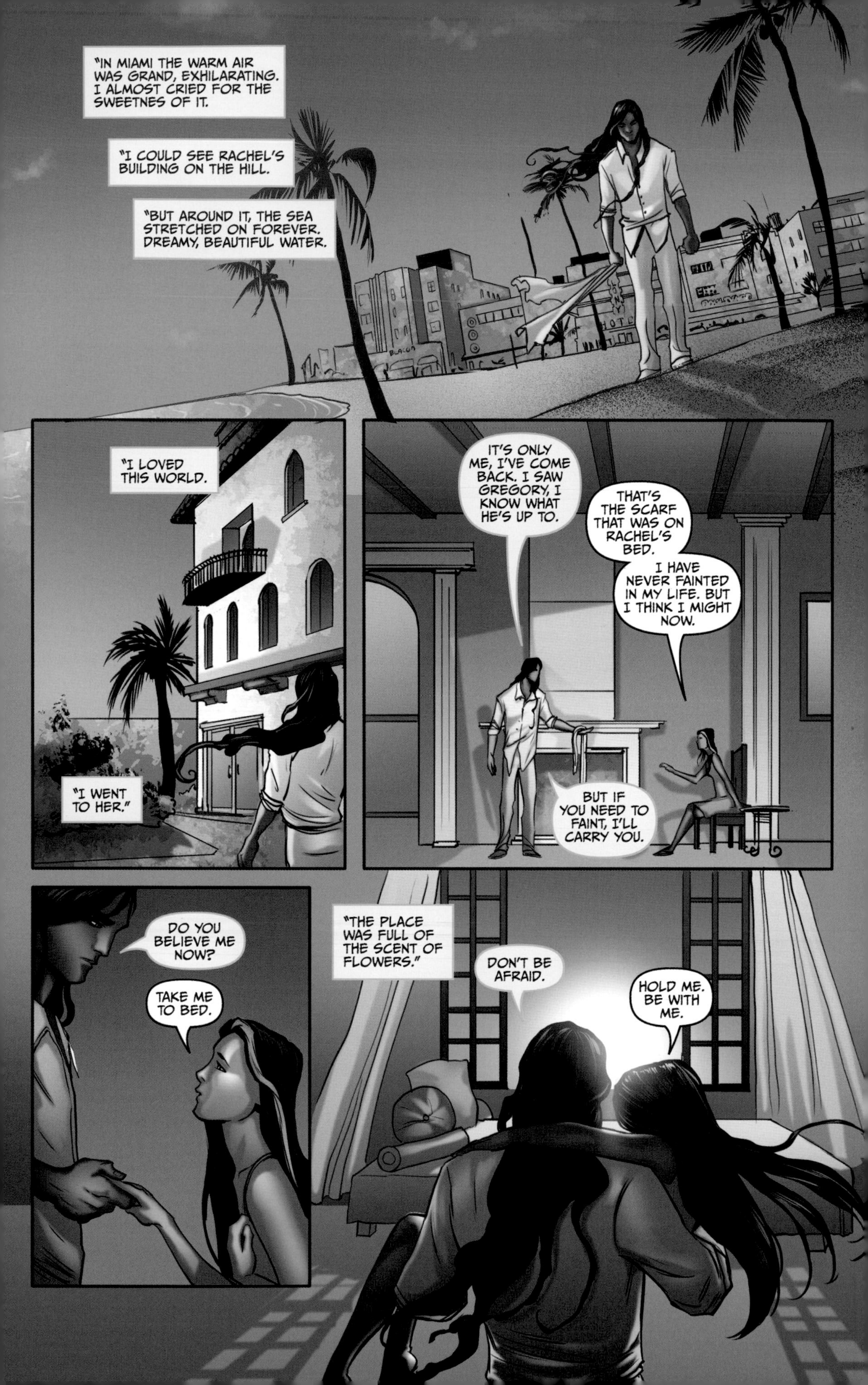
"IN MIAMI THE WARM AIR WAS GRAND, EXHILARATING. I ALMOST CRIED FOR THE SWEETNES OF IT.
"I COULD SEE RACHEL'S BUILDING ON THE HILL.
"BUT AROUND IT, THE SEA STRETCHED ON FOREVER. DREAMY, BEAUTIFUL WATER.
"I LOVED THIS WORLD.
"I WENT TO HER."
IT'S ONLY ME, I'VE COME BACK. I SAW GREGORY, I KNOW WHAT HE'S UP TO.
THAT'S THE SCARF THAT WAS ON RACHEL'S BED.
I HAVE NEVER FAINTED IN MY LIFE. BUT I THINK I MIGHT NOW.
BUT IF YOU NEED TO FAINT, I'LL CARRY YOU.
DO YOU BELIEVE ME NOW?
TAKE ME TO BED.
"THE PLACE WAS FULL OF THE SCENT OF FLOWERS."
DON'T BE AFRAID.
HOLD ME. BE WITH ME.

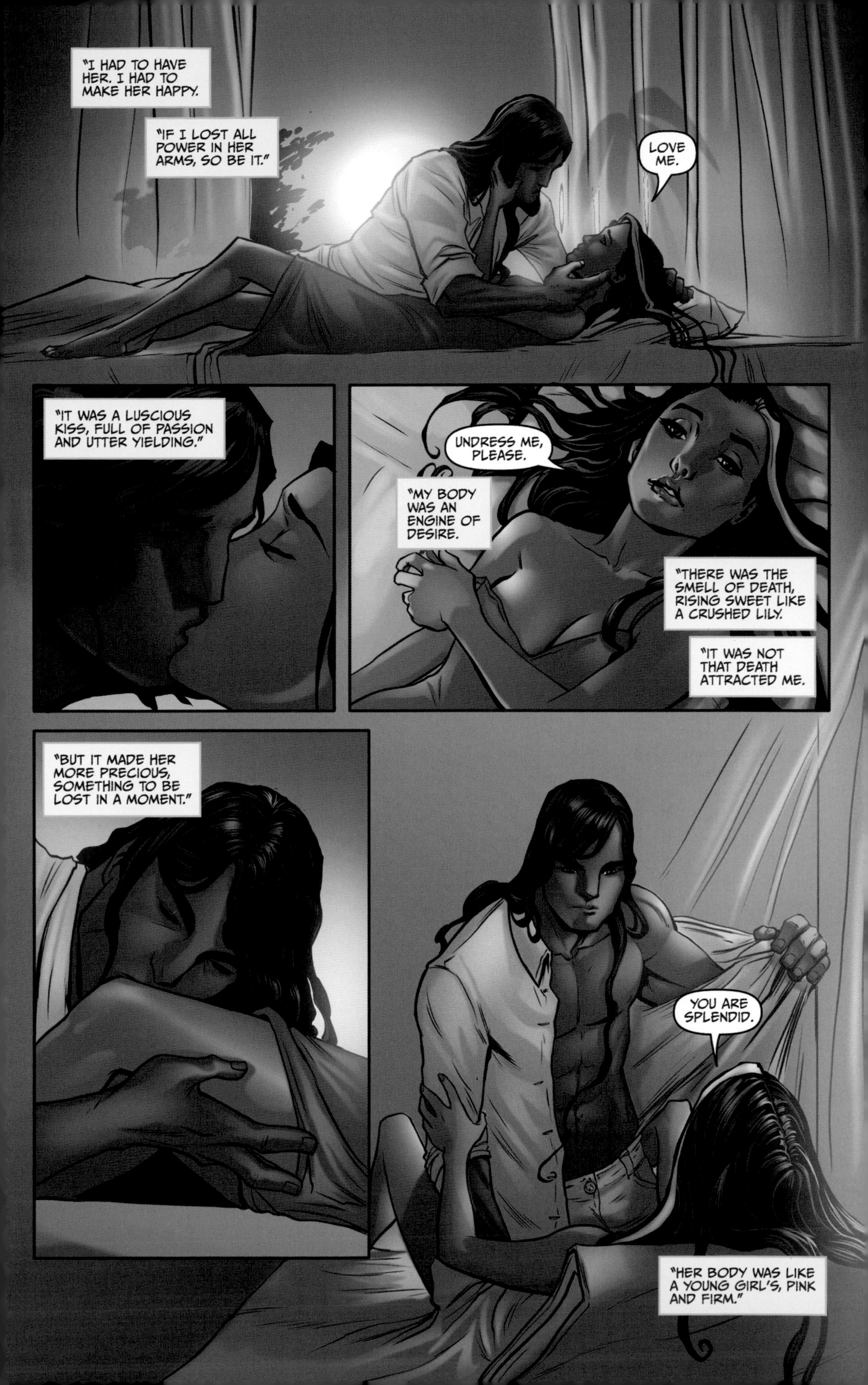
"I HAD TO HAVE HER. I HAD TO MAKE HER HAPPY.
"IF I LOST ALL POWER IN HER ARMS, SO BE IT."
LOVE ME.
"IT WAS A LUSCIOUS KISS, FULL OF PASSION AND UTTER YIELDING."
UNDRESS ME, PLEASE.
"MY BODY WAS AN ENGINE OF DESIRE.
"THERE WAS THE SMELL OF DEATH, RISING SWEET LIKE A CRUSHED LILY.
"IT WAS NOT THAT DEATH ATTRACTED ME.
"BUT IT MADE HER MORE PRECIOUS, SOMETHING TO BE LOST IN A MOMENT."
YOU ARE SPLENDID.
"HER BODY WAS LIKE A YOUNG GIRL'S, PINK AND FIRM."

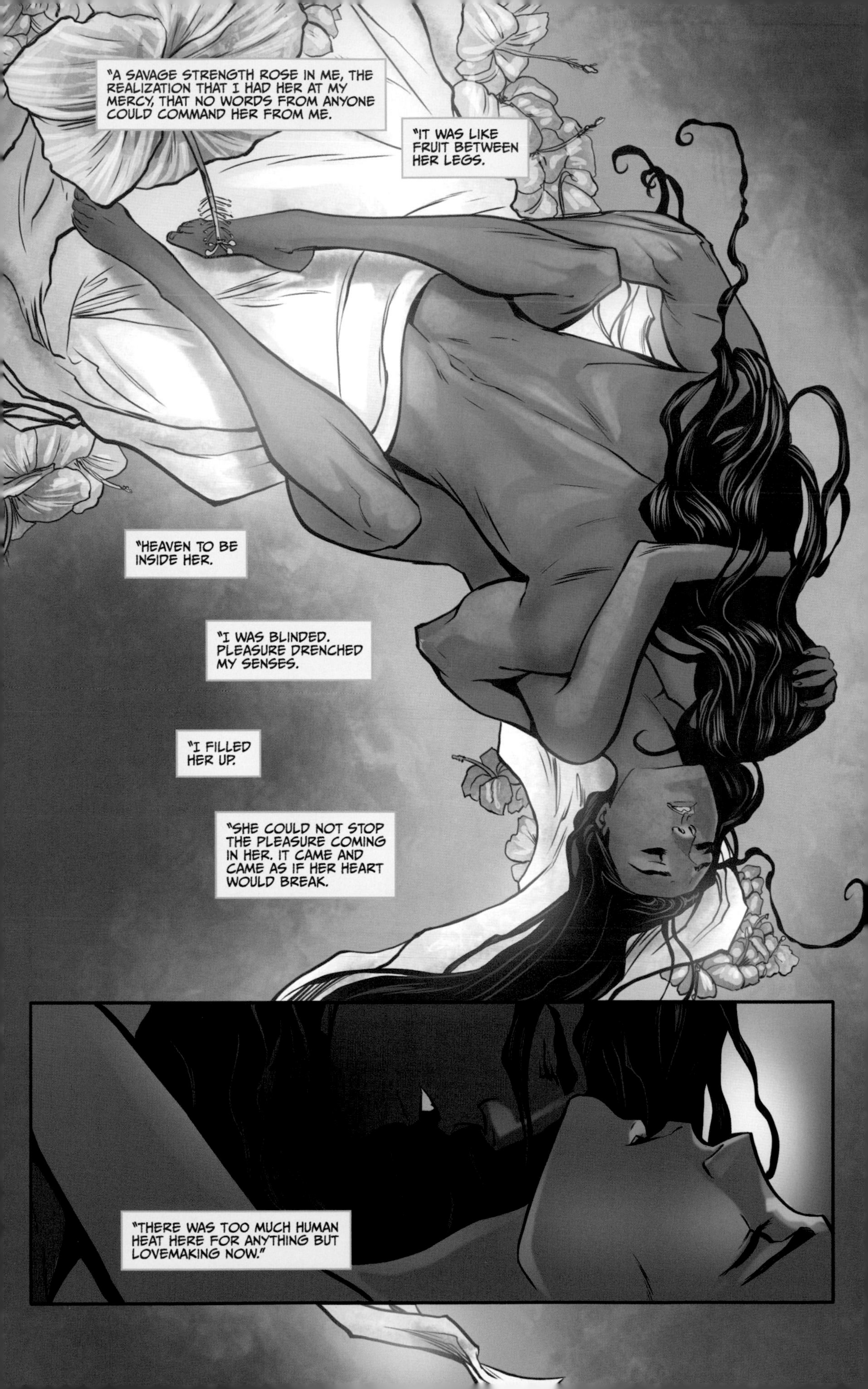
"A SAVAGE STRENGTH ROSE IN ME, THE REALIZATION THAT I HAD HER AT MY MERCY, THAT NO WORDS FROM ANYONE COULD COMMAND HER FROM ME.
"IT WAS LIKE FRUIT BETWEEN HER LEGS.
"HEAVEN TO BE INSIDE HER.
"I WAS BLINDED. PLEASURE DRENCHED MY SENSES.
"I FILLED HER UP.
"SHE COULD NOT STOP THE PLEASURE COMING IN HER. IT CAME AND CAME AS IF HER HEART WOULD BREAK.
"THERE WAS TOO MUCH HUMAN HEAT HERE FOR ANYTHING BUT LOVEMAKING NOW."

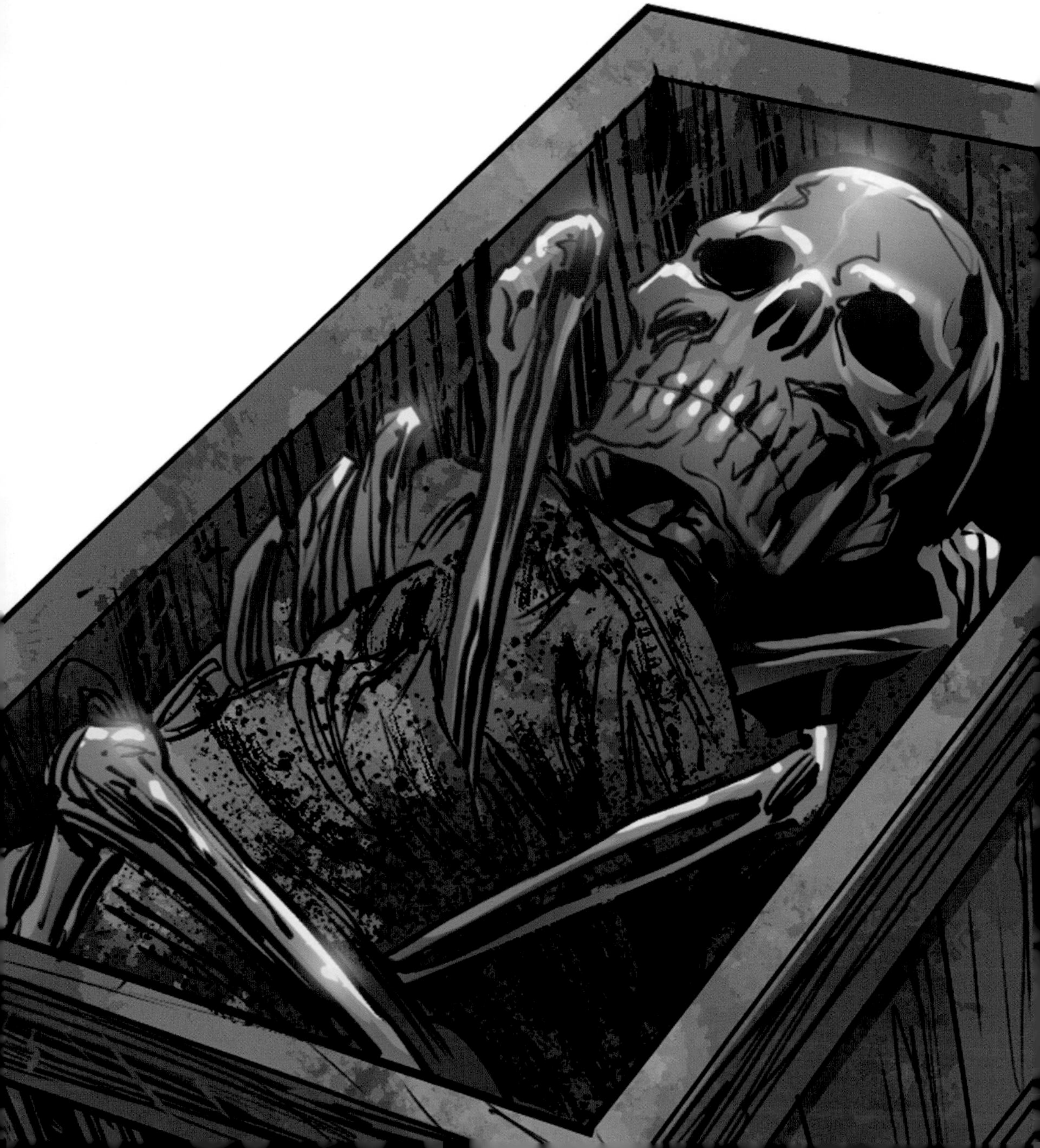

Chapter Six

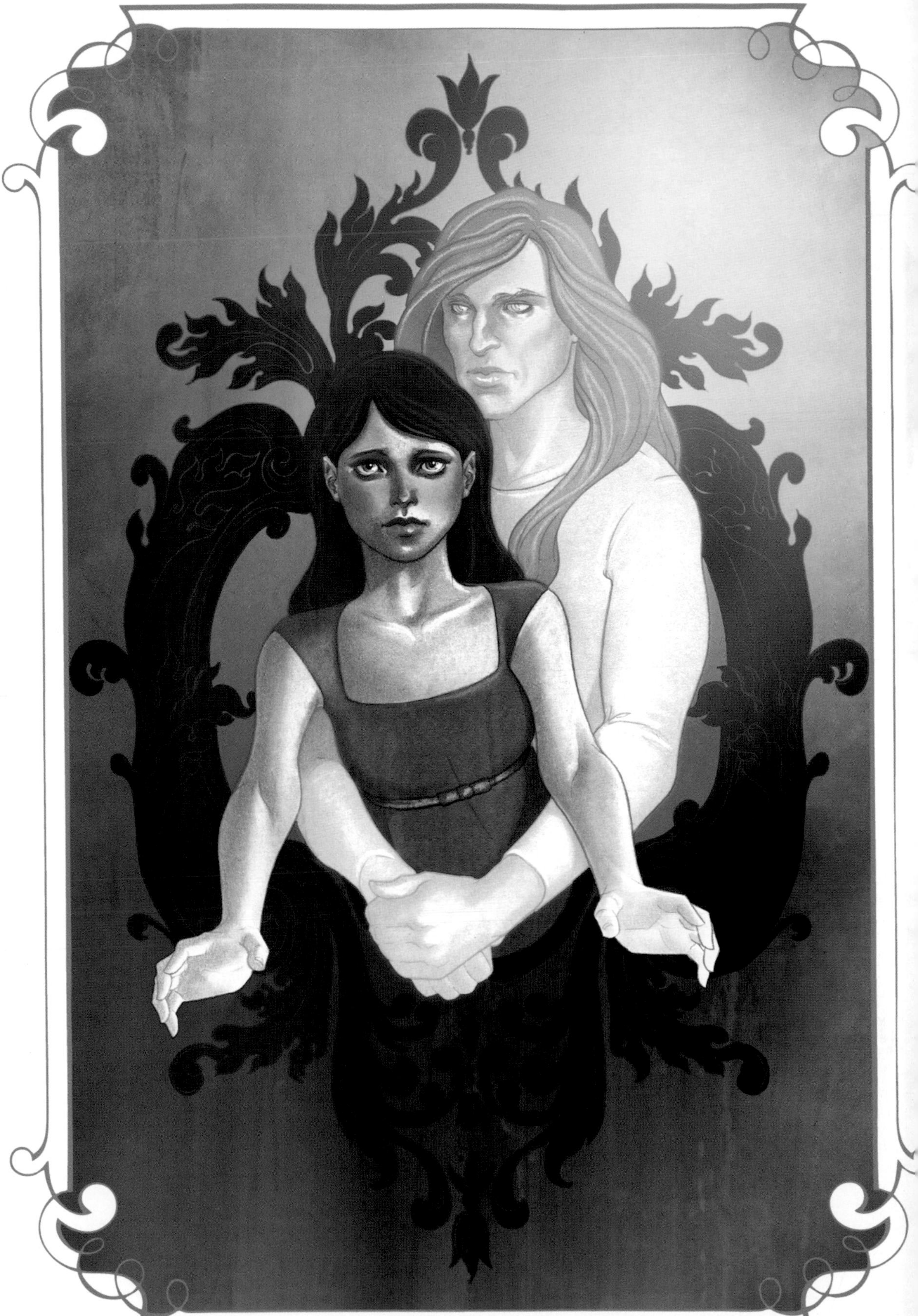

Art by Jenny Frison

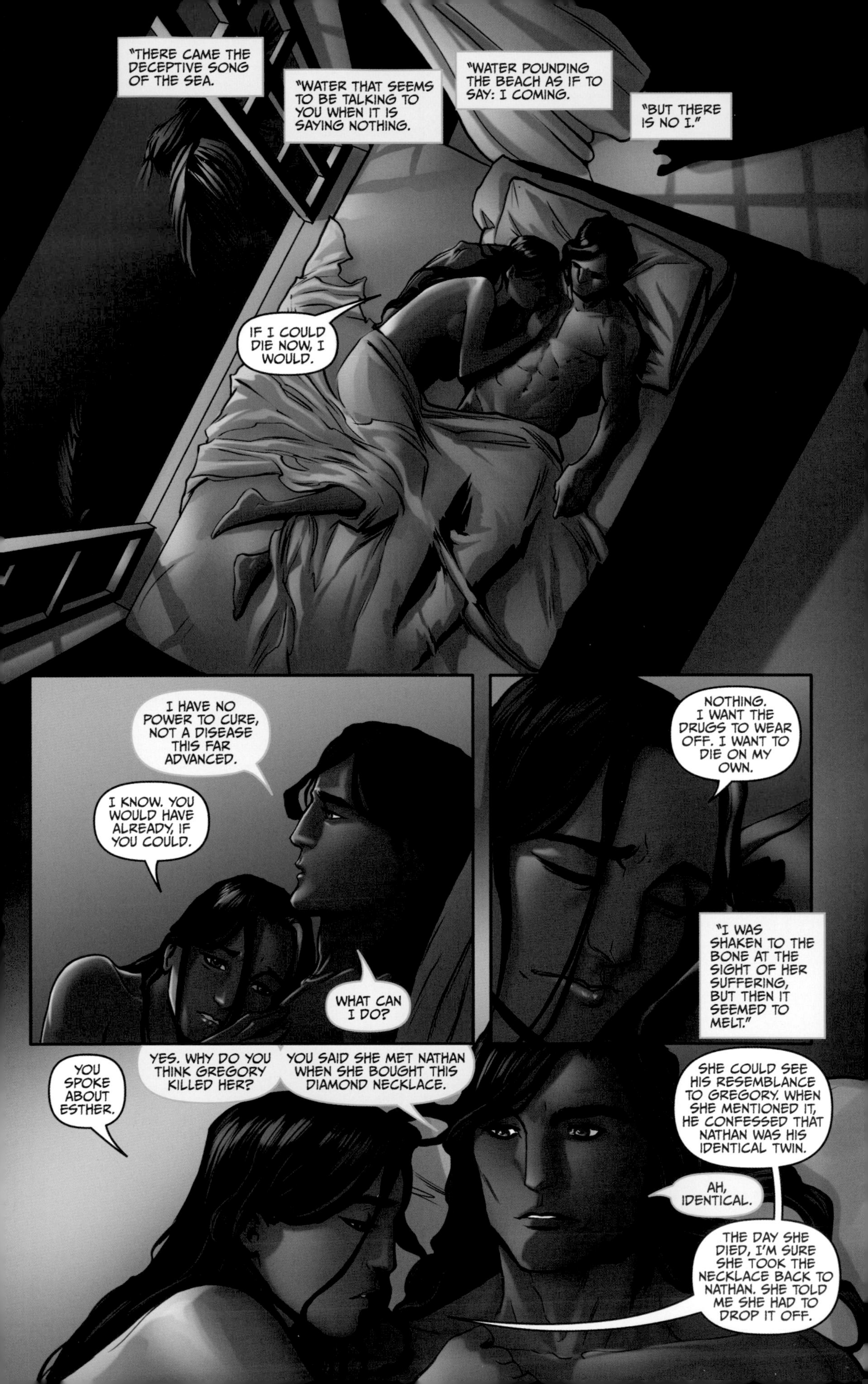
"THERE CAME THE DECEPTIVE SONG OF THE SEA.
"WATER THAT SEEMS TO BE TALKING TO YOU WHEN IT IS SAYING NOTHING.
"WATER POUNDING THE BEACH AS IF TO SAY: I COMING.
"BUT THERE IS NO I."
IF I COULD DIE NOW, I WOULD.
I HAVE NO POWER TO CURE, NOT A DISEASE THIS FAR ADVANCED.
I KNOW. YOU WOULD HAVE ALREADY, IF YOU COULD.
WHAT CAN I DO?
NOTHING. I WANT THE DRUGS TO WEAR OFF. I WANT TO DIE ON MY OWN.
"I WAS SHAKEN TO THE BONE AT THE SIGHT OF HER SUFFERING, BUT THEN IT SEEMED TO MELT."
YOU SPOKE ABOUT ESTHER.
YES. WHY DO YOU THINK GREGORY KILLED HER?
YOU SAID SHE MET NATHAN WHEN SHE BOUGHT THIS DIAMOND NECKLACE.
SHE COULD SEE HIS RESEMBLANCE TO GREGORY. WHEN SHE MENTIONED IT, HE CONFESSED THAT NATHAN WAS HIS IDENTICAL TWIN.
AH, IDENTICAL.
THE DAY SHE DIED, I'M SURE SHE TOOK THE NECKLACE BACK TO NATHAN. SHE TOLD ME SHE HAD TO DROP IT OFF.

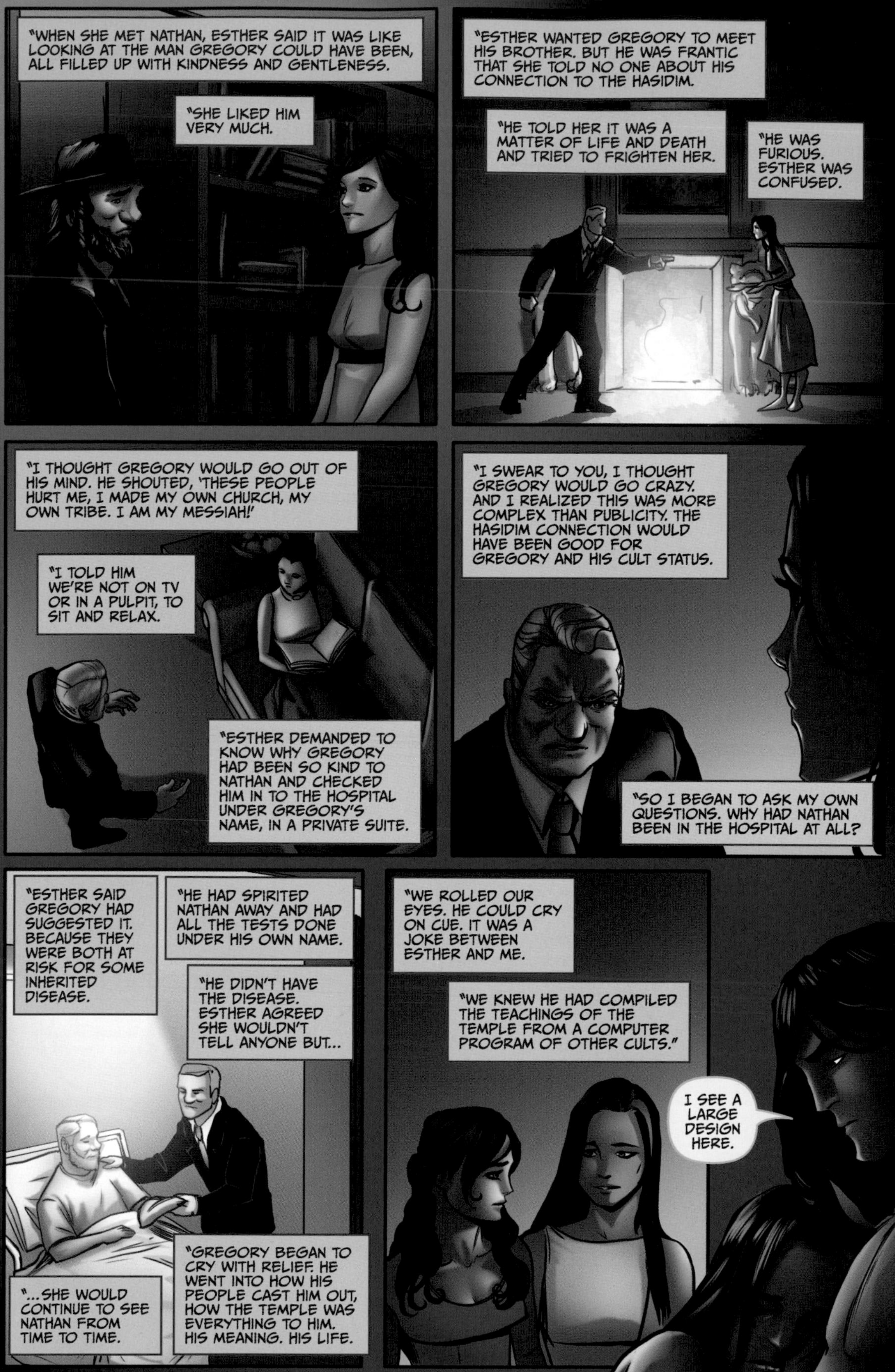
"WHEN SHE MET NATHAN, ESTHER SAID IT WAS LIKE LOOKING AT THE MAN GREGORY COULD HAVE BEEN, ALL FILLED UP WITH KINDNESS AND GENTLENESS.
"SHE LIKED HIM VERY MUCH.
"ESTHER WANTED GREGORY TO MEET HIS BROTHER. BUT HE WAS FRANTIC THAT SHE TOLD NO ONE ABOUT HIS CONNECTION TO THE HASIDIM.
"HE TOLD HER IT WAS A MATTER OF LIFE AND DEATH AND TRIED TO FRIGHTEN HER.
"HE WAS FURIOUS. ESTHER WAS CONFUSED.
"I THOUGHT GREGORY WOULD GO OUT OF HIS MIND. HE SHOUTED, 'THESE PEOPLE HURT ME, I MADE MY OWN CHURCH, MY OWN TRIBE. I AM MY MESSIAH!'
"I TOLD HIM WE'RE NOT ON TV OR IN A PULPIT, TO SIT AND RELAX.
"ESTHER DEMANDED TO KNOW WHY GREGORY HAD BEEN SO KIND TO NATHAN AND CHECKED HIM IN TO THE HOSPITAL UNDER GREGORY'S NAME, IN A PRIVATE SUITE.
"I SWEAR TO YOU, I THOUGHT GREGORY WOULD GO CRAZY. AND I REALIZED THIS WAS MORE COMPLEX THAN PUBLICITY. THE HASIDIM CONNECTION WOULD HAVE BEEN GOOD FOR GREGORY AND HIS CULT STATUS.
"SO I BEGAN TO ASK MY OWN QUESTIONS. WHY HAD NATHAN BEEN IN THE HOSPITAL AT ALL?
"ESTHER SAID GREGORY HAD SUGGESTED IT. BECAUSE THEY WERE BOTH AT RISK FOR SOME INHERITED DISEASE.
"HE HAD SPIRITED NATHAN AWAY AND HAD ALL THE TESTS DONE UNDER HIS OWN NAME.
"HE DIDN'T HAVE THE DISEASE. ESTHER AGREED SHE WOULDN'T TELL ANYONE BUT...
"...SHE WOULD CONTINUE TO SEE NATHAN FROM TIME TO TIME.
"GREGORY BEGAN TO CRY WITH RELIEF. HE WENT INTO HOW HIS PEOPLE CAST HIM OUT, HOW THE TEMPLE WAS EVERYTHING TO HIM. HIS MEANING. HIS LIFE.
"WE ROLLED OUR EYES. HE COULD CRY ON CUE. IT WAS A JOKE BETWEEN ESTHER AND ME.
"WE KNEW HE HAD COMPILED THE TEACHINGS OF THE TEMPLE FROM A COMPUTER PROGRAM OF OTHER CULTS."
I SEE A LARGE DESIGN HERE.

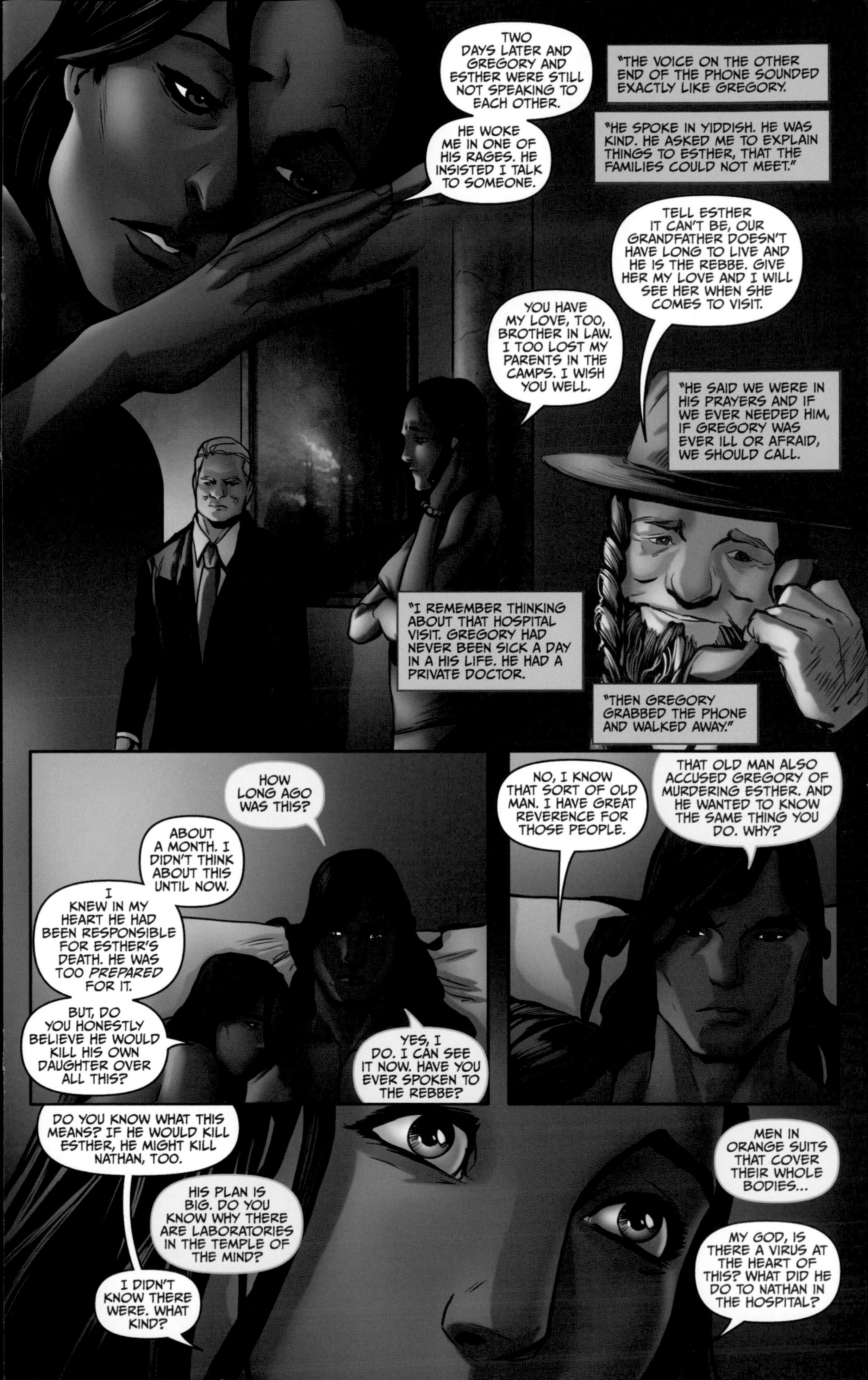

TWO DAYS LATER AND GREGORY AND ESTHER WERE STILL NOT SPEAKING TO EACH OTHER.
HE WOKE ME IN ONE OF HIS RAGES. HE INSISTED I TALK TO SOMEONE.
"THE VOICE ON THE OTHER END OF THE PHONE SOUNDED EXACTLY LIKE GREGORY.
"HE SPOKE IN YIDDISH. HE WAS KIND. HE ASKED ME TO EXPLAIN THINGS TO ESTHER, THAT THE FAMILIES COULD NOT MEET."
TELL ESTHER IT CAN'T BE, OUR GRANDFATHER DOESN'T HAVE LONG TO LIVE AND HE IS THE REBBE. GIVE HER MY LOVE AND I WILL SEE HER WHEN SHE COMES TO VISIT.
YOU HAVE MY LOVE, TOO, BROTHER IN LAW. I TOO LOST MY PARENTS IN THE CAMPS. I WISH YOU WELL.
"HE SAID WE WERE IN HIS PRAYERS AND IF WE EVER NEEDED HIM, IF GREGORY WAS EVER ILL OR AFRAID, WE SHOULD CALL.
"I REMEMBER THINKING ABOUT THAT HOSPITAL VISIT. GREGORY HAD NEVER BEEN SICK A DAY IN A HIS LIFE. HE HAD A PRIVATE DOCTOR.
"THEN GREGORY GRABBED THE PHONE AND WALKED AWAY."
HOW LONG AGO WAS THIS?
ABOUT A MONTH. I DIDN'T THINK ABOUT THIS UNTIL NOW.
I KNEW IN MY HEART HE HAD BEEN RESPONSIBLE FOR ESTHER'S DEATH. HE WAS TOO *PREPARED* FOR IT.
BUT, DO YOU HONESTLY BELIEVE HE WOULD KILL HIS OWN DAUGHTER OVER ALL THIS?
YES, I DO. I CAN SEE IT NOW. HAVE YOU EVER SPOKEN TO THE REBBE?
NO, I KNOW THAT SORT OF OLD MAN. I HAVE GREAT REVERENCE FOR THOSE PEOPLE.
THAT OLD MAN ALSO ACCUSED GREGORY OF MURDERING ESTHER. AND HE WANTED TO KNOW THE SAME THING YOU DO. WHY?
DO YOU KNOW WHAT THIS MEANS? IF HE WOULD KILL ESTHER, HE MIGHT KILL NATHAN, TOO.
HIS PLAN IS BIG. DO YOU KNOW WHY THERE ARE LABORATORIES IN THE TEMPLE OF THE MIND?
I DIDN'T KNOW THERE WERE. WHAT KIND?
MEN IN ORANGE SUITS THAT COVER THEIR WHOLE BODIES...
MY GOD, IS THERE A VIRUS AT THE HEART OF THIS? WHAT DID HE DO TO NATHAN IN THE HOSPITAL?

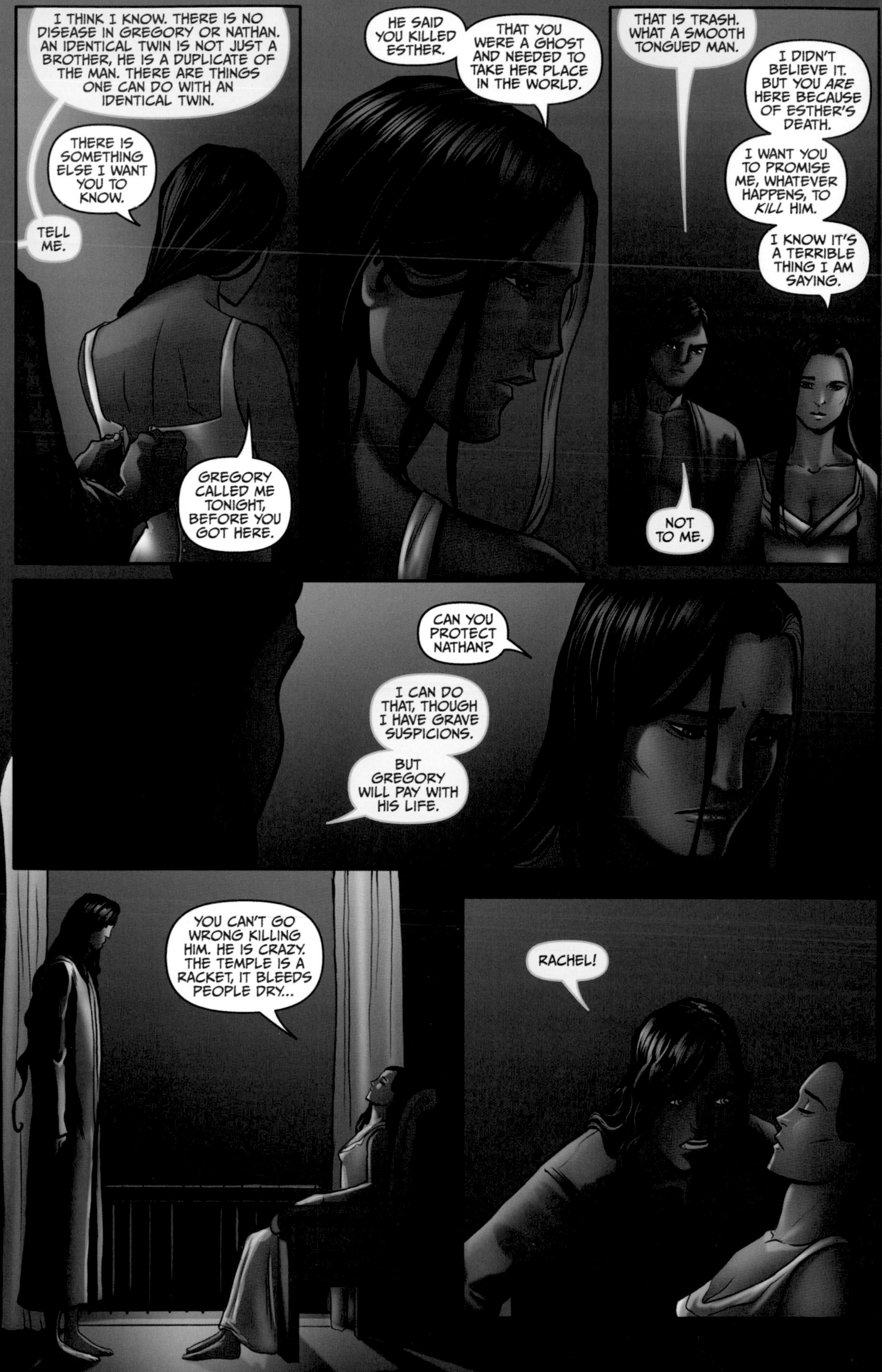
I THINK I KNOW. THERE IS NO DISEASE IN GREGORY OR NATHAN. AN IDENTICAL TWIN IS NOT JUST A BROTHER, HE IS A DUPLICATE OF THE MAN. THERE ARE THINGS ONE CAN DO WITH AN IDENTICAL TWIN.
THERE IS SOMETHING ELSE I WANT YOU TO KNOW.
TELL ME.
GREGORY CALLED ME TONIGHT, BEFORE YOU GOT HERE.
HE SAID YOU KILLED ESTHER.
THAT YOU WERE A GHOST AND NEEDED TO TAKE HER PLACE IN THE WORLD.
THAT IS TRASH. WHAT A SMOOTH TONGUED MAN.
I DIDN'T BELIEVE IT. BUT YOU ARE HERE BECAUSE OF ESTHER'S DEATH.
I WANT YOU TO PROMISE ME, WHATEVER HAPPENS, TO KILL HIM.
I KNOW IT'S A TERRIBLE THING I AM SAYING.
NOT TO ME.
CAN YOU PROTECT NATHAN?
I CAN DO THAT, THOUGH I HAVE GRAVE SUSPICIONS.
BUT GREGORY WILL PAY WITH HIS LIFE.
YOU CAN'T GO WRONG KILLING HIM. HE IS CRAZY. THE TEMPLE IS A RACKET, IT BLEEDS PEOPLE DRY...
RACHEL!

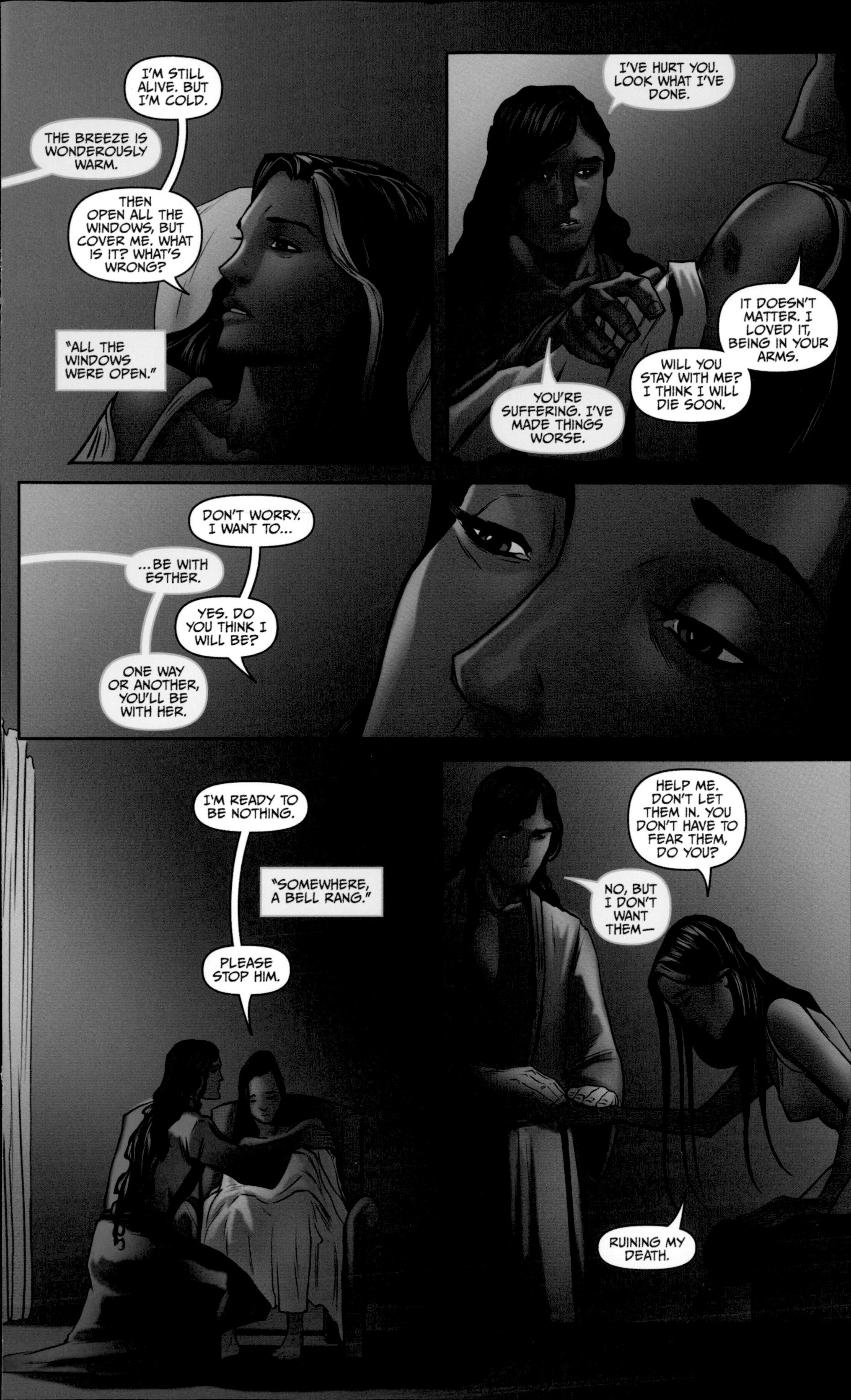
I'M STILL ALIVE. BUT I'M COLD.
THE BREEZE IS WONDEROUSLY WARM.
THEN OPEN ALL THE WINDOWS, BUT COVER ME. WHAT IS IT? WHAT'S WRONG?
"ALL THE WINDOWS WERE OPEN."
I'VE HURT YOU. LOOK WHAT I'VE DONE.
IT DOESN'T MATTER. I LOVED IT, BEING IN YOUR ARMS.
YOU'RE SUFFERING. I'VE MADE THINGS WORSE.
WILL YOU STAY WITH ME? I THINK I WILL DIE SOON.
DON'T WORRY. I WANT TO...
...BE WITH ESTHER.
YES. DO YOU THINK I WILL BE?
ONE WAY OR ANOTHER, YOU'LL BE WITH HER.
I'M READY TO BE NOTHING.
"SOMEWHERE, A BELL RANG."
PLEASE STOP HIM.
HELP ME. DON'T LET THEM IN. YOU DON'T HAVE TO FEAR THEM, DO YOU?
NO, BUT I DON'T WANT THEM—
RUINING MY DEATH.

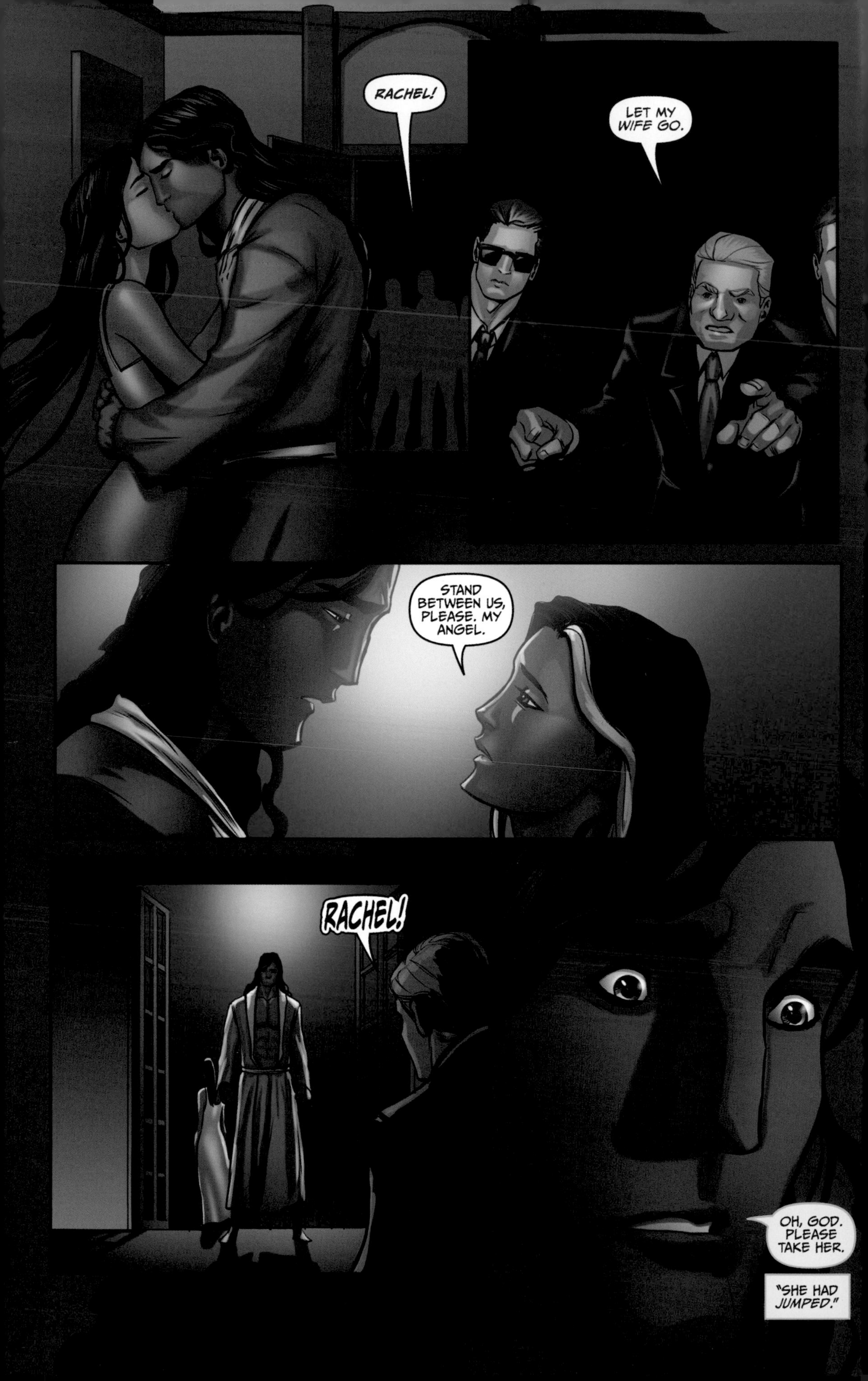
RACHEL!
LET MY WIFE GO.
STAND BETWEEN US, PLEASE. MY ANGEL.
RACHEL!
OH, GOD. PLEASE TAKE HER.
"SHE HAD JUMPED."

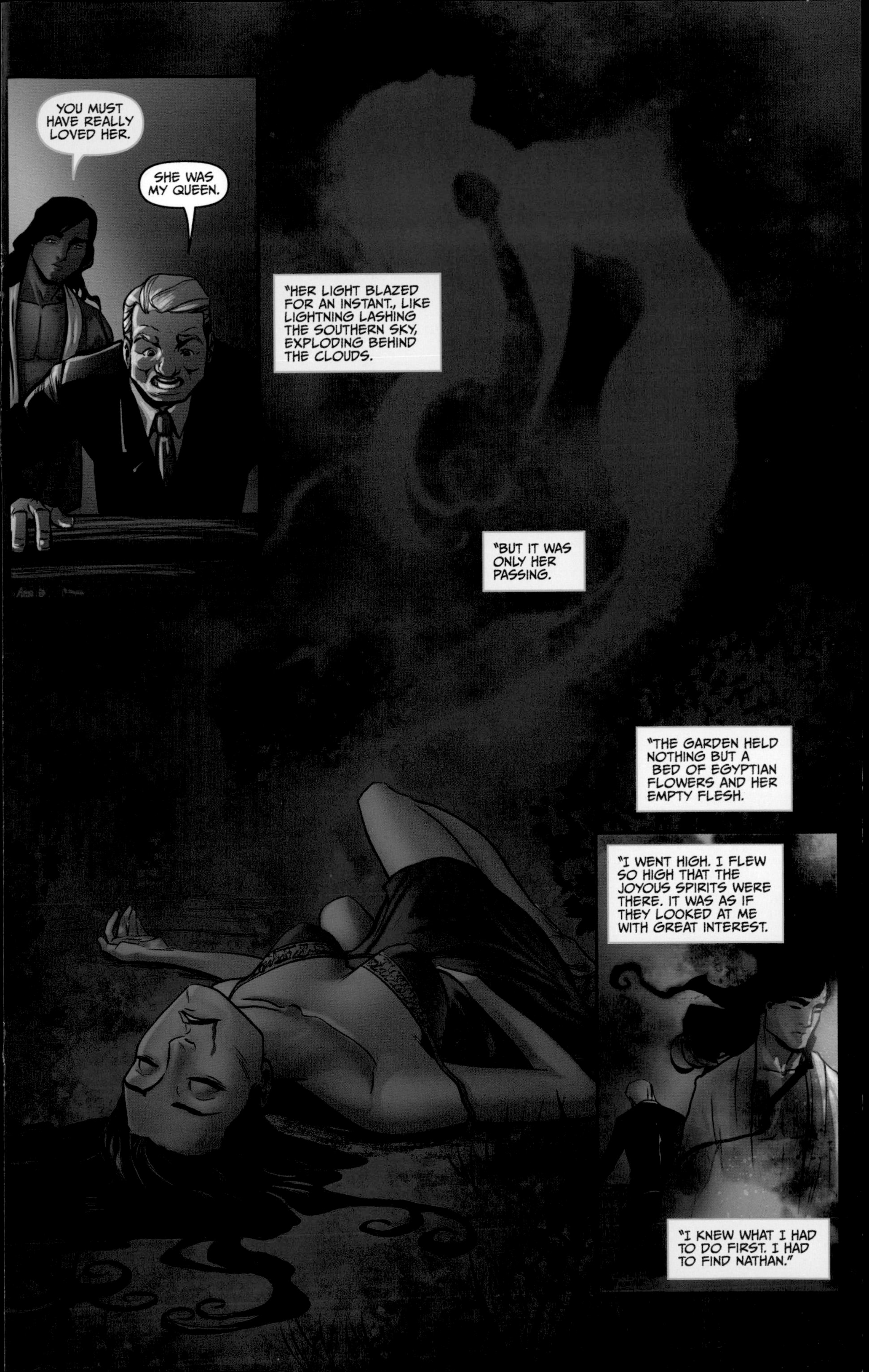
YOU MUST HAVE REALLY LOVED HER.
SHE WAS MY QUEEN.
"HER LIGHT BLAZED FOR AN INSTANT., LIKE LIGHTNING LASHING THE SOUTHERN SKY, EXPLODING BEHIND THE CLOUDS.
"BUT IT WAS ONLY HER PASSING.
"THE GARDEN HELD NOTHING BUT A BED OF EGYPTIAN FLOWERS AND HER EMPTY FLESH.
"I WENT HIGH. I FLEW SO HIGH THAT THE JOYOUS SPIRITS WERE THERE. IT WAS AS IF THEY LOOKED AT ME WITH GREAT INTEREST.
"I KNEW WHAT I HAD TO DO FIRST. I HAD TO FIND NATHAN."

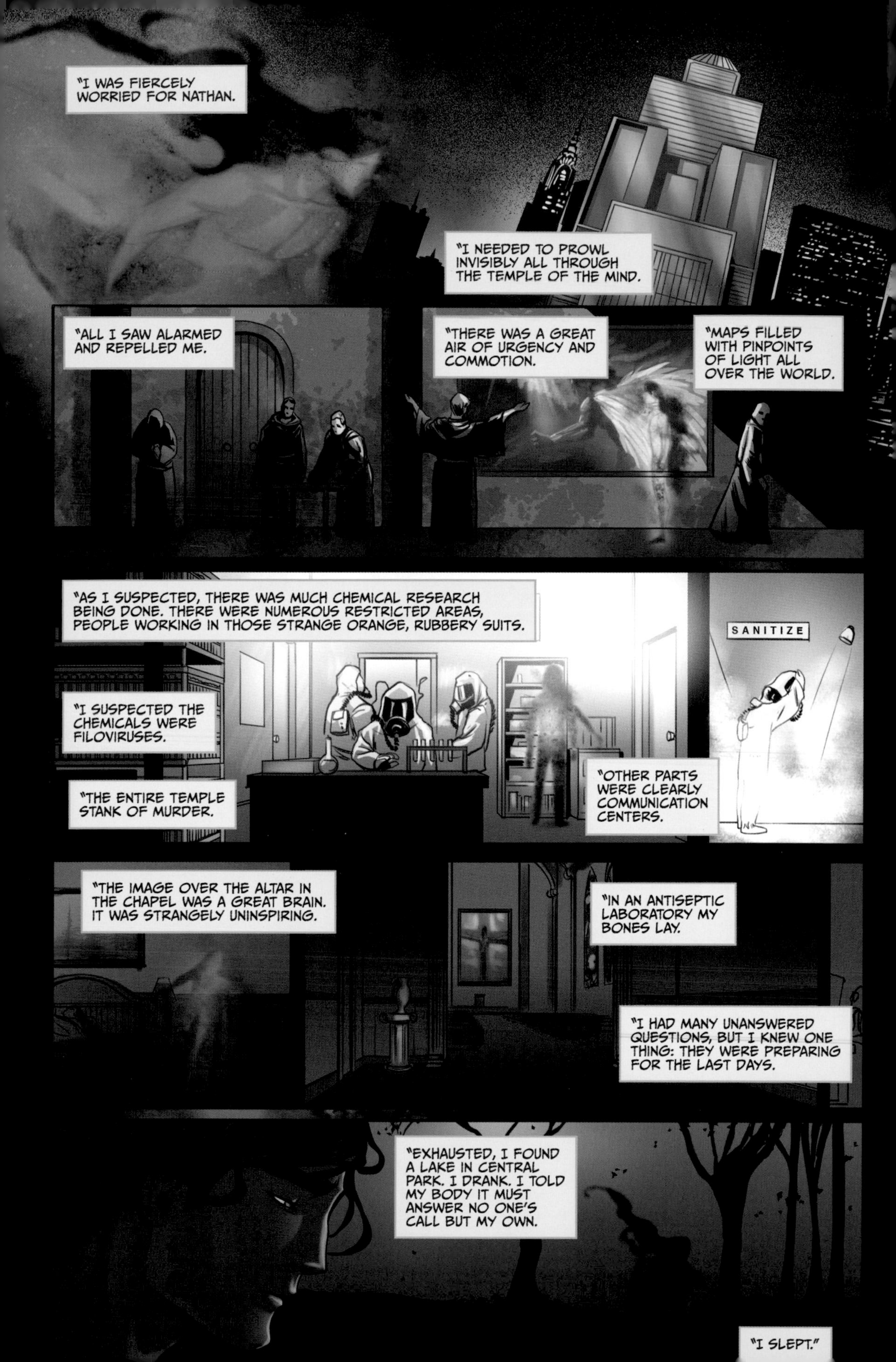
"I WAS FIERCELY WORRIED FOR NATHAN.
"I NEEDED TO PROWL INVISIBLY ALL THROUGH THE TEMPLE OF THE MIND.
"ALL I SAW ALARMED AND REPELLED ME.
"THERE WAS A GREAT AIR OF URGENCY AND COMMOTION.
"MAPS FILLED WITH PINPOINTS OF LIGHT ALL OVER THE WORLD.
"AS I SUSPECTED, THERE WAS MUCH CHEMICAL RESEARCH BEING DONE. THERE WERE NUMEROUS RESTRICTED AREAS, PEOPLE WORKING IN THOSE STRANGE ORANGE, RUBBERY SUITS.
"I SUSPECTED THE CHEMICALS WERE FILOVIRUSES.
"THE ENTIRE TEMPLE STANK OF MURDER.
"OTHER PARTS WERE CLEARLY COMMUNICATION CENTERS.
SANITIZE
"THE IMAGE OVER THE ALTAR IN THE CHAPEL WAS A GREAT BRAIN. IT WAS STRANGELY UNINSPIRING.
"IN AN ANTISEPTIC LABORATORY MY BONES LAY.
"I HAD MANY UNANSWERED QUESTIONS, BUT I KNEW ONE THING: THEY WERE PREPARING FOR THE LAST DAYS.
"EXHAUSTED, I FOUND A LAKE IN CENTRAL PARK. I DRANK. I TOLD MY BODY IT MUST ANSWER NO ONE'S CALL BUT MY OWN.
"I SLEPT."

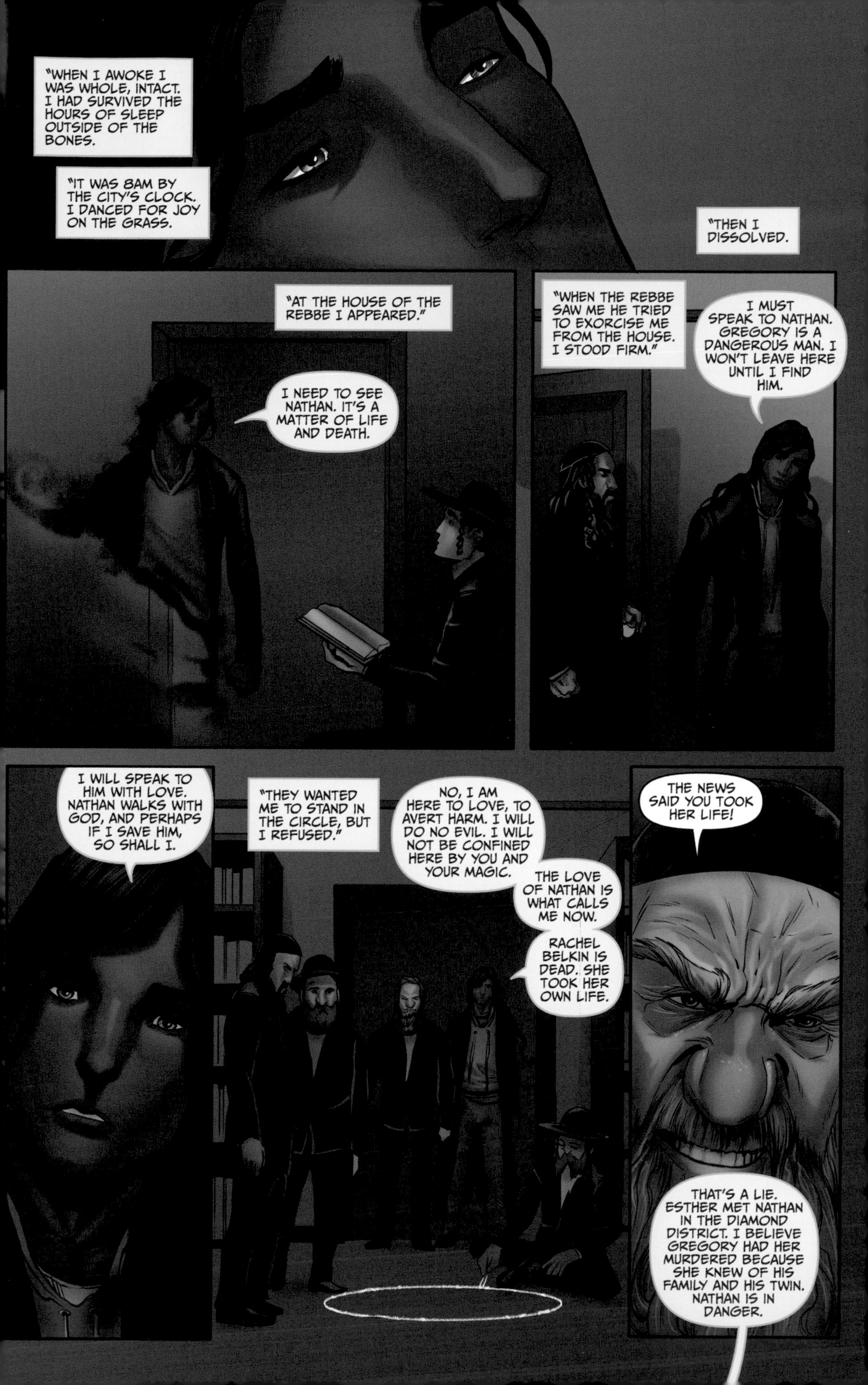
"WHEN I AWOKE I WAS WHOLE, INTACT. I HAD SURVIVED THE HOURS OF SLEEP OUTSIDE OF THE BONES.
"IT WAS 8AM BY THE CITY'S CLOCK. I DANCED FOR JOY ON THE GRASS.
"THEN I DISSOLVED.
"AT THE HOUSE OF THE REBBE I APPEARED."
I NEED TO SEE NATHAN. IT'S A MATTER OF LIFE AND DEATH.
"WHEN THE REBBE SAW ME HE TRIED TO EXORCISE ME FROM THE HOUSE. I STOOD FIRM."
I MUST SPEAK TO NATHAN. GREGORY IS A DANGEROUS MAN. I WON'T LEAVE HERE UNTIL I FIND HIM.
I WILL SPEAK TO HIM WITH LOVE. NATHAN WALKS WITH GOD, AND PERHAPS IF I SAVE HIM, SO SHALL I.
"THEY WANTED ME TO STAND IN THE CIRCLE, BUT I REFUSED."
NO, I AM HERE TO LOVE, TO AVERT HARM. I WILL DO NO EVIL. I WILL NOT BE CONFINED HERE BY YOU AND YOUR MAGIC.
THE LOVE OF NATHAN IS WHAT CALLS ME NOW.
RACHEL BELKIN IS DEAD. SHE TOOK HER OWN LIFE.
THE NEWS SAID YOU TOOK HER LIFE!
THAT'S A LIE. ESTHER MET NATHAN IN THE DIAMOND DISTRICT. I BELIEVE GREGORY HAD HER MURDERED BECAUSE SHE KNEW OF HIS FAMILY AND HIS TWIN. NATHAN IS IN DANGER.

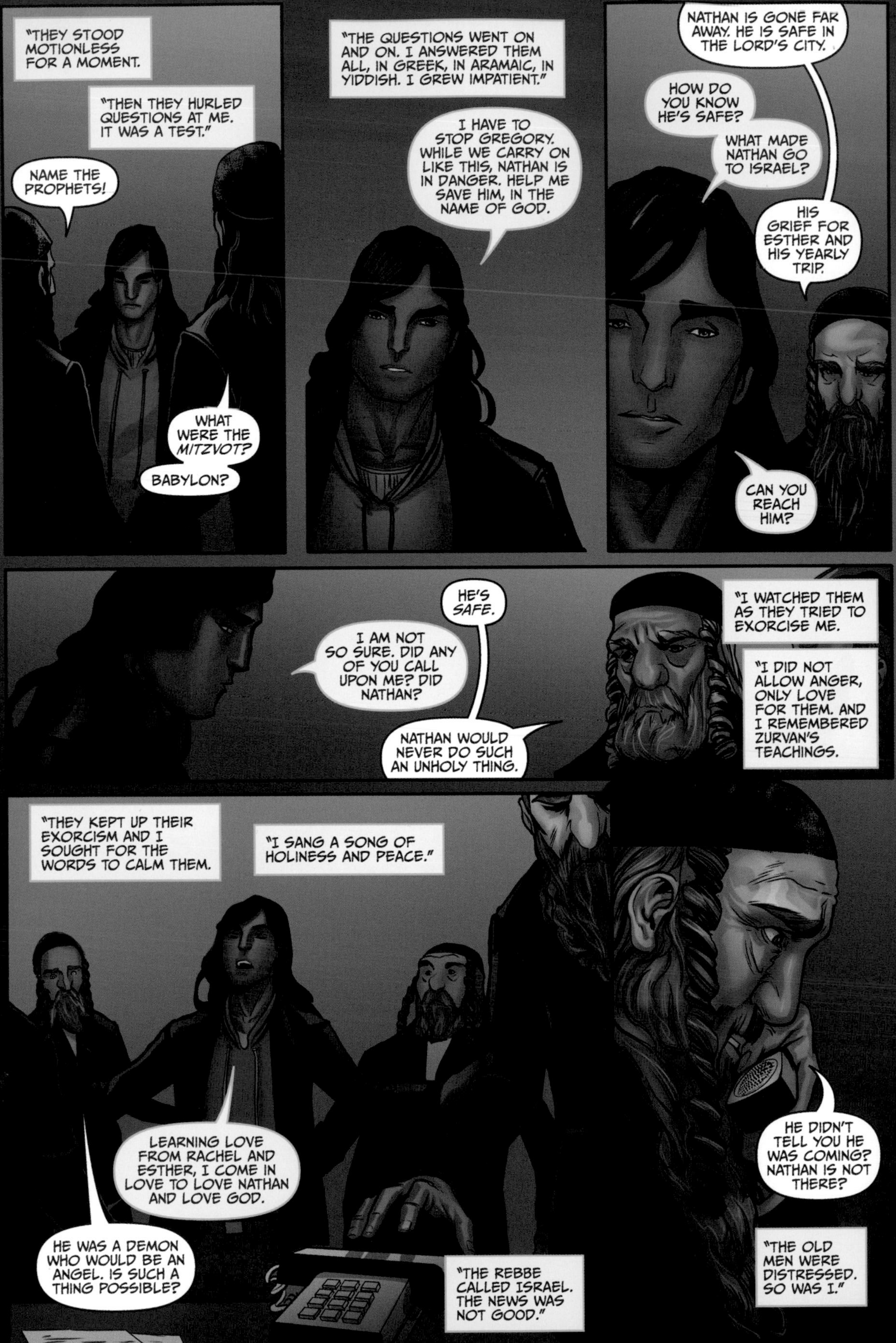
"THEY STOOD MOTIONLESS FOR A MOMENT.
"THEN THEY HURLED QUESTIONS AT ME. IT WAS A TEST."
NAME THE PROPHETS!
WHAT WERE THE *MITZVOT?*
BABYLON?
"THE QUESTIONS WENT ON AND ON. I ANSWERED THEM ALL, IN GREEK, IN ARAMAIC, IN YIDDISH. I GREW IMPATIENT."
I HAVE TO STOP GREGORY. WHILE WE CARRY ON LIKE THIS, NATHAN IS IN DANGER. HELP ME SAVE HIM, IN THE NAME OF GOD.
NATHAN IS GONE FAR AWAY. HE IS SAFE IN THE LORD'S CITY.
HOW DO YOU KNOW HE'S SAFE?
WHAT MADE NATHAN GO TO ISRAEL?
HIS GRIEF FOR ESTHER AND HIS YEARLY TRIP.
CAN YOU REACH HIM?
HE'S *SAFE.*
I AM NOT SO SURE. DID ANY OF YOU CALL UPON ME? DID NATHAN?
NATHAN WOULD NEVER DO SUCH AN UNHOLY THING.
"I WATCHED THEM AS THEY TRIED TO EXORCISE ME.
"I DID NOT ALLOW ANGER, ONLY LOVE FOR THEM. AND I REMEMBERED ZURVAN'S TEACHINGS.
"THEY KEPT UP THEIR EXORCISM AND I SOUGHT FOR THE WORDS TO CALM THEM.
"I SANG A SONG OF HOLINESS AND PEACE."
LEARNING LOVE FROM RACHEL AND ESTHER, I COME IN LOVE TO LOVE NATHAN AND LOVE GOD.
HE WAS A DEMON WHO WOULD BE AN ANGEL. IS SUCH A THING POSSIBLE?
"THE REBBE CALLED ISRAEL. THE NEWS WAS NOT GOOD."
HE DIDN'T TELL YOU HE WAS COMING? NATHAN IS NOT THERE?
"THE OLD MEN WERE DISTRESSED. SO WAS I."

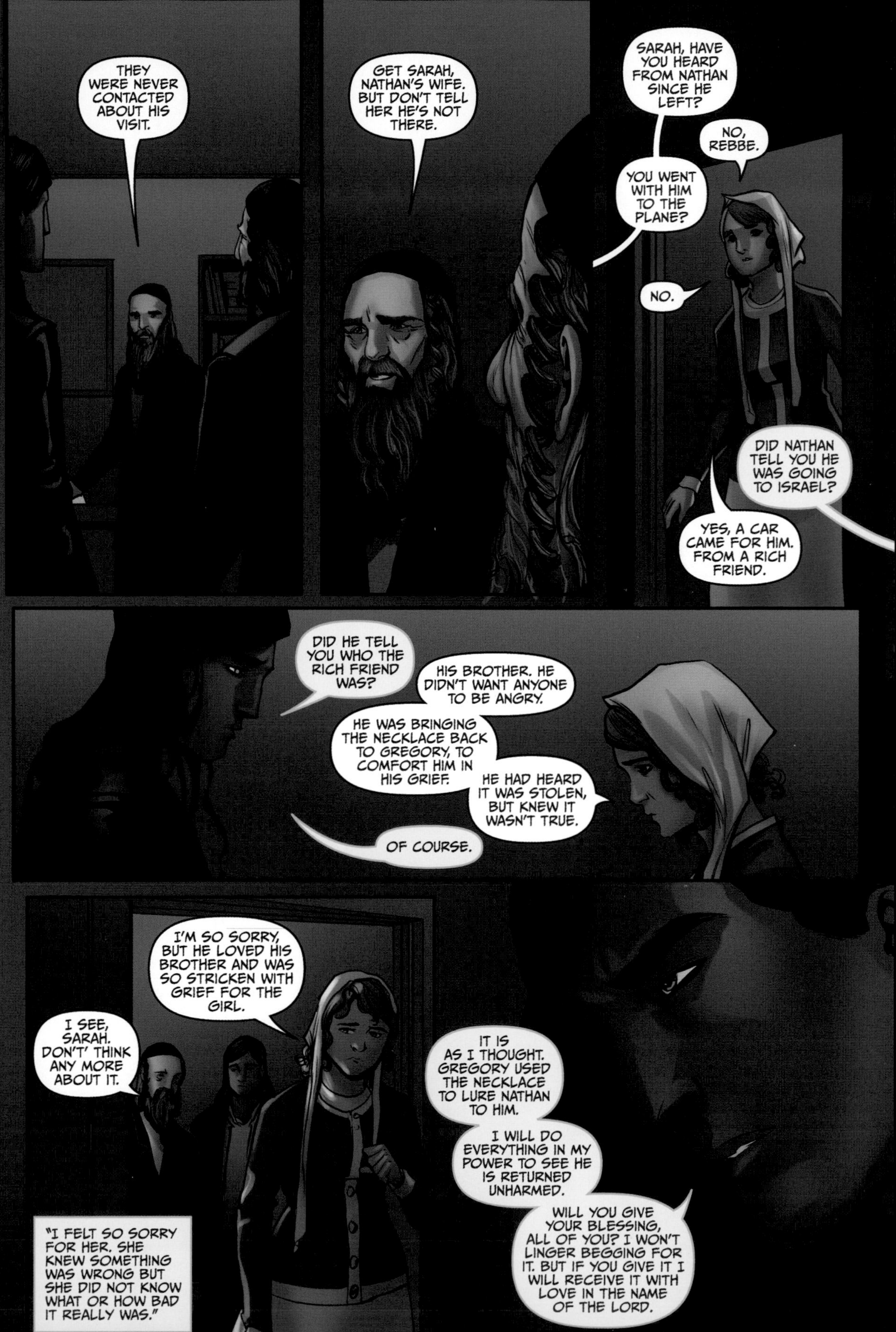
THEY WERE NEVER CONTACTED ABOUT HIS VISIT.
GET SARAH, NATHAN'S WIFE. BUT DON'T TELL HER HE'S NOT THERE.
SARAH, HAVE YOU HEARD FROM NATHAN SINCE HE LEFT?
NO, REBBE.
YOU WENT WITH HIM TO THE PLANE?
NO.
DID NATHAN TELL YOU HE WAS GOING TO ISRAEL?
YES, A CAR CAME FOR HIM. FROM A RICH FRIEND.
DID HE TELL YOU WHO THE RICH FRIEND WAS?
HIS BROTHER. HE DIDN'T WANT ANYONE TO BE ANGRY.
HE WAS BRINGING THE NECKLACE BACK TO GREGORY, TO COMFORT HIM IN HIS GRIEF.
HE HAD HEARD IT WAS STOLEN, BUT KNEW IT WASN'T TRUE.
OF COURSE.
I'M SO SORRY, BUT HE LOVED HIS BROTHER AND WAS SO STRICKEN WITH GRIEF FOR THE GIRL.
I SEE, SARAH. DON'T' THINK ANY MORE ABOUT IT.
IT IS AS I THOUGHT. GREGORY USED THE NECKLACE TO LURE NATHAN TO HIM.
I WILL DO EVERYTHING IN MY POWER TO SEE HE IS RETURNED UNHARMED.
WILL YOU GIVE YOUR BLESSING, ALL OF YOU? I WON'T LINGER BEGGING FOR IT. BUT IF YOU GIVE IT I WILL RECEIVE IT WITH LOVE IN THE NAME OF THE LORD.
"I FELT SO SORRY FOR HER. SHE KNEW SOMETHING WAS WRONG BUT SHE DID NOT KNOW WHAT OR HOW BAD IT REALLY WAS."

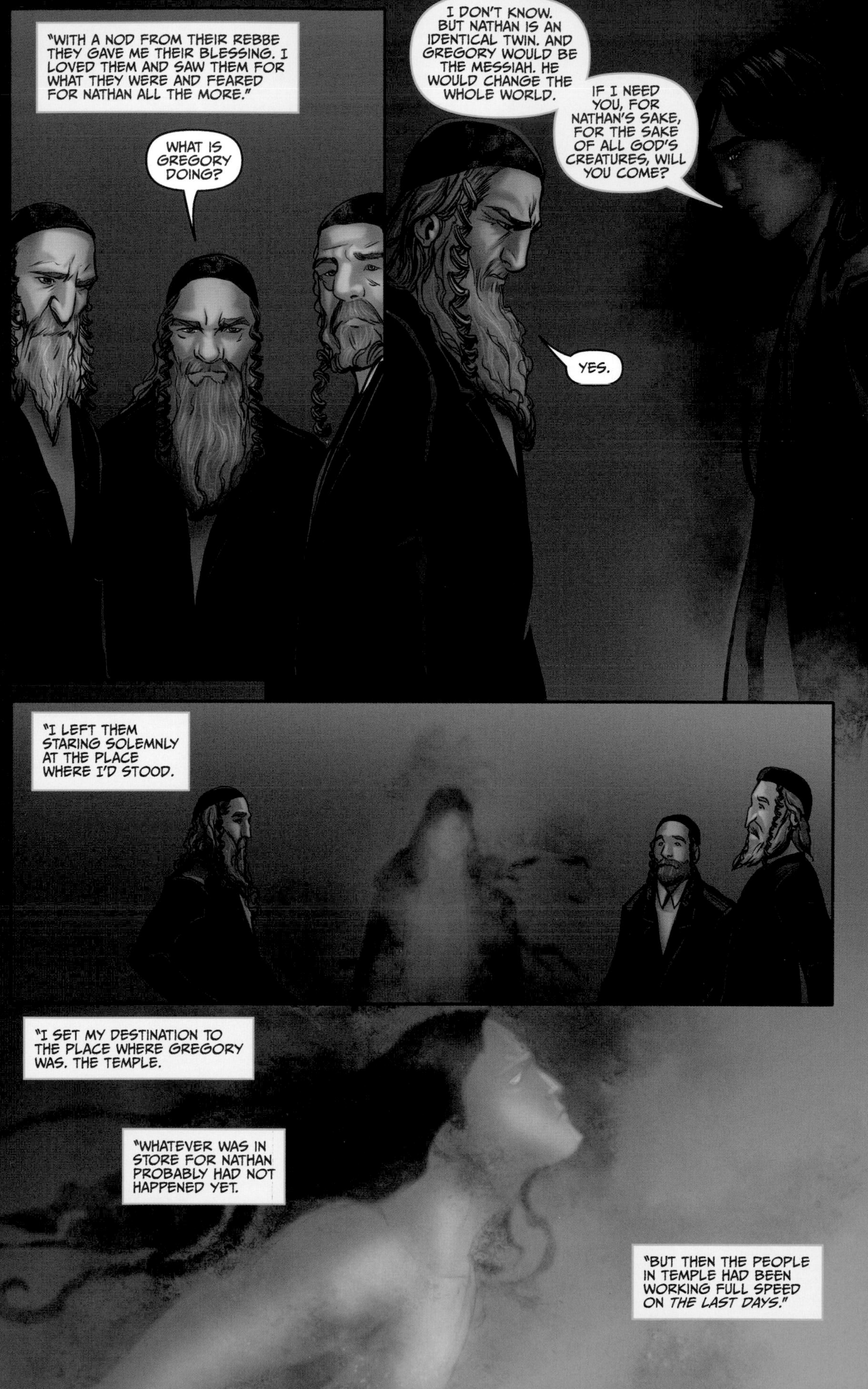
"WITH A NOD FROM THEIR REBBE THEY GAVE ME THEIR BLESSING. I LOVED THEM AND SAW THEM FOR WHAT THEY WERE AND FEARED FOR NATHAN ALL THE MORE."
WHAT IS GREGORY DOING?
I DON'T KNOW. BUT NATHAN IS AN IDENTICAL TWIN. AND GREGORY WOULD BE THE MESSIAH. HE WOULD CHANGE THE WHOLE WORLD.
IF I NEED YOU, FOR NATHAN'S SAKE, FOR THE SAKE OF ALL GOD'S CREATURES, WILL YOU COME?
YES.
"I LEFT THEM STARING SOLEMNLY AT THE PLACE WHERE I'D STOOD.
"I SET MY DESTINATION TO THE PLACE WHERE GREGORY WAS. THE TEMPLE.
"WHATEVER WAS IN STORE FOR NATHAN PROBABLY HAD NOT HAPPENED YET.
"BUT THEN THE PEOPLE IN TEMPLE HAD BEEN WORKING FULL SPEED ON *THE LAST DAYS*."

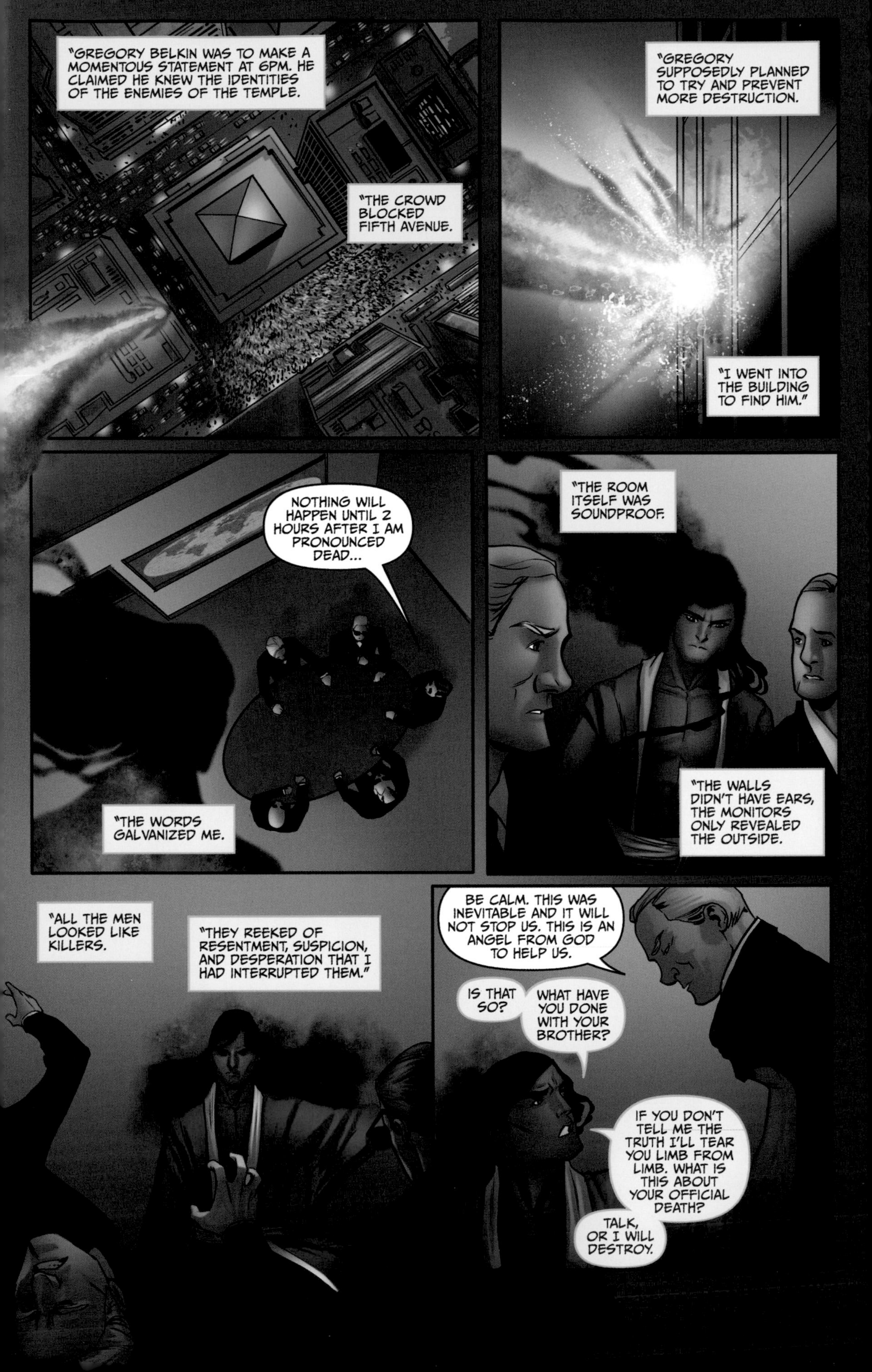
"GREGORY BELKIN WAS TO MAKE A MOMENTOUS STATEMENT AT 6PM. HE CLAIMED HE KNEW THE IDENTITIES OF THE ENEMIES OF THE TEMPLE.
"THE CROWD BLOCKED FIFTH AVENUE.
"GREGORY SUPPOSEDLY PLANNED TO TRY AND PREVENT MORE DESTRUCTION.
"I WENT INTO THE BUILDING TO FIND HIM."
NOTHING WILL HAPPEN UNTIL 2 HOURS AFTER I AM PRONOUNCED DEAD...
"THE WORDS GALVANIZED ME.
"THE ROOM ITSELF WAS SOUNDPROOF.
"THE WALLS DIDN'T HAVE EARS, THE MONITORS ONLY REVEALED THE OUTSIDE.
"ALL THE MEN LOOKED LIKE KILLERS.
"THEY REEKED OF RESENTMENT, SUSPICION, AND DESPERATION THAT I HAD INTERRUPTED THEM."
BE CALM. THIS WAS INEVITABLE AND IT WILL NOT STOP US. THIS IS AN ANGEL FROM GOD TO HELP US.
IS THAT SO?
WHAT HAVE YOU DONE WITH YOUR BROTHER?
IF YOU DON'T TELL ME THE TRUTH I'LL TEAR YOU LIMB FROM LIMB. WHAT IS THIS ABOUT YOUR OFFICIAL DEATH?
TALK, OR I WILL DESTROY.

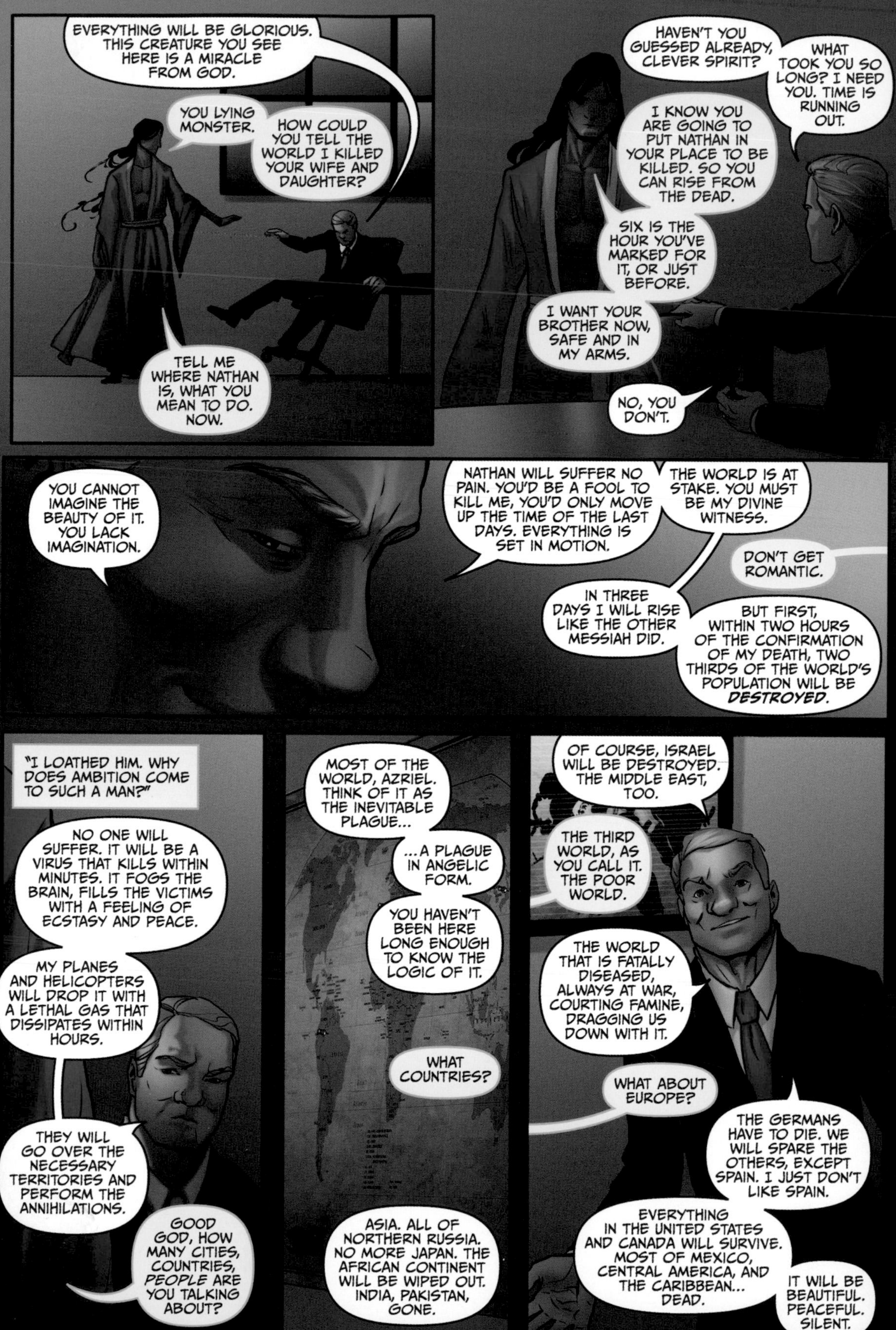
EVERYTHING WILL BE GLORIOUS. THIS CREATURE YOU SEE HERE IS A MIRACLE FROM GOD.
YOU LYING MONSTER.
HOW COULD YOU TELL THE WORLD I KILLED YOUR WIFE AND DAUGHTER?
TELL ME WHERE NATHAN IS, WHAT YOU MEAN TO DO. NOW.
HAVEN'T YOU GUESSED ALREADY, CLEVER SPIRIT?
WHAT TOOK YOU SO LONG? I NEED YOU. TIME IS RUNNING OUT.
I KNOW YOU ARE GOING TO PUT NATHAN IN YOUR PLACE TO BE KILLED. SO YOU CAN RISE FROM THE DEAD.
SIX IS THE HOUR YOU'VE MARKED FOR IT, OR JUST BEFORE.
I WANT YOUR BROTHER NOW, SAFE AND IN MY ARMS.
NO, YOU DON'T.
YOU CANNOT IMAGINE THE BEAUTY OF IT. YOU LACK IMAGINATION.
NATHAN WILL SUFFER NO PAIN. YOU'D BE A FOOL TO KILL ME, YOU'D ONLY MOVE UP THE TIME OF THE LAST DAYS. EVERYTHING IS SET IN MOTION.
THE WORLD IS AT STAKE. YOU MUST BE MY DIVINE WITNESS.
DON'T GET ROMANTIC.
IN THREE DAYS I WILL RISE LIKE THE OTHER MESSIAH DID.
BUT FIRST, WITHIN TWO HOURS OF THE CONFIRMATION OF MY DEATH, TWO THIRDS OF THE WORLD'S POPULATION WILL BE ***DESTROYED***.
"I LOATHED HIM. WHY DOES AMBITION COME TO SUCH A MAN?"
NO ONE WILL SUFFER. IT WILL BE A VIRUS THAT KILLS WITHIN MINUTES. IT FOGS THE BRAIN, FILLS THE VICTIMS WITH A FEELING OF ECSTASY AND PEACE.
MY PLANES AND HELICOPTERS WILL DROP IT WITH A LETHAL GAS THAT DISSIPATES WITHIN HOURS.
THEY WILL GO OVER THE NECESSARY TERRITORIES AND PERFORM THE ANNIHILATIONS.
GOOD GOD, HOW MANY CITIES, COUNTRIES, *PEOPLE* ARE YOU TALKING ABOUT?
MOST OF THE WORLD, AZRIEL. THINK OF IT AS THE INEVITABLE PLAGUE...
...A PLAGUE IN ANGELIC FORM.
YOU HAVEN'T BEEN HERE LONG ENOUGH TO KNOW THE LOGIC OF IT.
WHAT COUNTRIES?
ASIA. ALL OF NORTHERN RUSSIA. NO MORE JAPAN. THE AFRICAN CONTINENT WILL BE WIPED OUT. INDIA, PAKISTAN, GONE.
OF COURSE, ISRAEL WILL BE DESTROYED. THE MIDDLE EAST, TOO.
THE THIRD WORLD, AS YOU CALL IT. THE POOR WORLD.
THE WORLD THAT IS FATALLY DISEASED, ALWAYS AT WAR, COURTING FAMINE, DRAGGING US DOWN WITH IT.
WHAT ABOUT EUROPE?
THE GERMANS HAVE TO DIE. WE WILL SPARE THE OTHERS, EXCEPT SPAIN. I JUST DON'T LIKE SPAIN.
EVERYTHING IN THE UNITED STATES AND CANADA WILL SURVIVE. MOST OF MEXICO, CENTRAL AMERICA, AND THE CARIBBEAN... DEAD.
IT WILL BE BEAUTIFUL. PEACEFUL. SILENT.

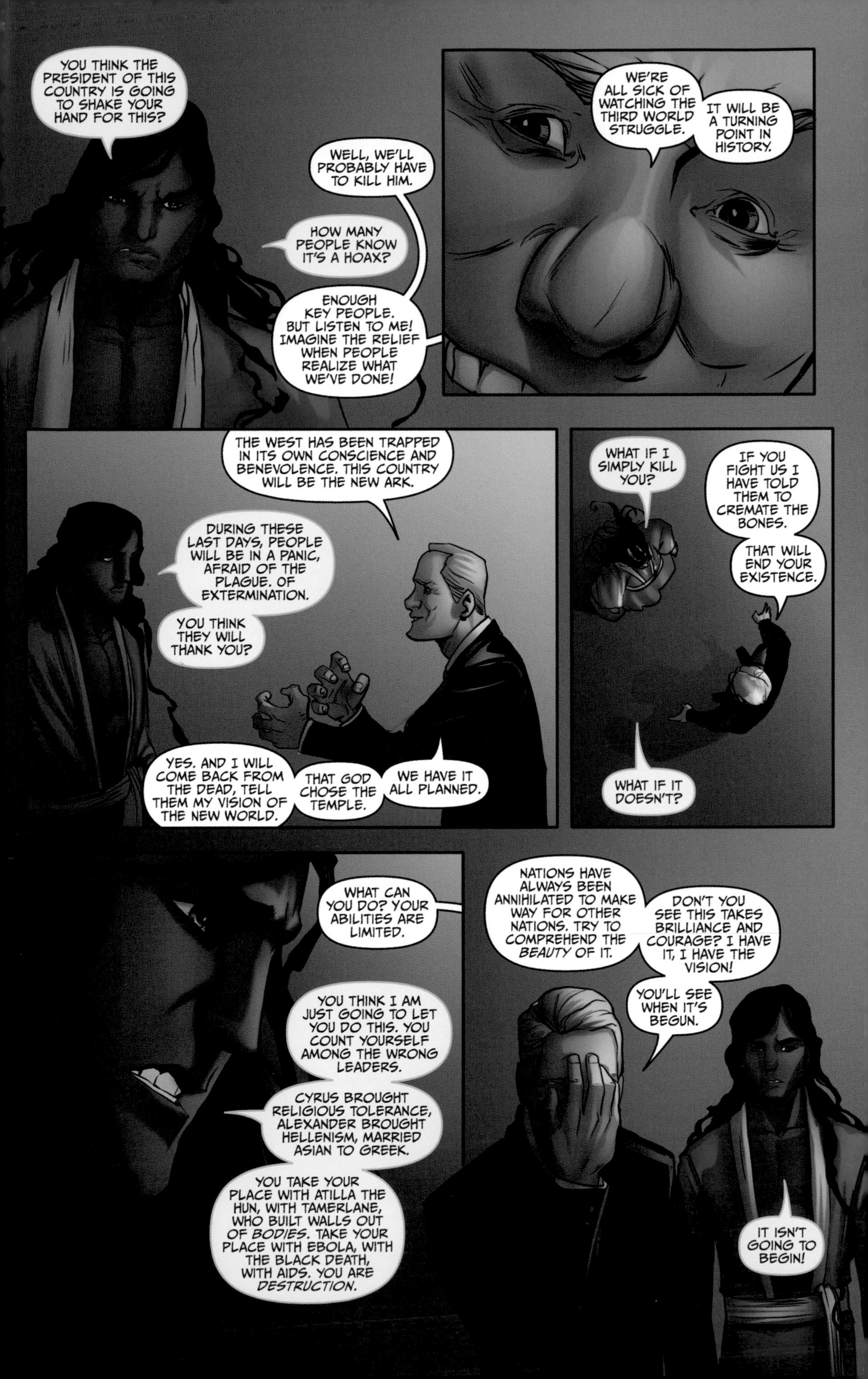
YOU THINK THE PRESIDENT OF THIS COUNTRY IS GOING TO SHAKE YOUR HAND FOR THIS?
WELL, WE'LL PROBABLY HAVE TO KILL HIM.
HOW MANY PEOPLE KNOW IT'S A HOAX?
ENOUGH KEY PEOPLE. BUT LISTEN TO ME! IMAGINE THE RELIEF WHEN PEOPLE REALIZE WHAT WE'VE DONE!
WE'RE ALL SICK OF WATCHING THE THIRD WORLD STRUGGLE.
IT WILL BE A TURNING POINT IN HISTORY.
THE WEST HAS BEEN TRAPPED IN ITS OWN CONSCIENCE AND BENEVOLENCE. THIS COUNTRY WILL BE THE NEW ARK.
DURING THESE LAST DAYS, PEOPLE WILL BE IN A PANIC, AFRAID OF THE PLAGUE. OF EXTERMINATION.
YOU THINK THEY WILL THANK YOU?
YES. AND I WILL COME BACK FROM THE DEAD, TELL THEM MY VISION OF THE NEW WORLD.
THAT GOD CHOSE THE TEMPLE.
WE HAVE IT ALL PLANNED.
WHAT IF I SIMPLY KILL YOU?
IF YOU FIGHT US I HAVE TOLD THEM TO CREMATE THE BONES.
THAT WILL END YOUR EXISTENCE.
WHAT IF IT DOESN'T?
WHAT CAN YOU DO? YOUR ABILITIES ARE LIMITED.
YOU THINK I AM JUST GOING TO LET YOU DO THIS. YOU COUNT YOURSELF AMONG THE WRONG LEADERS.
CYRUS BROUGHT RELIGIOUS TOLERANCE, ALEXANDER BROUGHT HELLENISM, MARRIED ASIAN TO GREEK.
YOU TAKE YOUR PLACE WITH ATILLA THE HUN, WITH TAMERLANE, WHO BUILT WALLS OUT OF *BODIES*. TAKE YOUR PLACE WITH EBOLA, WITH THE BLACK DEATH, WITH AIDS. YOU ARE *DESTRUCTION*.
NATIONS HAVE ALWAYS BEEN ANNIHILATED TO MAKE WAY FOR OTHER NATIONS. TRY TO COMPREHEND THE *BEAUTY* OF IT.
DON'T YOU SEE THIS TAKES BRILLIANCE AND COURAGE? I HAVE IT, I HAVE THE VISION!
YOU'LL SEE WHEN IT'S BEGUN.
IT ISN'T GOING TO BEGIN!

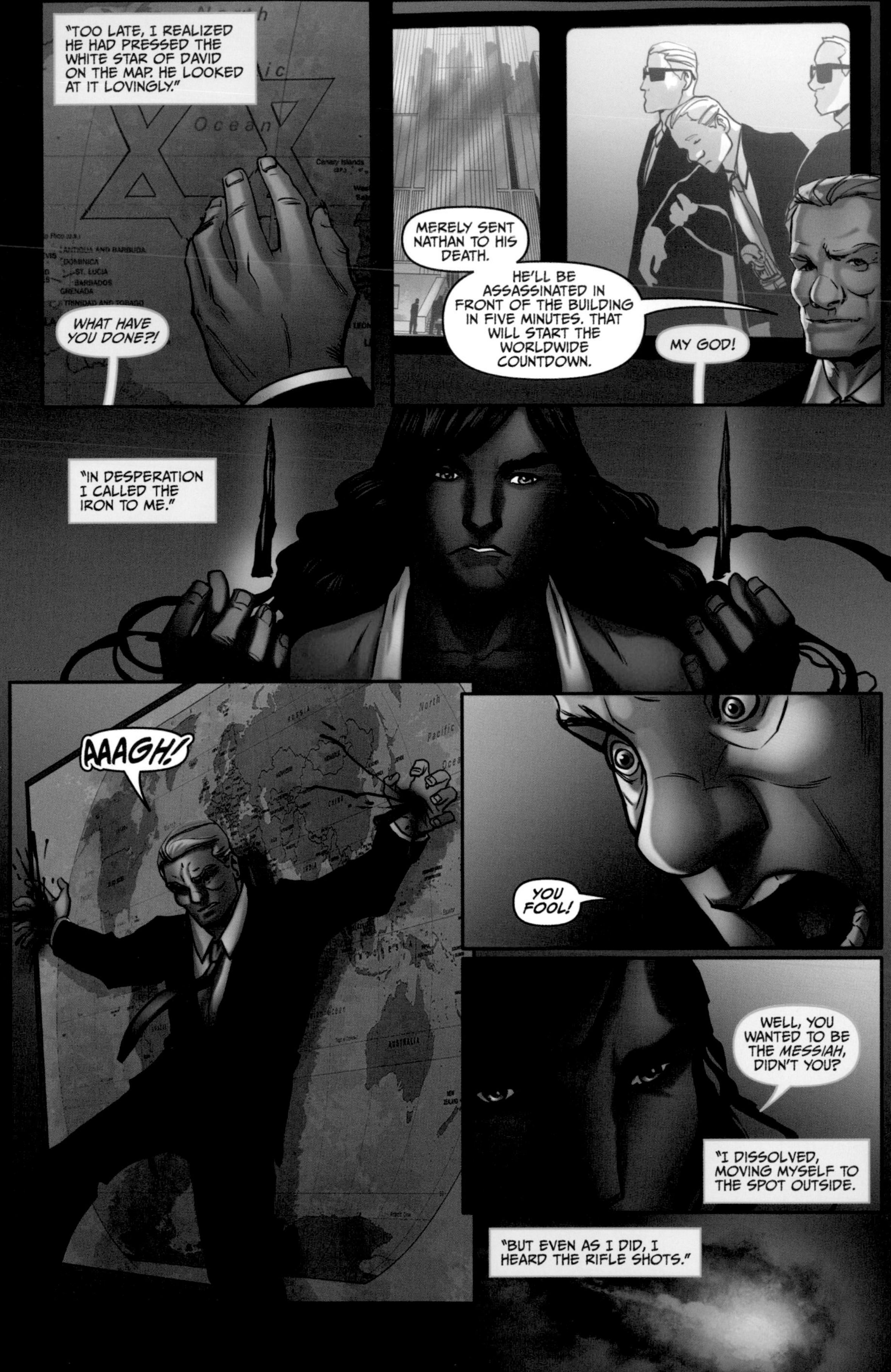

"TOO LATE, I REALIZED HE HAD PRESSED THE WHITE STAR OF DAVID ON THE MAP. HE LOOKED AT IT LOVINGLY."
WHAT HAVE YOU DONE?!
MERELY SENT NATHAN TO HIS DEATH.
HE'LL BE ASSASSINATED IN FRONT OF THE BUILDING IN FIVE MINUTES. THAT WILL START THE WORLDWIDE COUNTDOWN.
MY GOD!
"IN DESPERATION I CALLED THE IRON TO ME."
AAAGH!
YOU FOOL!
WELL, YOU WANTED TO BE THE *MESSIAH*, DIDN'T YOU?
"I DISSOLVED, MOVING MYSELF TO THE SPOT OUTSIDE.
"BUT EVEN AS I DID, I HEARD THE RIFLE SHOTS."

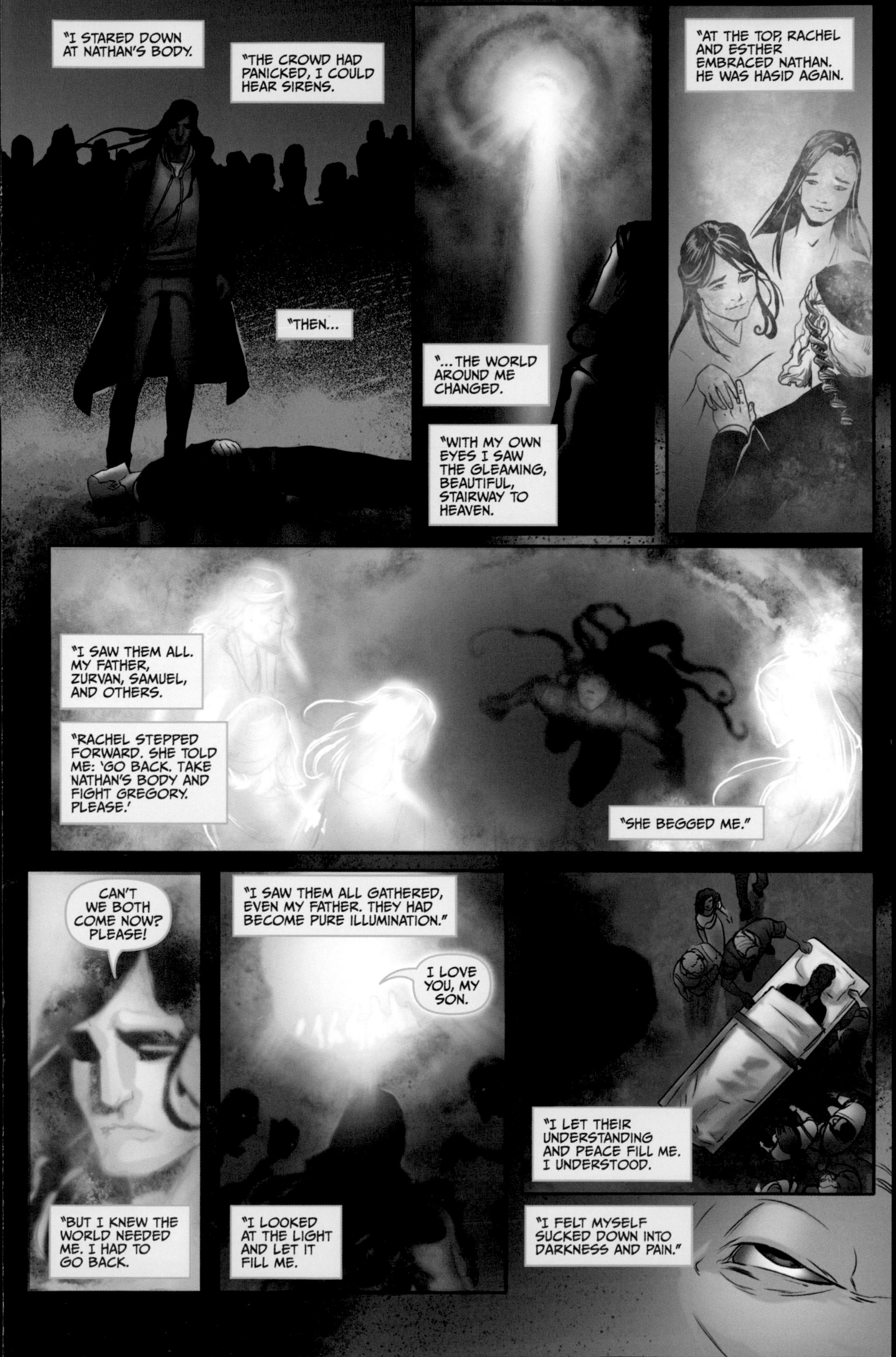
"I STARED DOWN AT NATHAN'S BODY.
"THE CROWD HAD PANICKED, I COULD HEAR SIRENS.
"THEN...
"...THE WORLD AROUND ME CHANGED.
"WITH MY OWN EYES I SAW THE GLEAMING, BEAUTIFUL, STAIRWAY TO HEAVEN.
"AT THE TOP, RACHEL AND ESTHER EMBRACED NATHAN. HE WAS HASID AGAIN.
"I SAW THEM ALL. MY FATHER, ZURVAN, SAMUEL, AND OTHERS.
"RACHEL STEPPED FORWARD. SHE TOLD ME: 'GO BACK. TAKE NATHAN'S BODY AND FIGHT GREGORY. PLEASE.'
"SHE BEGGED ME."
CAN'T WE BOTH COME NOW? PLEASE!
"BUT I KNEW THE WORLD NEEDED ME. I HAD TO GO BACK.
"I SAW THEM ALL GATHERED, EVEN MY FATHER. THEY HAD BECOME PURE ILLUMINATION."
I LOVE YOU, MY SON.
"I LOOKED AT THE LIGHT AND LET IT FILL ME.
"I LET THEIR UNDERSTANDING AND PEACE FILL ME. I UNDERSTOOD.
"I FELT MYSELF SUCKED DOWN INTO DARKNESS AND PAIN."

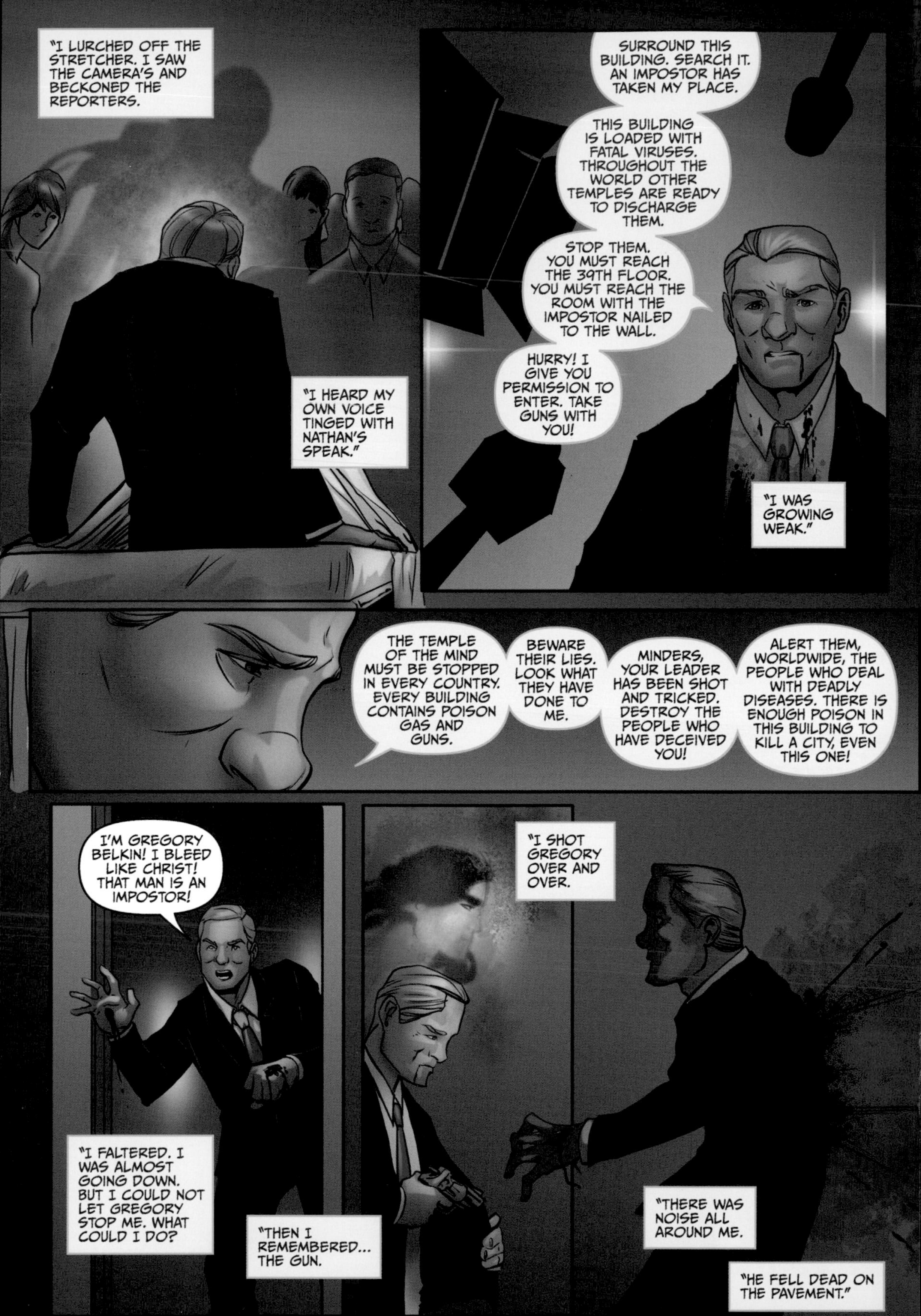
"I LURCHED OFF THE STRETCHER. I SAW THE CAMERA'S AND BECKONED THE REPORTERS.
"I HEARD MY OWN VOICE TINGED WITH NATHAN'S SPEAK."
SURROUND THIS BUILDING. SEARCH IT. AN IMPOSTOR HAS TAKEN MY PLACE.
THIS BUILDING IS LOADED WITH FATAL VIRUSES. THROUGHOUT THE WORLD OTHER TEMPLES ARE READY TO DISCHARGE THEM.
STOP THEM. YOU MUST REACH THE 39TH FLOOR. YOU MUST REACH THE ROOM WITH THE IMPOSTOR NAILED TO THE WALL.
HURRY! I GIVE YOU PERMISSION TO ENTER. TAKE GUNS WITH YOU!
"I WAS GROWING WEAK."
THE TEMPLE OF THE MIND MUST BE STOPPED IN EVERY COUNTRY. EVERY BUILDING CONTAINS POISON GAS AND GUNS.
BEWARE THEIR LIES. LOOK WHAT THEY HAVE DONE TO ME.
MINDERS, YOUR LEADER HAS BEEN SHOT AND TRICKED. DESTROY THE PEOPLE WHO HAVE DECEIVED YOU!
ALERT THEM, WORLDWIDE, THE PEOPLE WHO DEAL WITH DEADLY DISEASES. THERE IS ENOUGH POISON IN THIS BUILDING TO KILL A CITY, EVEN THIS ONE!
I'M GREGORY BELKIN! I BLEED LIKE CHRIST! THAT MAN IS AN IMPOSTOR!
"I FALTERED. I WAS ALMOST GOING DOWN. BUT I COULD NOT LET GREGORY STOP ME. WHAT COULD I DO?
"THEN I REMEMBERED... THE GUN.
"I SHOT GREGORY OVER AND OVER.
"THERE WAS NOISE ALL AROUND ME.
"HE FELL DEAD ON THE PAVEMENT."

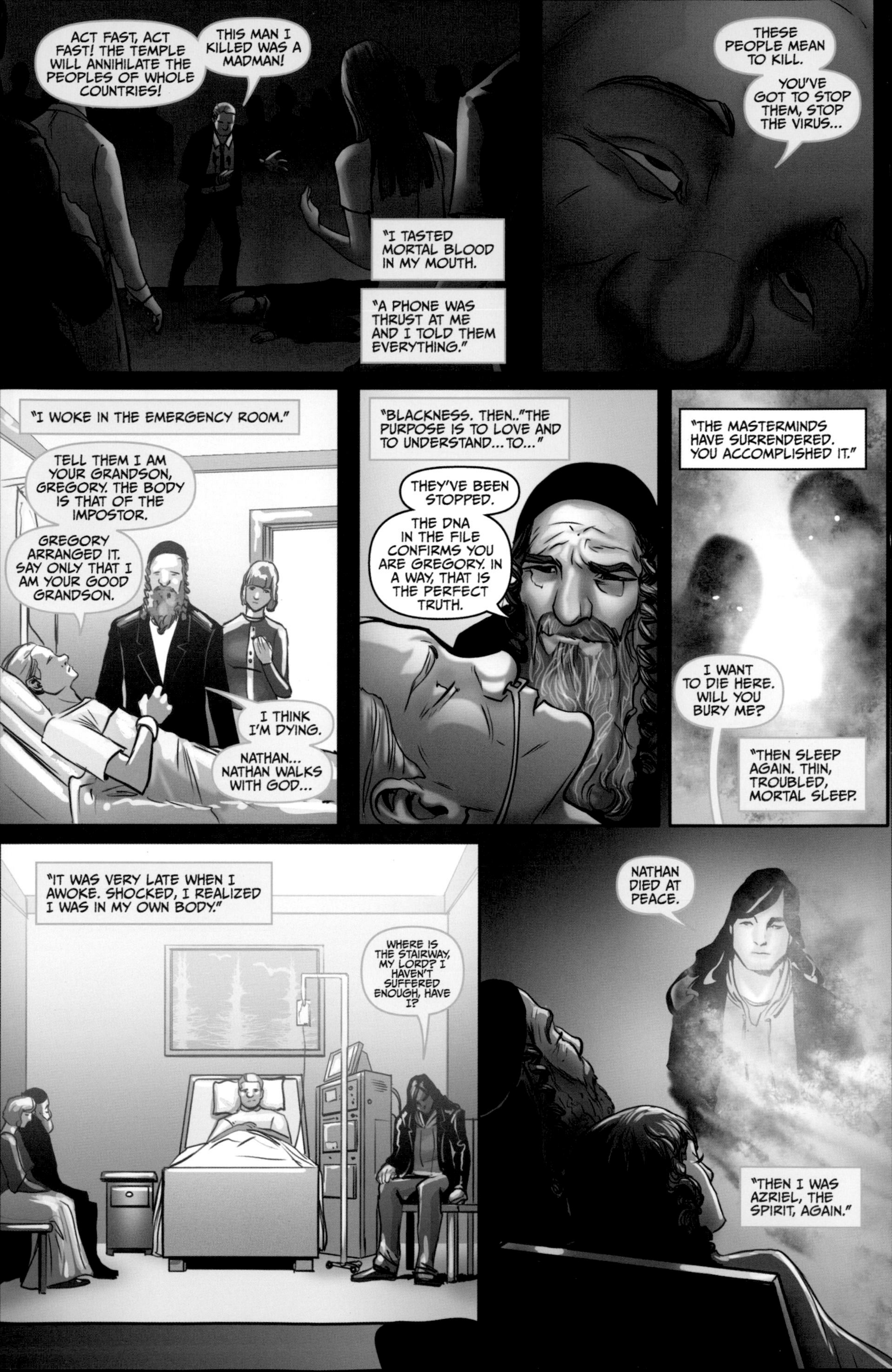
ACT FAST, ACT FAST! THE TEMPLE WILL ANNIHILATE THE PEOPLES OF WHOLE COUNTRIES!
THIS MAN I KILLED WAS A MADMAN!
"I TASTED MORTAL BLOOD IN MY MOUTH.
"A PHONE WAS THRUST AT ME AND I TOLD THEM EVERYTHING."
THESE PEOPLE MEAN TO KILL.
YOU'VE GOT TO STOP THEM, STOP THE VIRUS...
"I WOKE IN THE EMERGENCY ROOM."
TELL THEM I AM YOUR GRANDSON, GREGORY. THE BODY IS THAT OF THE IMPOSTOR.
GREGORY ARRANGED IT. SAY ONLY THAT I AM YOUR GOOD GRANDSON.
I THINK I'M DYING.
NATHAN... NATHAN WALKS WITH GOD...
"BLACKNESS. THEN.."THE PURPOSE IS TO LOVE AND TO UNDERSTAND...TO..."
THEY'VE BEEN STOPPED.
THE DNA IN THE FILE CONFIRMS YOU ARE GREGORY. IN A WAY, THAT IS THE PERFECT TRUTH.
"THE MASTERMINDS HAVE SURRENDERED. YOU ACCOMPLISHED IT."
I WANT TO DIE HERE. WILL YOU BURY ME?
"THEN SLEEP AGAIN. THIN, TROUBLED, MORTAL SLEEP.
"IT WAS VERY LATE WHEN I AWOKE. SHOCKED, I REALIZED I WAS IN MY OWN BODY."
WHERE IS THE STAIRWAY, MY LORD? I HAVEN'T SUFFERED ENOUGH, HAVE I?
NATHAN DIED AT PEACE.
"THEN I WAS AZRIEL, THE SPIRIT, AGAIN."

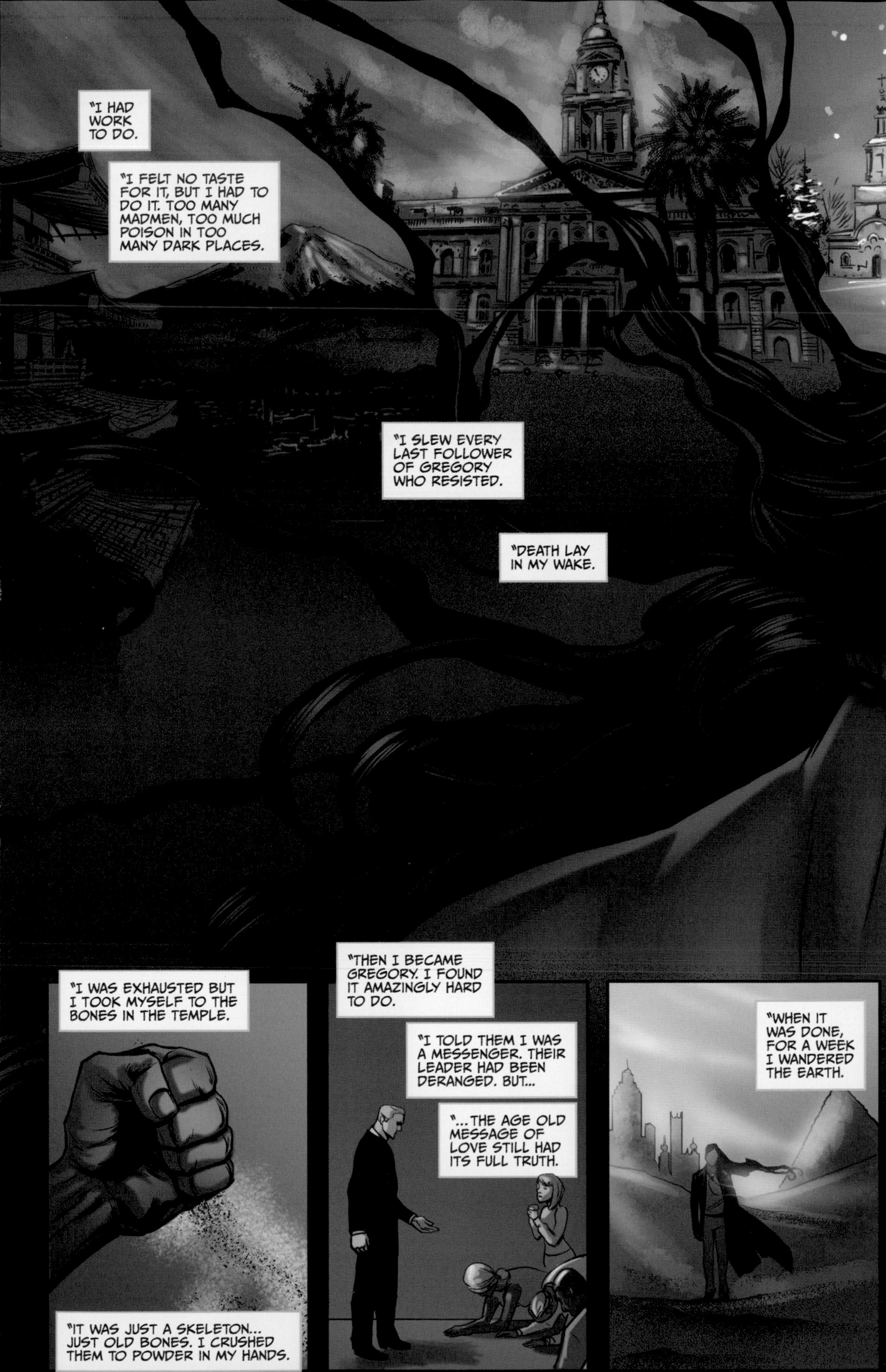
"I HAD WORK TO DO.
"I FELT NO TASTE FOR IT, BUT I HAD TO DO IT. TOO MANY MADMEN, TOO MUCH POISON IN TOO MANY DARK PLACES.
"I SLEW EVERY LAST FOLLOWER OF GREGORY WHO RESISTED.
"DEATH LAY IN MY WAKE.
"I WAS EXHAUSTED BUT I TOOK MYSELF TO THE BONES IN THE TEMPLE.
"IT WAS JUST A SKELETON... JUST OLD BONES. I CRUSHED THEM TO POWDER IN MY HANDS.
"THEN I BECAME GREGORY. I FOUND IT AMAZINGLY HARD TO DO.
"I TOLD THEM I WAS A MESSENGER. THEIR LEADER HAD BEEN DERANGED. BUT...
"...THE AGE OLD MESSAGE OF LOVE STILL HAD ITS FULL TRUTH.
"WHEN IT WAS DONE, FOR A WEEK I WANDERED THE EARTH.

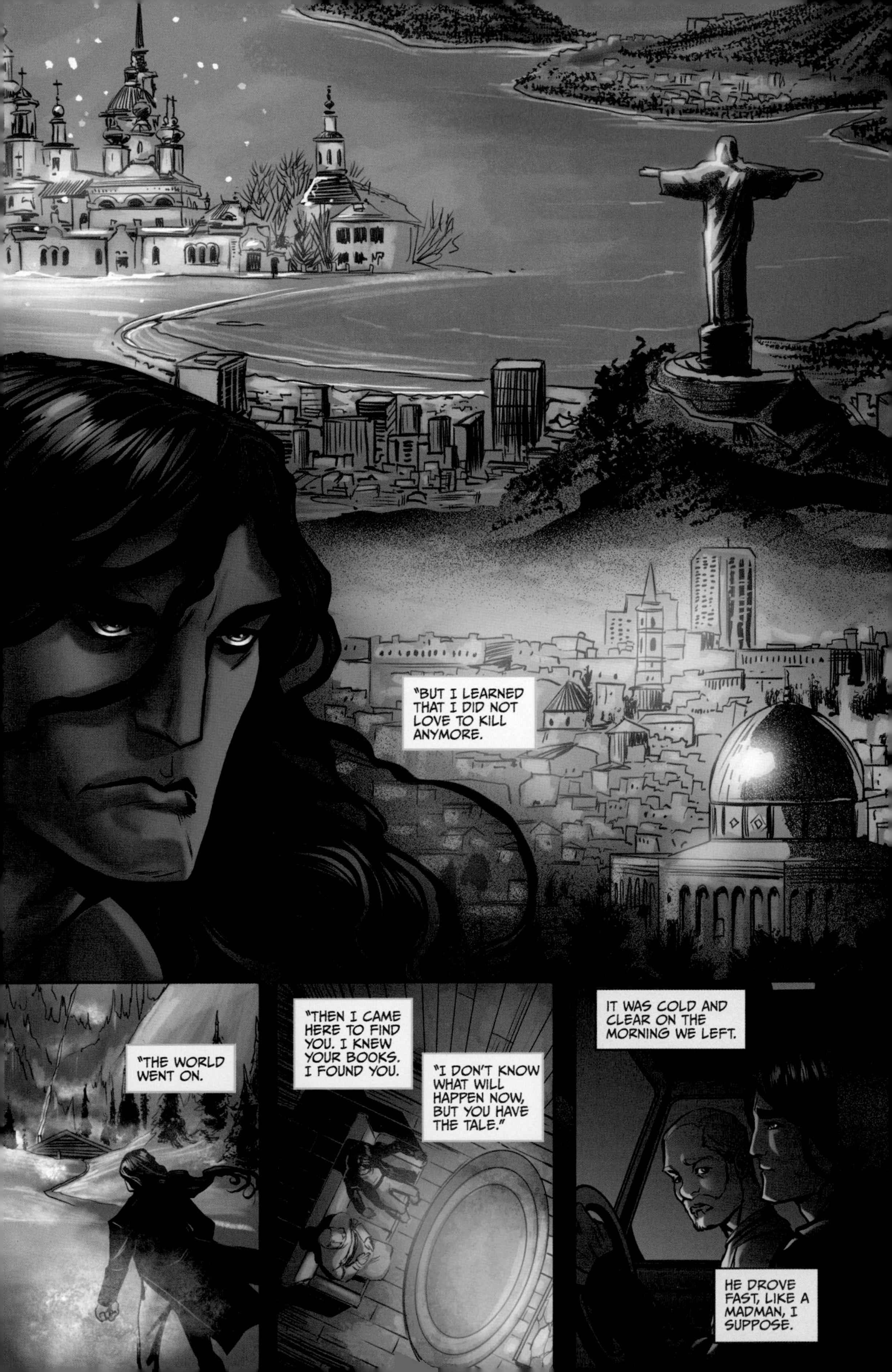
"BUT I LEARNED THAT I DID NOT LOVE TO KILL ANYMORE.
"THE WORLD WENT ON.
"THEN I CAME HERE TO FIND YOU. I KNEW YOUR BOOKS. I FOUND YOU.
"I DON'T KNOW WHAT WILL HAPPEN NOW, BUT YOU HAVE THE TALE."
IT WAS COLD AND CLEAR ON THE MORNING WE LEFT.
HE DROVE FAST, LIKE A MADMAN, I SUPPOSE.

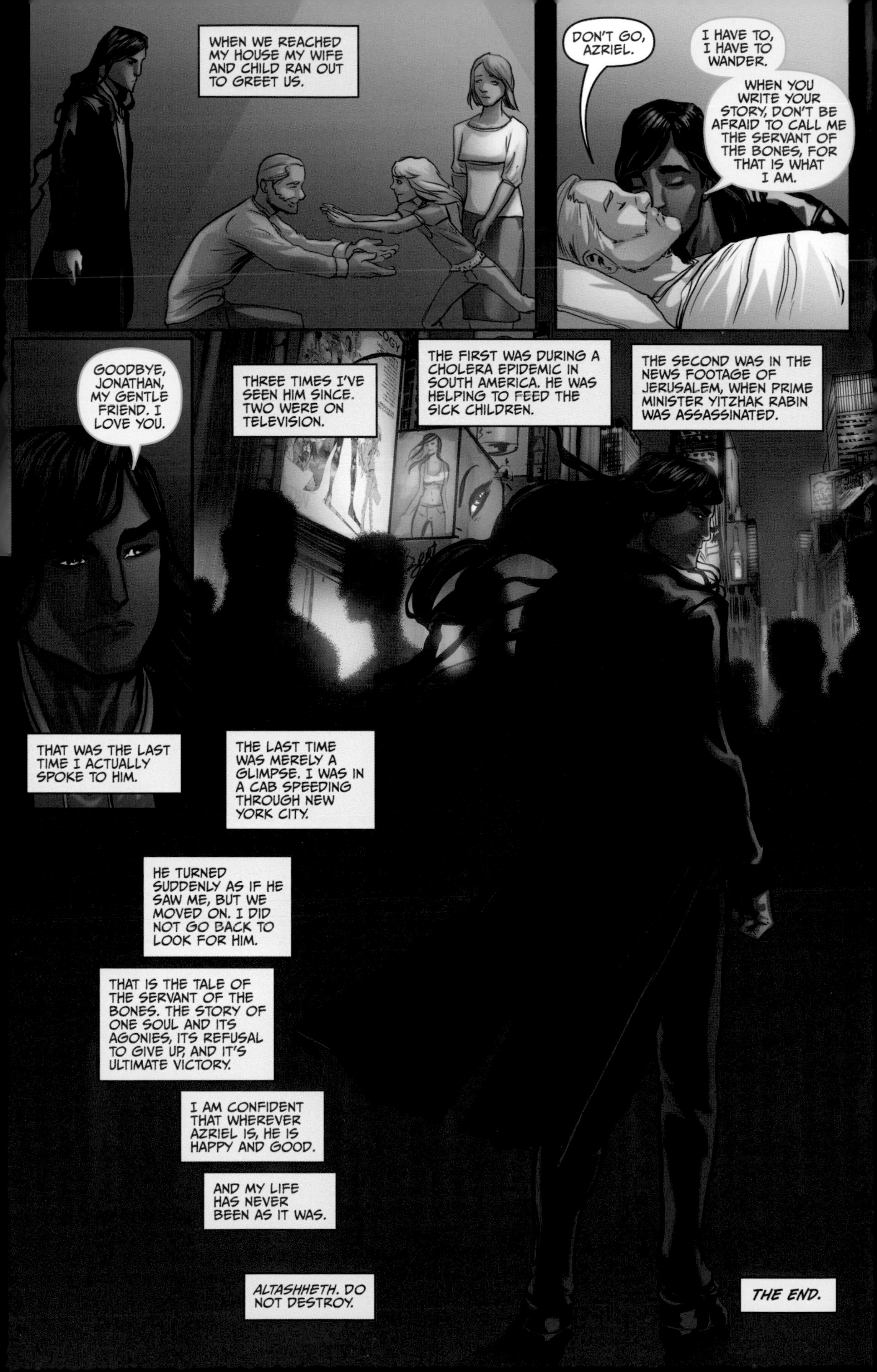
WHEN WE REACHED MY HOUSE MY WIFE AND CHILD RAN OUT TO GREET US.
DON'T GO, AZRIEL.
I HAVE TO, I HAVE TO WANDER.
WHEN YOU WRITE YOUR STORY, DON'T BE AFRAID TO CALL ME THE SERVANT OF THE BONES, FOR THAT IS WHAT I AM.
GOODBYE, JONATHAN, MY GENTLE FRIEND. I LOVE YOU.
THAT WAS THE LAST TIME I ACTUALLY SPOKE TO HIM.
THREE TIMES I'VE SEEN HIM SINCE. TWO WERE ON TELEVISION.
THE FIRST WAS DURING A CHOLERA EPIDEMIC IN SOUTH AMERICA. HE WAS HELPING TO FEED THE SICK CHILDREN.
THE SECOND WAS IN THE NEWS FOOTAGE OF JERUSALEM, WHEN PRIME MINISTER YITZHAK RABIN WAS ASSASSINATED.
THE LAST TIME WAS MERELY A GLIMPSE. I WAS IN A CAB SPEEDING THROUGH NEW YORK CITY.
HE TURNED SUDDENLY AS IF HE SAW ME, BUT WE MOVED ON. I DID NOT GO BACK TO LOOK FOR HIM.
THAT IS THE TALE OF THE SERVANT OF THE BONES. THE STORY OF ONE SOUL AND ITS AGONIES, ITS REFUSAL TO GIVE UP, AND IT'S ULTIMATE VICTORY.
I AM CONFIDENT THAT WHEREVER AZRIEL IS, HE IS HAPPY AND GOOD.
AND MY LIFE HAS NEVER BEEN AS IT WAS.
ALTASHHETH. DO NOT DESTROY.
THE END.

 **L** ament

Cry not, my baby.
Cry.
I know a frog ate a white moth.
That's why he's a frog.
Now moth is not.
My baby, cry not. Cry. There is much to do.
I will cry too.
I will cry for you.

Stan Rice, *Some Lamb* 1975

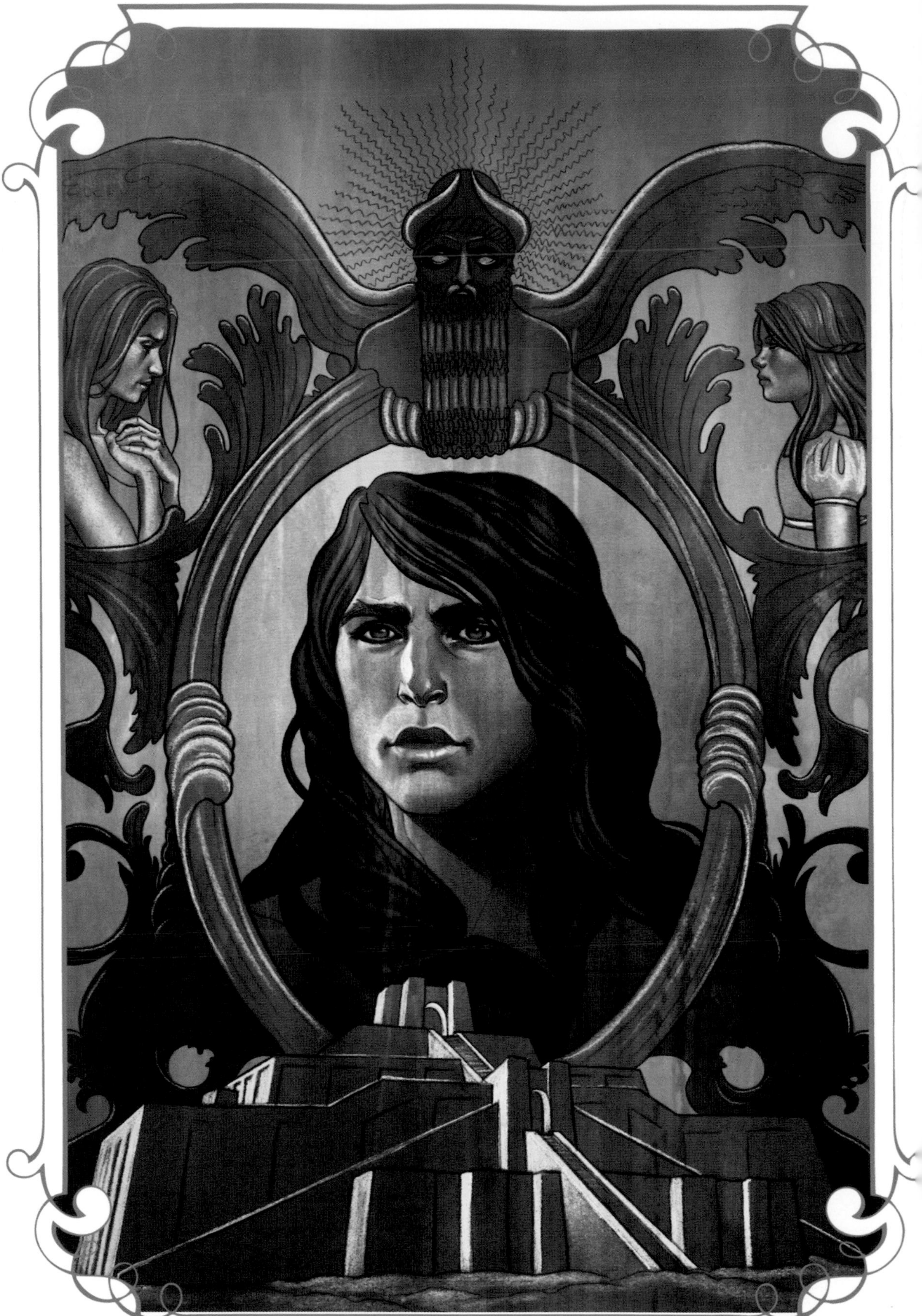

Art by Jenny Frison

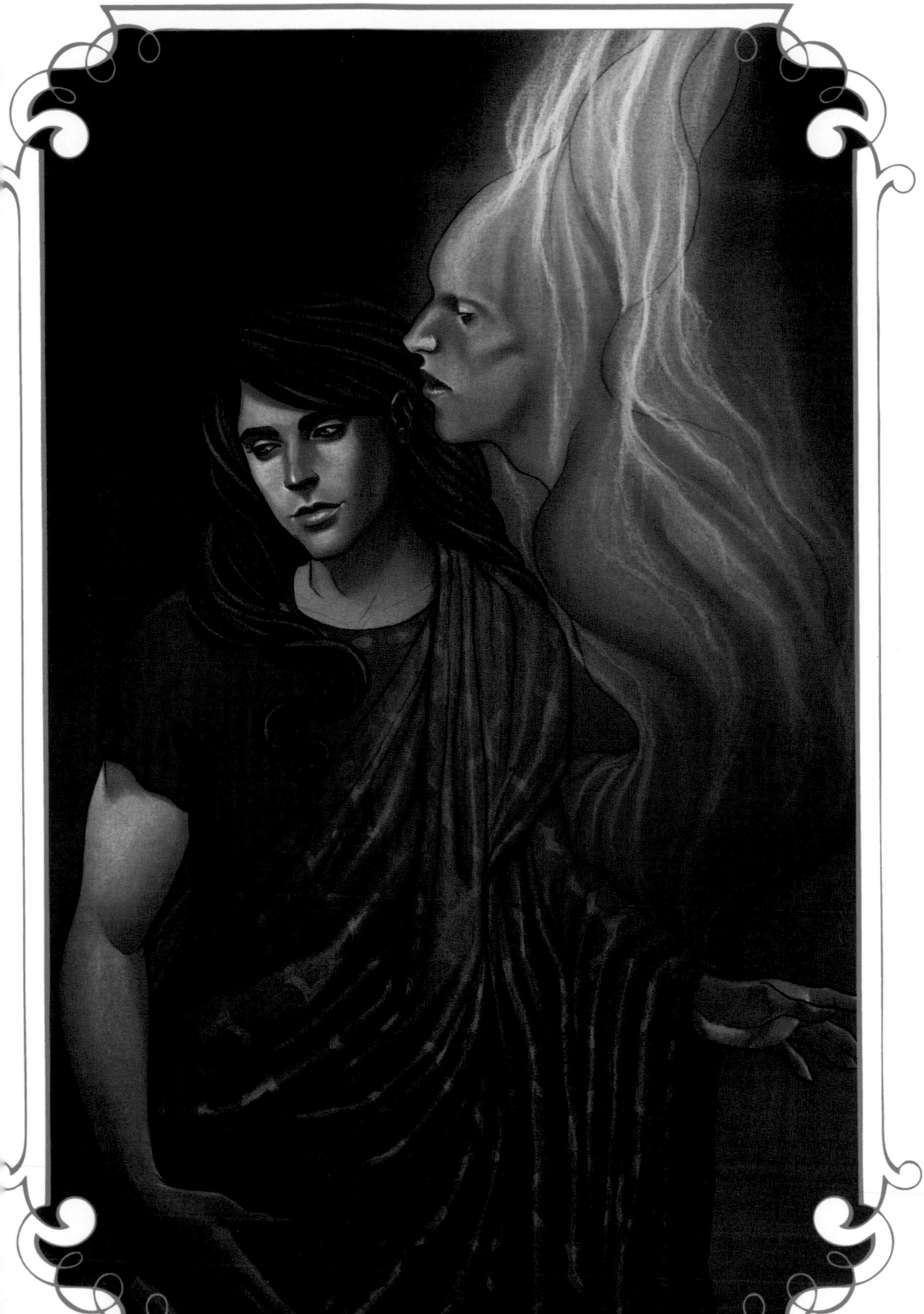

Art by Jenny Frison

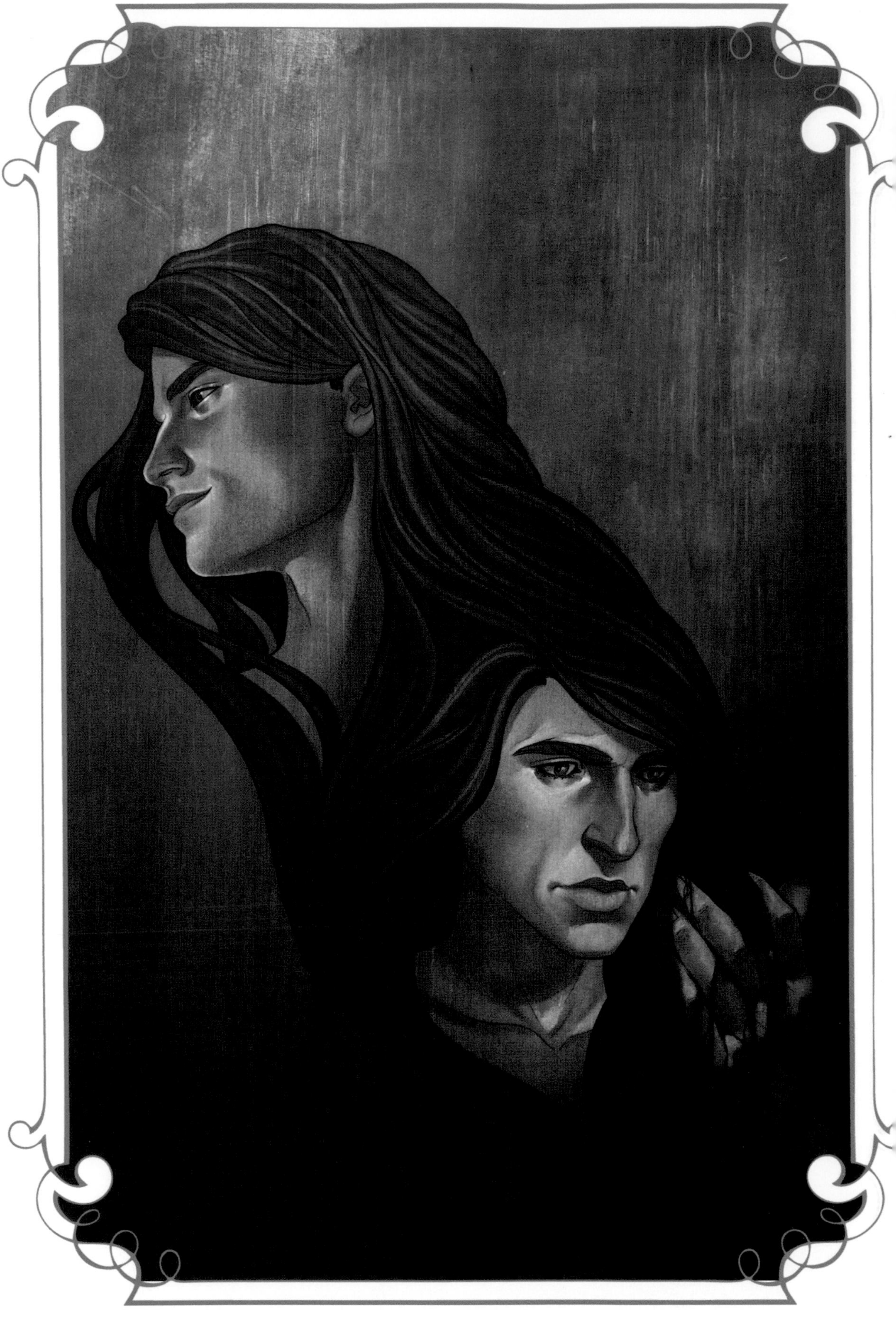

Art by Jenny Frison

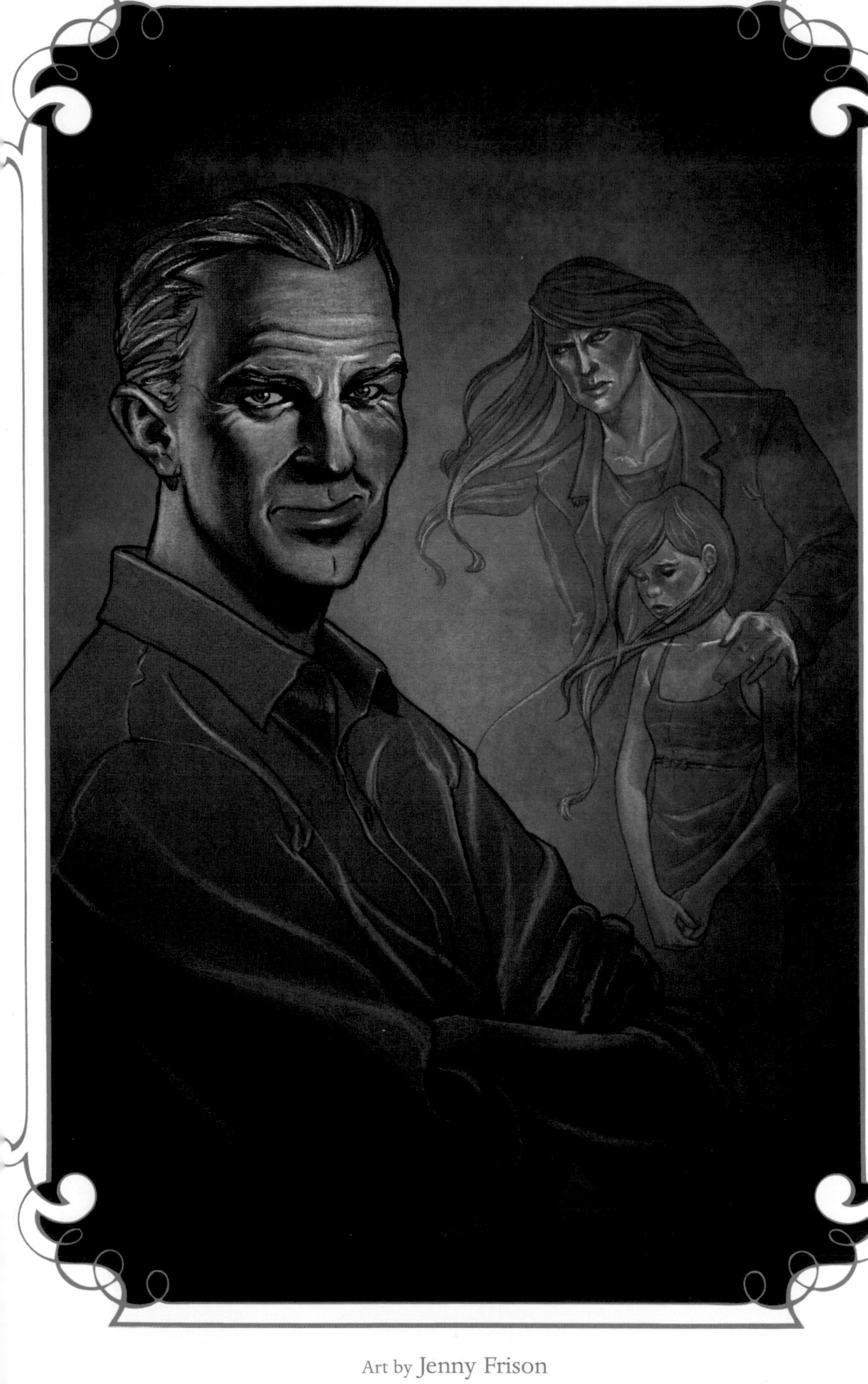

Art by Jenny Frison

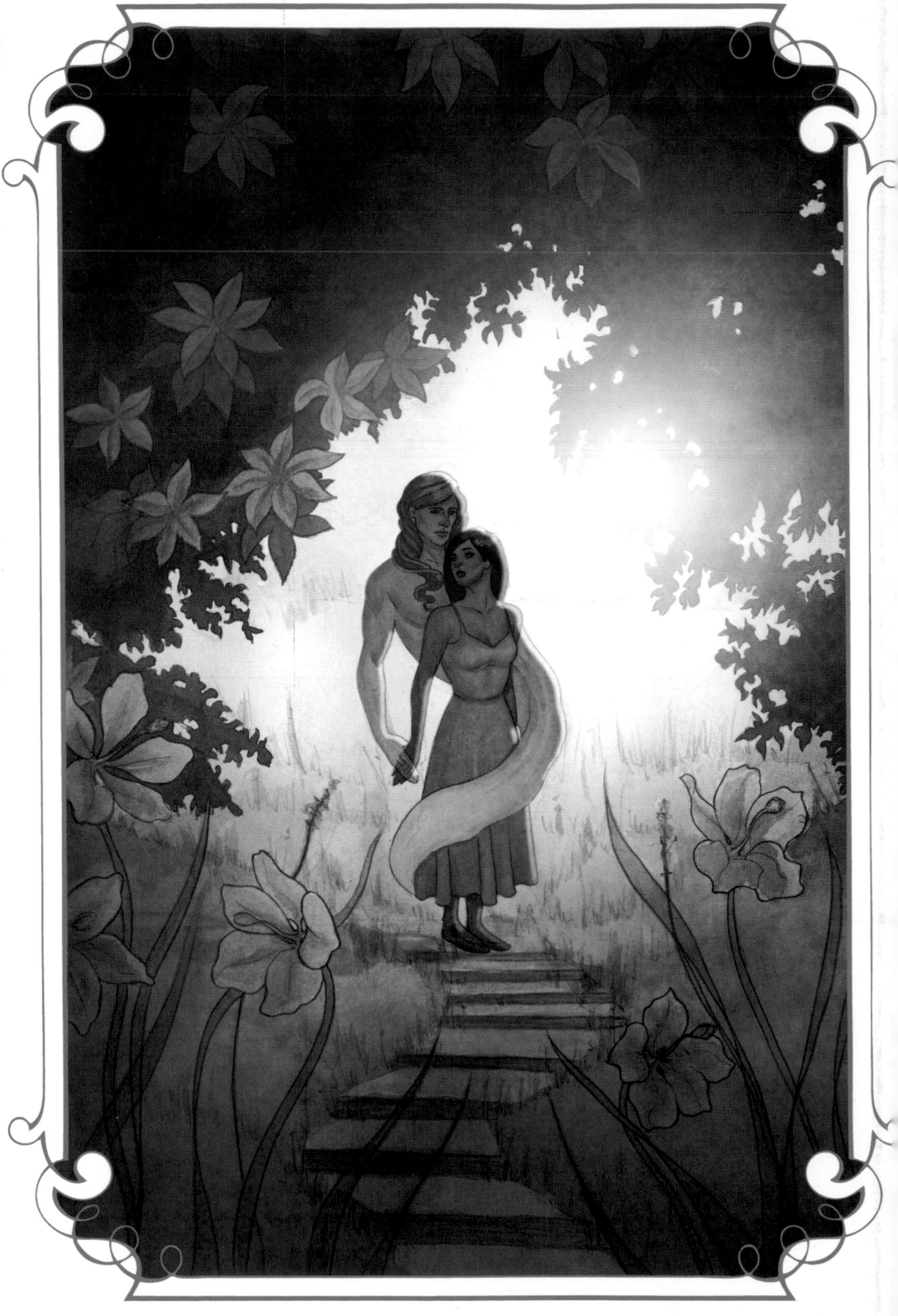

Art by Jenny Frison